PARAGON
Diamond Sharpened
edish Quality Steel

TOOLS

A COMPLETE ILLUSTRATED ENCYCLOPEDIA

Garrett Wade Company

With contributions by Mark Duginske, Kim Carleton Graves,
Bruce Marshall, Dick Onians, Mario Rodriguez

Photography by Dick Frank

SIMON & SCHUSTER SOURCE

NEW YORK LONDON TORONTO SYDNEY SINGAPORE

SIMON & SCHUSTER SOURCE
Rockefeller Center
1230 Avenue of the Americas
New York, NY 10020

A Marshall Edition
Conceived, edited, and designed by
Marshall Editions Ltd.
The Orangery, 161 New Bond Street
London W1S 2UF

Simultaneously published in Great Britain by Marshall Editions Ltd.

Project Editor	Theresa Lane
Art Editor	Sandra Horth
Picture Editor	Zilda Tandy
Designer	Paul Montague
Copy Editor	Eleanor Van Zandt
Indexer	Jill Dorman
Production Controller	Anna Pauletti
Editorial Coordinator	Gillian Thompson
Art Director	Dave Goodman
Editorial Director	Ellen Dupont

Library of Congress Cataloging in Publication Data
Garrett Wade Company
Tools: a complete illustrated encyclopedia
Garrett Wade Company
p. cm.
Includes index.
ISBN 0-7432-1348-3
1. Tools—Encyclopedias. I. Garrett Wade (Firm)

TJ1195.T627 2001
621.9'003—dc21 2001018378

Originated in Italy by Articolor
Printed and bound in Germany by Mohndruck
10 9 8 7 6 5 4 3 2 1

Front and back cover photography: Dick Frank

Contents

INTRODUCTION

The tools below are typical of those found in a cabinetmaker's toolbox in the early 1800s. About half of the tools were made in Britain, the remaining half in the United States.

GARRETT WADE IS A CATALOG BUSINESS SPECIALIZING IN SUPERB woodworking tools and other related high-quality craft and household tools. The company, now 25 years old, has customers in all 50 of the United States, as well as in 78 other countries. I am often asked why I started Garrett Wade. The simple answer has to do with a boy's inspiring experience in school. As a boy in the Midwest in the 1950s, I took the obligatory "manual arts training" class, also known as "wood shop." Not only did I gain confidence and self esteem by learning that I, too, could "make that and make it well," but I was blessed with a teacher who transferred his love of the material to his students, and he guided my hands as they gained skill in filing, cutting, planing, and joint making.

I kept those memories intact, but when I decided to resuscitate my skills years later, the obstacle that stopped me in my tracks was that I could not find any of those wonderful tools that I knew I needed

This 19th-century brace, made from a tree root, demonstrates the craftsman's ingenuity.

"There is no satisfaction quite equal to that which can come from the exercise of some personal skill: particularly the skill of the hands."

CHARLES HAYWORD, *WOODWORKER MAGAZINE*, 1956

to enjoy my hobby. Why this had happened is a story in itself, having to do with the trends in retail marketing at the time, which lies beyond the scope of this book. Suffice it to say, I eventually solved my personal tool supply problem; however, it was a struggle.

Some years later, it occurred to me that there were probably many other people who shared my frustration in trying to find good tools—which turned out to be true. So, I thought, here was work that could make a real difference in people's lives; and in time, the Garrett Wade Company was born. Many things eventually came together culturally to help produce a renaissance in amateur woodworking in the United States, but I know that it is not stretching the truth to say that, by simply being there, Garrett Wade has helped a great deal.

Working with wood is an old and honorable craft, enthusiastically practiced by hobbyists and professionals alike. As a material for habitat construction, for the making of furniture and other household necessities, and for works of art, wood has played a major role in all civilizations throughout the world—in Europe, the Americas, Africa, Asia, Oceania. So it follows that the craft of working wood has roots deep in all our histories.

The reason for the company's appeal has much to do with the important role that wood craftsmanship has always played. As Charles Hayward wrote in the British magazine, *Woodworker,* over 40 years ago: "Craftsmanship has always been one of the essential planks in bridging the gap between the world of ideas and the world of reality."

Choosing the suppliers and tools

So what is it that gets our attention? Garrett Wade's dominant criterion for tools has always been quality. However, it would be self-righteous to claim that the company has never been tempted off this path. If it was felt that a certain tool, although not perfect, was functionally important and the best

Over the years Garrett Wade has continuously supplied the best woodworking tools available, including these flatback chisels.

This Japanese woodblock print shows Japanese workers using traditional Japanese woodworking tools, including a chisel and saw (foreground, left) and a plane (center, right).

available—or was so good a value—then the company has relaxed its criteria a little.

I would be the last to say that all the tools you have in your home or shop should be the kind of high-quality tools that I have such enthusiasm for. There's always a place for lesser quality equipment—for the one-time task or a short-term piece of work that you are not likely to have to repeat. I have made such a choice myself countless times.

But barring such circumstances, it has always been my heartfelt conviction that good tools are simply inspirational—inspiring to the individual spirit and inspiring to the woodworker in the very act of using them. I have always believed that the use of a good tool in itself stimulates the user to do better quality work—and that better work is more satisfying work. But in the main, if Garrett Wade were to carry a tool, it simply had to be a very good tool, and this principle has stood us in very good stead indeed.

Garrett Wade looks all over the world for woodworking tools. We have been, or are now, sourcing from England, Germany, Italy, China, the Czech Republic, Sweden, France, Japan, Australia, Taiwan, Costa Rica, Zimbabwe, India, Spain, the Netherlands, Denmark, Austria, Switzerland—and, of course, Canada and the United States.

We like all the tools we carry, and have from our inception believed that displaying them in our catalog clearly, with good lighting and in sufficient size so that the woodworker can see the item in detail, treats the tools as they deserve—and is also respectful of the customer. And I note with some pride that since Garrett Wade pioneered this approach to tools merchandising over 25 years ago, many advertisers and marketeers have been inspired by us.

The development of tools

It is important to realize that tools have not developed historically the way that they have simply by chance. Darwin's principles of natural selection are at work here. The physical design and the materials used in all tools, hand as well as powered, have evolved in most cases over many years from the experience of hundreds of thousands of woodworkers.

Hand tools are generally the most highly evolved, because their mechanics are the simplest and because woodworkers have been using them the longest and the most intensively. But a similar evolution has been happening to power tool design—even as costs have been pushed down and the product cheapened by mass production

European cabinetmakers in a traditional Western-style workshop are shown in this 16th-century German woodcut.

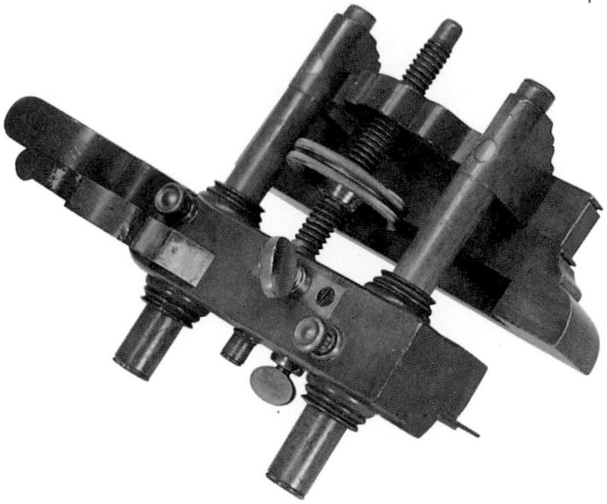

Made of boxwood and brass trimmings, this 19th-century plough plane exemplifies some of the attention given to detail and the high-quality craftsmanship found on woodworking hand tools.

in Asia—because woodworkers steadily reject less effective tool design and construction. The market demands both quality and a good price. The price stays sharp because of competition—and the quality and range of choices available generally improve over the long term.

You may notice that almost everything that is in this book is of Western European or North American origin. (Where it is not, it usually comes from a former United Kingdom colony.) These are the styles of tools that we in the United States are the most familiar with. The only notable exception is Japanese tools. A well-justified great interest has developed in the West regarding the unique design heritage and exceptional quality of traditional Japanese woodworking tools. (This subject is worth a book of its own. Did you know that Japanese planes and saws cut by pulling, not pushing, because Japanese woodworkers traditionally work sitting or kneeling—not standing at a bench, as in the West?) Otherwise, regrettably, practical considerations have precluded expanding our scope to include tools from, say, China or Egypt, and other parts of the world with long woodworking traditions.

In addition to getting your tools from trusted specialist merchants, you may find antique sales and flea markets useful sources of secondhand or old tools for your shop. Sometimes the bargains are terrific. Sometimes they are not—unless you are collecting tools for their historic or aesthetic value. When shopping for old tools to use, always make sure they are complete (no missing parts) and are clean enough so that you can assure yourself that nothing is broken. Beyond that, steel wool, mineral spirits, a sharpening stone, and elbow grease can turn what looks like a "pig's ear" into a "silk purse."

It is my singular hope that you will find this book a stimulating source of information about the traditional craft of woodworking and a primer on the tools of the craft, in all their rich and rewarding diversity.

STARRETT

Measuring and marking tools

1

Measuring tools
Marking tools

Measuring tools

Available in a huge array of shapes and sizes, measuring tools are used not only to determine size, but also for layout—as accurate guides in making marks.

There's one school of thought that says, "Never measure unless you have to," implying that a good eye, reference marks notched on a stick, and piece cut to match piece in a satisfying progression are all the guidance you need. After all, a woodworking project has a life of its own and does not need to conform to cold engineering tolerances. However, most of us need the comforting support of a straightedge metal rule minutely marked in 16ths of inches or millimeters, a try square, and a spirit level. We know that the axiom "Measure twice, cut once" has become the ultimate cliché of the woodworking craft only because it is true.

Woodworkers take great pride in their measuring tools—a glinting array of etched steel and burnished rosewood—and it is upon their precise application that the success and pleasure of a project ultimately depend.

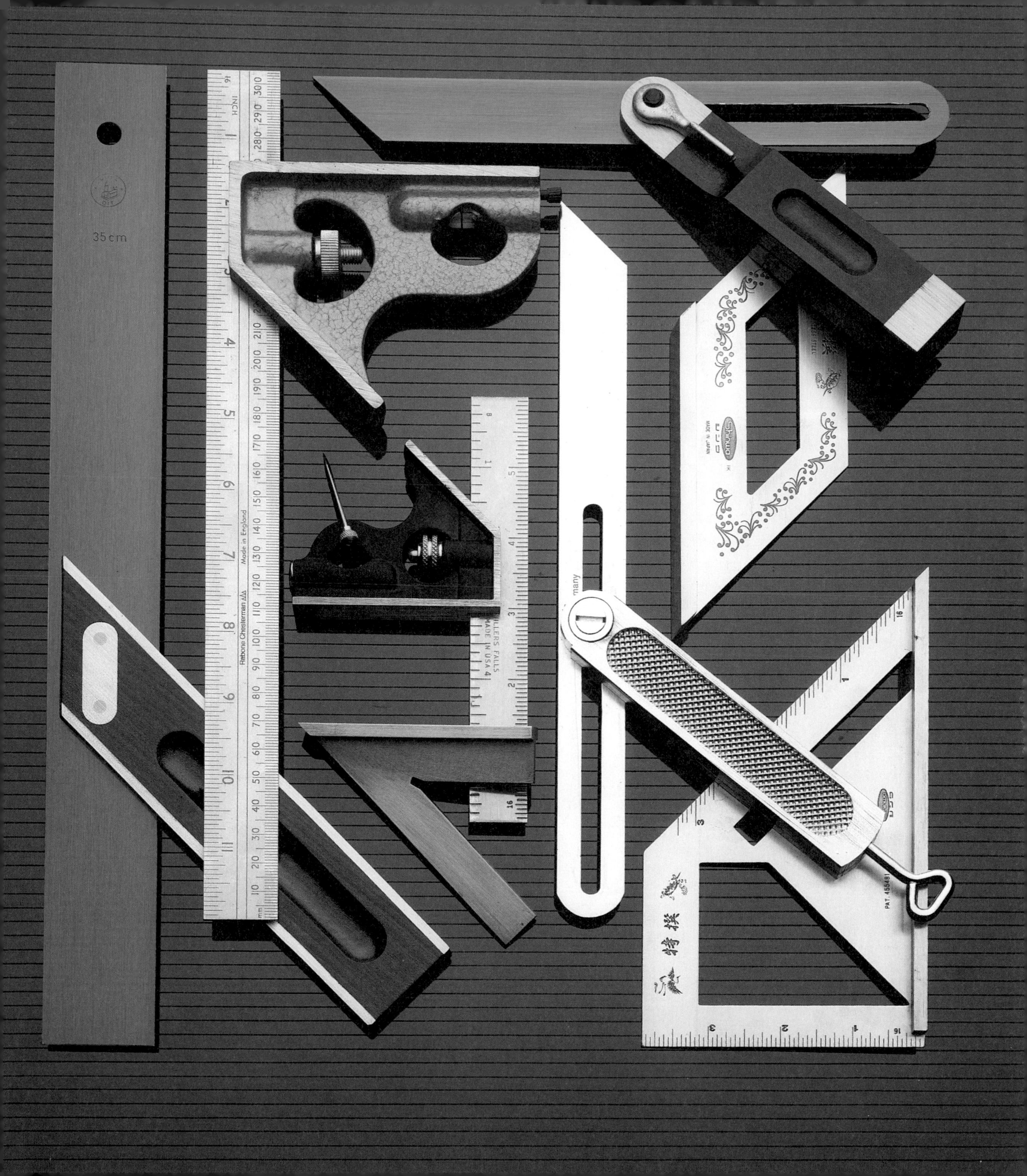
35cm
Rabone Chesterman
Made in England
INCH
MILLERS FALLS
MADE IN USA
Shinwa
MADE IN JAPAN
PAT. 455481

MEASURING TOOLS

WOODWORKERS CAME LATE TO THE DISCIPLINE OF MEASURING precisely. Until a few centuries ago, ergonomic sense dictated the size of things—a table at a comfortable height to eat from; chairs to fit beneath it; a storage dresser that fitted between two wall posts. Notches on a stick established the primary dimensions; thereafter, a stylish eye for proportions, attention to fit, and the rules of geometry guided the craftsman.

Rough-and-ready calibration had long been available. Linear measuring instruments found in Egypt's pyramids use as a unit the cubit, 20 inches (500 mm). Artisans in King Alfred's England knew the inch (a finger joint), 12 of which made a foot, and three of those made a yard (a man's stride). Under Queen Elizabeth I of England, the yard and its subdivisions were standardized, and those measures were taken to North America by the colonists. The last formalization, the Imperial Standard Yard, officially inscribed on a bronze bar (the most stable metal of the time), came in 1844.

France, meanwhile, established the metric system—decimal multiples and fractions of a meter, which was reckoned to be 1/10 millionth of a quadrant of the earth, drawn, naturally, through Paris. More practical and simple to use, it became the compulsory French standard in 1801 and was soon adopted throughout continental Europe, where at the time there were well over 200 regional variations of the length meant by "a foot."

Today, the United States still adheres to the old British system (with slight modifications), and even

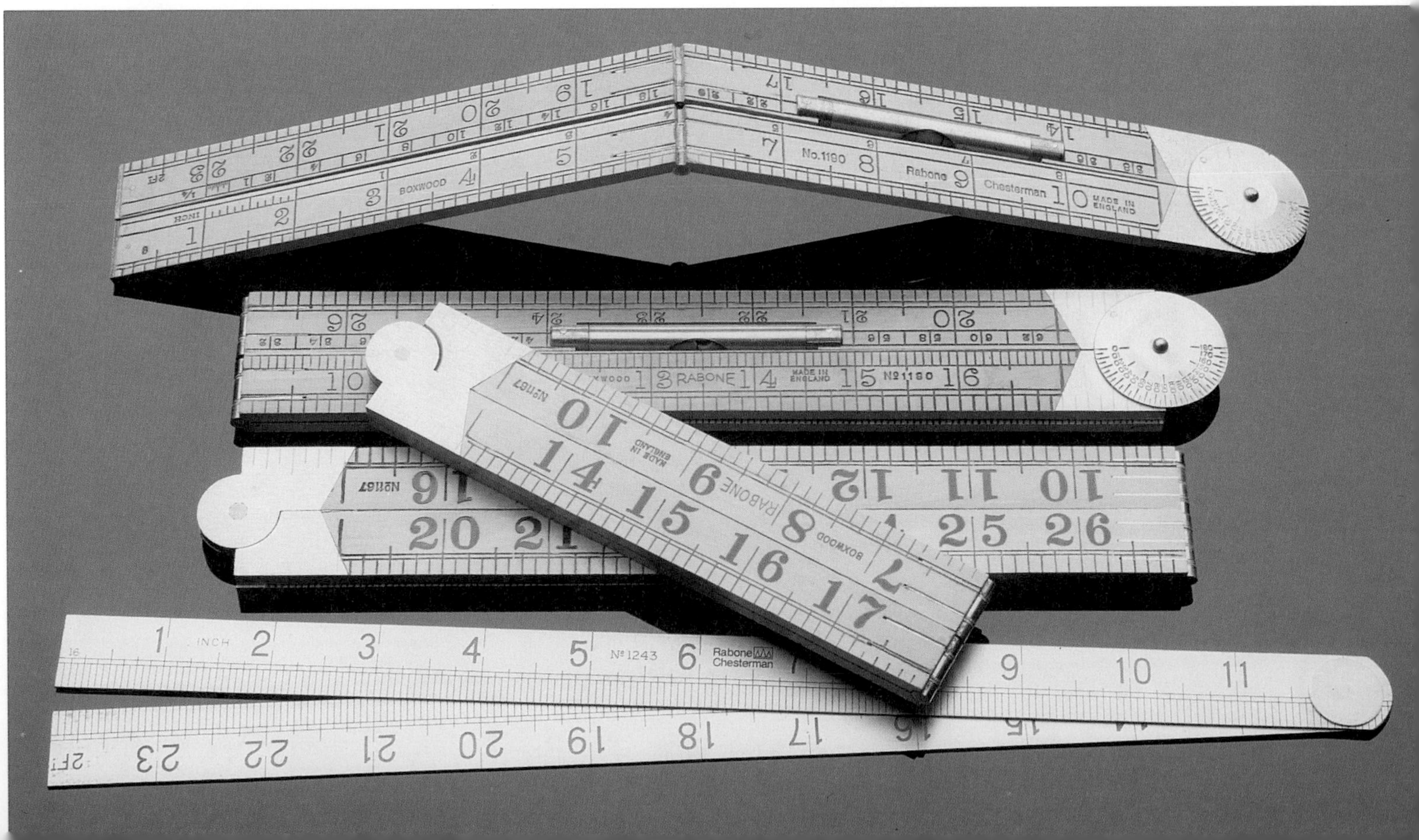

Folding rules come in a variety of styles, both in wood and metal. They have a pivot that allows the legs to slide into a closed or open position. Some models have a hinge to fold up the rule; others incorporate a level.

"While 'measure twice and cut once' is always pithy advice, it is more important to measure accurately and to know that you have."

ALDREN WATSON, *HAND TOOLS: THEIR WAYS AND WORKINGS*, 1993

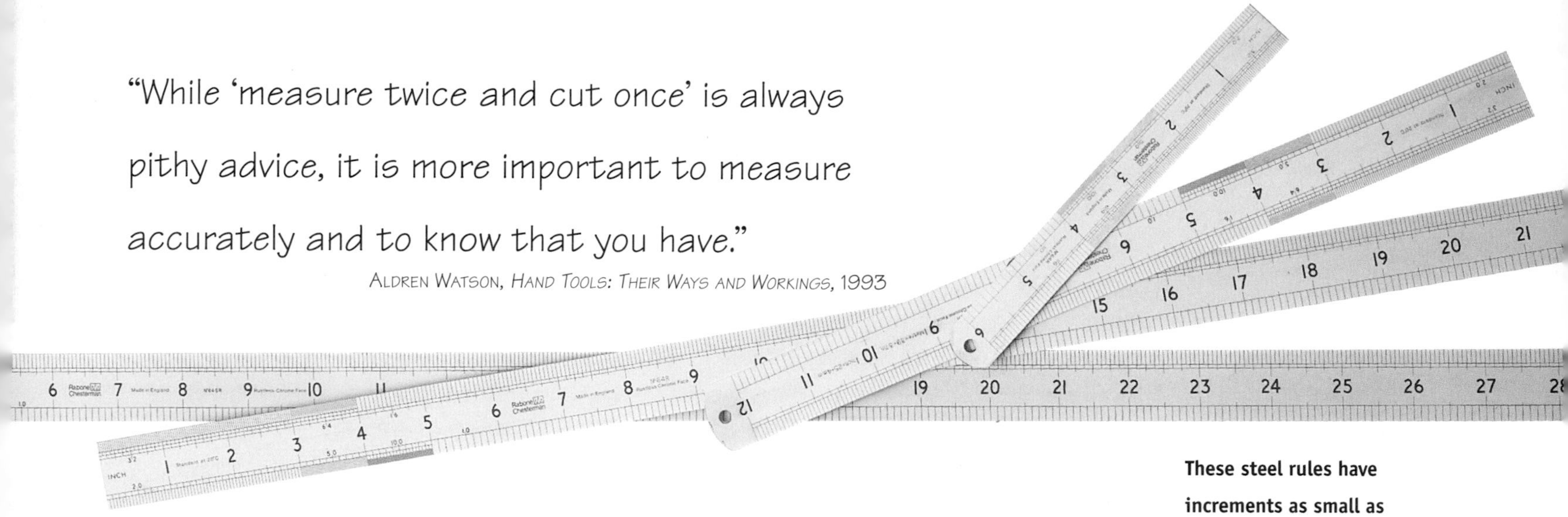

These steel rules have increments as small as 1/64th of an inch and half a millimeter.

here the yard is officially defined in terms of the meter (0.9144 m). However, commercial trading with other countries has led many American industries to also use metric. In fact, Americans will find metric measurements in the dosage of medicines, such as over-the-counter aspirin, and in liter bottles of soda pop.

With the Industrial Revolution, woodworkers, who had previously started their projects from the tree, now bought standard planks from the sawmill, and mass-produced lathe work was made to crisply defined dimensions. By that time, also, artisans were more likely to be able to read and write and less daunted by written symbols.

The engineers who built the metal machines that powered the new industries needed to work to precise tolerances—an ill-fitting piston slapping around in a cast-iron cylinder had a short and wasteful life—and their measuring instruments inspired those of the woodworkers. Although to this day purists among woodworkers prefer their measuring aids to be made of wood, their tool catalogs still deferentially acknowledge the superior accuracy of engineers' all-steel tools.

Today's woodworker

Although carpenters can satisfactorily do their work with tolerances of 1/16th of an inch (1.5 mm), the cabinetmaker must be more precise—only by using accurate measurements will joints fit snugly together. The handyman's retractable tape measure, for example, is too inaccurate for most woodworking jobs.

The measuring and marking of angles starts from a true face line, a straight edge. Before machined finishes, a woodworker would check that first sawn and planed face line with wooden straightedges of his own making—not one but two, so that one, which might have become warped, could be checked against the other.

Despite their authoritative good looks, even today's measuring tools can be imprecisely marked, inscribed, or engraved. Check your tools against

Craftsman's tips

The smallest calibrations generally available on woodworkers' tools are 1/16th of an inch or a millimeter. Seeking accuracy beyond that, woodworkers talk of "fat" or "thin" measures—"a fat 5/8ths (16 mm)," "a thin 3/16ths (5 mm)." "Full" or "bare" are other ways of expressing it. Or they make work to plus or minus "a hair."

each other. Always use the same measuring tool throughout a job. Switching from one rule to another, or from rule to tape—any of which might have imperfections—can result in compounding errors that may entail redoing all the work.

Rules

The steel straightedge is a necessity for most workshops. We often take for granted the trueness of the face line on a delivered board, but it is worthwhile to check it with a steel straightedge that is also inscribed to serve as a rule. A steel rule with etched gradations is more accurate than a soft aluminum one with painted markings—it is worth paying the extra cost for the better tool.

For smaller projects, that rule, or one with a single fold, gives the most confidence that measurements will be accurate. Over longer runs, a zigzag folding rule of wood or plastic is the favorite instrument. This is the successor to the classic hinged, folding ruler beloved of collectors, who sometimes find versions made of ivory with German silver hinges. The preferred length for a zigzag rule is 6 feet or 2 meters. Some models have a calibrated sliding bar set in one or both ends to help in accurately gauging inside dimensions.

For cabinet work, do not trust the ubiquitous flexible tape. Despite its historical progress from a (stretchable) fabric to rolled steel or aluminum, it is at best for approximate observation and reference marking, not for indicating definitive cut marks. That's because the end-hook seating wears loose. However, the flexible rule comes into its own as the only practical means of measuring around curves and reading circumferences.

When measuring, make sure you understand woodworking instructions. "Length" means along the grain, "width" across the grain, and "thickness" the distance between the board's faces. Usually, the length provides the true face line, the base for all laying-out measures and their markings.

Squares

If the board is to be square ended, the most basic and biggest tool is the frame square used by carpenters. It is a metal right angle, usually 24 inches (610 mm) along one side, 16 inches (405 mm) along the other, with inscribed 1/16th inch calibrations. Check the tool for squareness by drawing a line along it, then turn the tool over and check it against the line. If the angle is acute, hit the inside of the corner with a hammer; if it is open, aim the hammer at the outside of the corner.

In the workshop, the smaller try square is handier, an opinion confirmed by the fact that the try square that has been around in its present form for 200 years. Quality models have a hardwood stock with a brass face and a steel blade. The front—the fence—hooks onto the face of the work; the thin steel blade provides a 90-degree guideline. Some versions have the blade placed in a stock cut diagonally, so that a simple repositioning shows a 45-degree line. The fence is no more than a few inches (several cm) long, so precision work requires a 45-degree miter square with a full-length fence.

Many woodworkers opt for an adjustable combination square, which serves both purposes, and more. The fence unit, with faces at both angles and often incorporating a spirit level, slides along a calibrated steel blade. Accuracy depends on the quality of the slide-locking mechanism, operated by a hand-turned nut; it is well worthwhile for a woodworker to spend the extra money to invest in the engineer's model, which is built to higher standards of precision. Because the length of the blade can be set relative to the fence, it can check

Although a flexible tape measure is not standard in a woodworking shop, it can be useful for measuring around circular or irregularly shaped objects.

The classic folding rule (below) is perhaps one of the most familiar tools in woodworking. It has solid brass fittings, clear markings, and a rod that extends from one end.

Dos and don'ts

Do measure a second time after making a mark to confirm that the mark has been made at the right place.

Do allow for kerfs (width of the cuts) when calculating the overall measurement on a board to be cut into several sections.

Do check the end of a board for squareness by placing the blade of a try square along the edge of the board and looking for light between the blade and board. Aligning the try square at the corner of the board, with the blade along the face of the board, is a much less accurate method.

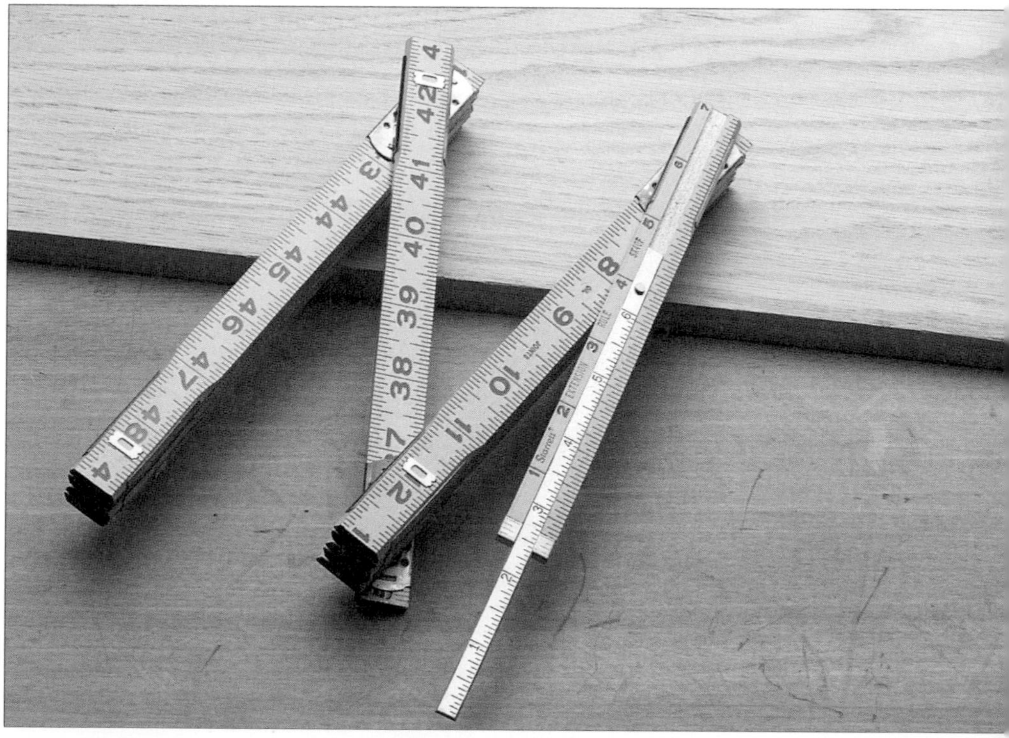

This first century bronze bricklayer's square is an indication of how long people have been using measuring tools.

The cast-iron level (below), patented in 1867, is a testimony to the pride that the Victorians placed in their tools. The center insert was made separately.

Precision engineering combination square sets (above) can also be valuable in the woodworker's shop.

A T square is formed by attaching a head to the steel rule (below, top).

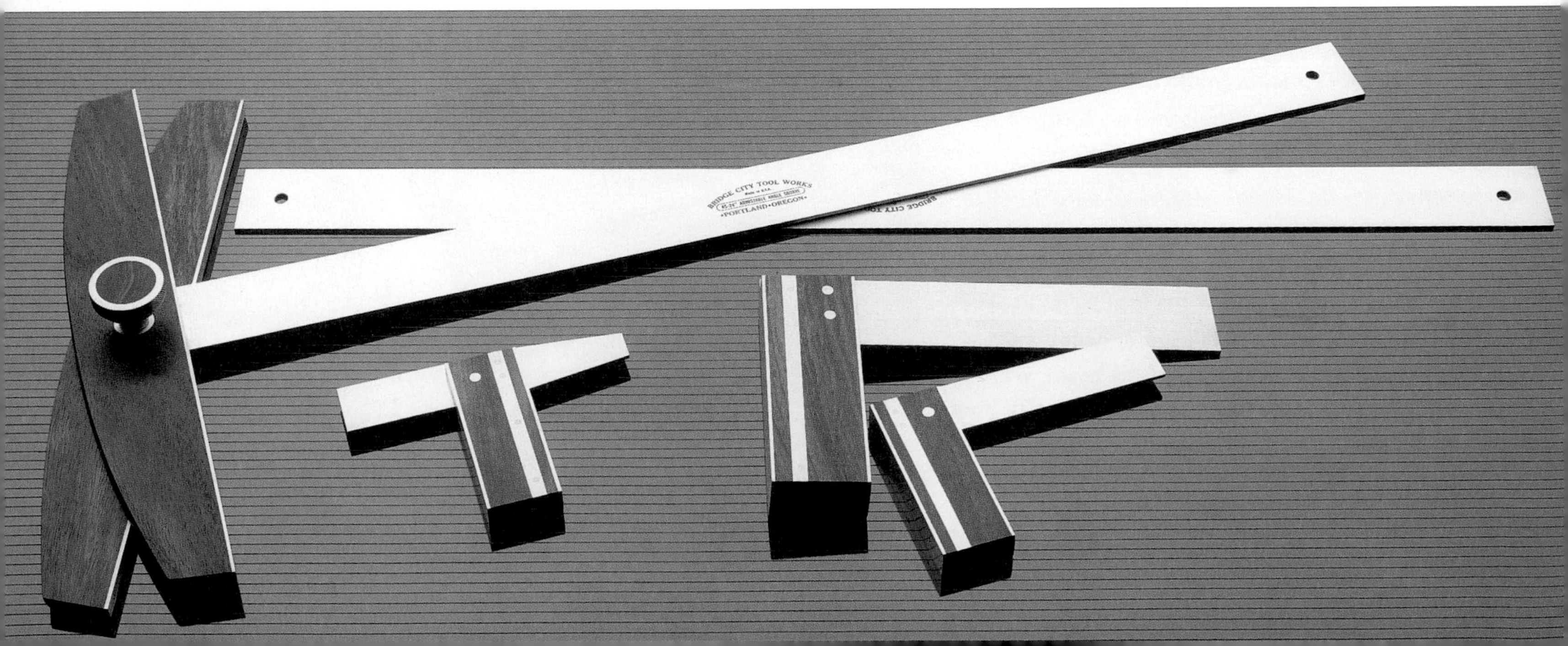

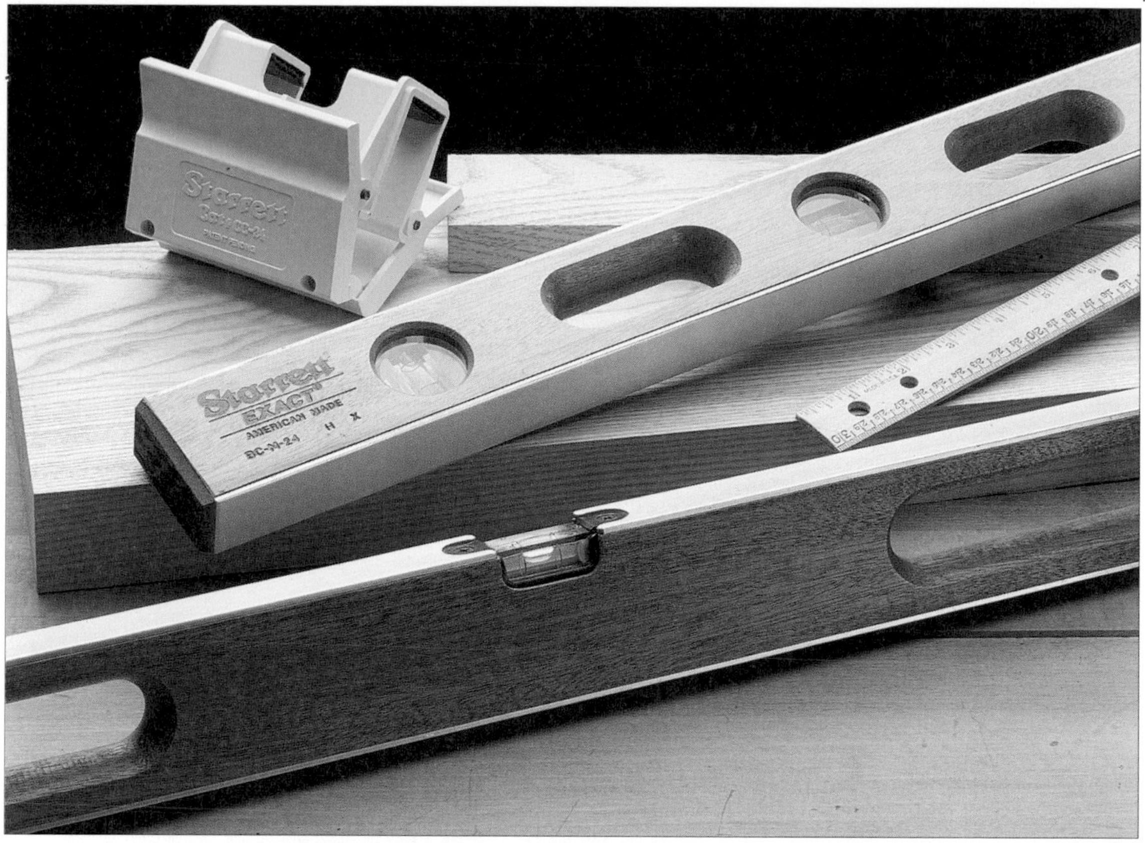

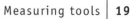

These superior mahogany and aluminum builder's levels (right) can also be used by cabinetmakers.

Traditional diamond-pattern squares and sliding bevel (right, bottom) are styled on presentation tools made in England from the 19th century until the 1940s. These examples are made of solid African ebony, and both edges of the squares are brass faced, so that both are square to the blade.

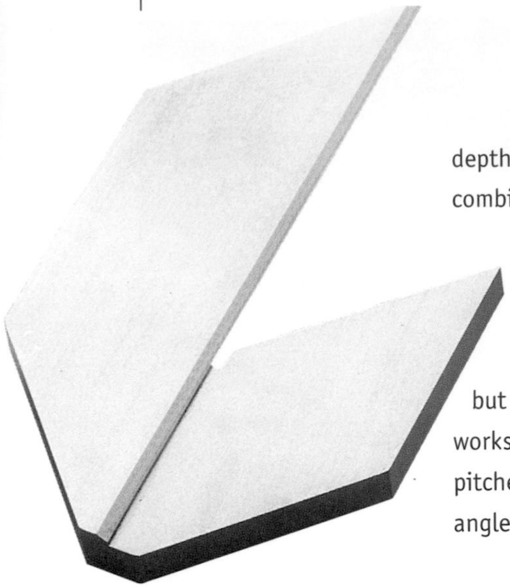

Woodworkers can use a steel center square to accurately find the center of a piece of round stock.

depths of housings, rabbets, and mortises. With the combination square, together with a sliding bevel, whose blade can be locked to any angle, and a protractor used to calculate angles, the woodworker can measure all angles and miters.

Dovetailing has become a task for the router, but dovetail "squares" are pretty tools for the workshop with everything. A good model has two pitches: 1:6 for softwood, 1:8 for hardwoods—the angles for making dovetails in the relevant woods.

Levels

The old way of checking the horizontal was to put water in a dish and check its relationship to a line painted inside the rim, parallel with the base. The spirit level, a rectangular tool with a flat top and bottom and a glass vial almost filled with a spirit or other liquid, was devised in the 1660s to help astronomers align telescopes. When a bubble in the vial floats in the center, the work is level. It took a few centuries before carpenters began to use them.

Mahogany levels have been revered, but even traditionalists may now admit that plastic and metal bodies are more accurate. Even the most hi-tech spirit levels should be regularly checked by comparing the position of the bubble in the vial before and after reversing the level.

Calipers and other measuring tools

Working on the same principle as compasses (see pages 26–35), calipers often have turned-out feet or bow legs. Double calipers have both; others have straight legs. The first are used to transfer internal measurements; the second adjust to the outside of the workpiece. Woodturners use them for checking the diameters of bores and spindles from the lathe. A hazard is that if the hinge pin holding the legs together is free enough to allow easy adjustment, it can also accidentally move. Calipers with screwthread adjustment against spring-tensioning are more accurate.

Woodturners need a quick way of finding centers on circular pieces. A center square does that. And if there is a vacant area in your tool rack behind the workbench, it can take an angle divider. This can be preset to give and bisect angles and to indicate the cut lines for multisided figures. French curves, transparent plastic stencils, supply a range of curves to be used as templates for laying out.

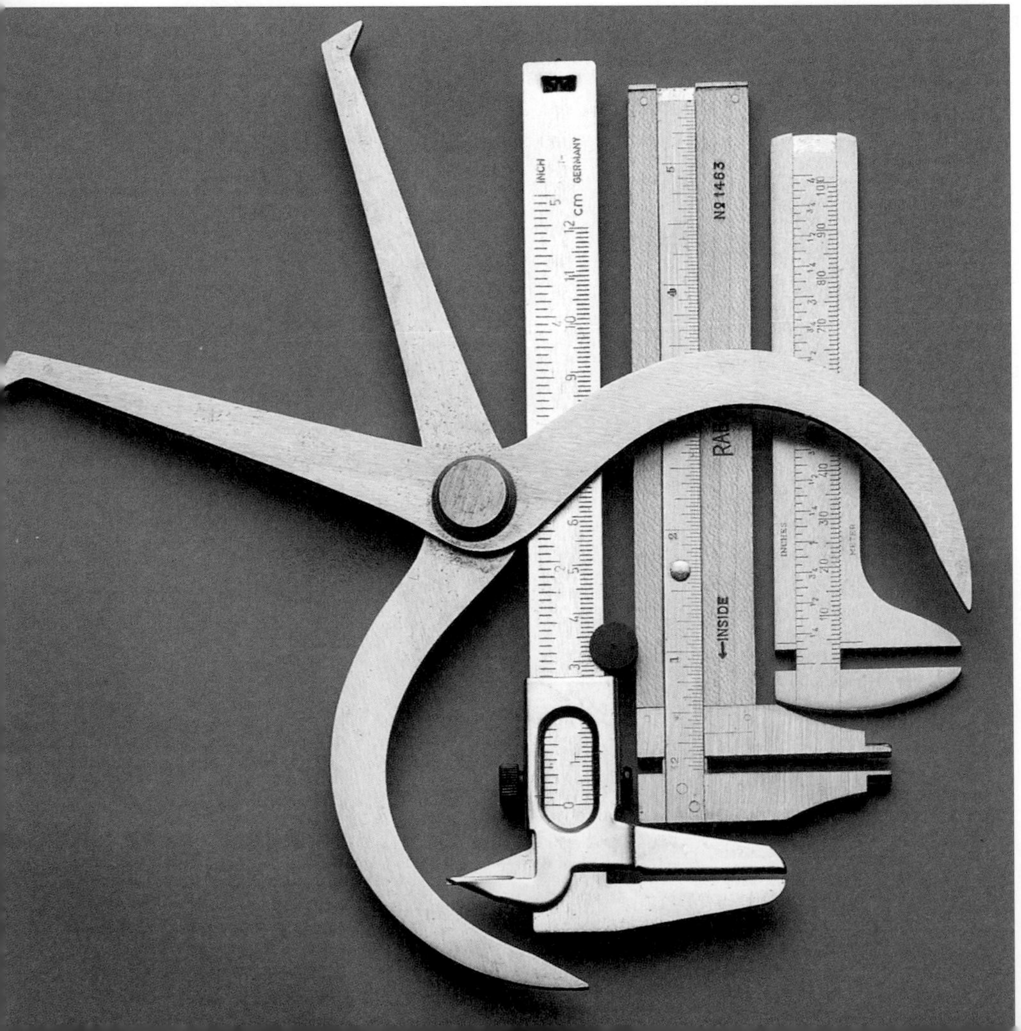

The top calipers are special calipers for woodturners. Below it are (from left) a steel caliper, a brass caliper in a maple frame, and a solid brass caliper.

French curves are an ideal way of transferring a curved shape to a piece of stock, simply by tracing around the appropriate edge.

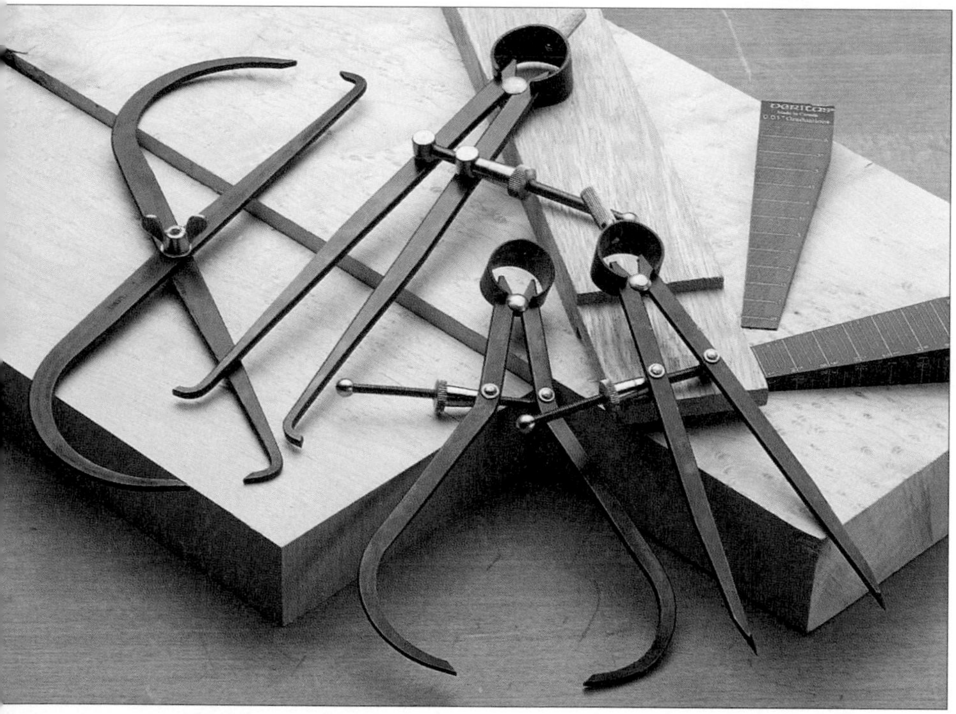

These French tools includes (from left to right) a bowtie caliper, inside and outside calipers, and a divider. They have ferro-blackened steel shanks and brass fittings.

These 19th-century calipers illustrate the decoration that was once applied to many tools. Some calipers were formed literally in the shape of a pair of legs.

Many standard types of measuring tools can be found in home centers and hardware stores, and these are often used for home improvement jobs. However, for true accuracy in a woodworking shop, you will get better results by investing in high-quality measuring tools—perhaps, even including some of the tools designed for engineering. You will find these tools in some better-quality hardware stores and in mail-order catalogs.

1 Starrett precision dial caliper and hook rules

Designed to make machine setup easy, the dial on this instrument (left) has easy-to-read numbers in minute increments. You can make adjustments with one hand, and the tool has a built-in depth gauge. The hardened steel rules (right) hook over the edge of the work to permit you to take accurate measurements without having to visually align the edge of the rule with the edge of the piece you are measuring.

2 Folding square

An accurate, fully functional measuring tool with an angle protractor, this square folds up for storage in the toolbox.

3 Miter square

The brass and rosewood miter square (bottom) is a popular tool in Europe. The blades provide precise 90-, 60-, 45-, and 30-degree angles.

4 Sliding bevel

This heavyweight brass bevel has a rosewood handle.

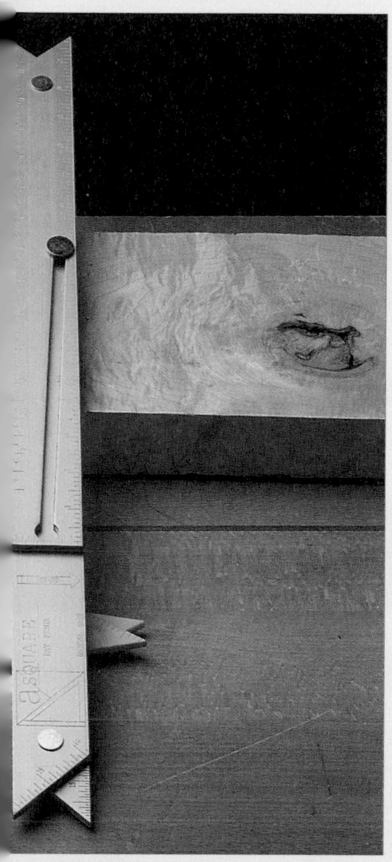

5 Veritas bar gauge heads

Bar gauges, traditionally made of two strips of wood held in place with rubber bands, are ideal tools for transferring inside measurements, such as in the sizing of shelves, and in comparing diagonals to check squareness. They are invaluable as "story sticks" when doing an assembly in which nothing is square. These heads are an accurate replacement of the rubber bands and prevent the strips from slipping out of position.

6 Japanese miter square

The Western-style woodworker will find the Japanese miter square an asset in the workshop. The 45-degree miter (left) has 45-degree faces on all sides. The graduated miter (right) is a combination tool with both 45-degree and 90-degree faces. Both tools have a flat base, which allows the tool to stand upright or to hook on a lip.

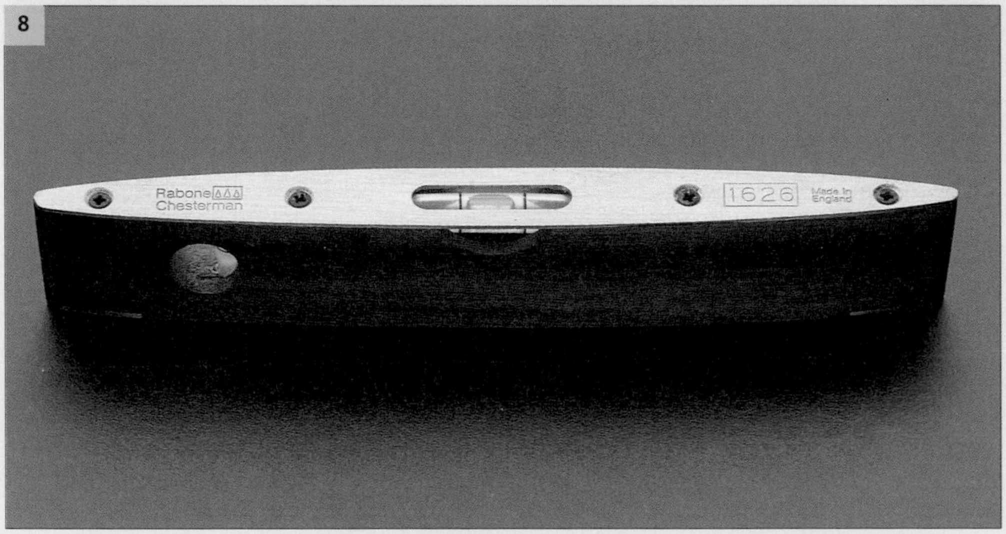

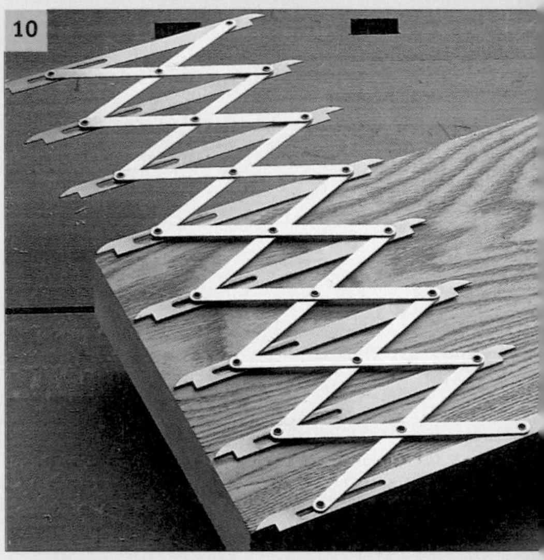

7 Starrett squares

From left to right are a combination square, with an attachment so it can be used for laying out centers and parallel lines; a pattern maker's square, with a blade that can be tilted; and double squares, with adjustable sliding blades.

8 Torpedo level

A small carpenter's level made in the traditional "torpedo" boat shape, this level is ideal for woodworkers. The tool here has a teak body and brass fittings.

9 Squares and dovetail layout tool

This group of tools include a small brass quick check square (top left), engineer's squares (bottom) to set up stationary power tools, and a dovetail tool (top right) to lay out dovetails on both hardwood and softwood.

10 Point-to-point proportioning tools

By extending this tool across the work, you can quickly work out points for dowels, screws, or biscuits at accurate, equal distances.

11

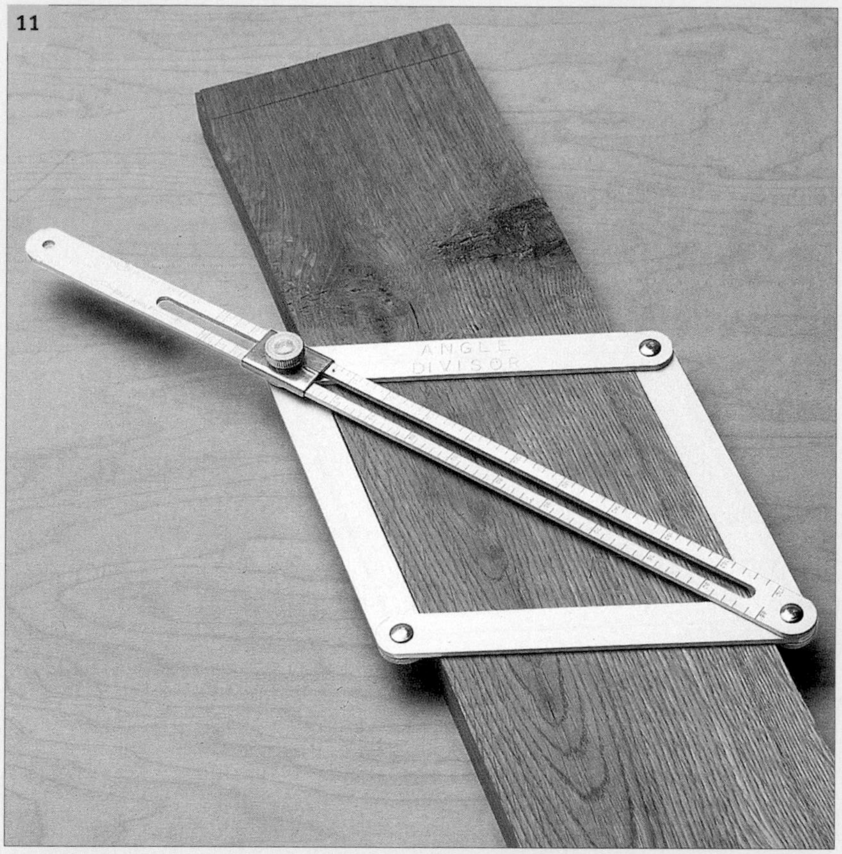

11 Angle divider

As handy as any square, this tool will precisely divide any angle—a necessity for accurate miters. It also acts as a protractor and layout tool. It can directly read angles from 5 to 170 degrees.

12 Nobex miter angle setter

Simple to use and very accurate, the miter angle setter allows you to transfer a precise corner angle, whether inside or outside, to any hand or power miter saw.

13 Stanley's no. 1 odd-job layout tool

Old-timers used to say, "All you need is a no. 1 Odd Job, a hammer, and a saw, and you can build anything." Originally made by Stanley from 1888 to the 1930s, this tool is in production again. It's an inside miter and try square, a depth gauge, a scribing tool for arcs and circles, a T square, a depth marking scribe, a plumb level, and a 6-inch (150-mm) rule. You can also purchase a 12-inch (300-mm) rule to use in addition to the shorter rule.

12

13

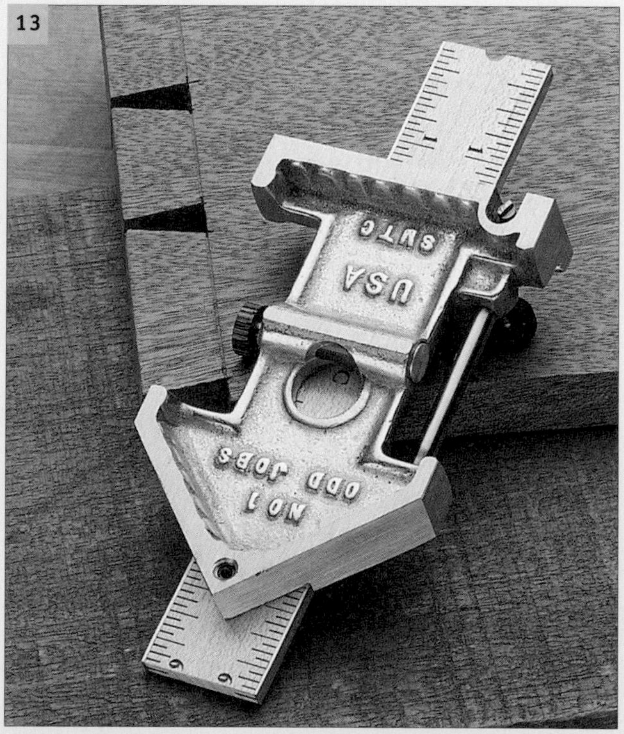

Marking tools

Marking and cutting gauges look similar, but the real difference is whether the tool is supporting scribing points or cutting blades.

Just as it is important to measure accurately, it is equally vital that all your marks be made with exact precision. Although badly fitting pieces and the resulting wobbly construction are often caused by a blunt chisel or dull saw teeth, the same problem can also be due to slightly inaccurate marks—for example, thick lines produced by a dull pencil. Many of the best woodworkers have created their finest masterpieces only after painstakingly careful measuring and marking.

Choosing the marking tools for your workshop is a simple matter of taste, budget, and function. The beginning woodworker will need just a handful of basic marking tools in the workshop, including an awl, a scribe, and a marking gauge. Other marking tools can be added as they are required for particular woodworking projects.

MADE STANLEY IN U.S.A.

MARKING TOOLS

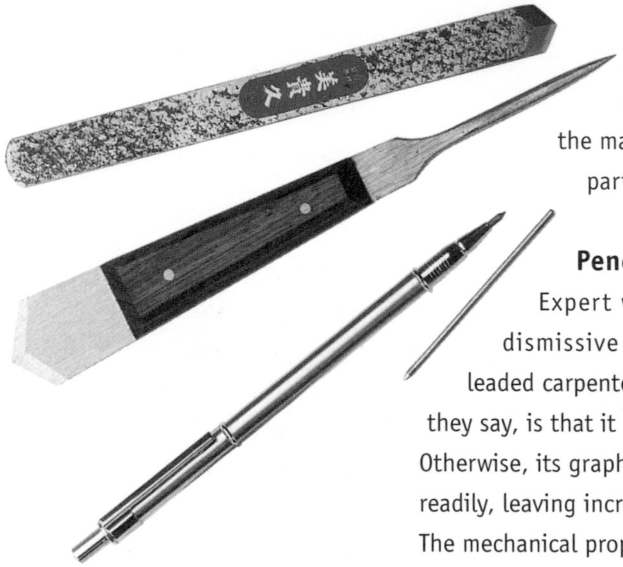

Desirable tools include (from top to bottom) the Japanese marking and striking knives and the marking pen, which also holds the scriber.

WOODWORKERS HAVE ALWAYS USED SOME METHOD TO MARK their work, as a guide for cutting. The tools used for marking are often very simple—although in the past they might be highly decorated. The choice of the marking tool will depend partly on the user.

Pencils and chalk lines

Expert woodworkers are often dismissive of the classic oval, thick-leaded carpenter's pencil; its one virtue, they say, is that it doesn't roll off the bench. Otherwise, its graphite chisel point crumbles too readily, leaving increasingly thick, blurred lines. The mechanical propelling pencil also has few adherents: when the lead is extended beyond the depth of a straightedge it will snap. Much better is the architect's leadholder, whose thicker lead projects farther without breaking.

In truth, the best is the everyday pencil with an HB or H (or no. 2) lead kept sharpened. With softer lead, the lines are thicker and darker and may be difficult to erase from a fine piece of wood; harder lead may scar the wood. Colored leads can be useful on dark materials.

An old-fashioned chalk line can still have its uses—for example, for rough cutting a 4- x 8- foot (120- x 240- cm) sheet of plywood in half. The line is reeled out from a chalk-filled canister, hooked to a nail at one end of the intended cut line, tensioned at the other end, and snapped against the board.

Incising tools

The most precision a woodworker can expect is to 1/64th inch (0.375 mm). To get close to that, marking lines must be incised, not surface daubed. Use tools with points to cut along the grain or end grain and blades to cut across it so that the wood fibers are severed, not torn. Either way, these incisions create guide channels for a saw or chisel.

Awls are the simplest, and most essential, pointed tools. The kind with a stubby shank and a broadly ground point marks hole centers for drilling and is sturdy enough to be hit with a mallet. The more elegant style, with a thinner, longer shank and a sharper point, is for scribing cut lines. Premium awls have wooden handles, which are more pleasing to the eye, but plastic handles serve just as well.

An everyday penknife, well sharpened and preferably with a blade lock, is a perfectly adequate marking tool, but most workshops will have a utility knife with replaceable blades. Choose a model with

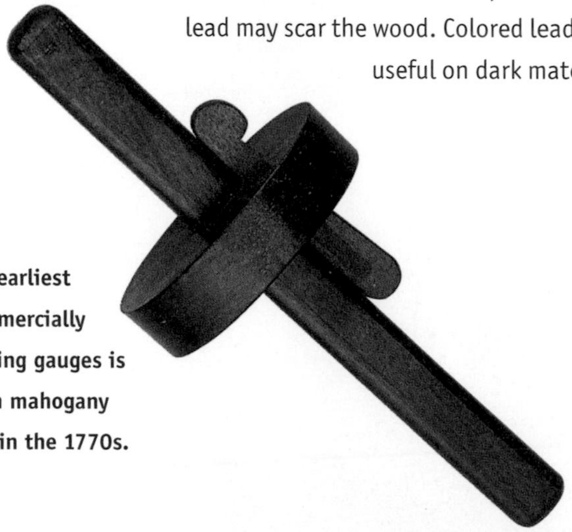

One of the earliest known commercially made marking gauges is this English mahogany tool, made in the 1770s.

Craftsman's tips

Scribing across wood grain makes erratic markings, because the tool jumps at changes in the density of the wood, which fluctuates with soft summer growth and the harder winter wood. Always use a very sharp tool to mark across the grain.

IDENTIFYING MARKS

The first marks to make are symbols indicating the face side and face edge of the material to be used. Do this after checking that the face side and face edge have the grain direction and appearance required, without sapwood, blisters, and splits marring displayed surfaces.

A right-handed worker should measure and mark from the left, so that waste is always to the right of the cut mark (vice versa for left-handers). Pencil or chalk an arrow up to the mark, so that it's easy to find the mark if the cutting process is delayed. Draw a squiggle or cross on the waste side, so there's no confusion about which pieces are part of the project. Erase that mark if and when the waste material comes back into service.

Scratch awls can make incredibly fine marks, and the width of the lines will not vary. The scratched line can help you guide a chisel or saw.

These French-made marking knives have carbon surgical steel blades and handles made of ebony. The set includes a righthand bevel, lefthand bevel, and double bevel for every possible situation and personal preference.

The tri-scribe markers come with steel scribe points. They can be clamped onto the edge of a try square and used as a marking or mortise gauge. If the scribe point is replaced with a pencil, the marker can act as a trammel point to mark out a radius.

Among a variety of tools, this *Sheffield List,* printed in England in 1889, shows marking, cutting, and mortise gauges. This is only a small selection of the numerous gauges available at the time.

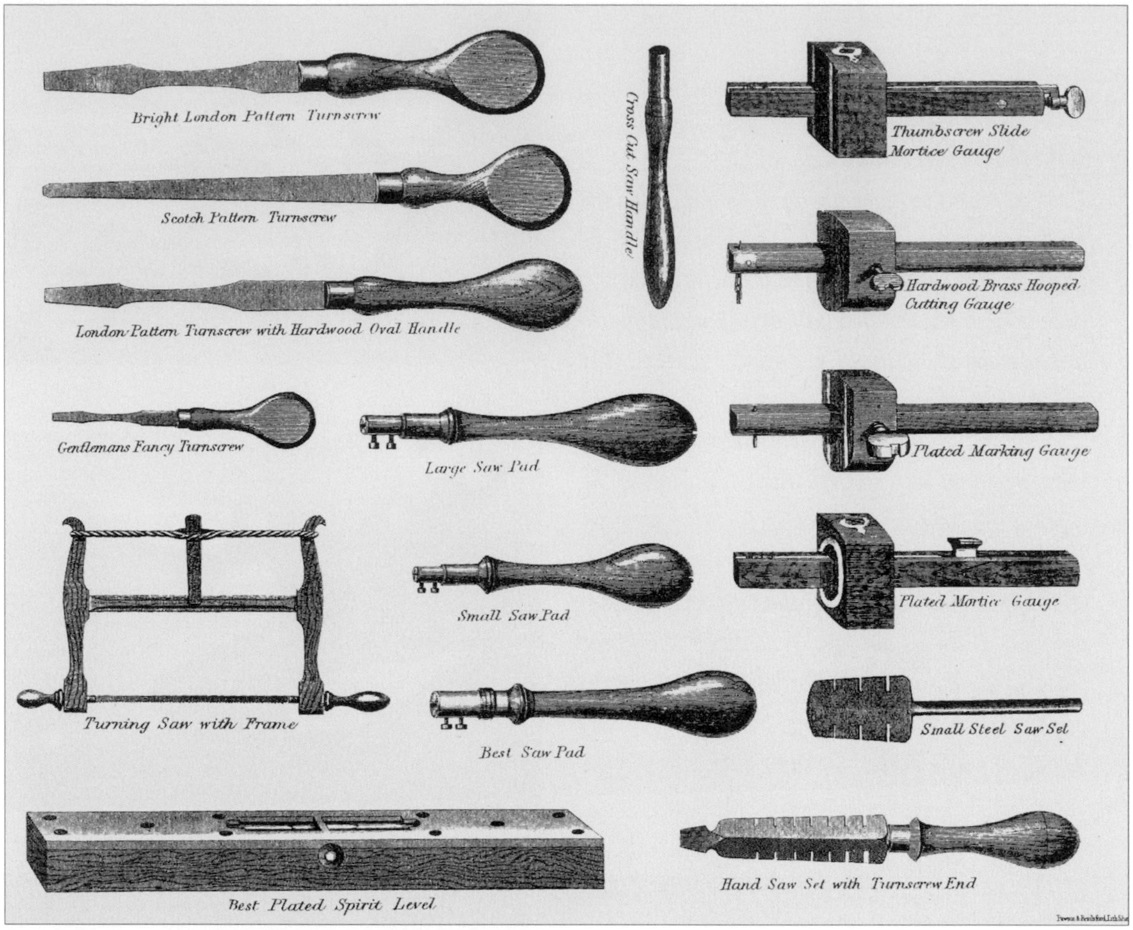

Excellent Japanese design and craftsmanship are exhibited in this pair of cutting/marking gauges. The single-beam gauge (below) is easy to control and adjust. The double-beam model is more versatile—it can also be used as a mortise gauge.

a blade-retracting mechanism, which makes it safer to carry. Hobby, or craft, knives, while seeming to promise precision, are too flimsy for use in general woodworking. Japanese knives have a cutting edge of high carbon steel laminated into a surround of softer metal; they can be honed to cut-throat sharpness. For maximum accuracy, sharpen blades on one side only, cutting with the flat side against the straightedge.

Marking and cutting gauges

Other tools that follow the principle of using points and blades according to grain direction are marking and cutting gauges. These tools are used to cut

From left to right, are two combination gauges (with a pin on one side for marking and a set of two pins for marking mortises), a cutting gauge, and a marking gauge. The first two gauges differ in the way the pins are adjusted—by a pull slide (top) or thumbscrew (bottom).

parallel to a nearby edge, with the stock or handle held firmly against this guide.

Old catalogs show scores of these gauge styles, for coopers and coachbuilders, shipwrights and wheelwrights. Those specialists used to make their own tools, and, to this day, gauges retain the handsome appearance established by those artisans. Once, they might have been constructed in ebony or rosewood; now it is usually beechwood. Top-quality models have long-wearing brass face inserts in the fence, and the fence-adjusting screw tightens against a metal inlay in the beam, so that it does not scar the wood. There is sometimes a calibration panel in another side of the beam.

Fasten or sharpen the spike of a marking gauge so that it protrudes no more than 1/8th inch (3 mm) from its seating; this allows the beam to rest as closely parallel as possible to the work. Pushing or pulling a gauge is a matter of preference; it is easier to see the line as it is scribed by pushing it away.

The blade of a cutting gauge is wedged into the beam so that it can be removed for sharpening. Grind it on one side only, and fit it in position with the bevel facing the stock. Because the knife will tend to follow the grain, this positioning will help to pull the stock into the work and prevent wobble. When marking for a channel or groove, reverse the blade so that the edges are clean-cut. A rounded

The 19th century trammel points above have brass fittings and steel points.

The trammel points below are fitted onto a steel rule, so that they can be accurately positioned along the measurements.

knife edge cuts more gently and is safer for veneer work. Some gauges use a cutting disc that revolves on a spindle. A double-nubbed gauge has a projection on each side of the stock face so that it will steadily follow a curved edge.

Mortise gauges have two spikes, one on a sliding bar, allowing the gap between them to be set to the width of the chisel. The more complicated tenon gauge, for repetitive work, has four calibrated beams to mark both mortise and tenon.

The beams of these gauges are no more than 10 inches (255 mm) long—longer ones can wobble and distort the mark. For larger work, a panel gauge is required. A wide stock sits against the face edge, the spur housing slides along two rigid steel bars.

Marking circles

Compasses (the smallest versions are called dividers), the favorite items in the schoolroom geometry set, have a place in the workshop when circular measurements are needed. One steel leg ends in a point; the other may have a point or a fitting to hold a pencil. Compasses are also useful for "walking" equal spaces along a line.

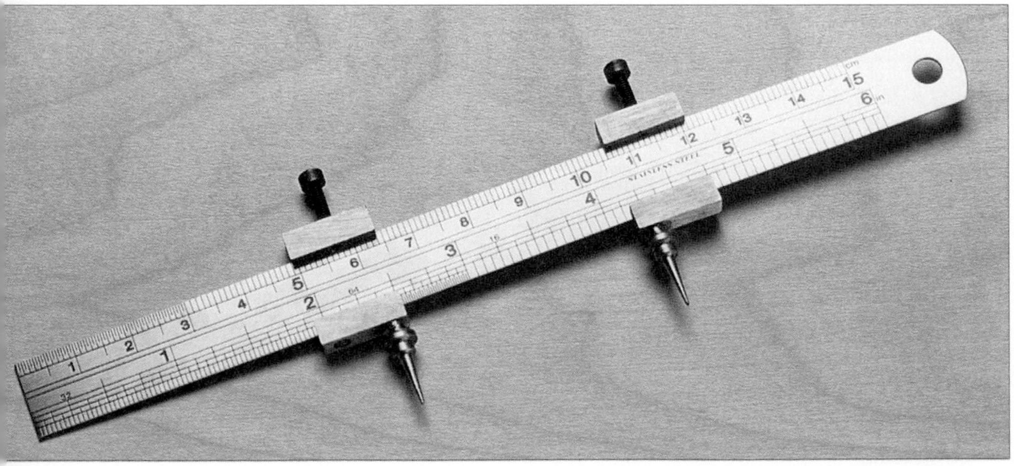

To mark large circles beyond the range of dividers or a compass, a trammel gauge is the tool to use. Two heads fitted with steel pins (trammel points) are clamped to a wooden bar of the desired length. One trammel head is set at the center of the circle, the other head is positioned at the desired radius. (For a one-time-only job, you can use a homemade device—drill two holes in a stick, and use one to take a nail for the center position, the other to house a pencil at radius distance.) A trammel gauge is also useful for transferring dimensions from one piece to another.

There are several tools that mark the center of a circle. For door hanging, a butt gauge is valuable; it transfers hinge positionings and lock housings. Use a center punch to mark screw holes, using the hardware as templates. Dowel centers can mark the ends of dowels and the insides of the holes for pegs.

Dos and don'ts

Do always use only a sharp blade in a knife. A dull blade will not leave a reliable mark.

Do overlay an incised line with a pencil line to make it easier to see.

Don't use a pencil with a dull point. The mark left will not be precise enough to judge where to make an accurate cut.

Do use the right marking tool (points for with the grain, blades for across the grain) to avoid chipout in the work.

Do make sure you hold a compass upright.

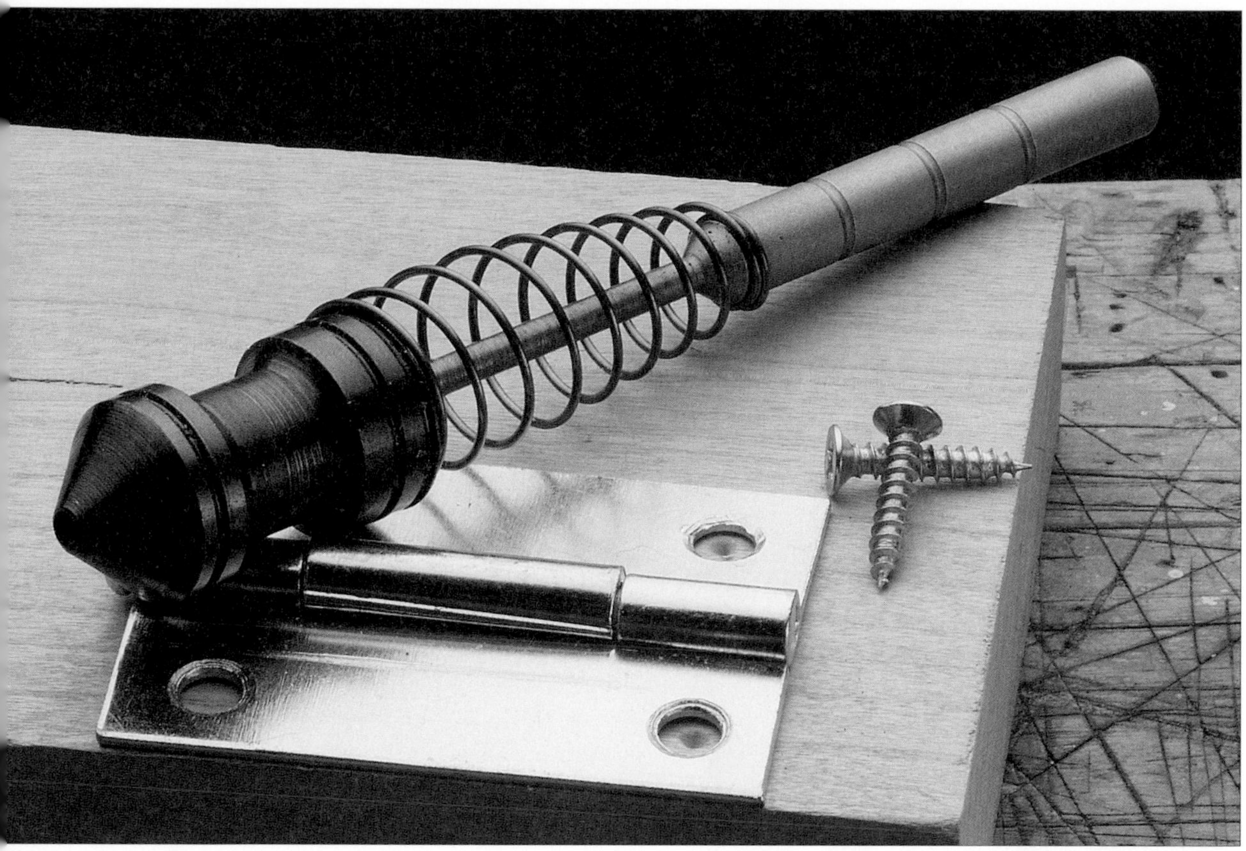

The spring-loaded self-centering punch will help you center pilot holes to mount hardware. Simply tap the end of the tool with your hammer and the mark is true.

These dowel centers are hollow, so that you can use them to transfer the mark of a dowel, as well as a hole. Each of these centers has a point on both the inside and the outside. Dowel centers are availabe in several standard sizes.

It's not necessary to spend a vast sum of money on most marking tools. Your basic awl, for example, shouldn't set you back by much. In comparison, marking and mortise gauges can be moderately expensive if you want to buy good-quality models; however, once you buy one, you should expect it to last for many years to come.

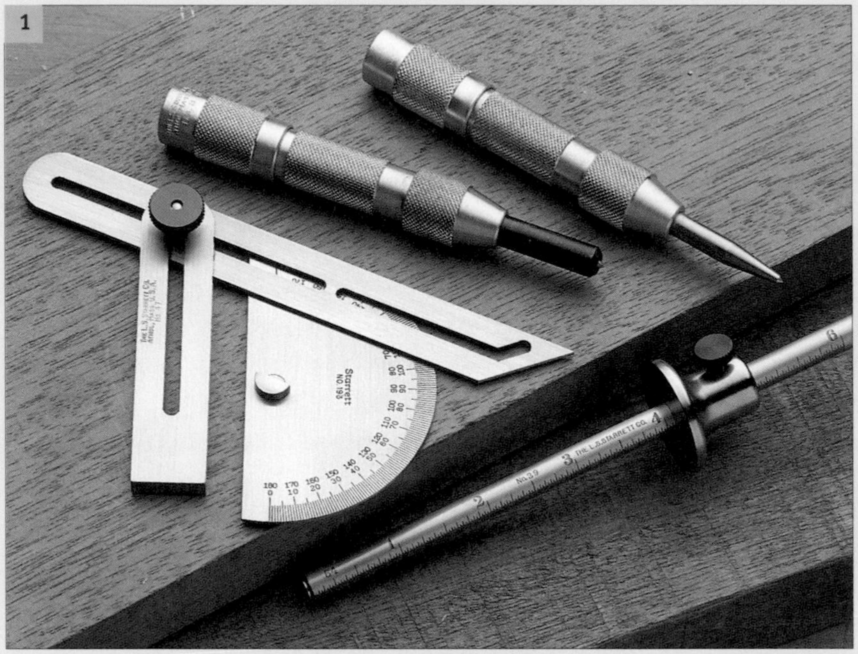

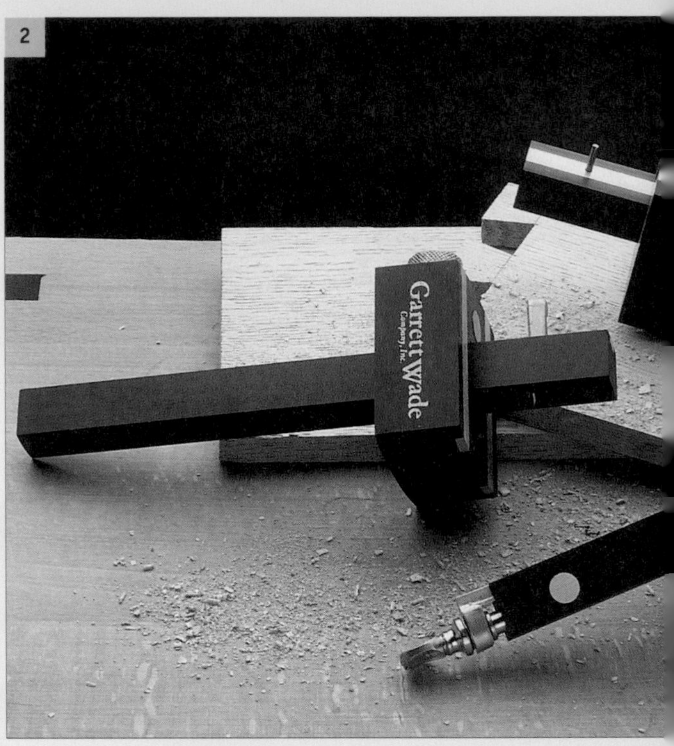

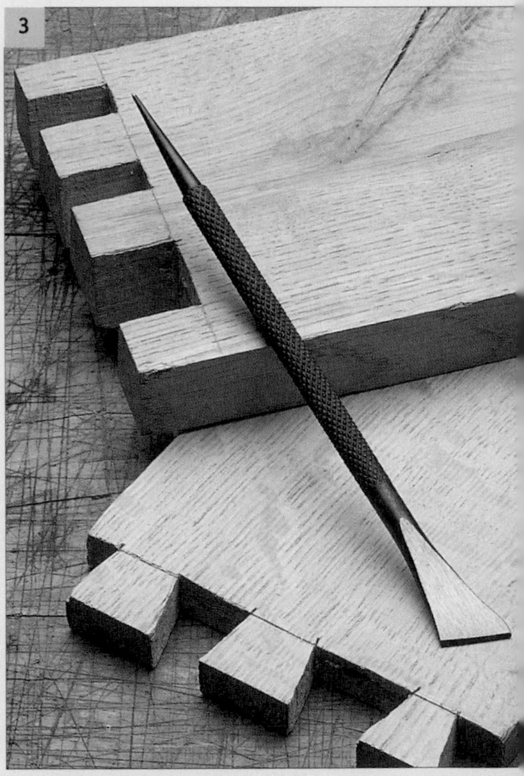

1 Center and centering punches and all-steel marking gauge

Every woodworking shop can use these metalworking tools. The center punch (top right) has a spring mechansim, which allows you to strike a perfect mark. Position the punch point and press the handle down. The self-centering punch (top center) works in the same way, but it has an external locating sleeve, which locates a mark in the center of a countersunk screw hole. The all-steel gauge (bottom right) has a sliding head, and the scratch marker is set firmly in the beam.

2 Marking, cutting, and mortise gauges

Styled on the gauges made in England before the 1940s, these tools are made from a renewable source of African black ebony. The originals were once given as gifts to artisans for long and loyal service, and they are prized by collectors.

3 Double-ended steel scribe

The broad tip of this tool works just like a striking knife or cutting gauge. The point tip acts as a single point scribe, scratching a mark on any steel, wood, or composite surface needed.

4 Veritas trammel points

Trammel points slide smoothly on the supplied rod. The exterior point can be easily adjusted with the knurled nut. The end stop keeps the point from sliding off the rod.

5 Circle cutter and cutout compass

This is a simple French tool. The movable pivot locks anywhere on the bar to adjust the size of the circle, and the cutter will slice through or mark any wood or soft material.

6 Workshop compass and Japanese awls

A first-class tool available in a wide range of sizes, the workshop compass (left) bears no resemblance to those used in school. These are rugged, industrial workshop grade tools. Made in a traditional Japanese style, these Japanese awls (right) have beautifully tapered blades fastened to white oak handles.

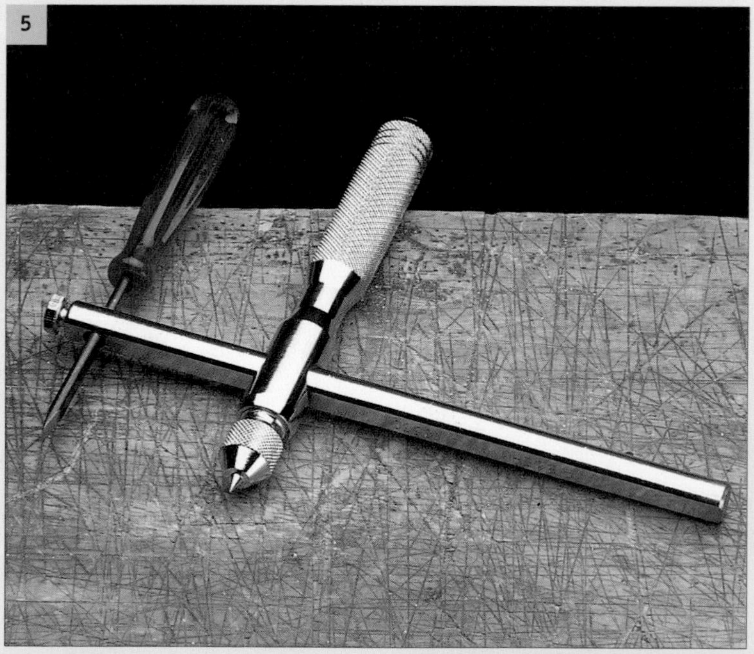

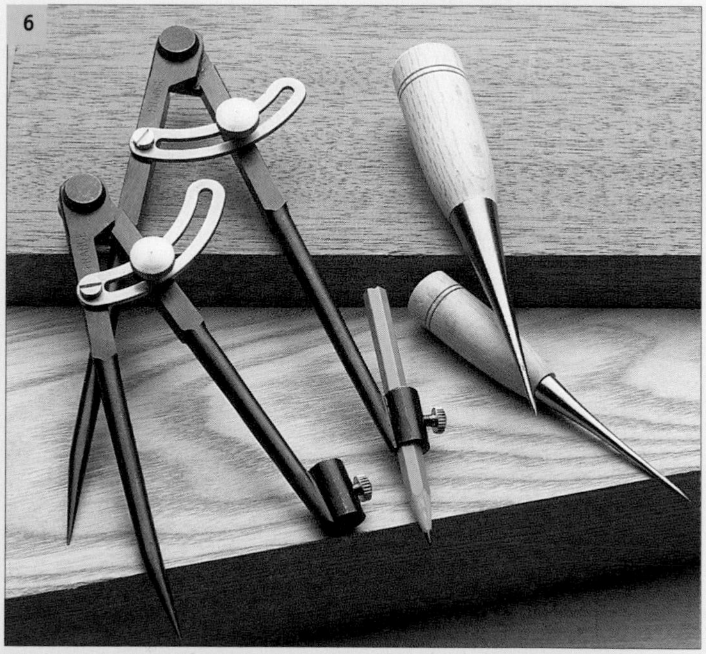

Swedish Quality Steel
PARAGON
3/4"

Cutting tools

2

Saws

The difference in saw blades can be seen in the design of the framed saw (foreground) and the panel saw (background).

All saws have a metal blade with teeth running along its length. The teeth are designed to cut wood fibers and, sometimes, other materials. Whether manually or electrically powered, some saws are better at cutting in a straight line and others are better adapted to cut to a curved outline.

There are three basic handsaw designs. The panel saw has a thick, wide blade for cutting a straight line, especially in thick, hard wood. The backsaw has a spine along the top edge of the blade to keep the blade stiff as it makes an accurate, straight cut. The framed saw, has a blade held in a frame. If a thin blade is used, it has more flexibility for turning as it makes a curved cut.

Following the same principles as their hand-powered counterparts, the table saw has a thick blade for making straight cuts. The thinner blades on the band and scroll saws can be used to make curved cuts.

PAX
THE PROFESSIONAL SAW
HIGH CARBON ALLOY STEEL

HANDSAWS THAT MAKE STRAIGHT CUTS

USING THE PROPER SAW—ONE THAT IS SHARP AND STRAIGHT—a woodworker can cut precisely to a line. He can remove several pieces of equal dimensions from a larger, thicker plank, or he can efficiently reduce the thickness of a wood plank in one operation, instead of tediously planing it. Saws are also used to cut thin veneer from a thick slab of wood.

The basic form of the handsaw has not changed much since the Bronze Age, some 4,500 years ago. The bronze blade was made of thin metal and had teeth shaped similarly to those on today's counterpart. However, to overcome the inherent weakness in the blades of the time, these saws were used with a pull stroke, like traditional Japanese saws. With the change of material to iron and, later, to steel, the saw was designed to cut on the push stroke, which allowed the user to get behind the stroke, making it easier to support the work.

This illustration of Sheffield saw grinders was printed in the *Illustrated London News* in 1866.

In earlier times, the handsaw was the most technically difficult of the hand tools to produce. The blades need a fine balance of several qualities to work well. Western-style saws had to be hard to remain sharp, smooth to prevent binding in the cut, stiff to allow the tool to be pushed through the work, and flexible so that the blade would not break, but bend, under stress. Heavy forges or rolling mills were necessary to produce the sheet steel for the blades, and great skill was necessary to harden, temper, straighten, and grind the blades.

Until 1860, few American tool manufacturers made saws. Most saws were made in England, where Taylor Brothers was one of the most productive manufacturers in the mid-19th century. It was the 1860 Morrill Act, which placed a large tax on foreign iron and steel imports, that sparked the making of handsaws in the United States. Henry Disston was the first major American saw manufacturer.

The design of the saw teeth

There are two basic tooth shapes, which are distinguished by their orientation to the blade. On a rip saw the teeth are more pointed; their cutting edge is nearly in the same plane to the blade and their face is sharpened square to the blade, making an aggressive cut. On a crosscut saw the teeth are pyramid shaped and beveled, moving more slowly through the wood and producing a cleaner cut.

The specific function of either type of saw is determined by the size and number of teeth per inch (referred to as "tpi"). Because cutting along the grain is easier and produces a smoother cut, a rip saw has teeth fewer per inch, and each

From top to bottom are a backsaw with 12 tpi, crosscut saw with 10 tpi, and rip saw with 6 tpi.

individual tooth will be larger. By the same token, a crosscut saw would need a greater number of smaller teeth to cut across the grain, severing the wood fibers, to produce a clean and accurate cut. For example, a typical rip saw might have 4–6 tpi compared to a crosscut saw with 10–12 tpi.

The teeth of a saw are purposely "bent" away from the line of the blade, producing a kerf—the cut, or groove, created by the saw teeth—that is wider than the saw blade's thickness. This "set" is essential to the smooth and easy performance of the saw. It ensures that the saw will move through the material being cut and not bind or become stuck. A saw with numerous small teeth will have less set than a saw with fewer large teeth.

The panel saw

Also referred to as a hand saw, the design of the panel saw is probably the most common and recognizable of all handsaws. It has a wide, tapering blade with teeth cut along one edge and a handle riveted to the wide end. There are basically two types of panel saws: crosscut saws, which are used to cut across the grain (the width of the material), and rip saws, which are used to cut along the grain (the length of the material). Each of these woodworking operations makes specific demands on a saw. The panel saw is most effectively used to cut large, wide, or thick pieces of wood. The sturdy handle provides a comfortable and safe grip, and the thin, but wide blade provides stiffness and reasonable accuracy. Its time-tested design makes the panel saw a model of efficient performance.

When selecting a panel saw, look for a supple blade that can take a good amount of flexing but

Dos and don'ts

Do pause and consider how the task will progress before beginning work. Is the workpiece set up so that you will you be able to maintain your balance throughout the operation? Will the work progress in an efficient way that will not waste time or material?

Do make sure that you use a saw that has sharp teeth. Dull teeth can damage the work and lead to an accident.

This *c.*1816 joiner's handsaw has a steel blade and brass handle. The blade shows the humped shape along the top of the blade typical of saws of the time. The saw blade has corroded with age.

will also spring back straight and true. This quality is a good sign of a saw that will sharpen easily and stay sharp longer.

New vs. old saws

Although panel saws are commercially available today, many seasoned woodworkers prefer to acquire older saws through tool dealers or at yard and garage sales, scrap dealers, and flea markets. The reason for this is that the best saws were manufactured about 70 years ago, at a time that combined developing industrial technology with disappearing craftsmanship.

Even with modern-day promises of perpetually sharp teeth and a sleek plastic handle, cradled in a cardboard sleeve, a new panel saw often leaves much to be desired. Modern saw blades are made of pretempered cold rolled steel, and their teeth may be induction hardened, a process that produces longer-lasting "hardpoint" saw teeth. However, these teeth are so hard, they're impossible to resharpen. So, the panel saw has essentially become a throwaway tool; once it gets dull, you throw it away—and buy a new one.

The old way of producing a panel saw was to shape the blade and cut the teeth from soft (annealed) steel, then harden and temper the blade, concentrating on the teeth. This often meant that the back (the edge opposite the teeth) was softer and more flexible than the teeth. Because the low-tech heat treatment sometimes warped the blade, it then had to be straightened with carefully controlled hammer blows. After all this, the saw teeth were sharpened, the blade was polished, and the handle was attached.

Some of these antique saws were also taper-ground. With this procedure, the blade's thickness was reduced behind the teeth, making the saw better able to cut through wood without binding. This meant that the saw required less set to accomplish the same thing. A saw with less set will cut more easily, be easier to control, and leave a finer cut.

What to look for in an old saw

The most desirable of the old panel saws are the 1930 vintage Disston or Atkins brand saws. If you encounter an old saw, inspect it closely—underneath the rust and the dirt may be a real gem, just in need of a cosmetic cleanup. If a saw is dark with rust and deeply pitted, pass it by. Superficial rust can be easily removed, but a deeply pitted saw blade can never be sharpen properly.

Sight down the length of the saw blade. It should be straight, without any kinks. Although some woodworkers claim to be able to remove kinks, it is rarely, if ever, possible to completely restore a crooked panel saw. Don't let the condition of the saw's teeth deter you. Ignore them. Wavy, dull, or chipped teeth can be easily restored.

Craftsman's tips

When cutting a large sheet of man-made material or a long length of board, as you reach the end of the cut you will need to turn around and cut from the end of the work toward the kerf already made, or you can reverse the saw and, holding the handle with both hands and the saw perpendicular to the work, continue the cut.

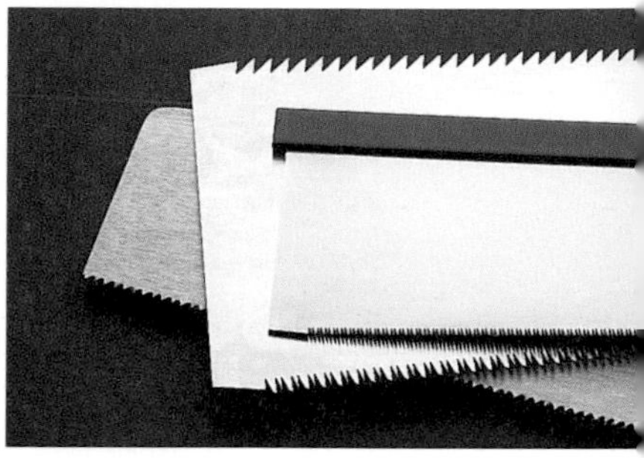

The tiny, precision teeth of Japanese saws leave small kerfs.

This set of Japanese pull-stroke saws includes (from top to bottom) a flush-cutting saw, a replaceable-blade ryoba saw—with one side of the blade for ripping and the other for crosscutting—a trim saw for detailed work, and a dovetail dozuki saw.

Keep an eye open for interesting, detailed handles. Often made of unusual woods, such as curly maple or apple wood, and decorated with elaborate grips and cutouts, the handles on some early saws rival sculpture. Even if the handle is in poor condition, there may be enough of it remaining for an experienced woodworker to reproduce the design.

Japanese handsaws

The popularity of Japanese handsaws among American and European woodworkers has soared in the past 25 years. Japanese saws are razor-sharp, with very fine, slender teeth capable of cutting the thinnest kerf—there is no Western saw that comes close to producing the same results. Japanese saws are strikingly different in appearance from European and American saws, and they also differ in the way in which they cut. Western-style saws cut through wood when pushed, while Japanese saws cut on the pull stroke.

The thin kerf produced by a Japanese saw is due mainly to the thinness of the blade. A thin blade is susceptible to bending or breaking when it is pushed. However, if the blade is pulled, not only can it be made of thinner steel, but the teeth can be set closer together, resulting in a thinner kerf. A thin kerf leaves a clean cut with less clean-up work later.

However, before you discard all your old handsaws and replace them with Japanese tools, you should consider several aspects that are unique to the ownership and use of these special tools.

First of all, they can be expensive. Like any other tool, Japanese saws can range in quality from cheap manufactured tools to expensive custom-made instruments. Second, most Japanese saws are designed for use with soft woods. So when the teeth encounter hard wood, they can break if used incorrectly. And a few missing teeth is all it takes to render one of these saws useless. Third, because of their unusual tooth configuration, Japanese saws are almost impossible to sharpen. The better saws are often sent back to Japan for careful tuning and resharpening—an expensive and time-consuming practice. However, there are less expensive saws that have replaceable blades. When the teeth become dull or damaged, the blade can be changed in a couple of minutes.

The backsaw

In woodworking, there are many operations that require a fine, accurate cut—for example, dovetailing. The backsaw, which includes the dovetail saw and tenon saw, holds a prominent place in the woodworker's tool chest for this purpose. There are several characteristics that distinguish a backsaw from other types of handsaws. The most obvious is a stiff length of brass or steel set over the top edge of the saw blade, providing support for the blade and preventing the blade from flexing or twisting. This spine allows the use of thinner steel, which produces a narrower and cleaner kerf.

The backsaw's appearance—and performance—are given careful consideration, and there are several firms dedicated to reproducing rare 18th- and 19th-century examples for today's woodworkers. These tools are carefully constructed, using the finest steel for the blades and exquisite hardwood for the handles.

The thickness of the blade can vary from a thin $\frac{3}{125}$ inch (0.5 mm) to a stout $\frac{1}{20}$ inch (1.25 mm). The thinner blades, yielding a thinner kerf, are filed for smaller teeth and used for finer cutting. Ideally, the blade should possess some resilience. In the event that the blade is compressed, it should not kink.

Backsaws come in several sizes, including the tenon saw, gent's saw, dovetail saw, and slotting saw. They measure from 5 to 16 inches (125 to 405 mm) in length, but they can be as long as 24 inches (610 mm) for use in a miter box (basically, a frame that guides the saw to make cuts at specific angles). The teeth can number from 12 to 25 tpi.

The variety of backsaws includes (top to bottom) a gent's saw with 17 tpi, a tenon saw with 14 tpi, a dovetail saw with 19 tpi, a standard backsaw with 15 tpi, a slotting saw with 25 tpi, a tenon saw with 13 tpi, and a slotting saw with 21 tpi.

Backsaw handles

Long noticed by collectors, saw handles on older backsaws are more than a place to grip the tool. They are often minor works of art. Their flourishes, sweeping tails, and swirling cusps suggest

WHAT TO LOOK FOR—THE BACKSAW

Regardless of the saw's design, it should be well balanced. It should rest comfortably in the hand and not tip forward or back. The back or spine should be milled from a solid piece of metal instead of simply being bent over the blade. A carefully milled spine will be straight and not exert undue pressure upon the blade, causing it to bend or wander from the cut.

These lightweight dovetail saws come with (from top to bottom) an offset handle, an offset handle with reversible blade, and a typical straight handle. The gent's saw (bottom) has a polished brass back.

movement and speed. The handle of a backsaw is different from one on a panel saw. It is smaller, more delicate, and often made of rare wood. Some examples of backsaw handles are almost like sculpture, exhibiting wonderful details. These tools are a pleasure to hold and provide an unbelievable degree of control and comfort.

The choice of handle is a personal matter. Comfort, not beauty, should be the determining factor. You should be able to grip the saw securely for long periods without your hand becoming cramped. In the past, better-quality saws often had handles made of mahogany or walnut, and some had applewood or curly maple grips.

The handle of a saw can often make a practical difference in how the saw performs. A more expensive saw, besides having a handle of an exotic wood species or cut from an unusually figured wood (the decorative quality of the woodgrain), will exhibit more detail in its design—and more care in its construction. The handle might be better sculpted and carefully shaped to provide blister-free comfort. It might also be better balanced or have more brass rivets or screws, which attach the blade to the handle. Often, a better-quality handle is a good indicator of superior steel in the blade.

The dovetail saw and slotting saw

The most important of the backsaws—and one of the smallest—is the dovetail saw. This saw is almost entirely dedicated to one function—that of cutting dovetails, where a clean and accurate saw cut is the hallmark of fine work. Dovetail saws are available in three handle designs: a closed handle, as on a panel saw; an open- or pistol-grip handle; and a turned spindlelike handle. They all perform alike—which one to choose is a matter of personal preference.

The smallest of the backsaws measures about 5-inches (125-mm) long with a turned handle and has around 25 tpi. Because of the fine teeth, this saw is employed for the smallest tasks in the shop such as for cutting dowels to length, trimming edging to length, or cutting tiny dovetails. Because the teeth on slotting saws are so small, the blades are discarded when they become dull.

Sharpening saws

If most woodworkers routinely sharpen their chisels and plane irons, why don't they sharpen their saws? Saw sharpening is an art, but one that can be easily learned. It requires just a few special but inexpensive tools and a small amount of ability, some experimentation, and a lot of practice. Once you have had enough practice, you will see an immediate improvement in the condition and performance of your saws.

The offset handle on this French flush-cutting saw allows for easier cutting. This tools has a double-sided blade, which makes it more versatile than other flush-cutting saws.

When you sharpen your own saw, you can alter almost every aspect of its configuration. You can customize the pitch, bevel, and set of the teeth to suit the wood, your sawing technique, and the desired result. For example, minimizing the set of the teeth improves the quality of the cut, but causes binding. You can compensate for this by filing a deeper gullet (the intersection of the face of one tooth and the back of the adjacent tooth). A deeper gullet creates more room to chamber the sawdust, which relieves binding.

Tools for saw sharpening

Sharpening a saw is no haphazard affair and requires accuracy and control at every step. Although sharpening may seem like a difficult task, assembling a kit that contains the proper tools will help make the job more easy. Having the proper tools in good condition is an essential first step. The teeth of a sharp saw must be carefully and uniformly prepared. If the teeth on one side of the saw are sharper or have more set, the saw will drift to that side. If the height of the teeth is uneven, the saw will skip or bump along, making a fluid and accurate stroke nearly impossible.

Employ an 8-to-10-inch (200-to-255 mm) mill file to joint and dress the tops of the teeth and to ensure all the teeth are the same height. Don't skimp here—buy a top-quality file. Besides being used to dress saw teeth, a mill file is handy around the shop for general filing.

Use the saw set to bend alternate teeth away from the blade, enabling the saw to cut a kerf wider than the blade's thickness. Setting the saw teeth properly is essential to the smooth, effective, and safe performance of the saw. To accomplish this, place the saw set at 90 degrees to the saw blade and directly over a single tooth. As you squeeze the handle, a pin advances toward a beveled anvil, pressing the saw tooth caught between the pin and the anvil and bending it to a particular degree, or "set." On one side of the blade, bend, or set, every other tooth in the same direction; then repeat the operation from the other side of the blade.

Most saw sets have a circular numbered gauge that corresponds to the tpi count of the saw. Use this scale only as a guide; in no way should it dictate a specific setting. The exact amount of set varies with the task at hand. For example, cutting dry hardwood, such as maple, requires less set than freshly cut softwood such as pine.

The saw file is a triangular file dedicated for shaping and sharpening saw teeth. The file's shape allows the woodworker to file the cutting face of one tooth and the back of the next tooth at the same time, which helps to maintain proper tooth size and spacing. Always fit a file with a handle of an appropriate size that is also comfortable. This will make filing easier and safer. Saw files should be sharp and cut easily; this removes metal quickly and allows the user to maintain a particular angle. If a file is dull, it will skim over the teeth and not remove any metal. You can use a saw file for about three to four saw sharpenings before discarding it.

How to use a saw

Using a hand-powered saw can be a demanding task, requiring physical effort, accuracy, and attention to safety. The first step is to select the proper saw for the job. There are two things to consider when selecting a saw. One is the type and size of the saw. You should choose a saw designed for the task. Hand sawing is physically demanding work, and you want to produce the maximum result for your effort.

The other point to consider is whether the material is being cut along the grain (ripped) or across it. Ripping is generally a little less demanding, in that wood fibers will separate more easily along the grain. So, you might select a saw with fewer, larger teeth. If you were crosscutting, a clean cut would result only from using a saw with

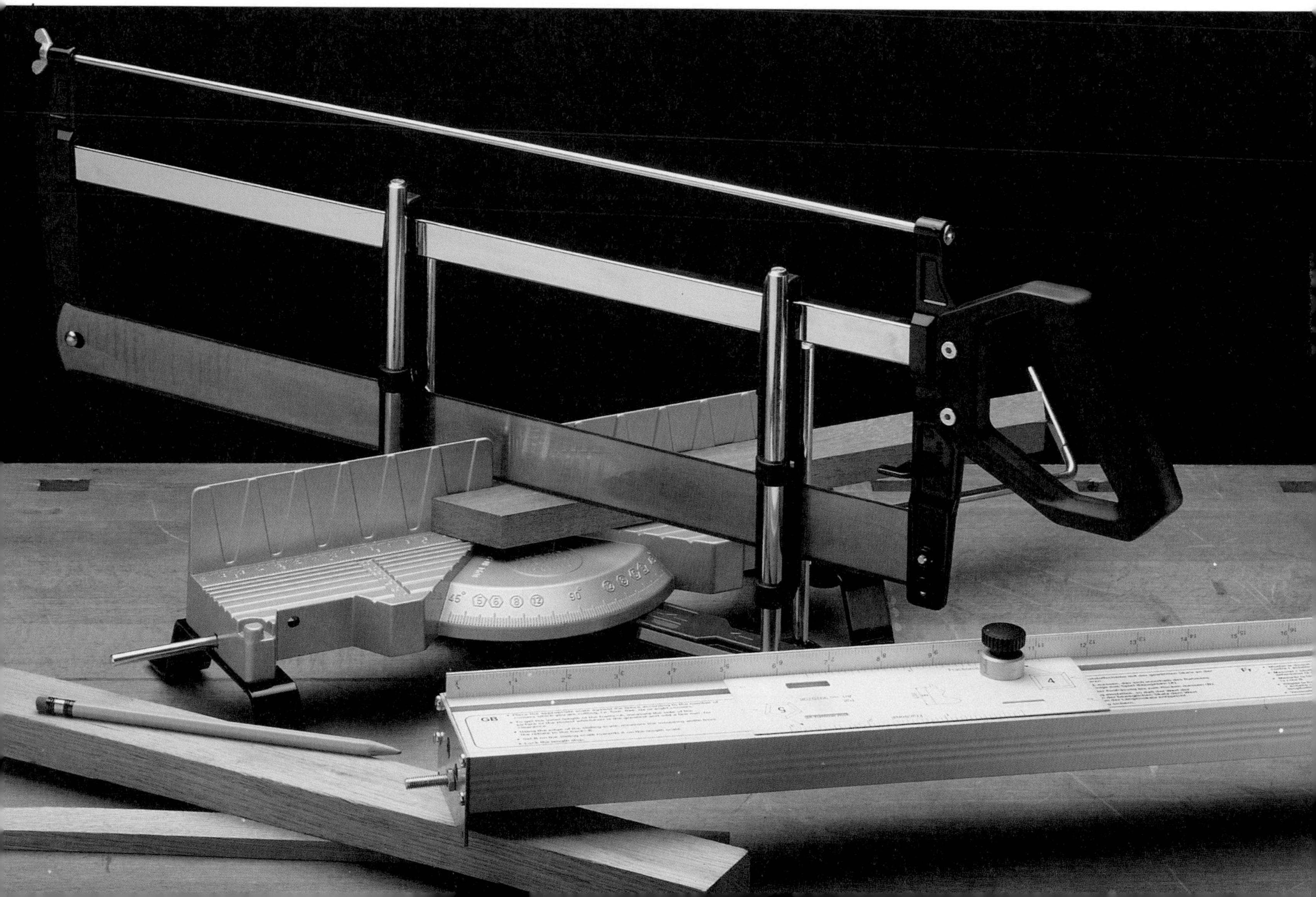

The compound miter saw (below), designed to make compound-angle miter cuts, comes with a standard clamp. A measuring accessory to assist in cutting frames is available.

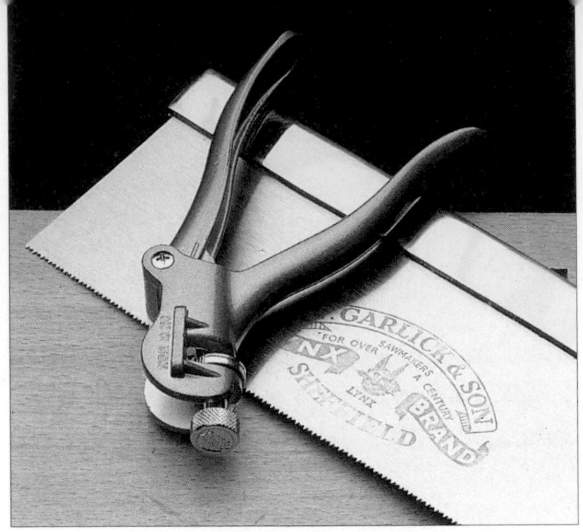

The saw set is designed to reset the saw teeth before they have been sharpened with a file.

smaller, more numerous teeth that are filed correctly. Try to match the type of saw (rip or crosscut) and the number of teeth to the task at hand. This approach is one of trial and error and may require that you switch tools a few times.

The next step is to secure the workpiece. You don't want the wood bouncing around or slipping while being cut. If it is a small job, a workbench vise (see pages 234–237) should be adequate to secure it. A large workpiece might need to rest upon saw horses. A comfortable and safe working height is also important. The workpiece should be placed where it will allow you easy access without causing you to strain yourself or damage either the saw or the material.

It is important that the saw moves freely, without binding in the wood. Despite the proper amount of set, a saw can bind in the wood if the cut is not properly supported. You must make sure that as the cut progresses, the wood does not close in on the saw. To ensure that the cutting operation proceeds safely, always make sure that the waste piece can separate from the larger section easily. This usually involves the careful utilization of work surfaces and, on occasion, saw horses.

Making the cut

The most common mistake beginners make is to both push and pull the saw vigorously, using only the middle section of the saw blade. This practice produces only discouraging results, a dull handsaw, and a sore shoulder. Novices often also experience trouble beginning the cut. The saw, pushed into the cut, often bounces around and skips. The cut line is obliterated and the edge of the work is chewed up.

The proper technique is to place the saw blade on the cut line at the far corner of the workpiece, with about one-quarter of the back of the blade above this point. The blade should be at an approximately 45-degree angle. Rest the thumb of your other hand against the blade to support and guide the saw cut, then draw the saw back lightly, without applying any real pressure. Repeat this several times until you have cut a small, shallow kerf, or notch, into the wood. This notch should be adequate to support and guide the saw and begin the cut.

Most Western saws are designed to cut on the push stroke, and the most effective cuts are achieved with smooth, steady forward strokes. On the pull stroke, return and reposition the saw to cut again on the push. The return pass offers the woodworker a chance to catch his or her breath and make small adjustments in the orientation and angle of the saw to the wood. Once you establish the cut, keep the saw at the 45-degree angle to the

THE VENEER SAW

This specialized French saw is used for cross-cutting and ripping veneer, thin sheets of decorative wood that cover less decorative materials. The teeth are flat with no set on one side and only a slight set on the other. The blade is angled slightly away from the beech handle to give sight lines. The teeth are pointed toward the center to allow you to score the veneer with a stroke before beginning the cut. Other types appear similar to the flush-cutting saw (see page 46), but are smaller in size and have an offset handle veering away at an angle from the double-edged blade.

Which handsaw should you use?

The type of handsaw to choose will depend on the type of wood and direction of the wood grain. Below are a few suggestions.

ACTIVITY	TYPE OF HANDSAW
Rough cutting stock along the wood grain	The rip saw has teeth designed to quickly cut along the grain of the wood. In general, choose a rip saw with 5–8 tpi, ideally about 20 to 26 inches (510 to 660 mm) long. A thick slab of freshly cut oak is best ripped with a 5-tpi rip saw.
Rough cutting wood against the wood grain	The crosscut saw, with 9–11 tpi, has finer teeth than a rip saw. These teeth are designed for cutting across wood grain. The crosscut saw can be used in construction or for making or repairing case furniture, tables, and chairs.
Cutting sheet material (plywood and MDF, or medium-density fiberboard)	Choose a panel saw with 9–11 tpi. Because of the abrasive nature of these materials—they quickly dull standard teeth—you should use only a saw with hardpoint teeth. For reclaimed materials, where nails may be sunk in secondhand wood, use a general-purpose saw.
Making cuts in small planed wood	Choose a backsaw with 8–14 tpi, in lengths from 8 to 14 inches (200 to 355 mm). For making fine cuts, you can use a Japanese-style pull saw, with 14–24 tpi; look for one with a 10-to-12-inch-(255-to-305-mm-) long blade.
Cutting dovetails	The dovetail saw, with 15–21 tpi, is a type of backsaw specifically designed for this purpose. You can also use it for other work requiring fine cuts.
Cutting dowels to length, trimming edging to length, and cutting tiny dovetails	With only 25 tpi, the slotting saw is ideal for making these fine cuts and for modelmaking. To cut dowels flush to the work, you can also use a flush-cutting saw. For thin sheet work, employ the veneer saw, which can be used close to the surface.
Cutting logs into short lengths for firewood	You can use a special log saw, which has large teeth that are designed for cutting on both the push and pull stroke.

wood, with your weight directly behind the saw and the cut line in sight to align the blade with it.

Grip the saw firmly but comfortably with one hand. Some woodworkers employ a four-finger grip with the forefinger placed along the handle. This helps to "aim" the saw and keep it upright and square to the cut. It also prevents the woodworker from gripping the saw too tightly and tiring his arm. If you become tired, your attention to the task will suffer, and controlling the saw will become difficult. Sometimes, depending on the wood, you can place your other hand on top of the handle and exert a little pressure to accelerate the cutting without adversely affecting the result.

The novice should practice sawing in order to develop a steady and effective stroke that is fluid and easy. Try to saw a thick plank in half without pausing while also carrying on a conversation. The result should be both a coherent and interesting chat with a friend and a straight cut. With practice, and as you gain experience and confidence, your sawing will become faster and more accurate.

Every woodworker should be in possession of at least one general-purpose panel saw that both crosscuts and rips, or two panel saws—one for crosscutting and one for ripping. He or she should also possess a standard-size backsaw and a smaller model for detail work. Other handsaws can be acquired as the need arises, for either making rough cuts or fine, detail work. Furniture makers will appreciate a flush-cutting saw for trimming dowels.

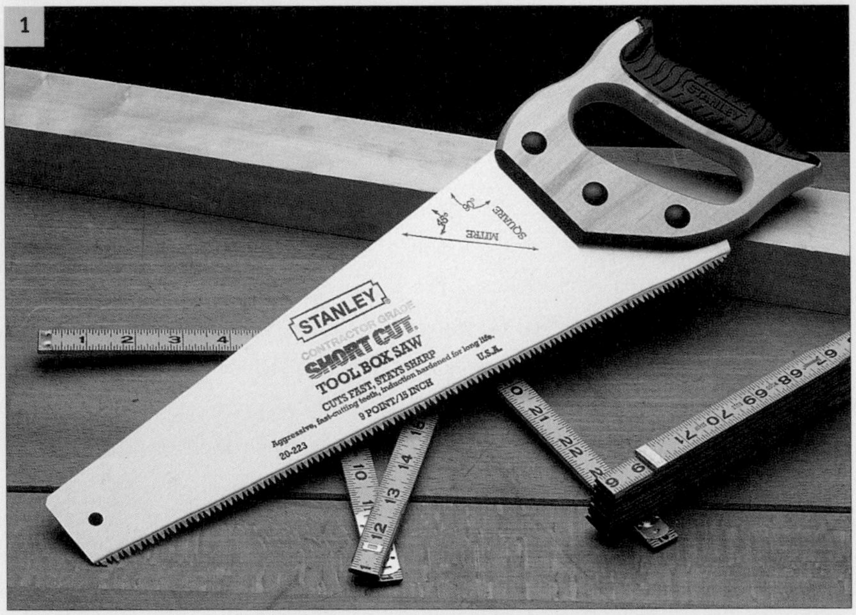

1 Stanley's "short cut" handsaw
With a blade only 15-inches (380-mm) long, this tool will fit into a tool box. It has 9 tpi, and the teeth are specially hardened to resist abrasive artificial materials found in MDF (medium-density fiberboard) and wallboard.

2 Hardpoint saw and "The Chainsaw"
The hardpoint saw (left) has special impulse-hardened teeth (7 tpi) and a soft-grip handle, which is comfortable to use. The teeth resist dulling by most abrasive materials. The French-made saw (right) has a saw blade covered with a special slick black coating and diamond-sharpened teeth (5 tpi). There is nothing refined about the cut it makes, but it is a large, fast-cutting utility saw that is handy to have in the shop.

3 Extra-fine dovetail saw
This extremely fine-tooth saw has an amazing 60 tpi, which produces a very smooth finish. The teeth have virtually no set, so the kerf is minute. The hardened blade can cut soft metals and plastics, as well as wood. The blade is replaceable.

5

4 Japanese tenon saw

By combining the best of Western and Japanese saw styles, this saw works astonishingly well, with a smooth finish and exceptionally fast cutting action—but on the push stroke. The tool follows the classic style of a tenon saw but has precision diamond-cut Japanese-pattern teeth.

5 "Independence" trimming saws

The dovetail saw (foreground) is filed with a rip pattern for a ripping operation; it has 15 tpi to produce fast, smooth results. The carcass saw (background) has 14 tpi and is used for precise cuts across the grain and cutting tenon shoulders.

6 Plywood saw and log saw

The plywood saw (top) has hardened teeth (14 tpi) on the upper, curved edge to allow you to cut into a panel without a drilled hole to start. The log saw (bottom) is a splendidly made saw for cutting logs and lumber. The blade has both starting teeth and main teeth.

4

6

POWER SAWS THAT MAKE STRAIGHT CUTS

CUTTING WOOD ACCURATELY IS ESSENTIAL FOR GOOD craftsmanship. The material should be cut as precisely as possible to insure tight joints. For many years there were basically two types of straight-cutting machines, the table saw and the radial-arm saw. Gradually, a portable motorized miter saw was developed that cuts moldings and narrow boards accurately. Because of its accuracy and compact size, the miter saw has replaced the radial-arm saw, especially among contractors, who did not like carrying a heavy tool to the job site. The accuracy of the miter saw led to the next development in saw technology, the sliding compound miter, which improves on the miter saw by including a telescoping arm that rotates for a bevel cut.

A "circular-saw bench" driven by steam- or water- power turbines is shown in this 19th-century advertisement.

Dos and don'ts

Do make sure the table saw is kept in a "tuned" condition so that it will run well and safely. Accidents and close calls can often be traced directly to a saw or accessory that was not correctly adjusted.

Do not let the push stick, which applies side pressure, move past the front of the blade. This would apply too much side pressure to the blade, which could cause kickback.

Do not rip a badly twisted board, because it will bind and may kick back.

The table saw

The first machine a woodworker acquires is usually the table saw. The tool is simply a table with a circular saw blade in the middle. With this power tool you can make any straight cut in wood. Two jigs are available to support and control the wood during the cut. The rip fence is used for making rip cuts (these are cuts made parallel to the face edge of the board, with the grain), and the miter gauge is used for crosscuts (these are cuts made perpendicular to the face edge of the board, across the grain). The miter gauge can be angled to make angled crosscuts such as miters. The blade can also be tilted to make bevels with the rip fence or miters and compound miters with the miter gauge.

With specialized blades, such as a dado head, the table saw can cut grooves, dadoes, and rabbets. The molding head produces professional-looking decorative moldings, and the variety and combination of cutters allow an almost unlimited choice. With jigs and fixtures, the saw can also cut finger joints, tenons, and dovetails.

Table saw anatomy

The internal components of a contractor-style table saw include the saw cradle (or carriage), trunnions, and the arbor assembly, which is bolted to the underside of the saw table. The cradle supports the arbor assembly, which holds the arbor. The arbor assembly consists of a shaft held in place by bearings. The arbor has a pulley on one end for a V-belt, and the saw blade is held by a flange and nut on the other end. The cradle also holds the motor, which is in the back of the saw on the contractor design and below the cradle on the cabinet style. Two trunnions, one at each end of the assembly, align the cradle and the motor. They make it possible for the cradle to be tilted for bevel cuts.

Two crank wheels change the height and angle of the blade. The tilt wheel on the side of the saw adjusts the angle of the blade to the table. The tilt mechanism generally has a worm gear, which engages a semicircular rack on the front trunnion. When the saw's tilt wheel is rotated, the angle of the cradle and blade changes. Two adjustable screw stops limit the range of trunnion travel and are usually set at 90 degrees and 45 degrees. Another hand wheel at the front of the saw drives another worm gear, which raises and lowers the blade.

This contractor's table saw has an open base to make the machine lighter for transportation, yet the table extends to a reasonable width to handle sheet materials.

Table saw design

Two styles of tilting arbor table saws predominate. The cabinet saw is a relatively large industrial saw with a solid base, or cabinet, and a correspondingly large and heavy tilt mechanism. The motor is enclosed in the base and often drives the arbor with three belts. The contractor's saw is lighter and has an open base. It has a lighter undercarriage, and the motor hangs off the back of the saw on one belt. Contractor-style saws usually cost about half of the price of a more substantial cabinet saw.

There is an ongoing controversy over which way the blade should tilt. On most American, European, and Taiwanese saws the blade tilts to the right. On some American saws, however, the blade tilts to the left. No saw tilts both ways. Blade tilt direction has safety implications. Most people crosscut with the miter gauge in the left table slot, so it is best to have the blade tilt to the right for crosscutting bevels. However, most people rip with the fence on the right side of the blade, which makes the left-tilting saw better for ripping bevels, so the workpiece doesn't bind between the fence and the blade, and kick back. Neither tilt direction presents an insolvable problem. On right-tilting saws, you can move the rip fence to the left side of the blade when you make a bevel cut. With a left-tilting saw, use the right miter slot when crosscutting a bevel.

By fitting a top-quality miter guide to a table saw, you can increase the accuracy of the cuts made with the saw.

The rip fence and miter gauge

The rip fence is basically a straightedge aligned parallel to the blade. It positions and guides the workpiece. The distance between the blade and the fence, which is adjustable, determines the width of the workpiece. The wood remains in contact with the fence during the saw cut. To rip safely and accurately, the wood must lie flat on the table with a straight edge against the fence.

The miter gauge is an adjustable protractor, which slides in one of two miter slots on either side of the blade. The miter gauge supports the work as it is crosscut. The face of the protractor remains square to the bar for the square crosscut and the bevel crosscut. The face of the miter gauge is angled in relation to the blade for the miter cut and the compound miter cut.

Tuning a table saw

All working parts of a table saw must be adjusted and aligned. This includes the trunnions, the table and undercarriage, the square and bevel stops, and the miter gauge and rip fence. Machinery always slips out of adjustment. Just moving the saw in your shop can lose a critical few thousandths of an inch (tenths of a millimeter) in accuracy. Vibration also takes a toll on the accuracy of your table saw. In the case of a new saw, it is possible that your saw was not properly tuned at the factory. A yearly checkup is a good idea. It is important that you go through this tune-up process in proper sequence, because each step builds on the completion of the previous step. A well-tuned table saw exhibits the following characteristics:

- The table and the table extensions are flat.
- The saw arbor is solid and turns smoothly.
- The blade is at 90 degrees to the table.
- The table slots are parallel to the blade.
- The miter gauge is at 90 degrees to the blade and the table.
- The rip fence is aligned parallel to the blade, with the back of the fence angled away from it very slightly, about the thickness of four sheets of paper or 1⁄64 inch (0.375 mm). This prevents binding during a rip cut.

This cabinet table saw has an extended table, which makes it easier to handle large pieces of material.

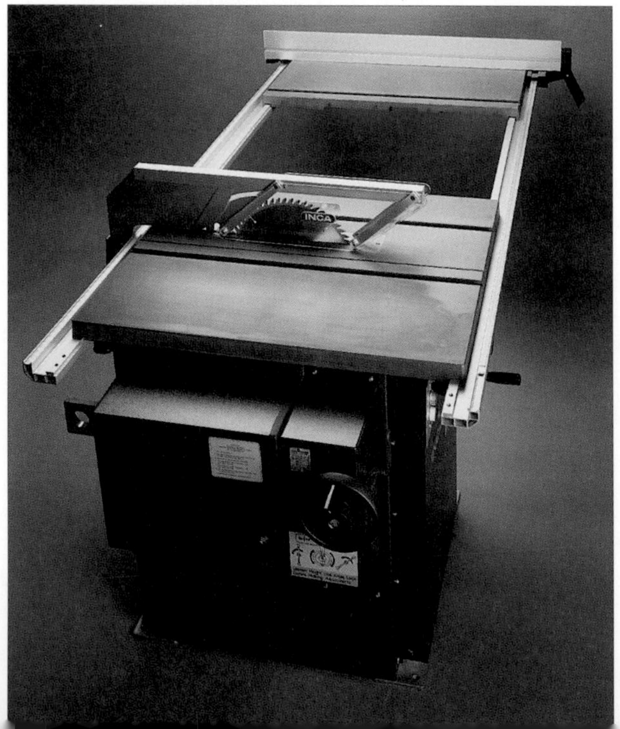

Table saw adjustments

The table top must be flat. A new saw should be checked for flatness with a straightedge and a flat, automotive-type feeler gauge as soon as you get it. Recheck it every few months, especially while still under warranty. The cast top should not be more than 1⁄64 inch (0.375 mm) out of flat. Replace a warped table if it is still under warranty.

Most saws have extensions attached to the table, which expand its surface area. The extension tables are often made of cast or stamped sheet steel. They should be adjusted so that they are level with the table. Check the alignment with a straightedge. If the outside of the extension table is too high or too low, insert a metal shim (or a cut-up piece of aluminum soda can) between it and the main table.

Check and adjust the saw's throat plate, or table insert, regularly. It should be a few thousandths of an inch (tenths of a millimeter) lower than the saw table in front and the same amount higher in back. This prevents the workpiece from hitting the plate before the cut or binding on the table after the cut.

WHAT YOU SHOULD LOOK FOR IN A TABLE SAW

Table saws are made to a variety of standards, and you get what you pay for. The one shown here is a high-quality, professional-style table saw. Better saws have larger, stronger, and more accurately machined parts. Manufacturers are under tremendous pressure to keep the initial cost of a machine as low as is possible. Generally, they want to minimize liability, maximize profit, and sell as many units as possible. Compromises are often made on the standard accessories.

The guards, rip fences, and miter gauges are made economically to lower costs. However, manufacturers of retrofit guards, fences, and luxury miter gauges are compelled by the marketplace to make the safest, most accurate fences possible with little regard for cost. The replacement rip fences have a large front rail and a wide T-fence, which maintains a consistent alignment. (These fences are standard on some saws.)

European miter gauges and American retrofit miter gauges are equipped with auxiliary fences and flip stops. The advantage of these metal stops is their hinge mechanism, which allows them to flip out of the way. This allows multiple stops to record multiple positions. Retrofit miter gauges provide accuracy and convenience at a reasonable price.

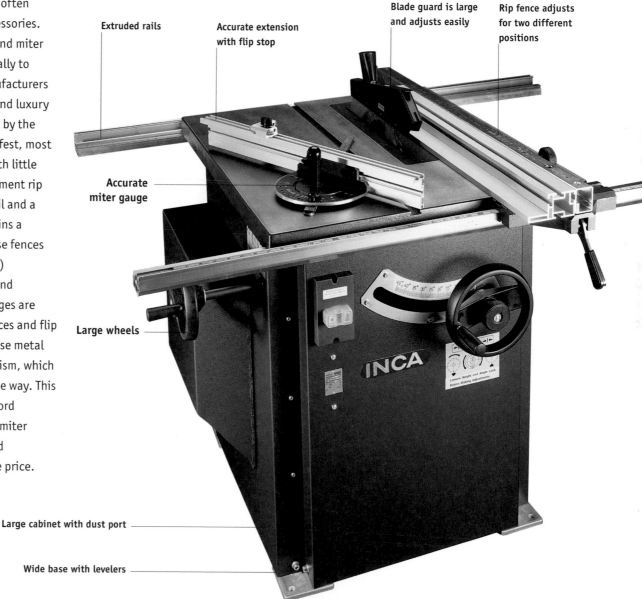

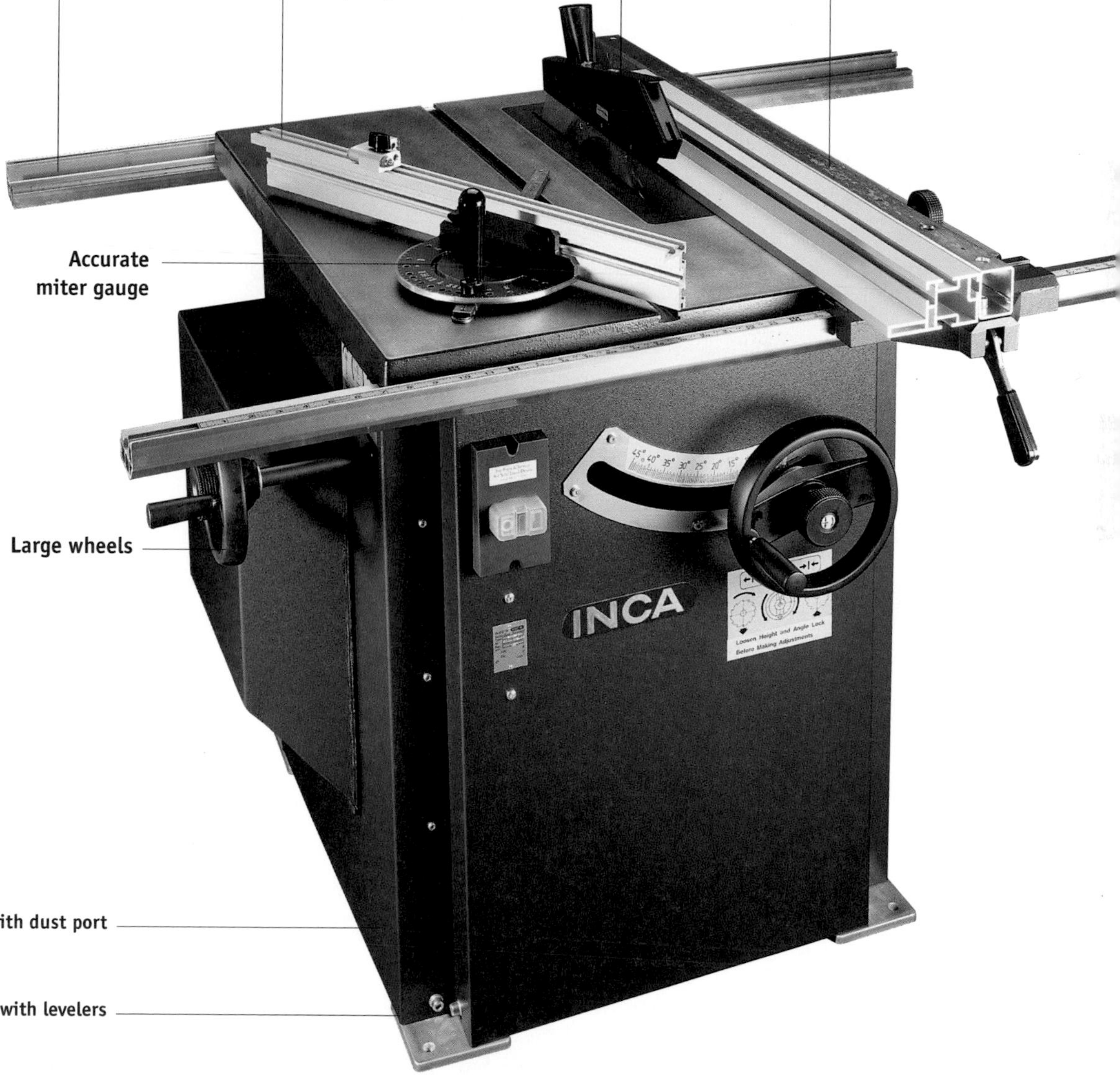

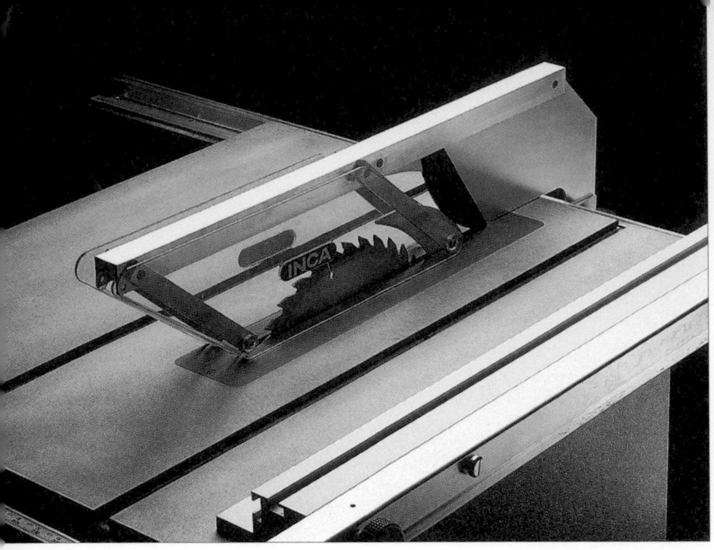

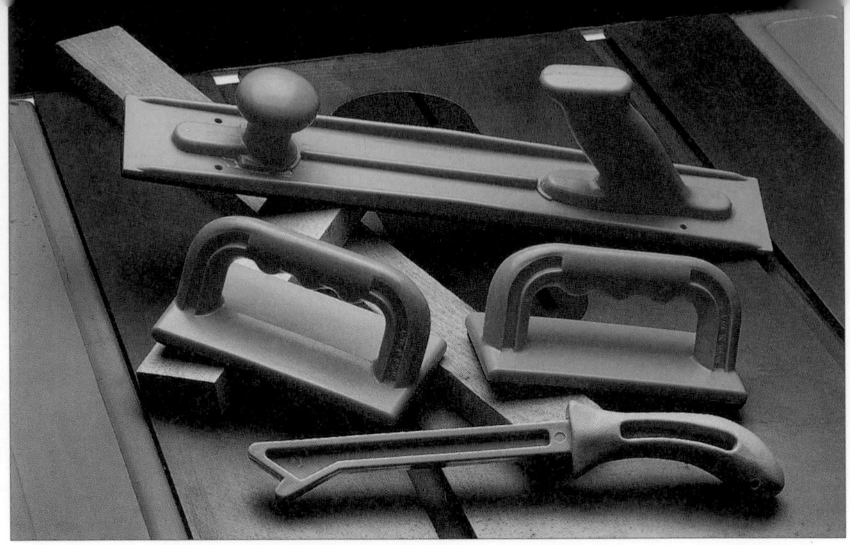

For extra safety, replace a standard safety guard with one rated as one of the best (above).

Keep your hands out of harm's way by using (above right, from top to bottom) a pusher, single-hand push plates, or a push stick. These tools are rubber based.

Adjusting the tilt mechanism

During square and bevel cutting operations, the trunnions and cradle must be solid for true, accurate cuts. To check for cradle play, unplug the saw. Turn the tilt mechanism until it is against the 90-degree stop. Grab the motor and try to shake it back and forth. If it is solid, make one more test. Tilt the saw to 70 degrees and shake the motor again. The cradle may be solid when at the 90-degree stop, but loose in the angled position. If the cradle is loose in either position, you should work on the saw. Occasionally lubricate the tilting mechanism with a dry lubricant such as graphite.

Squaring the blade to the table

For square cuts the blade must be square to the table. Raise the blade as high as it will go. Check the blade's squareness with a high-quality metal or plastic square. Place the blade of the square vertically against a flat carbide-tip saw blade, with the square against the body, not against a tooth. Look for a gap between the square and blade. To get the most accurate reading of the surface of the table and the blade, put the square on the side of the table that has the least amount of space between the blade and the table edge. Turn the saw's tilt adjustment handwheel until the gap of light between the blade and the square disappears. Don't force it. If it is hard to see the gap, lay a flashlight on the table.

Next, adjust the stop for 90 degrees. The blade should reach this angle just as you feel resistance at the tilt wheel, which is a sign that the trunnion is hitting the stop. Never apply excess pressure to square the blade. Use this process for setting the 45-degree stop. Finally, realign the pointer on the front of the saw. This makes the angle scale fairly accurate for quickly setting angle cuts. Never assume that this scale is precise. Always check angles with a square or bevel gauge on the blade.

"Woodwork reflects...the changing face of history. From the first primitive tribesman to hollow the trunks of trees into seaworthy canoes...to the cabinetmaker some thousands of years later having at his finger tips all the technical skill of the workshop, is a long story of progress."

CHARLES HAYWARD, *WOODWORKER* MAGAZINE, NOVEMBER 1962

The feather board (above left), which is best used in pairs, safely positions the work during the ripping process.

A precision miter-setting jig (above) is the tool to use when you want to quickly set an absolutely precise angle.

Adjusting the miter gauge

The miter gauge bar usually fits too loosely in the slot of the saw table to yield accurate crosscuts. To adjust the bar to fit more snugly, you can buy a kit that allows you to install an adjustment mechanism. Some of these miter guides have an adjustable bar. The bar should slide smoothly along the length of the slot with a minimal amount of side-to-side play. Check the fit in the table slot you use most often.

The angle of the miter gauge is adjusted to correspond to the desired number of sides of the project. A four-sided object requires a 45-degree angle of the miter gauge. The protractor on the miter head has a degree scale, but you will get more accurate angles if you adjust the miter gauge using a square or an adjustable drafting square. There is a special accurate square that is made for adjusting the fence for 4-, 6-, 8-, and 12-sided objects.

Aligning the blade to the miter slots

For the miter gauge to crosscut accurately, the blade must be parallel to the miter slot. If they are not parallel, the saw blade can produce a wide workpiece at the back of the blade. This is dangerous, and the back of the blade can lift the binding workpiece and cause kickback (where the work jerks back violently from the blade).

The first step in adjustment is to test the saw's alignment. Most woodworkers think the best reading comes directly from a saw cut. Raise the blade as high as it will go, and clamp a piece of wood to the miter gauge. A 1-x-2-inch- (25-x-50-mm-) square piece of hardwood works well. Crosscut the test piece and move it past the back of the blade. Is it resawn when it touches the back of the blade? If it is resawn, the back of the blade is closer to the miter slot than the front of the blade. Unplug the saw, then slide the miter gauge, with the test piece still clamped to it, next to the front of the saw blade. Rotate the blade by pulling the belt or turning the motor pulley. Don't grab the blade because your hand may deflect it.

As you rotate the blade, one or two teeth will rub against the wood the hardest, making the loudest sound. Mark those teeth and slide the test piece to the back of the blade. The same teeth that rubbed against the workpiece at the front should rub against it at the back, making the same sound. If the sound is the same, the table slot and the blade are in alignment. If you get a louder or softer sound at the back than at the front, the distance between the blade and the slot will have to be increased or decreased accordingly.

Rip fence alignment

For all rip cuts, the work must be guided by the rip fence. In theory, the rip fence is parallel to the blade. In practice, it is best if the fence is slightly canted away from the back of the blade. This

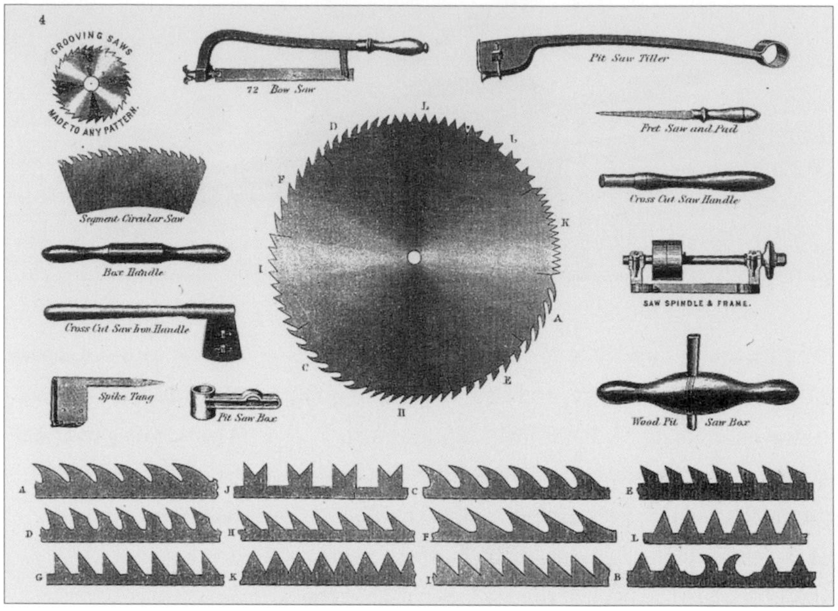

This 1889 *Sheffield list* shows a variety of saw components. The circular blade in the center is used on table saws, and it shows the different types of teeth available on these blades.

prevents the wood from binding between the blade and the fence, particularly if the workpiece warps slightly as it is ripped.

Use the same test piece for crosscut alignment. Lower the saw blade below the table, then move the miter gauge with the test piece to the front of the saw. Lock the rip fence against it. Slide the test piece over the back of the saw's throat plate. There should be about 1⁄64 inch (0.375 mm) clearance between the piece and the fence. To test the amount of clearance, slide a feeler gauge or a piece of paper folded over twice between them.

Blades

The part of the saw that actually does the cutting is the blade. As cutting technology has evolved and cutting speeds have increased, there has been specialization in the design and manufacture of blades. There are a number of types of grinds, and a single blade may be a combination of grinds.

At one time, all blades were made entirely of steel. Tungsten carbide tips are now added to the blade for durability. A steel blade with tungsten carbide tips will stay sharp about 50 times longer in solid wood than with all-steel. With man-made materials, it will outlast a steel tip by 200 or 300 times. In the past, carbide tips had the reputation of being durable but producing an inferior quality of finish cut on the wood. If you wanted a top-notch finish on the board, you had to use a steel blade. With new grinding techniques, today's carbide tips can produce a perfect finish cut on a board.

The old rule—the more teeth, the smoother the finish, but the slower the cut—is still somewhat relevant today. In the past, woodworkers used either finer blades with more teeth for crosscutting or coarser blades with less teeth for ripping. The blade was often changed for ripping and crosscutting operations. Now, with the advent of "combination" blades, one blade can be used for every task.

A dado set of blades and shims (right, top) can cut dadoes, rabbets, and grooves. The saw-setting gauge (right, bottom) is ideal for setting blade heights.

Choosing a blade for the job

You can get the best results from a blade by choosing the correct one for a particular job.

ACTIVITY	TYPE OF BLADE
Crosscutting	The ATB blade is the best blade for crosscutting, but it is also adequate for occasional ripping.
Ripping	The FTG blade is specifically designed for ripping. You should have one FTG blade that you change to if you have a lot of ripping to do. This doesn't have to be the highest quality blade, because the surface of the work should be jointed or planed.
General use	The ATB blade with 50 teeth is the best choice for a general-use blade. It is designed for crosscutting, but it can be used for ripping and cutting man-made materials. Choose a high-quality blade. This blade is the most common one used on the table saw and is used almost exclusively on miter saws and radial-arm saws. Keep two blades in the shop so you have a blade to use when the other one is being sharpened.

ACTIVITY	TYPE OF BLADE
Cutting man-made materials	Although an ATB blade can be used to cut man-made materials, they are best processed with a triple-chip blade. The triple-chip grind is an expensive blade and is used almost exclusively for cutting man-made materials such as particleboard, plastic laminate, and aluminum. If you cut a lot of these materials, this blade is a good investment because this design will produce higher-quality cuts with a very clean, chip-free edge. This blade functions well for crosscutting solid wood, but it has a tendency to burn and be slow when used for ripping.
Finish cuts on exposed ends	Ideally, you should have one really high-quality ATB blade for the finish cut on exposed ends. A high-quality one can leave a beautiful finish, especially on end grain. Some makers suggest that you send these premium blades back to them for sharpening.

Types of blades

An alternative-top bevel (ATB) blade with 40 or 50 teeth is a blade you can leave on your saw without changing. It is often referred to as a "combination blade." The front and the face of the tooth are both angled, creating a point. The point of the tip alternates sides, from one tooth to the next.

The flat-top grind (FTG) blade, as the name implies, has a tooth with a flat face and a flat top. The combination of a large gullet and few teeth allows a efficient ripping action in solid wood. These blades usually have 24 to 32 teeth, but some of them have as few as 12 teeth. This is the roughest cutting blade.

The triple-chip grind is a sophisticated blade using two different types of teeth. One group of teeth has a flat face and a flat top, similar to the flat-top grind; the difference is that the top corners of the teeth are chamfered. The alternating group of teeth are either flat-top or alternative-top bevel. There are a number of combinations available. The one thing they have in common is that the chamfered teeth are taller than the others. They cut out the middle of the kerf; the other teeth clean up the sides. These blades usually have over 60 teeth.

A miter board has fences and gauges to guide a circular saw to make miters and crosscuts.

The compound miter saw tilts and rotates to make bevel and miter cuts.

Safety equipment

Most table saws sold in North America are equipped with a "cage"-style saw guard. This is a see-through plastic or metal guard with a sheet metal spine. The metal spine also serves as a splitter. An attached toothed, anti-kickback mechanism swings backward over the workpiece. This type of guard offers a high degree of protection, but it is unwieldy when ripping narrow pieces, and it is difficult to slide a push stick past the guard if the fence is close to the blade. Sometimes, when crosscutting thick stock, the piece wedges under the anti-kickback fingers and cannot be easily pulled backward after the cut. Also, the cage guard must be removed if a dado or rabbet cut is made. Consequently, despite the best intentions, guards are often left off the saw. Some manufacturers make superior guards to retrofit on an older machine, which overcome these problems. Most of these guards are similar to the European design, which is suspended over the blade.

Wood is unpredictable. During the tree's growth, stresses develop, and these are relieved anytime you cut wood, particularly when ripping. The splitter is the thin piece of metal directly behind the saw blade. It helps solve kickback problems caused by wood pinching the sawblade as it is ripped. If the wood closes after the cut, it pinches the splitter instead of the back of the blade, thus keeping the kerf open. There are two designs for splitters. One, a small piece of metal attached to the back trunnion, is independent of the guard. This splitter is common on European saws. Independent splitters are often found on machines with overhead guards. On some European saws a guard is mounted on top of the splitter. The second type of splitter incorporates the splitter into the guard. This is the most common type of splitter on American table saws.

The guard or splitter must be perfectly adjusted or it will be difficult and dangerous in operation. Using a straightedge, check that the arbor, splitter, and guard lie in the same plane as the blade.

Push sticks and feather boards

If the distance between the blade and the rip fence is less than 3 inches (75 mm), push the workpiece past the blade with a push stick instead of your hand. Push stick designs are varied, but all have in common a notch, which hugs the corner of the workpiece. The notch allows you to push the workpiece forward and hold the back of the workpiece down on the table. About 6 inches (150 mm) before the end of a rip cut, use the push stick to complete the cut. On narrow boards feed the work with two push sticks.

You may want to make a long-nosed push stick, which also holds down the front of the board. These are particularly good for controlling short boards, where the upward force from the back of the blade has a tendency to lift the board off the table.

A feather board applies side pressure to the workpiece. Clamp the feather board to the table so that light pressure is applied just in front of the saw blade. It works best to make the feather board out of a softwood with a lot of cuts. This produces a more flexible feather board and allows some latitude for adjustment. Feather boards and push sticks are good partners, and two feather boards working in tandem are a good team.

The circular saw

Although it is usually thought of as a carpentry tool, the circular saw is indispensable in the wooworking shop. For example, it is a lot easier to cut sheet goods to size with a circular saw than to try to handle them on a table saw. The circular saw cut does not have to be perfectly accurate. If the panel is cut in half, the factory edge can be used against the fence for an accurate cut.

A number of guides are available for controlling the circular saw cut. An inexpensive drywall square can be clamped to sheet goods with the guarantee of being square. A simple shop-made guide of two pieces of wood screwed together in a T-shape is indispensable. There are a number of manufactured jigs and guides available that are designed to make the circular saw more accurate. Some of these guides are aluminum extrusions or injected molded plastic. Some feature crosscut and mitering functions, which help the saw perform the task of a miter saw and a radial-arm saw.

A power miter saw can be customized by adding an extension track system.

Professional installers often use the circular saw in conjunction with the router for cutting panels and doors to length. A rough cut is made with a circular saw using a straightedge. The cut line is often covered with masking tape to prevent chipping, or tear-out. With the straightedge still clamped to the workpiece, a router with a straight bit is used to trim the edge to the final dimension.

Electric miter saw

Some technologies are winners, and one wonders why someone didn't come up with the idea earlier. This is the case with the motorized miter saw. During the 1970s and 1980s manufacturers produced a variety of portable tools, including the miter saw, which is basically a circular saw on a large hinge. The blade is lowered into the work much like a manual miter saw. A large protractor

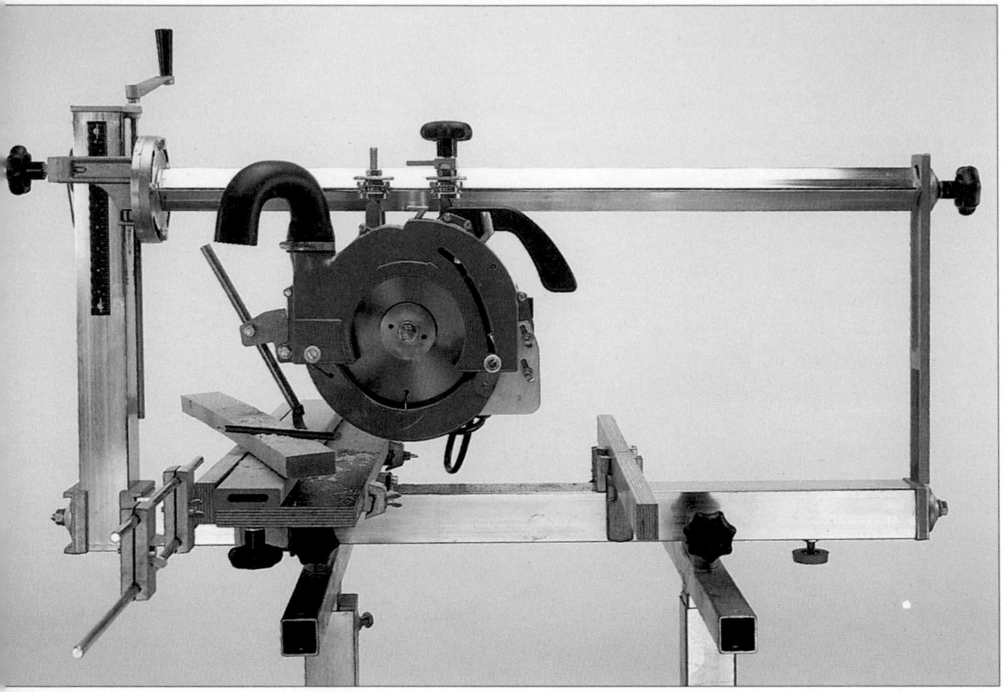

The radial-arm saw is designed so that the motor and blade move along an extended arm. This particular model has a closed frame.

mechanism angles the saw in relation to the fence. This simple design is dependable and accurate and requires essentially no adjustment or maintenance. Some manufacturers have developed a tilt mechanism, which allows a compound angle cut.

The miter saw can be accurately readjusted in minutes. The fence is usually solid; the angle is adjusted by loosening the fence and placing a square between the fence and the blade. The blade is squared to the table with a simple single-bolt mechanism. The only drawback is that the saw does not cut wider than 4 inches (100 mm).

The sliding compound miter saw

The design of the miter saw was fine, except that it needed more crosscut capacity. The sliding compound saw solves the problem. It is a combination of the radial-arm and miter saw. Instead of being hung from an arm, like the radial-arm saw, the motor is suspended from telescoping tubes. It has the pivoting feature of the miter saw and the width capacity and the compound angle cutting ability of the radial-arm saw. It comes in a compact design so that it easy to carry, stays accurate for a long time, and is easy to adjust.

A huge advantage of the saw is the very large protractor, which is easy to see and locks in place quickly. Combined with a good stop system, it is capable of cutting hundreds of accurate parts exactly the same size in a short period of time.

A unique feature of the saw is that it can perform three different sawing techniques. As with the radial-arm saw, it can be pulled through the work. As with the miter saw, the blade can be lowered through the work. It also allows the third option of pushing the saw through the work—a European concept. When it is used on wide stock, the saw is first lowered onto the work and pushed forward through the remaining material. The chop-and-push technique is possible because the motor and hinge are supported by a sliding arm, which allows the saw to move in and out.

It may take some time to get used to the push technique, but once you do, it will seem very natural. When you think about it, pushing is the best option. Like the radial-arm saw, the sliding

Craftsman's tips

To rip wood where the edge is not straight, joint it straight before making the cut, or make a jig to hold the wood securely while making a straight cut. If the wood is not flat, face-joint it to establish a flat surface, or position the workpiece so that it does not rock during the saw cut.

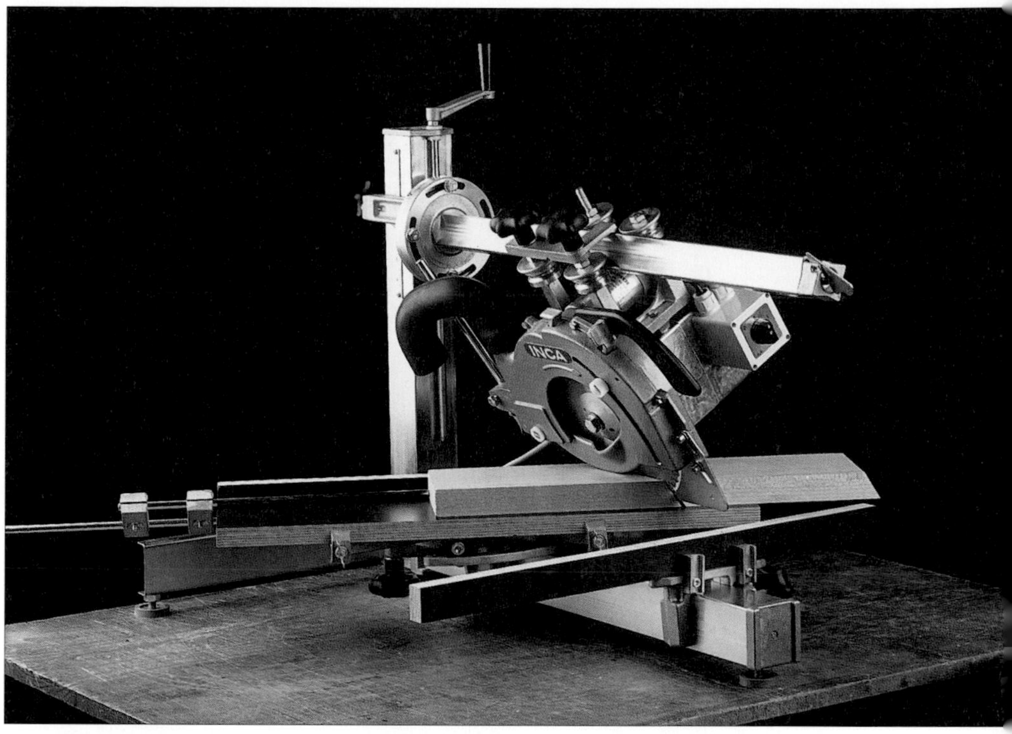

The motor and blade on a radial-arm saw can be adjusted to make miter cuts and rip cuts. This is a European model.

compound saw can also be used to cut a compound angle. This is accomplished by a simple design, which allows the whole motor mechanism to rotate at an angle. The mechanism is easily readjusted and the scale is easy to reset.

Radial-arm saws

The radial-arm saw was developed in the late 1920s and was first used at lumber yards and on construction sites, where its ability to crosscut large pieces of material efficiently was especially valued. When you study the design, it is easy to see how the saw evolved from the handheld circular saw. The blade attaches directly to the motor shaft. The motor hangs from a movable, or radial, arm, which is supported by a post. The motor is supported by the yoke which allows it to be rotated and angled.

The great advantage of the radial-arm saw is its versatility. As in the table saw, the motor is held stationary for rip cuts and beveled rip cuts. The saw is pulled (or pushed) through the work for crosscuts (this is easy to do on long pieces), miters, bevel cuts, and compound angle cuts.

As with all machines, however, the radial-arm saw has some drawbacks. It has a reputation for being less than accurate. The motor hanging from an arm is the source of some of its weaknesses. More care and attention are required to make it accurate, and it needs frequent cleaning and maintenance. Because the saw has a number of parts, adjusting it is more time consuming, and the adjustments must be done in the proper sequence.

The radial-arm saw incorporates several different parts, and if there is any movement in any of the parts, the accuracy of the cut suffers. The greater the movement, the greater the inaccuracy. To get precise cuts, the saw blade must be held securely by the arm, table frame, and yoke. Dirt and rust are the enemies of precision on any machine, but particularly on the radial-arm saw, because it has so many moving parts. The single most important thing that you can do for your saw is to keep it clean. Clean the roller track and bearings often with a thin coat of light machine oil. If you detect any roughness in the movement of the saw on the arm, wipe off the dust or chips with an oily rag.

The radial-arm saw has a place in many shops, but it is in decline. Its many parts are expensive to make, which causes the price to increase. Its forte—crosscutting long pieces—has been taken over by the electric miter saw and sliding compound saw. These saws are more accurate, less expensive, and more portable, which gives them an edge with the contractor and the hobbyist. In the future, the radial-arm saw will probably be relegated to professional shops and lumber yards.

There are dozens of accessories available for the table saw. Some of these are replacements for standard accessories supplied with the saw; others are additional accessories to provide more flexibility when using your table saw. The accessories that you choose to purchase will depend on how often you will use your saw, how accurate you want your cuts to be, and the type of work you want to do with the tool.

1 Table saw trueing disc

Blade runout or wobble is a chronic problem when trying to do accurate joinery. Sometimes the problem is with the table saw's arbor, bearings, or blade flanges; more often, it is with the blade itself. The trueing disc, which is inserted between the existing flange and washer, acts as an extra flange to improve the cutting performance.

2 Tenoning jig

This steel and cast-iron jig simplifies cutting tenons on a table saw and makes the cuts more reliable. The adjustable jig has a clamp to hold the stock in position.

3 Height gauge attachment

The ruler of an ordinary combination square can be turned into a height gauge with this attachment. You can use it to set up any power tool.

4 Taper jig

A built-in scale is included in this fully adjustable, aluminum taper jig. It can be assembled for either left-hand or right-hand use. You can use it with your rip fence to cut tapers of up to 15 degrees.

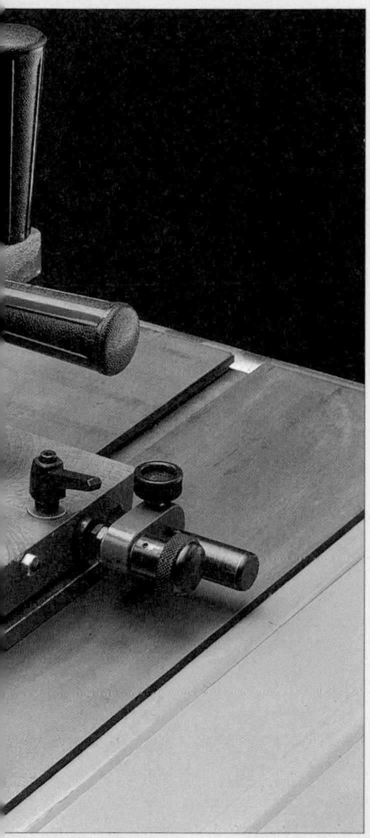

5

5 Electronic blade gauge

To get spot-on height readings, you can use this electronic blade gauge. The main body has electronic contact points, which are finished with printed circuit-board material. When the tip of the saw tooth touches the contact as you "dial in" the height, the LED light goes on. A nickel plating prevents wear to extend the liftetime of the tool for many years.

6 Blade-locking device

Changing table saw blades is almost always a tricky proposition. Made of tough nylon, this blade-locking device is a secure and safe way to "grab" the blade and hold it firmly while unlocking, then relocking, the arbor nut on your table saw. The device will "rock off" the blade if the nut is being overtightened.

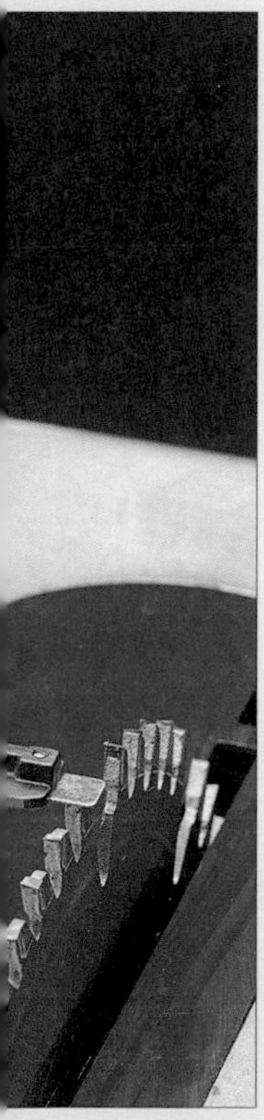

4

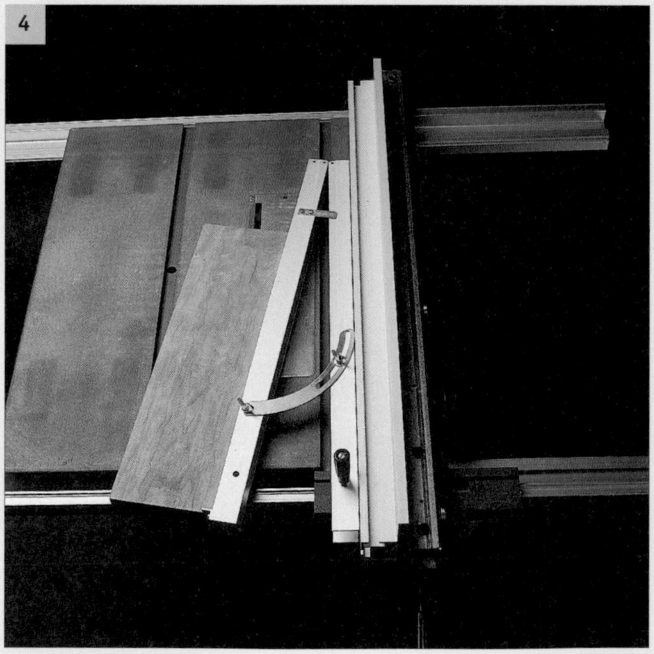

6

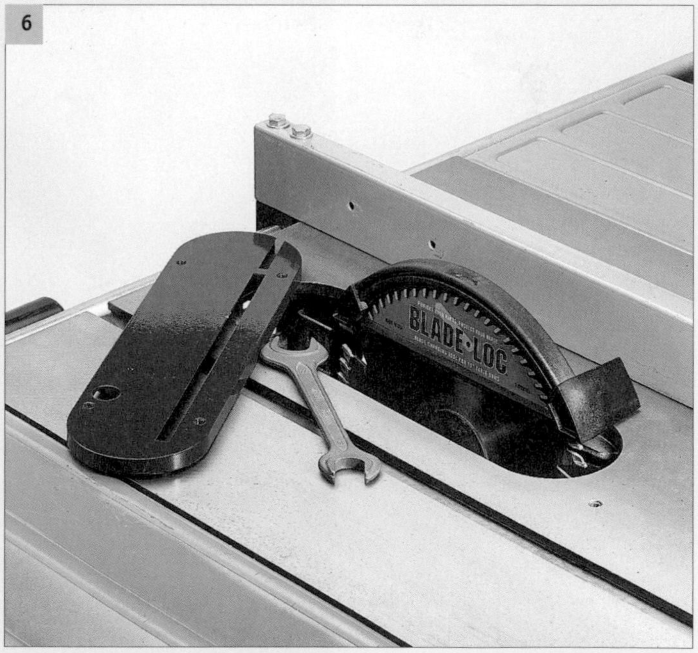

HANDSAWS THAT CUT CURVES

IN 5000 BC, THE EGYPTIANS WERE MAKING SAWS FROM IRON, copper, and bronze—sometimes fitted with jeweled teeth for stonecutting. But these metals lacked rigidity, so saws made of these materials could be used only on the pull stroke, instead of the pushing action more commonly used today (except in Asia). These early tools were really abrading tools. They had unraked teeth, which rubbed instead of cut.

It took the Iron Age and the Romans to bring about major advances in saw manufacture, in which the saw teeth were "set"—bent slightly to the left or right. They also developed the framed saw. Much of this development took place in Mediterranean areas, but there have been many fine examples of Iron-Age cutting tools found in Great Britain, Scandinavia, Switzerland, and Russia. The Middle Ages saw few major technological advances, but it is thought that the change from pull to push blades took place during the late 11th to early 12th centuries.

In the saw's early history, the metal used in the blades was soft and often needed a stout frame to hold the blade rigid during heavy cutting; otherwise, it was susceptible to breaking. It was only in the 17th century, when improvements in steelmaking came about, that it was possible to make the unframed handsaws (see pages 40–51) that are more commonly used today. However, the width of the blade makes these tools unsuitable for cutting curves.

A woodsman uses a framed saw to cut a log in this painting by the French artist Camille Pissarro (1831–1903).

The framed saw

With few exceptions, most of the handsaws that are best suited for cutting curves belong to the framed saw category. This ancient design consists of a narrow blade, also known as a web, which is held rigid within a frame. The variety of jobs for which the framed saw is used is reflected in their wide range of sizes—from the small bow saw, with blades 6-inches (150-mm) long, to the 10-foot- (350-cm-) long pitsaw, which was used by two men, one inside a pit dug in the ground. Naturally, the smaller saws are used for jobs that require precise cuts.

The most important characteristic of a framed saw is its ability to cut along a curved outline if fitted with a narrow blade. This feature is one reason you'll find these saws popular among antique restorers, museum conservators, and furniture makers who favor traditional forms. Another characteristic is that a blade can be changed, as work changes, or it can be replaced if it becomes damaged. Wider blades used in a framed saw can be good for long, straight cuts. Today, several types of framed saw, such as the bow and coping saws, are still available.

The smaller of the two frame saws (background) cuts like the two bow saws (foreground) but with a longer stroke.

Dos and don'ts

As with all saws, always make sure you only use a sharp blade. A dull blade will only damage the work. It can also cause a greater injury to the user then one made with a sharp blade. You'll find it much easier to cut with a sharp blade.

When using a framed saw, do always hold the saw with two hands. Because of their light weight, these saws are difficult to control and require extra guidance to follow the cut line.

Don't use the saw too aggressively. By doing so, you can damage the teeth of the blade or the blade itself.

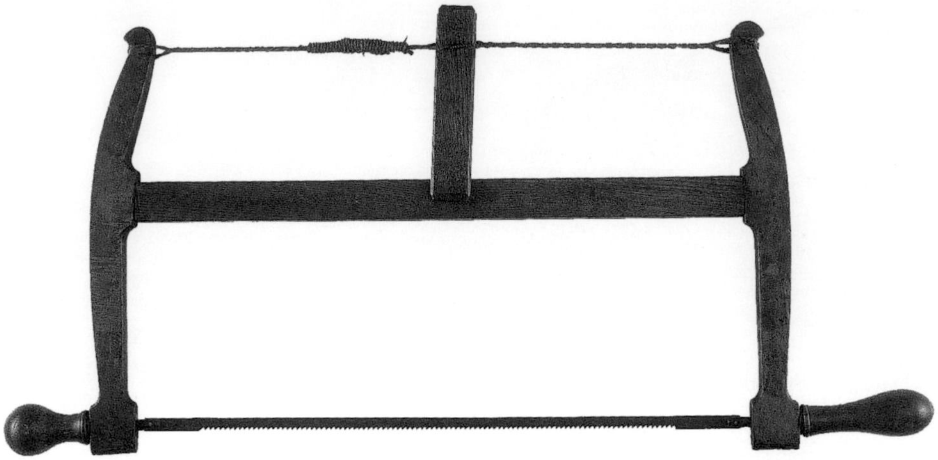

This late-19th-century English bow saw (above) has a frame made of mahogany. Some homemade examples have elaborate decorative carving incorporated into the frame.

A blade within a frame

The basic design of the frame saw consists of a four-sided frame, with a blade held parallel between the two long stretchers and attached to the two shorter ends. This saw is essentially an early version of the band saw (see pages 72–81). The sizes vary from a two-man-operated saw that is large enough to cut logs roughly into lumber to a small saw with delicate teeth for cutting thin sheets of veneer.

In parts of the world where electric power is unavailable or power machinery is unobtainable, the frame saw (or bow saw, as it is known when smaller and with a very narrow blade) is still popular. The side pieces of the frame are known as cheeks, or arms. The blade is held taut between the bottom ends of the arms, and a tensioning wire or rope—sometimes called a Spanish windlass—is stretched between the tops of the arms. A toggle—basically a wooden stick—is entwined in the wire or rope and rests on the center stretcher. By turning the toggle, the wire or rope is tightened. When the wire or rope is tightened, the center stretcher acts as a fulcrum, exerting tension on the blade, keeping it taut. Some versions use a rod in place of the wire or rope, with a wing nut or turnbuckle to create the tension.

Fittings hold the blade to the frame. On some models, turning the handles will rotate the blade to make curved cuts. In continental Europe frame saws are fitted with wider blades for making straight cuts, as well as with narrow blades for cutting curves, which are the only blades used in Great Britain. (A narrow blade makes it easier to use the saw to cut across the grain of the wood.) Both styles are used in North America.

Historically, cabinetmakers and carpenters used this saw to cut curved parts such as chair legs and arms and arches; and wheelwrights used it to cut curved parts of wheel rims. The frames were often homemade, which can make it difficult to date them. Chair makers once referred to this saw as a "dancing Betty" or a "Jesus Christ" saw, because of the bowing motion necessary to use it.

Another type of framed saw is known as the bucksaw—it has one arm longer than the other, which serves as a handle. This is the framed saw of choice for rough everyday work and chores such as pruning limbs and cutting firewood.

ABOUT THE FRAME

The frame of the bow saw may have a center stretcher that is tenoned to the arms, usually with shouldered tenons. These tenons should press against the cheeks evenly when the tensioning wire or cord is the correct tightness. After time, you may need to replace the stretcher or shorten the blade to maintain the same relationship. To shorten the original blade, simply cut it with a hacksaw and drill a new hole for the pin to secure it in the fitting on the frame.

Another type of stretcher has open housings that fit over the arms of the saw, which causes more movement in the frame. Unless the stretcher is correctly centered in the frame, it will be difficult to tension the blade correctly.

The coping saw with the beech handle (left) has hardened, high-carbon steel blades. The fret saws (right) have an extra-rigid, cast aluminum frame for good blade tensioning.

Using a frame saw correctly and efficiently can take some practice before you get it right. You must make sure that the blade is properly tensioned. The amount of tension necessary will depend on the length and width of the blade, the size of the saw frame, and the type of wood being cut. Too little tension will produce a poor cut, but too much tension can damage the blade, as well as the frame. You will know that the tension is correct when you can make a cut on the push stroke and it "feels sweet."

Coping and fret saws

One of the smaller of the framed saws is the coping saw. This saw is a relative newcomer to the tool industry, first making an appearance in tool catalogs only in the 1920s. The coping saw has a narrow metal frame, which supports a thin blade held in place with a hook, loop, or pin on each end of the blade. The blade can be rotated in the frame to make intricate curved cuts. A wing nut is used to adjust the blade's tension. A wooden handle is attached to the frame.

THE HACKSAW

A variation of the frame saw, the hacksaw was manufactured in factories beginning in the 19th century. Some inventive homemade versions incorporate a section of a scythe blade. Although typically a metalworker's tool for cutting metal, the hacksaw can be found in woodworking shops for cutting metal hardware such as bolts. It has a detachable blade. There is a range of blades available with different sizes of teeth to suit different materials: from fine teeth for thin sheet metal to coarse teeth for soft metals. If you are likely to do little metalwork, a junior hacksaw will suffice; they take only special small blades.

You can use the coping saw to make interior cuts in a workpiece. After drilling a hole in the waste area of the work, insert an unsupported blade end into the hole, then attach the end to the frame. You can also use the saw for small general-purpose jobs, such as cutting joints of baseboard and window trim and for cleaning out waste between dovetails and tenons.

The blades for coping saws are available with 10 to 28 tpi (teeth per inch); 15 tpi is reasonable if you work with hardwoods. The blades, which are disposable, are very thin and susceptible to damage, especially if it becomes overheated. Avoid being too aggressive with the saw and take short breaks to allow the blade to cool down. Always keep extra blades in stock.

The fret saw is similar to the coping saw, in that a slender metal frame supports a blade. But the fret saw has a deeper throat, which allows it a deeper reach to cut further away from the edge of the work. This saw also uses a much thinner blade then the coping saw, and it is suitable for fine detailed work, such as fretwork and marquetry and veneer work, where there is often a need to execute precise curved cuts in very thin material. You should purchase only premium-quality blades. Although they are more expensive, their performance justifies the cost.

An adjustable-frame fret saw, which woodworkers have borrowed from the jeweler's saw, is also available. The length of the frame can be adjusted to take blades of different lengths. This saw is available in a number of throat depths, up to 8 inches (200 mm) deep.

Compass saw

Although not a framed saw, the compass saw does similar work to the coping saw, but more heavy duty. It has a thin blade set into a pistol-grip-style handle. The blade quickly cuts curves, circles, and cut outs in wood, plywood, and wallboard. A smaller version is the keyhole saw, which also cuts light metal. The Western-style keyhole saw cuts on the push stroke, but the Japanese saw uses a better pull stroke.

This late-19th- to early-20th-century hacksaw has a curved end that holds one end of the blade and a thumb turn at the other end to tighten the blade. Similar saws were often used by butchers.

Most woodworkers will benefit from having at hand a bow saw and a coping saw for making general curved cuts in wood and a hacksaw for cutting metal, even if it is used only for cutting off bolt heads and other nonwoodworking "shop" tasks. A compass saw can be useful when working with sheet materials. Other saws can be acquired for more specialized jobs as the need arises.

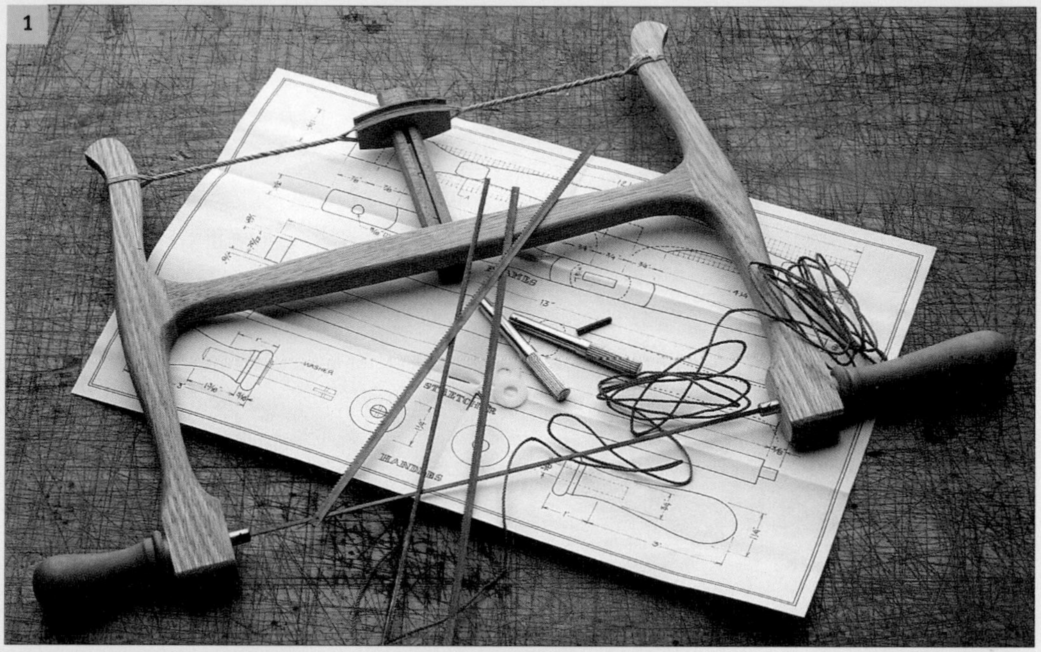

1 Classic bow saw kit

Make your own bow saw using this kit. It comes with a full scale plan, brass stems and washers, tapered fixing pins, cord for the Spanish windlass, and blades.

2 Japanese trim and keyhole saws

The trim saw (center left) is essentially a small keyhole saw with a fine-tooth narrow blade and walnut handle. The keyhole saw (center right) is based on the Western-style saw but has a shorter, narrow blade with a tight turning radius.

3 Fret saws

The adjustable-frame fret saw (foreground) can hold blades of lengths up to 6 inches (150 mm), which allows you to use broken blades. The deep fret saw (background) can cut tight curves far from the edge of a piece of thin wood.

In this 1881 print by Louis Poyet, a man is operating a scroll saw by pumping a pedal with his foot.

POWER SAWS THAT MAKE CURVES

CURVES ARE USED IN WOODWORKING FOR DECORATIVE AND structural reasons. The cabriole leg on a chair is chosen for aesthetics, while the round dining room table design allows more room for diners than one with corners. No matter what kind of woodworking you plan to do, you will eventually want to make curves of some type. There are three machines commonly used for making curves. The band saw and the scroll saw are stationary machines, and the saber saw is a handheld tool. Each has advantages and disadvantages. None of these tools does every task—in fact, they complement each other.

The scroll saw

The scroll saw is a stationary machine that is usually smaller than the band saw. A blade of about 6 inches (150 mm) is held in a clamping mechanism that keeps it taut. The blade is suspended between two arms located above and below the table. A drive mechanism moves the blade up and down, which provides the cutting action. Scroll-saw blades are very narrow and are best used for intricate designs such as puzzles. The blade can be threaded through a hole in the workpiece, allowing inside cuts.

There are a several features that make the scroll saw easy to use. Because the blade is held in a frame that goes up and down, there is no need to make adjustments to the saw. Changing the blade is simple. The sawing speed is often variable, which makes it easy to match the sawing speed to the material and allows the cutting of hard materials such as metals. With the right combination of speed and blade, the saw cut can be the finish surface with no need for sanding, which makes the scroll saw popular. It is the ideal saw for small projects that require curves such as puzzles, toys, jewelry, marquetry, intarsia (a type of inlay decoration), furniture repair, and decorative furniture elements.

The scroll saw is not as efficient as the band saw, because the blade is cutting only half of the time it's in operation. It cuts on the downstroke but doesn't cut on the upstroke. In addition, the blade is limited to small sizes, which restricts the type of work that it can be used for.

A clamp is usually engaged to keep the workpiece flat on the table, so that the upstroke of the blade doesn't lift it off the table. If the workpiece is lifted off the table, it will start to vibrate, which often breaks the blade. The hold-down clamp has to be adjusted correctly, which can be tedious.

From precision joinery to metal cutting to fretwork, a good scroll saw can be an enormously useful addition to any shop.

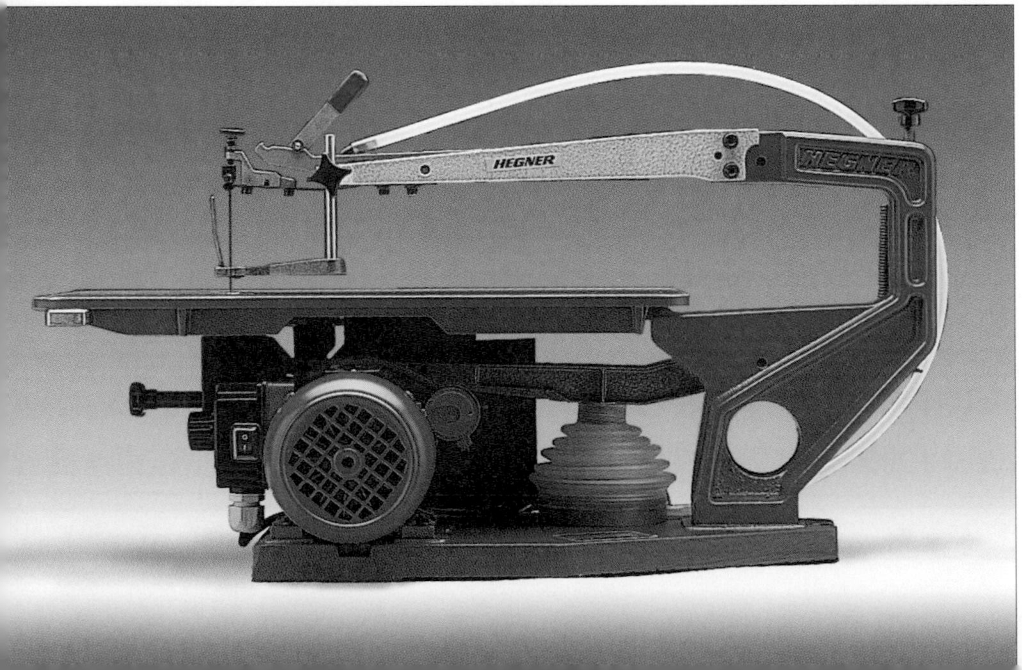

Scroll-saw blades

The blade size is designated in numbers. The fine blades no. 00 and no. 2 are best run at slower speeds to avoid breakage from metal fatigue. The thicker blades no. 5 and no. 7 can tolerate faster speeds. Inexpensive blades are stamped out of a

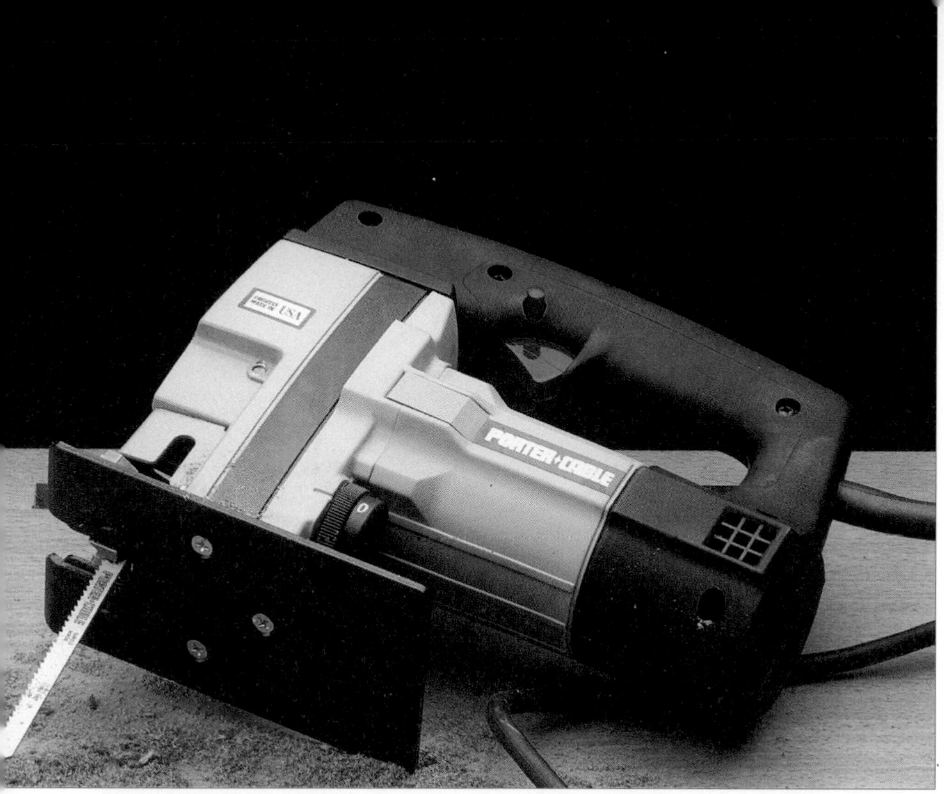

Although you can use a saber saw to cut straight lines, this tool excels in making curves. The depth of the cut varies with the model, so you should make comparisons before purchasing one.

Dos and don'ts

Do use the correct blade for a given task—and make sure it is sharp.

Don't force the wood and cause it to bind.

Do adjust the guard and use it.

Do think ahead, plan your work, and use relief cuts. Build a jig or fixture to control small pieces.

blank, whereas more expensive blades are ground. This explains why two packages of blades may look similar except for the price. Blades are relatively inexpensive, and the better blades are well worth the investment. You should experiment with different blades and speeds for the types of work that you want to do.

The saber saw

Also known as a jigsaw or a bayonet saw, the saber saw is a portable tool that is held in one hand and rotated to cut curves. The blade is usually about 3 inches (75 mm) long and is held on one end. The drive mechanism moves the blade up and down, creating the cutting action. Because the blade is attached on only one end, it can be easily used for a variety of tasks, including making inside cuts.

Its greatest strength is its portability. It can be used with a fine blade to make intricate scrollwork or with a coarse blade to do rough cutting, particularly in construction and remodeling. The blades range in size from ⅛ inch (3 mm) to ½ inch (13 mm). Some models have a variable speed, which allows you to use fine blades to cut metals.

As for the scroll saw, the blade for the saber saw cuts only half of the time. Better saws have an adjustable mechanism so that the blade goes through an arc during the cut. During the cycle, the blade moves forward as it cuts, then moves backward on the downstroke. This greatly increases cutting efficiency and decreases vibration.

Almost any carpentry task can be tackled with one of these handy tools. Although it is usually considered a construction tool, the saber saw has many uses in the woodworking shop. It excels at architectural decorative work, and its portability makes it an easy choice for cutting large pieces to size and for interior cuts.

Band saw

The band saw is the largest of the curve-cutting machines and has the most applications. It is named for the type of blade that it uses, which is a thin band with teeth on one side. The blade is suspended around either two or three wheels. As the wheels rotate, the band moves, providing the cutting action. The workpiece can be rotated around the blade to create a curved cut.

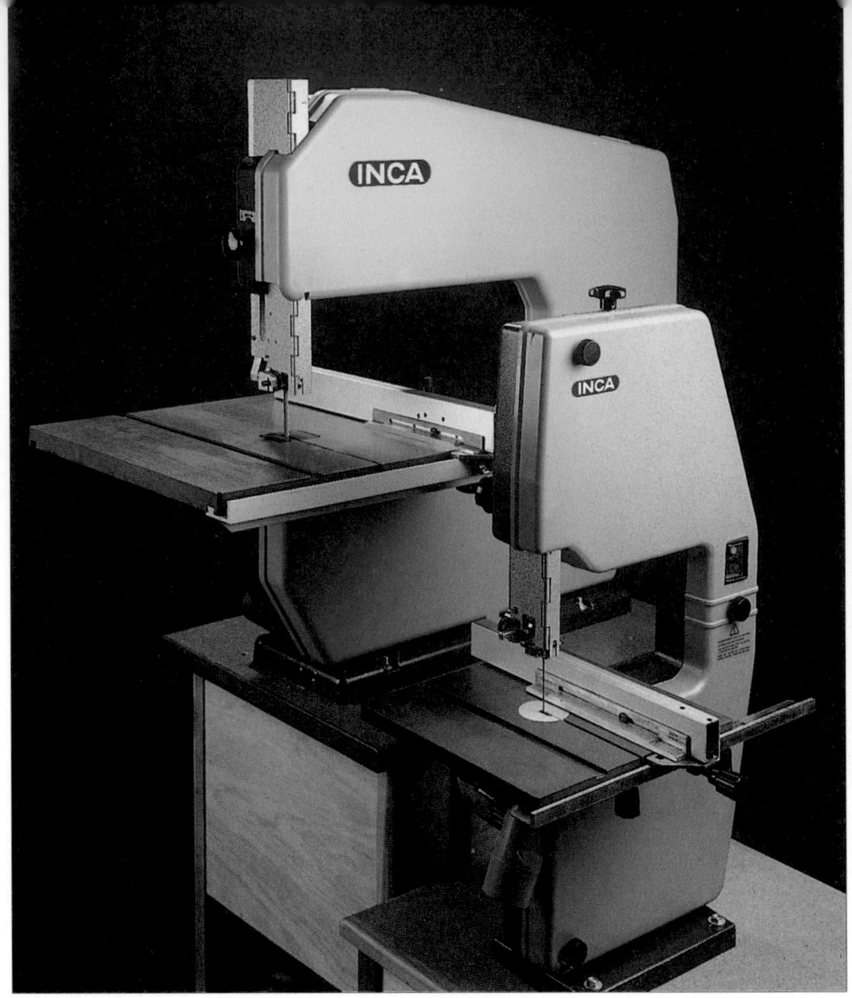

Band saws cut curves more efficiently than any other machine. The blade is thin enough to cut stock with a minimum of effort and waste. Woodturners use it to cut round bowl blanks out of logs. Furniture makers use it for decorative curves. With a small blade and the proper guide system, it can be used to cut very tight curves for craftwork.

With a wide blade, the band saw can also make straight cuts. Thick boards are easily cut to the desired size. Boards can be resawed, which is a technique of splitting the board from one edge to the other into thin strips. The matching pieces can be glued together so that one side of the board is a mirror image of the other. This is called book-matching and is popular in high-quality furniture. The band saw blade can be used to mimic hand tools. It easily cuts traditional joints such as dovetails and tenons. Jigs are used to cut circles or segments of circles.

Choosing a band saw blade

The blade of a band saw plays a more important role than in any other machine. A fine 1⁄16 inch (1.5 mm) blade performs like an expensive scroll saw. A coarse blade cuts like a chain saw. There are now hundreds of different types of blades available. Some are for highly specialized tasks. Each style of band-saw blade is good at one or more task. In order to use your band saw to its fullest potential, you need to understand blades well enough to pick the the correct blade for the task at hand.

The design of a band-saw blade is determined by a number of characteristics. Blade pitch refers to the number of teeth. It is usually designated with a number and the letters "tpi," which is short for teeth per inch. A coarse blade has fewer but larger teeth. A fine blade has many small teeth. A coarse blade with fewer large teeth cuts faster, because a big tooth can cut and carry away more wood than a group of small teeth. These blades often have a hook tooth with a raker set and a coarse pitch.

Band saw blades are sometimes classified as large, medium, and small. This classification refers to more than just blade width. Width, tooth form, and pitch are combined within each group classification. Each group offers unique cutting characteristics, which are only partially attributable to the width of the blade. You will be prepared for most cutting operations if you have at least one blade from each group.

When you are deciding which blade to put on your saw, there are two primary considerations: tightness of curves and the grain of the workpiece. Coarse blades cut best with the grain for ripping and resawing. Fine blades work well for crosscutting or multigrain sawing, as in making circles.

If you don't have space for a large, full-size band saw, a compact band saw made to high standards can be a reasonable substitute.

Most woodworking can be done with four different sizes of band-saw blades. A large, coarse hook tooth blade that is the maximum width for your saw is recommended for stock preparation. The hook tooth is good at long curves when cutting with the grain, and it is especially good at cutting with the grain when making straight cuts such as when ripping or resawing. This blade is useful for cutting rough material for woodturners, especially if the wood is green or wet.

Medium blades usually have a skip tooth with a raker set and a medium to coarse pitch. The best general-purpose blade is a ¼ inch (6 mm) width with 4 to 6 tpi. These blades are usually a skip tooth blade, which is less aggressive than the hook tooth. This blade can make a great variety of cuts, including curves, circular work for turning, and joinery. It will function well in crosscutting, diagonal cutting, and multigrain cutting.

Small blades usually have a standard (regular) tooth form and a fine pitch. The ⅛ inch (3 mm) blade with 14 tpi is ideal for tight turns and scrollwork and can also be used for joinery such as dovetails. The 1/16 inch (1.5 mm) blade with 24 tpi is ideal for very tight curves and also makes straight cuts. This is useful when cutting out a pattern that has both straight and curved cuts.

Adjusting the band saw

The band saw is the most complex of the curve-cutting tools. Like a musical instrument, it must be tuned for good performance. A poorly adjusted saw breaks blades, does not cut accurately, and vibrates. There is a sequence to follow. First of all, you have to pick the appropriate blade. Next, you have to change and track it to get the maximum performance. It is an easy habit, which can be quickly developed with practice and patience. After tracking and tensioning the blade, you have to adjust the guides.

Guides prevent the blade from deflecting sideways during the saw cut. Two sets of guides are located above and below the table. These are either solid blocks of material or bearings. The solid blocks have traditionally been made of metal, but in recent years a high-tech phenolic with graphite has been used with great success. These blocks, called Cool Blocks, decrease friction and heat, thereby increasing blade life. Adjust them so that they are directly in contact with the blade. This decreases twist and deflection and improves the accuracy of the cut. The blocks are a must for 1/16 inch (1.5 mm) blades and help with ⅛ inch (3 mm) blades.

Blade performance and blade life are improved if you round the back of the blade with a stone. Turn the saw on and gently hold a dry stone to the back

With the insides of the band saw exposed, it is easy to see how the continous band of saw blade is looped around the wheels.

of the blade. A round blade back creates smooth interaction between the bearing and the blade. If the blade rotates slightly, no sharp blade corner can dig into the thrust bearing. Rounding smooths the weld, helping to decrease problems associated with a poor weld. It also improves performance when making tight turns, because the round back has smooth contact with the saw kerf.

The band saw can be fitted with a fence for straight cuts. However, band saws often do not cut straight. Recently a curved extruded aluminum fence has been introduced, which is designed to be attached to the fence. The curved fence allows the workpiece to be rotated slightly as it is fed into the blade in case the blade is not cutting straight. This greatly simplifies rip or resaw cuts.

Choosing a blade for cutting curves

Although the band, scroll, and saber saw are completely different tools, the blades that are used in each machine have similar characteristics. When you are deciding which blade to put on your saw, there are two primary considerations: tightness of curves and the grain of the workpiece.

Width is the most important factor when choosing a blade. Blades are usually described by blade width, or the distance from the back of the blade to the front of the teeth. This measurement determines how well the blade will resist deflection and how tight a curve the saw will cut. The wider the blade, the more it will resist deflection, which is important when making straight cuts, especially joinery such as tenons or dovetails. The narrower the blade, the tighter the turn that can be made. Ideally, you want a blade that is narrow enough to make curves the size you want but no narrower.

The types of work you do, as well as the grain direction, hardness, and thickness of the wood you work with, will affect blade selection. Contour charts can help you to determine which size blade to install for a specific application. It is a good idea to keep samples of the type of cut that you get from each blade. Make test cuts in the different types of wood that you use.

Pitch

How fast and smooth the blade cuts is determined by pitch. The word "pitch" refers to the size of the tooth. The words "coarse," "medium," and "fine" also describe the number of teeth in a blade, but are less specific and precise. A coarse blade has few teeth, and a fine blade has many teeth per inch. The coarser the blade, the faster the cut, but the cut is rougher. The finer the blade, the smoother the cut, but the cut will be slower.

The teeth on the curve-cutting blades are bent or set sideways. The saw kerf is, therefore, wider than the body of the blade. The wider kerf lets you rotate the workpiece around the blade when cutting a curve. The side clearance of the blade created by the

It is important to keep the upper blade guides and thrust bearings in good condition. Worn ones can be replaced.

You can attach a good-quality rip fence to your band saw to make accurate rip cuts.

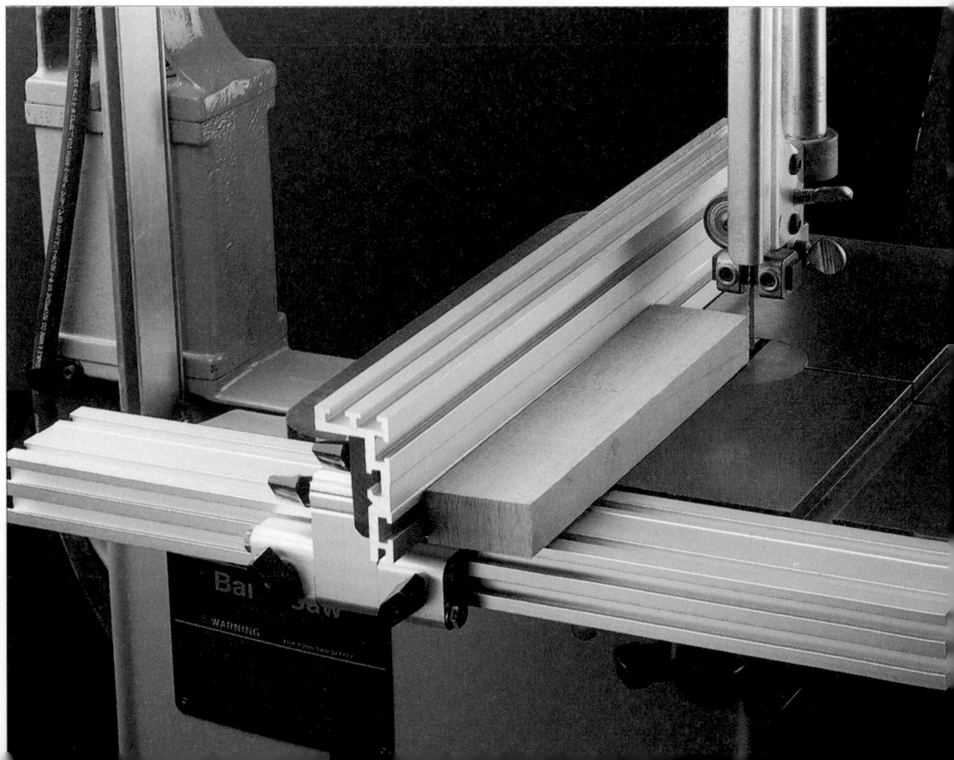

WHAT YOU SHOULD LOOK FOR

The band saw is acknowledged by experts and teachers alike as perhaps the single most useful machine you can have in a woodworking shop. However, in trying to please everyone by creating a "compromise" machine that can do it all and cut everything, many band saw makers end up creating a seccond-class piece of equipment. But the band saw can be first rate, and the best ones are very well made and will give you performance to match.

When purchasing a band saw you should look for a machine that has adequate power, a substantial thrust bearing, a good guide system that is easy to adjust and that will support both large and small blades, and, if possible, a dust-collection system. You should make sure the band saw takes blades that are readily available, and that it also has a good warranty.

If you need the machine to be portable, you should also consider its size, but take into account, too, the size of the work you plan to do. The machine should have an adequate throat capacity—this is the distance between the blade and the rear vertical support. There are several small band saws available that provide reasonable results.

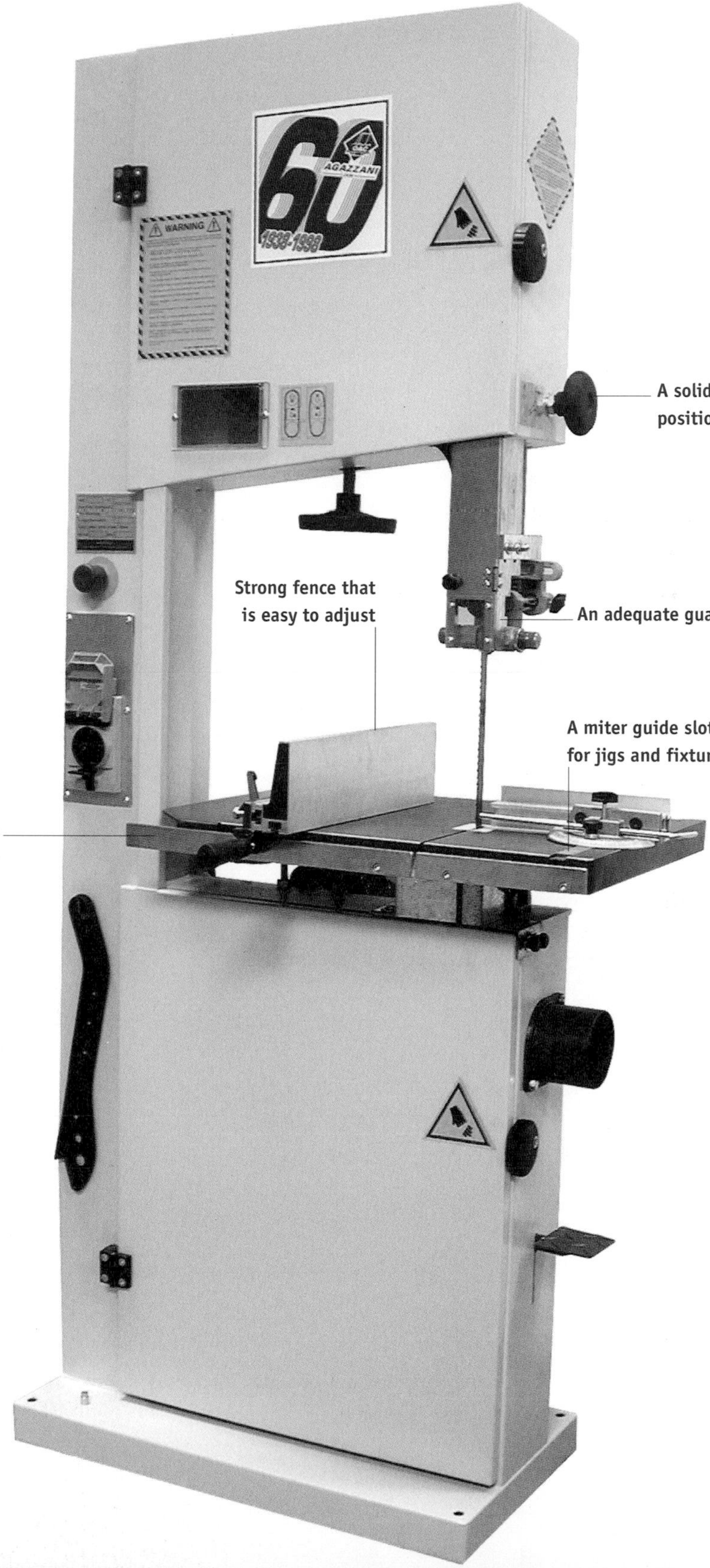

"Craftsmanship is a combination of knowledge on how to use tools and of skill with the hands."

STANLEY RULE AND LEVEL, *HOW TO WORK WITH TOOLS AND WOOD*, 1927

Choosing a saw blade with the right teeth and the correct width for the job you want it to do will give you the best results.

set of the teeth also decreases friction between the blade and the workpiece.

Generally, the harder the material, the finer the pitch should be. For example, extremely hard woods, such as ebony and rosewood, require a finer pitch than oak or maple. Softwoods, such as pine and poplar, are best cut with a fairly coarse blade. In gummy woods, such as pine, a fine blade will soon load with pitch and overheat.

It is important for you to match the blade to your work. Pitch is one aspect of this match. At least three teeth must be in the material at any given time during the saw cut. More teeth give you a smoother cut, but too many teeth will overheat and cut slowly. Overheated teeth soften and dull quickly. Heat also shortens the life of the saw itself. Too few teeth make for extremely rough cuts, stalled cuts, and blade breaks.

PROPER PITCH =
1. Fast cutting
2. Minimum heat
3. Minimum feed pressure required
4. Minimum horsepower required
5. Best blade life

PITCH THAT IS TOO FINE =
1. Slow cutting
2. Excessive heat causing premature blade breakage
3. Unnecessarily high feed pressure
4. Unnecessarily high horsepower
5. Excessive tool wear

PITCH THAT IS TOO COARSE =
1. Short blade life
2. Excessive tooth wear
3. Vibration

Which saw and blade should you use?

The band saw, scroll saw, and saber saw can be fitted with fine, medium, or coarse blades for the activities listed below.

ACTIVITY	TYPE OF BLADE
Making crosscuts, rip cuts, and miters, and resawing	Use the band saw or saber saw with a fine blade to make crosscuts; the same saws, but with a coarse blade, can make rip cuts. To make miters, you can use the band saw with a fine blade. The band saw fitted with a coarse blade excels at resawing.
Making dovetails and tenons, and cutting round stock	You can make adequate dovetails with a band saw fitted with a fine blade. Use the band saw with a medium blade to make tenons and cut round stock.
Cutting curves and circles	Any of these saws can cut curves. The type of blade will depend on the material. A fine blade is best for tight curves; use a coarse blade with a band saw or saber saw for thick material. To cut circles, the band saw is the best choice, although you can use a scroll saw or saber saw with a medium blade.
Making puzzles and toys	The scroll saw excels at cutting puzzles, but you can also use the band saw with a fine blade. If you use a medium blade, both the band saw and scroll saw are adequate for making toys.
Marquetry and intarsia	The scroll saw is the best tool for marquetry and intarsia. Marquetry requires a fine blade, but intarsia can be done with a medium blade. You can also use a band saw with a medium blade for intarsia.
Scrollwork	The scroll saw, as it name implies, is the best saw to choose when doing scrollwork. A band saw can sometimes also turn out adequate work. For either type of saw, use a narrow, fine blade.

ACTIVITY	TYPE OF BLADE
Shaping a cabriole leg	The band saw is an excellent tool for shaping a cabriole leg, using a coarse blade.
Making jewelry	You can do fine detail work on a scroll saw that has been fitted with a fine blade.
Cutting aluminum and brass	The tool of choice for cutting aluminum is a band saw with a medium blade, but you can use a scroll saw or saber saw. For brass, a scroll saw with a medium blade is best; you can also use a band saw, again, with a medium blade.
Cutting cloth and cardboard	Both of these materials can be cut with a band saw. The blade to use will depend on the material. You should experiment with scrap material.
Cutting cork and foam	The band saw can do an adequate job when cutting cork. It is better at cutting foam.
Cutting plastic	The best saw to use when cutting plastic is a scroll saw; however, both the band saw and saber saw will do an adequate job. Whichever saw you use, fit it with a medium blade.
Cutting rubber	Your best option is to use a band saw with a medium blade. If the rubber is hard, you can also use a scroll saw with a coarse blade or a saber saw with a medium blade.
Cutting construction materials	The saber saw's portable size makes it ideal at the construction site, but a small band saw can also be used. A coarse blade is suitable for this type of work.

To get the best use out of your band saw or scroll saw, you should consider fitting it with some of the many high-quality accessories available. You may want some of these to replace "standard" accessories that came with your saw, but some of these accessories are additions that will enhance its performance. Think carefully how you will use the machine before you start making your investment. You may want to make purchases as an accessory becomes useful for particular types of work.

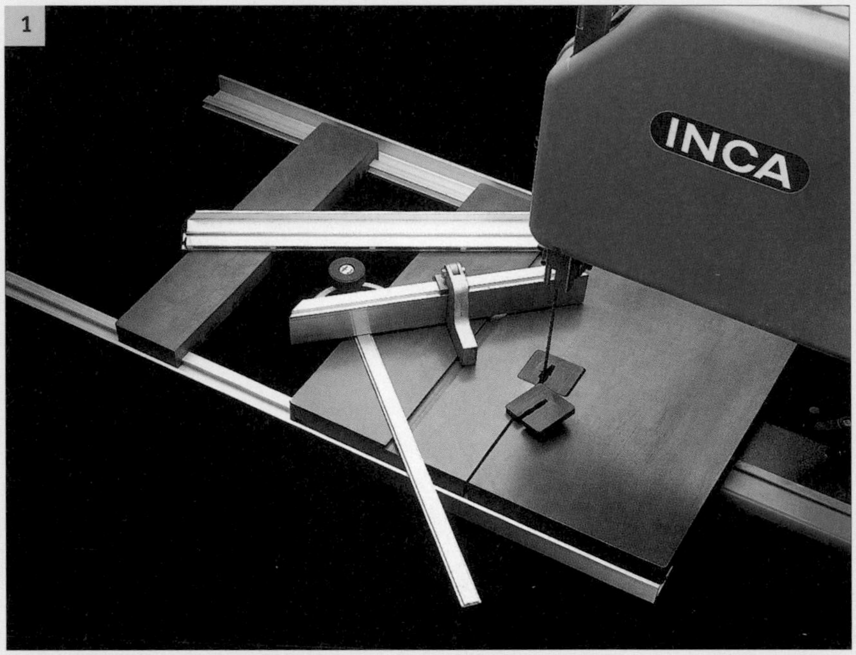

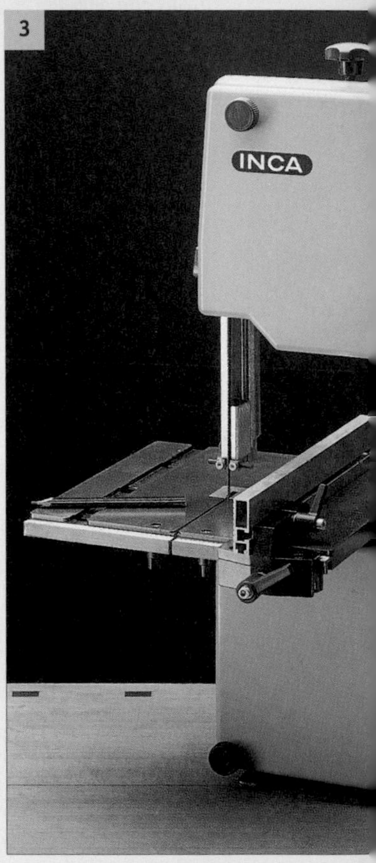

1 Band saw extension table and miter guide
If you work with large panels or do a lot of long rips, a table extension can make your life easier. The table will have extension rails and a support leg. The miter gauge will help guide work for making crosscuts on your band saw.

2 Band saw resaw guide
Even using the best-designed straight rip fence, it can sometimes be a challenge to rip a stright line in thick stock. This resaw guide attaches to a rip fence. It has a curved face that is designed to guide a board with a difficult or wavy grain pattern.

3 Small-scale band saw
This miniature band saw has the flexibility of a larger model but has an 8-inch (200-mm) throat and 5½-inch (140-mm) resawing capacity. It is equipped with a number of features, including a powerful motor and the standard guides.

4 Coolant fluid reservoir
This special accessory is used to feed cooling water when using diamond-coated blades or cutting fluid when doing extensive sawing of metals.

5

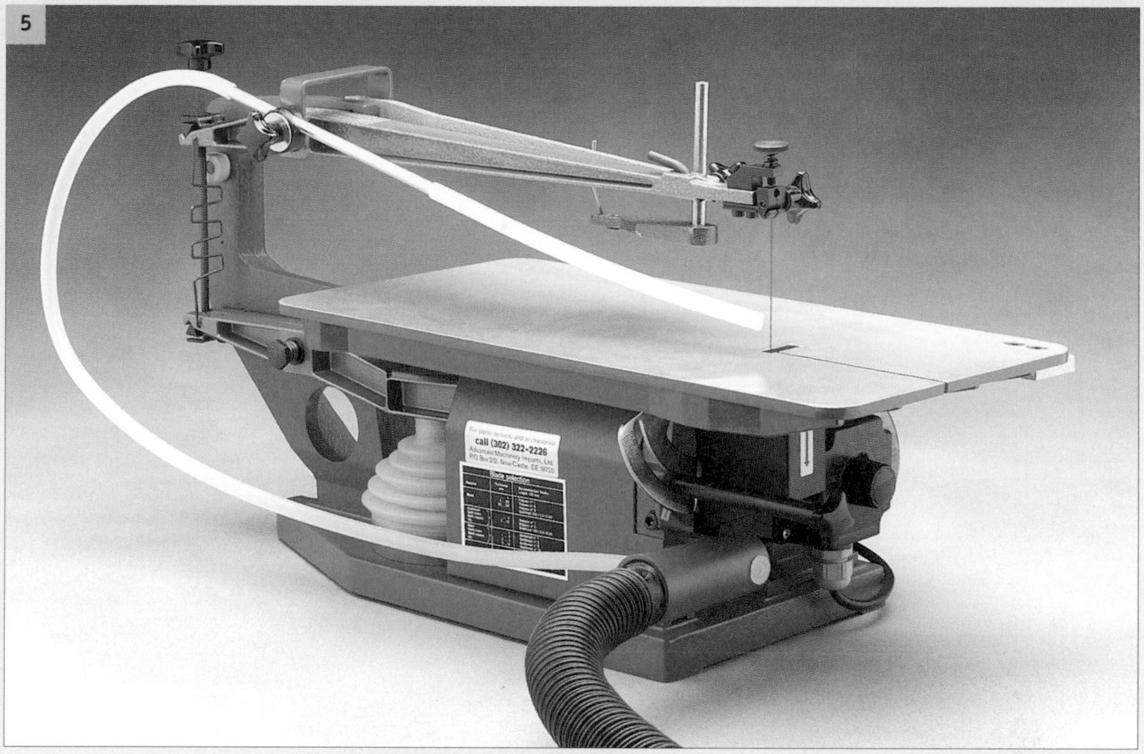

5 Scroll saw with dust-blowing system

This scroll saw is fitted with a dust-blowing system. It blows away the sawdust as you make a cut, allowing you to have a constantly clear view of the blade and the work.

6 Band saw circle-cutting guide

Basically a jig for cutting circles, this guide is fitted into the miter gauge slot, and it has multiple pivot points and a slide adjustment to fine-tune the radius to exactly the size circle you want to cut.

4

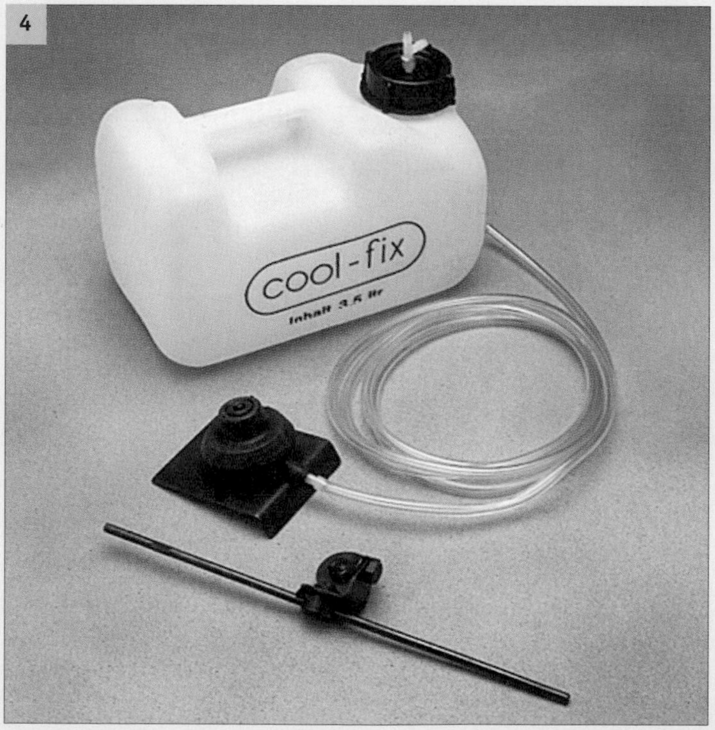

6

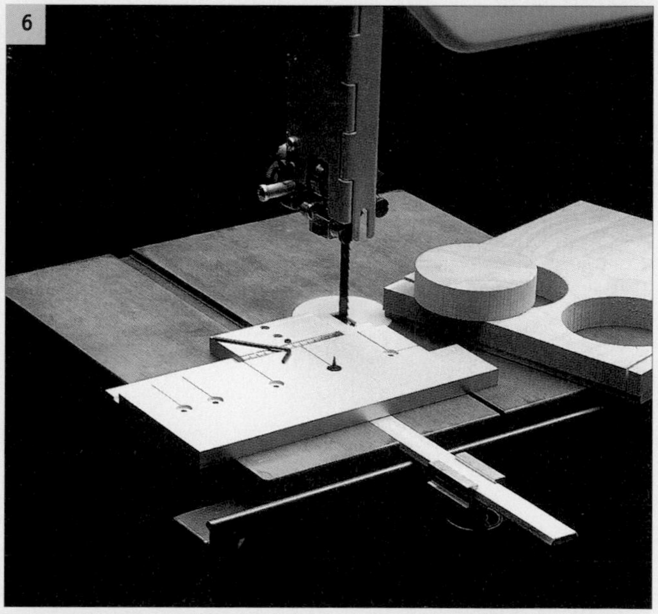

Planes

Planes (opposite page) can be divided into two groups: surface planes, including the long-body plane and the shorter planes to its right, and trimming planes such as the two planes in the top left corner.

There are a greater variety of planes than of any other type of tool, and they are often the "engine" that drives the quality of the end result. A 1966 survey by the British magazine *Woodworker* listed more than 40 different types (not counting the variety of sizes) of planes.

These days some power tools, such as thickness planers, are used to do work that until the 20th century had to be done by hand planes. However, hand planes remain unsurpassed in their ability to produce beautiful flat surfaces. And because of machinery set-up time, even the most mundane work, such as smoothing a board, can often be done faster with a hand tool.

This section is devoted to hand planes and the art of planing wood. It will help you understand what planes do and how, along with power tools, they fit into the woodworking picture today.

REGULATOR
CHROM-VANADIUM
REGULATOR
CHROM-VANADIUM

SURFACE PLANES

IN THIS DAY OF POWER-DRIVEN TOOLS, WE ARE APT TO FORGET how important hand planes, especially surface planes, are to woodworking. They have been in existence, in one form or another, since man first began to work with wood, and, because of their central role in this craft, they have been dubbed the "violins" of the workshop. Today, planes have lost this status, but they are no less important to good craftsmanship than they were when at their peak, about 150 years ago.

There is no substitute for a sharp blade shearing the wood fibers cleanly to produce a final surface that is flat and smooth. Boards planed flat with a hand plane will have a quality of appearance that testifies to fine hand craftsmanship. The reason for this is that the very slight unevenness of the surface when finished by hand will reflect light in a beautiful and subtle way that is far more pleasing than is possible with a surface that has been mechanically flattened "to perfection" or one that has been heavily sanded or scraped.

An experienced woodworker can do more careful (and better) work with a hand plane and can often work faster than with power tools, which

A large wooden bench plane with a front horn-style handle (below) is being used in this illustration, *The Four Conditions of Society,* by the French artist Jean Bourdichon (1457–1521).

These high-quality no. 1, no. 2, and no. 4 planes (left) have solid cast manganese-bronze or cast ductile iron bodies, adjustable frogs, and wooden parts made of cherry.

GREENFIELD TOOL COMPANY.
FABRICANTES DE PLAINAS DE TODA A CASTA, COMO SIMPLES E DE TORNEIO.
Unicos Fabricantes dos celebres
Ferros de Plainas,
MARCA
"DIAMOND"
De tempera uniforme e de gume finissi-simo, com cabos de fino aço, —tudo garantido;—
E TAMBEM DAS
FERRADURAS DE PATENTE PARA BOIS,
as mais em conta que ha, e reconhecidas universalmente como as melhores do mercado.
FERRAMENTAS DE TODA A QUALIDADE,
FROM GREENFIELD TOOL CO. GREENFIELD, MASS.
Para informaçõos, catalogos illustrados, etc., dirijam-se a Greenfield Tool Company,
Armazem em New York, 37, Chambers Street.
Greenfield, Massachusetts, E. U. d'America.

An 1874 advertisement in *O Novo Mundo* illustrates the international popularity of an American tool company. These surface planes were sold as a set.

usually require setup time. Another advantage is that the hand plane is a more forgiving tool. Skill at hand planing is one of the most important skills of any woodworker.

Experience with hand planes will help you understand what a power thickness planer (see pages 102–107) is doing when using it for a particular job. This is an important consideration if you are to achieve consistently good results with power tools, which do have their place in the workshop. For example, a rough board can be initially smoothed with a thickness planer, then given a finish with a hand plane to create a reflective surface.

The plane basics

A prerequisite for good wood assembly and construction is to always work with boards that have been made flat, parallel sided, and straight. To skimp on this critical step is to invite real trouble in the assembly process. Surface planes, the workhorses of any woodworking shop, are critical to achieving flat, parallel-sided, straight wood. These comprise all those planes that are used to "work" the surface of a board—from the beginning of initial dimensioning and flattening of rough stock to the final production of a polished smooth surface, ready for assembly and finishing.

Surface planes are also known as bench planes because they are usually used "at the bench." They are the most important tools in any woodworker's tool chest—an assertion that is not made lightly. These planes are used for (1) flattening a surface, (2) making a long edge straight, (3) producing a bevel, and (4) working on end grain.

Like all hand planes, a surface plane (which is always used two-handed) is a basic tool, consisting of a wooden or metal body with an opening, into which is inserted a steel cutting edge—the blade, or iron. This is held in place by some form of clamping mechanism, either a sliding wooden wedge or a fixed pressure clamp, typically made of steel or cast iron. Most woodworkers generally prefer a bench plane with a wooden handle. It simply feels better in the hands than a plastic one. However, with few exceptions, surface planes are now made with only plastic handles for reasons of cost control. Wooden handles are sometimes available to replace those plastic parts—make the swap if you can find them.

Until the 1950s, when power tools became popular, a woodworker could obtain dozens of different types of surface planes. Even today, there is a great variety available, both in size and style and in different levels of quality; however, surface planes are most often available with the familiar cast-iron body and adjustment mechanism. Most well-equipped shops will have two to four surface planes and the woodworker will develop the habit of reaching for the one that best suits the job at hand.

A carpenter trimming the edge of a length of wood with a long-body surface plane is the subject of this 1870 illustration, printed in the British publication *The Cottager and Artisan*.

The transition from wooden planes

Before the 20th century, surface planes, like all planes used by fine cabinetmakers and carpenters, were made entirely of wood, except for the cutting blade. A wooden block wedged into the body of the plane held the cutting iron, or blade, in position, and woodworkers quickly grew skilled at adjusting this cutting iron. Sometimes there was only a single iron in the plane, but when toolmakers discovered that the use of a second (or back) iron, used solely as a stiffener and support for the cutting iron, created superior results, most planes were converted to the "double-iron" style.

In the 17th century, the variety of architectural and furniture styles expanded as greater wealth was created in society. As a result, woodworking became a specialized skill. A homeowner was no longer satisfied with the decorative skills that a regular carpenter provided. In addition to the carpenter, special classes of artisans evolved such

METAL-BODY PLANES

These planes have several parts that will need adjusting from time to time. As you become more familiar with these parts, making these adjustments will become an easier task.

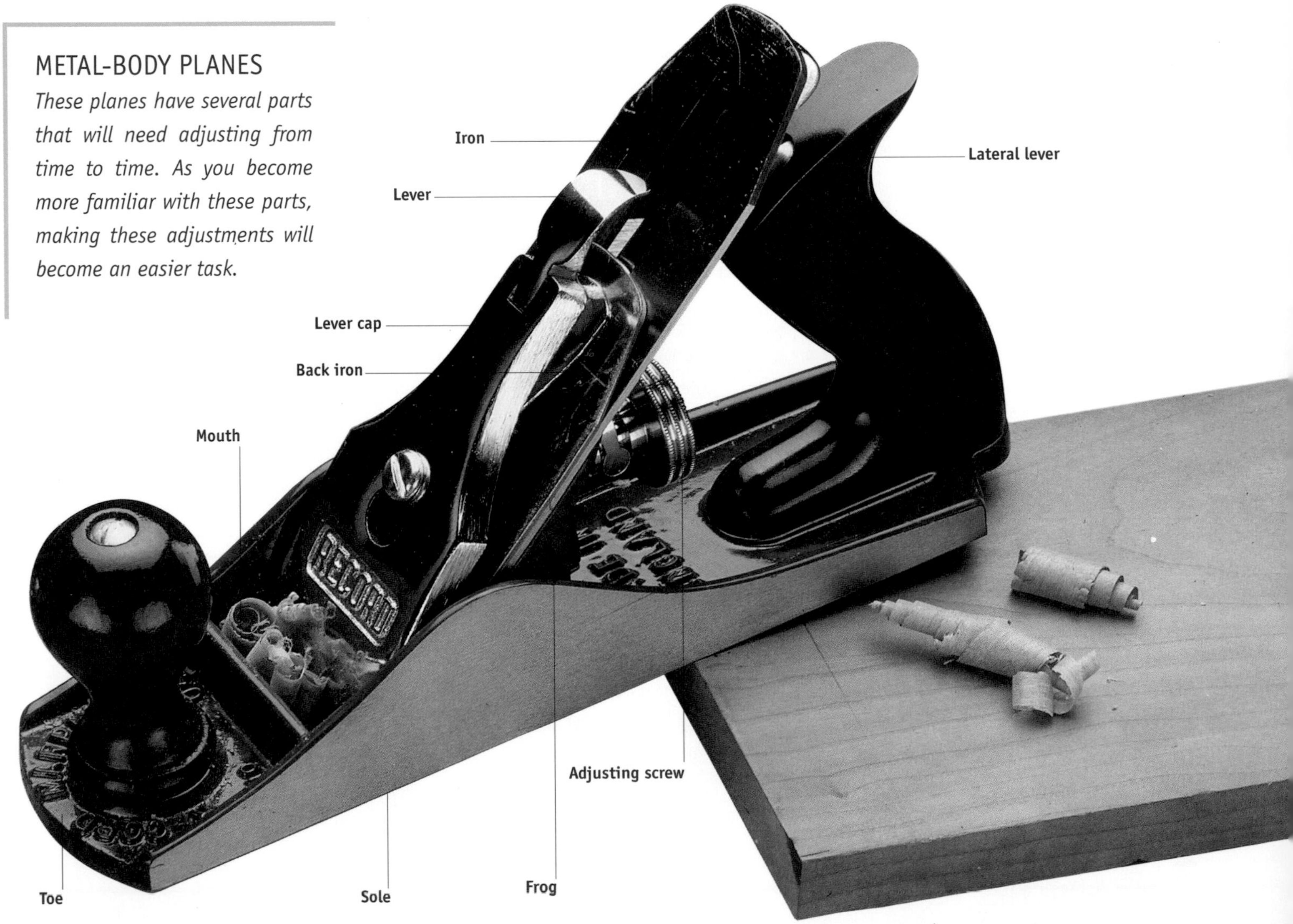

WHAT YOU SHOULD LOOK FOR

There is a great range in the quality of surface, or bench, planes on the market. Some are really low quality and should never be considered except for the most casual do-it-yourself use. Unfortunately, simple appearance is not necessarily a reliable guide to quality. The best general guide for the beginning customer looking for the best-quality tool is to buy the top end of a familiar general brand, to invest in a "premium" line of tools from the beginning, or to rely on a trusted retailer who specializes in high-quality tools.

Acquire the best planes that you can afford, and take care of them. In the days when a craftsman depended entirely on his planes, a good working tool might cost a full week's wages—and would last a lifetime. A best-quality bench plane will be a source of pleasure to its user, but, inevitably, it will be more costly than a merely good one.

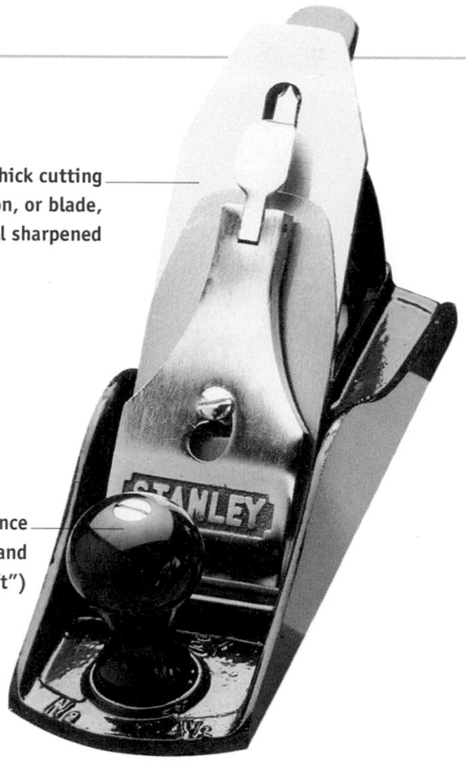

GOOD

The good tool will have a well-finished flat bottom, good balance in the hand, and comfortable handles.

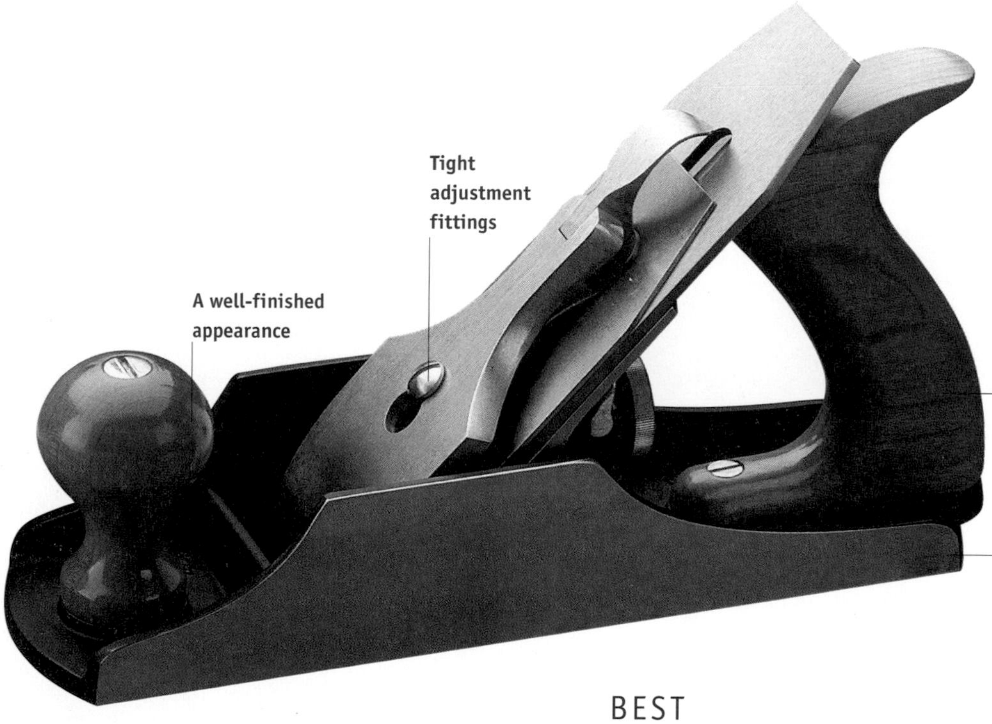

BEST

The premium tool will have an extremely heavy iron casting or one made of bronze, a fine wooden handle, carefully machined mating surfaces, and a heavier-gauge blade.

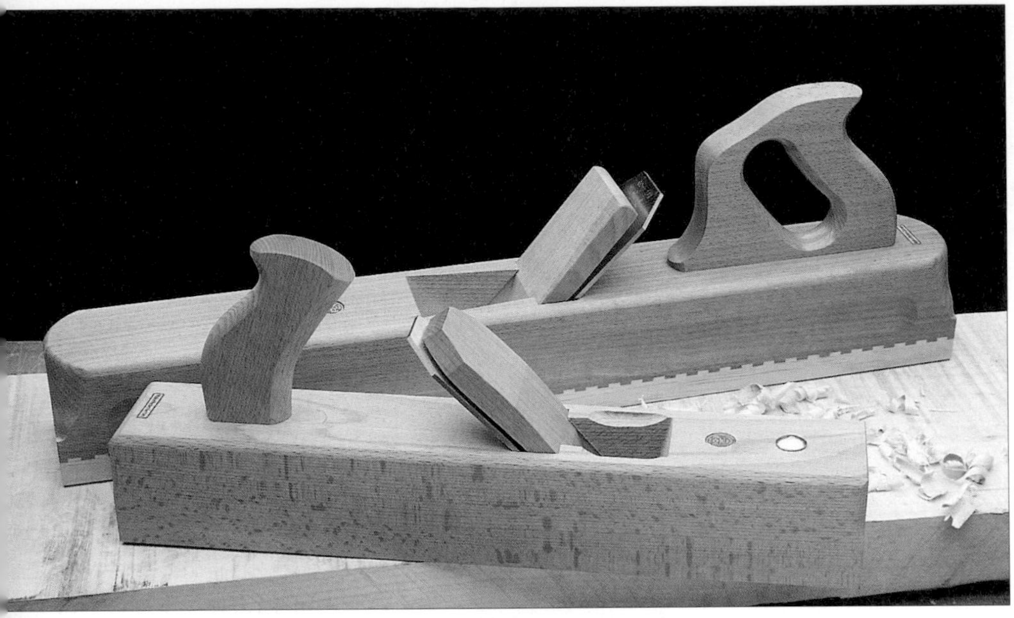

Wooden trying and jack planes (above) use a traditional wooden wedge to hold the blade in place.

The scrub plane (below) has a convex-shape blade to remove large amounts of stock quickly.

Before the Industrial Revolution, a raised panel plane (right) was popular for shaping a panel.

"The good craftsman sticks it out, makes his mistakes, learns, registers having mastered another facet of his craft..."

CHARLES HAYWARD, *WOODWORKER MAGAZINE*, OCTOBER 1961

as the joiner, the cooper, and the stair builder. Each of these trades (supported by the craft guilds) formed its own needs for specialized planes. The close cultural and commercial ties between Britain and the American colonies naturally led to the British tradition of woodworking tools in general and planes in particular setting a pattern for the style of tools that dominated in the United States. In both countries, as well as in other European countries, a fully equipped workshop might contain more than 100 planes—one for every function and shape needed. (Many of these were molding planes, a type of trimming plane; see pages 108–115.)

There are some contemporary Continental European makers, as well as traditional Japanese makers, of surface planes with a 100 percent wooden body. A few of these wooden-body planes have metal adjustment mechanisms, but most use the traditional wooden wedge to hold the blade firmly in place. Although they are no longer familiar to today's British or North American woodworker, this style of plane is the type that all woodworkers used for many hundreds of years until the cast-iron version was developed.

There are many advantages to the wooden body when compared to the steel-pattern plane—that is, a plane with a metal body. For example, a wooden sole (the plane's bottom) will never mar the surface of your work, and the wood-to-wood contact between the sole and the stock allows the plane to slide more easily over the surface and is, therefore, less tiring to use. Modern woodworkers who would like to use these traditional planes can feel fully confident that they will quickly develop the skill necessary to adjust the cutter quickly and precisely; it is easy to do once you get the knack of it.

Even after the steel-pattern planes were introduced, the wooden-body planes remained popular. In the early days of the Industrial Revolution, iron or steel of a suitable quality was a much more expensive material to use than the wood it would be replacing. More importantly for the woodworker, a wooden plane requires far less energy to push than a metal plane—a valid reason to stick with the wooden version at a time when virtually all work was done by hand. However, as

Craftsman's tips

To ensure that you maintain good control in guiding the plane, extend the forefinger of the hand holding the handle alongside the frog or iron. Use your free hand to hold the knob, or horn, at the toe (front) of the plane. To avoid rounding the work, start a pass with pressure on the toe, then shift it to the back of the plane as it makes contact with the work; maintain even pressure throughout the pass, moving your body forward with the plane if necessary.

The best way to plane rough wood is to hold the plane with its iron positioned at a 60-degree angle to the wood grain. This technique, known as skewing, creates a slicing action that can shear through difficult-to-cut grain.

A corrugated sole (foreground) on this metal-body jointer plane is designed to break any suction that might otherwise be created between the sole and the smooth wooden surface, thus reducing the effort needed to use the tool.

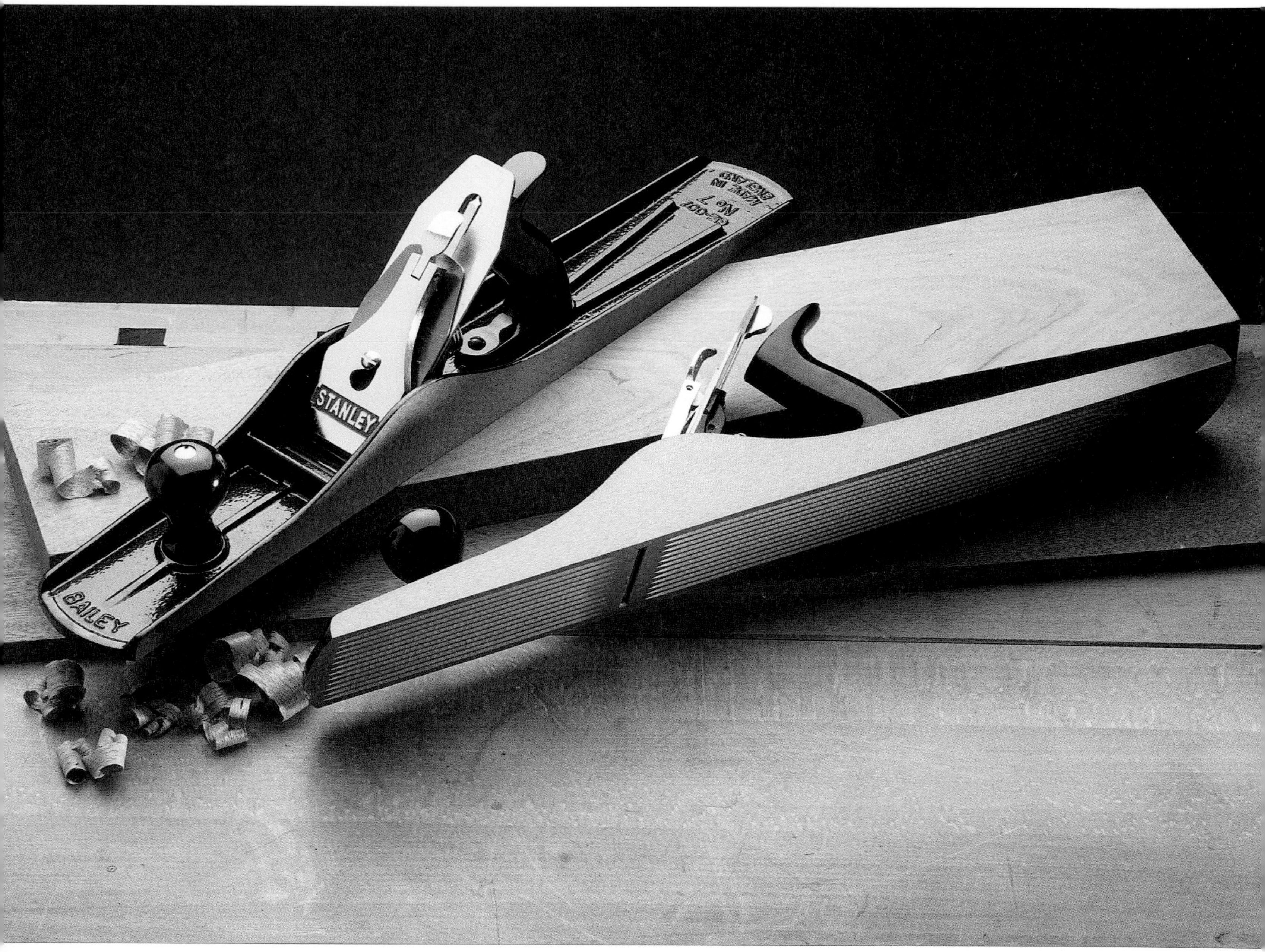

THE IMPORTANCE OF A SHARP BLADE

A well-sharpened plane blade will shave the hair off your forearm as easily as a razor would. If you keep your plane blades that sharp, you will be amazed by how fast and satisfyingly your plane does its work.

No new plane (without exception) will arrive in your shop with its blade properly sharpened, nor should it be the manufacturer's job to provide this step in preparation of the tool. The edge of a sharp blade is subject to shipping and handling damage. Only after you lap the last ½ inch (13 mm) of the back of the blade (the part nearest the cutting edge) on a stone until it is absolutely flat, should you then sharpen and hone the bevel edge *(see page 96)**.*

machines, such as the thickness planer, began to take over the role of basic stock preparation, the hand plane came to be used mainly as a finishing tool, and metal planes began to be used more frequently.

Metal-body planes

During the latter part of the 19th century, an inventor and toolmaker in the United States named Leonard Bailey developed an iron frame to hold and adjust the blade. This was first attached to a wooden bottom (the plane's sole), but soon engineers developed the ability to make reliable iron castings for the entire body of the plane—a design that survives today in the form of the common 9½-inch- (240 mm-) long no. 4 bench plane. Although not all of these sizes remain in production today, 14 different styles (and even more sizes) of Bailey cast-iron body planes were eventually developed.

Bailey's work reached its ultimate success with the development of the "Bedrock" pattern. These exceptional cast-iron planes were designed with a much more refined frog (the part of the plane that supports the blade) and a machining process that "bedded" the frog securely. This improvement reduced blade chatter to a minimum. Sadly, these refinements are costly for manufacturers to retain, so they are no longer found on new planes, except on premium brands.

Bailey's cast-iron planes were initially more expensive than their all-wooden brethren, but costs eventually came down and they became more commonly used for good reasons. They are

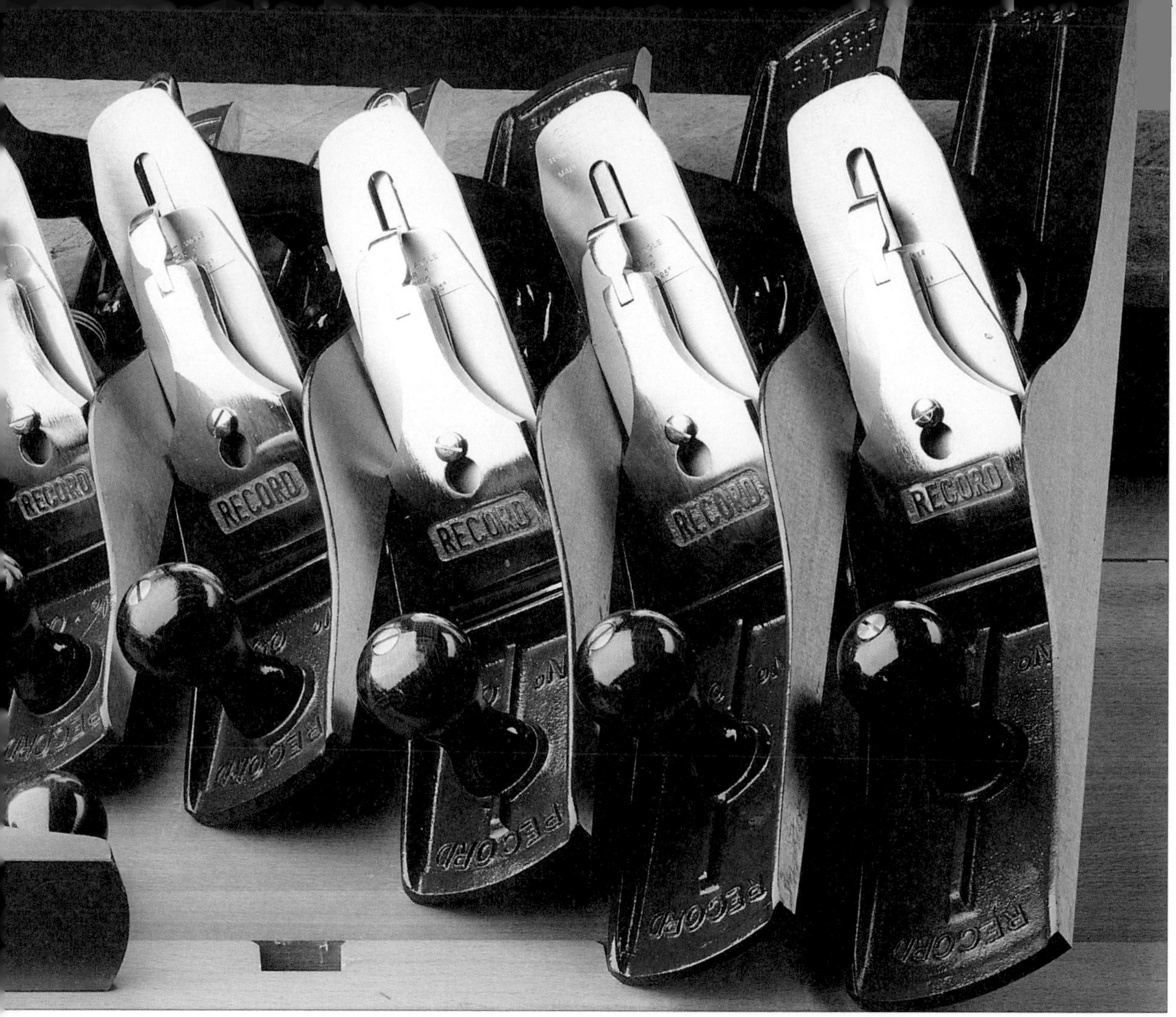

This row of surface planes demonstrates the variety of sizes available: from left to right are a corrugated jointer plane, three smoothing planes, two jack planes, a fore plane, a trying plane, and a long jointer plane. A bench rabbet plane (foreground) completes the picture.

inherently easier to adjust and use, they stay true, and the sole does not need maintenance. (The mouth, or throat, of an all-wooden plane becomes enlarged after heavy use and the sole is subject to movement due to humidity changes—both of which will entail maintenance.) Bailey's firm was eventually bought by the well-known toolmaker Stanley Works.

The models

The variety of surface planes available can be confusing for the novice. Although functions can sometimes overlap, each surface plane is designed for a different job. Used for flattening, smoothing, or leveling wide surfaces or long edges, they vary in width, length, and weight. Whether steel or wooden, Western or Japanese (see pages 94–95), surface planes are characterized by relatively wide blades and large, flat soles. Sizes, which are indicated by the length of the plane's body, range from 9 inches (230 mm) to 22 inches (560 mm). The blade's width varies between 1¾ inches (45 mm) and 2⅜ inches (60 mm).

There is a typical sequence in which surface planes are used. The jack plane (14 in/355 mm long) is usually the first one to be put to work, although it can sometimes be preceded by the scrub plane if the wood is very rough. For large surfaces or long edges, a jointer plane (18 to 22 in/460 to 560 mm long) is the preferred choice. The relatively short smoothing plane is then used for final smoothing of the flat surfaces. A surface well finished with a smoothing plane will require no further work prior to staining and finishing.

In fact, any sanding would reduce the overall quality of the surface.

You will find it useful to have at least three surface planes—one each of a short, medium, and long length. A few makers produce surface planes with a "corrugated" sole—that is, a sole with lengthwise grooves (see page 91).

Surface planes are known by model numbers, traditionally between no. 1 and no. 8, with no. 1 being the smallest and no. 8 the largest. Fractional numbers have been assigned to specialized planes that have been added over time. Shorter-bed models (no. 3, no. 4, and no. 5) are best for general work or for final surface smoothing. Longer-bed models with wider blades (no. 6 and no. 7 and the rare no. 8) are best for removing more stock and for straightening the edges of boards that will be glued up. The no. 5 jack plane and no. 6 fore plane are tools of intermediate size and are most frequently used in heavy cutting work. Consequently, they are usually "tuned" with the mouth set a bit wider than others, so that the thicker shavings can pass easily.

The longer bed on the no. 7 jointer plane is used to true up, or flatten, a surface initially roughed out to shape. The long bed allows it to "ignore" any highs and lows on the surface of the work as it begins to cut. The no. 7 jointer is also important for preparing a long edge for joining, a function at which it excels for the same reason as for truing a rough shape.

The no. 4 or no. 3 smoothing plane is typically used last, because its function is, in effect, to polish the surface. The best smoothing planes were produced in Britain (Norris and Spiers are two of the better-known manufacturers) in the early part of the 20th century. At that time, an ambitious craftsman would willingly pay a week's wages for one and would use it for the rest of his life. These planes were deliberately made heavy, with narrow mouths. Today, they are prized as collector's items, and they can achieve a high price at auction.

Japanese planes

Traditional Japanese planes are made of wood and have a different appearance from that of the Western planes we are used to seeing. The earliest planes were used to smooth wood with a push stroke. However, in the 17th century the Japanese started to make planes to be pulled instead of pushed (because Japanese craftsmen worked sitting down or kneeling instead of at a high bench), and they are still used with a pull stroke today. The art of plane making and plane-blade making evolved to its highest level in Japan, and the best-quality planes are treasured by the woodworker who uses these fine tools.

Tuning a plane

If you are using wooden planes, try to avoid denting the soles. But if you do get a dent (this is almost inevitable), just ignore it. A few dents will not have the slightest impact on the planes' function. If the sole of a wooden plane becomes slightly warped due to humidity changes, you can simply re-flatten it by taking a few light passes over your power jointer, or use another, longer body plane (clamped upside down on your bench) for the same purpose. Make sure you don't remove too much wood, which can increase the width of the mouth. Flatten the back of a plane blade in the same way as for a metal-body plane.

All metal-body planes will need tuning at some point. As all woodworkers know, working with a well-tuned surface plane is one of this craft's greatest and most sublime pleasures. Use a pair of winding sticks (see page 247) across the ends of

These Japanese planes (left) are made of Japanese red oak and have blades of laminated steel construction, with a very hard cutting edge laminated to a soft back for strength. Among the Japanese planes are a bench plane (below left) and a chamfering plane (below right), a type of trimming plane (see pages 108–115).

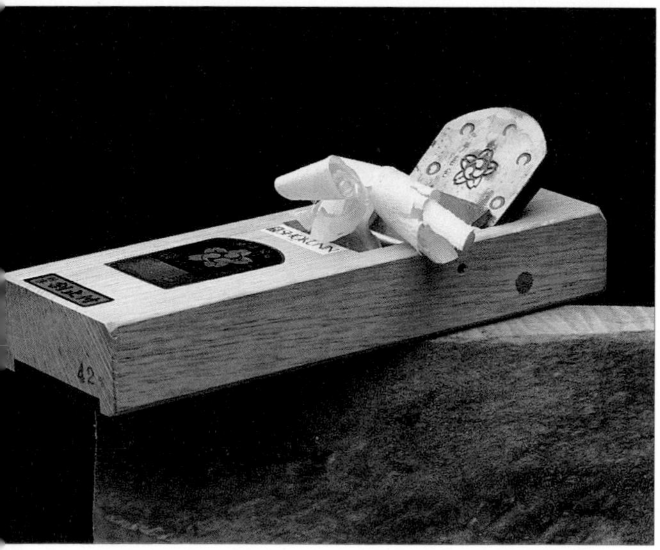

the sole to determine if it has a twist. Follow these straightforward steps to tune a surface plane:

- Start by flattening the sole of the plane. With the iron and frog backed off but still intact with the plane, lap, or smooth, a metal sole by gently rubbing it, using even pressure, on aluminum-oxide or silicon-carbide sandpaper that has been adhered to a plate of glass, starting with about 100-grit paper and working your way to 220-grit paper or finer. Or use silicon-carbide powder on the glass, lubricated with soapy water. Keep lapping until the sole is a consistent color.
- If possible, adjust the mouth for the type of work that you will be doing. For example, set it to a narrow opening for final smoothing or use a wider setting for initial heavy cutting.
- Fit the frog to the base of the plane, with the frog and the bevel of the sole aligned. Make sure that the adjustment mechanism on the frog has as little "wobble" in it as possible.
- Carefully fit the iron and iron cap to the frog; a loose iron will chatter.

This jack plane (left) and jointer plane (right) have bodies made of red beech; the body of the smoothing plane (foreground) is made of pearwood, an especially beautiful wood.

By using a modest amount of common sense, your planes will last a lifetime. Be careful not to drop a steel plane. Unless it is a plane with a ductile iron body, this may cause the casting to crack or break. Also, keep a light coating of oil on the exposed surfaces to prevent rust spots and to avoid stains from the natural acids in your fingers. Rubbing a small amount of paraffin or paste wax into the sole can reduce friction during use.

Sharpening plane blades

Having a sharp plane blade, or iron, is important. There are two steps in putting a proper edge on a plane blade: the initial grinding of the edge to shape it, then honing it to razor sharpness. Grinding may be necessary when a blade has been badly maintained or is nicked. If you use a bench grinder (see pages 228–229), keep the blade cool as you work, so that you do not overheat and ruin the hardness of the steel. Use a water-cooled grindstone, or keep a small glass of water next to the machine and dip the blade in it often.

You can round the corners of a blade that is used for preliminary or coarse work very slightly (by 1/64 in/0.375 mm or 1/32 in/0.75 mm) to help prevent it from digging in. For most final work and for jointing, the edge should be absolutely square. The blade should have a bevel of close to 25 degrees, and the bevel should be flat or have a very slight concavity produced by the grindstone.

After grinding, hone the edge razor sharp, using water- or oilstones. Start with a 1,000-grit stone until you can feel a wire edge along the back; then switch to a 6,000-grit stone. Once you have initially prepared your plane blade, the only work that it should need is an occasional re-honing.

What hand plane should you use?

All of these planes, if not available locally, can be acquired from a well-supplied mail order firm.

ACTIVITY	TYPE OF PLANE
Initial "cleanup" work on rough boards	Use a scrub plane with a convex blade if you want to remove a lot of wood fast. Work diagonally, as well as with the grain. A scrub plane will leave overlapping grooved cuts in the surface, which you can remove with a plane with a straight blade. Or use a no. 5 jack plane with a blade that has the corners slightly rounded. This will be slower work.
Flattening and planing to desired thickness	You can start by using a scrub plane or a jack plane as described above. This is a natural continuation of any initial cleanup work. When flattening, you should plane off the high spots to eliminate any cupping, bowing, or twist (all these are variations of warping). Use winding sticks (see page 247) placed at the ends of the board to determine visually when the board is flat. Finish off with as long-bodied a plane as you have (ideally a no. 6 or no. 7) to eliminate any remaining hard-to-see "valleys" in the surface. It is in this type of work that a plane with a corrugated sole can be helpful.
Smoothing the surface	Do this only after the board has been made flat. Use a smoothing plane (no. 3 or no. 4 or its wooden-body equivalent). The blade should be absolutely square, as sharp as you can get it, and the mouth opening set very small. A heavy plane is better here. If you want to invest in a premium-quality tool, this is the plane in which to make this initial investment. Work only with the grain when you take final strokes. As an alternative to a standard smoothing plane, you can use a low-angle jack plane or low-angle smoothing plane.

ACTIVITY	TYPE OF PLANE
To prepare a straight edge	The usual purpose in this step is to prepare an absolutely straight and square edge for gluing or other joinery. Use a no. 7 jointer plane on most boards; however, you can use a no. 5 jack plane on short boards (24 in/610 mm and under). A specialist tool called an edge trimming block plane is also available (see pages 114–115); because of its shearing cut, it works especially well on boards that have been laminated such as plywood.
Trimming small surface areas	Use a very small smoothing plane (no. 2 or no. 1) or a block plane (see pages 115).
To clean up the interior corners of a joint	A variety of planes can be used for this—the main requirement being that the blade is located at the very front edge of the body. Any bull nose plane or chisel plane will do this kind of work (see pages 109 and 112).
To smooth especially difficult surfaces	Sometimes a local, wild wood-grain pattern can make it especially difficult to get an area really smooth. Instead of sanding it, you can use a scraper plane (see page 99).
Planing curved surfaces	Use a special circular plane (the sole curves to conform to the surface, which can be either convex or concave) if the surface is large. Otherwise, use a spokeshave (see pages 116–117), but make sure you choose the correct shape and size.
Cutting decorative raised panel edges	You can use a special wooden raised panel plane, with its skewed blade, for this work.

Although surface planes have remained relatively the same through the years, some of the features found on them have evolved to meet the demands of the woodworker. The planes shown here are only a sampling of the variety available. These planes also include ones that manufacturers have made to very high standards. You should acquire at least one jointer plane, jack plane, and smoothing plane.

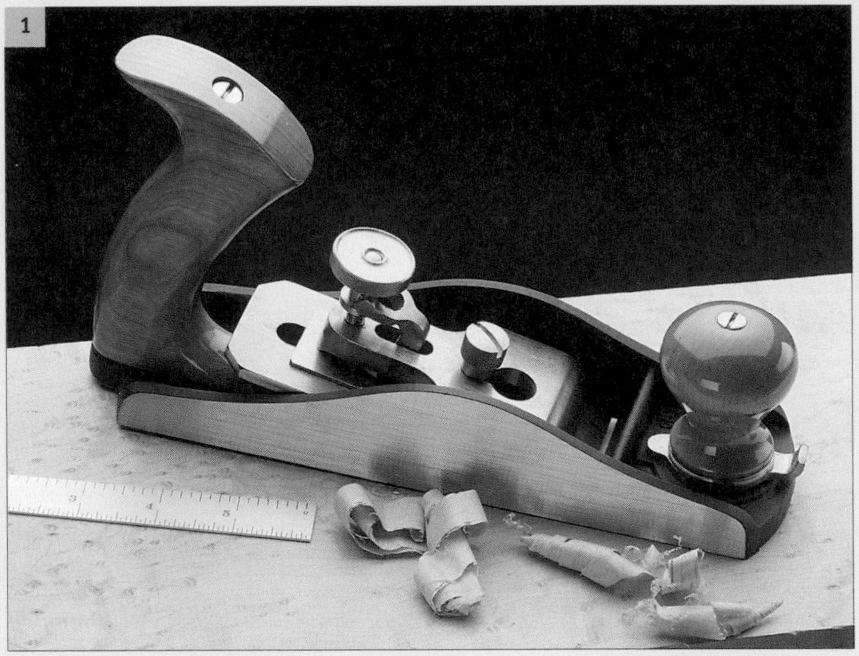

1 Lie-Nielsen low-angle smoothing plane
Based on the rare Stanley no. 164 plane, this plane has an iron, or cutting blade, that is set at a very low angle, which makes it ideal for heavy cutting across the grain. This model can also be easily converted to do finish work.

2 Clifton bench planes
Made in Sheffield, England, these premium-quality planes are made by Clifton and have especially well-finished iron castings, bubinga wood handles, Bedrock-style frogs, special stay-set back irons, and thick, hand-forged blades. They are available in sizes no. 3 through no. 7.

3 Record circular plane
This invaluable plane has an adjustable flexible sole, which allows it to work on a convex or concave surface, much like a very large spokeshave.

4 Mahogany scrub plane
Made by a third-generation European-trained craftsman, this scrub plane has a separate handle fitted to the body with a sliding dovetail. A brass striking button is set at the front of the plane, and the body is decorated in the French style. The plane is unique in its ability to quickly remove a lot of wood from a board.

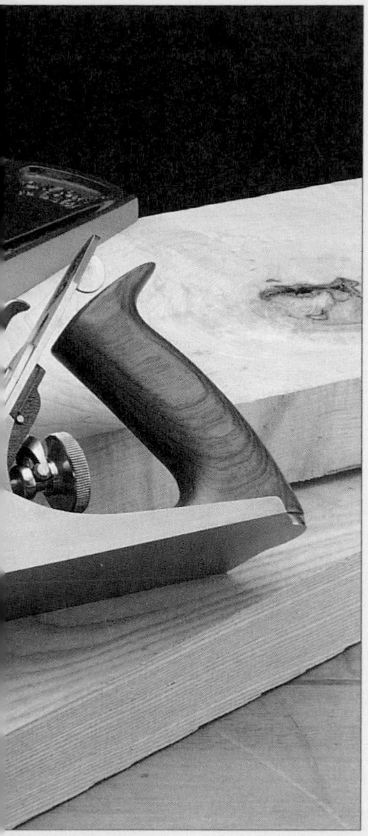

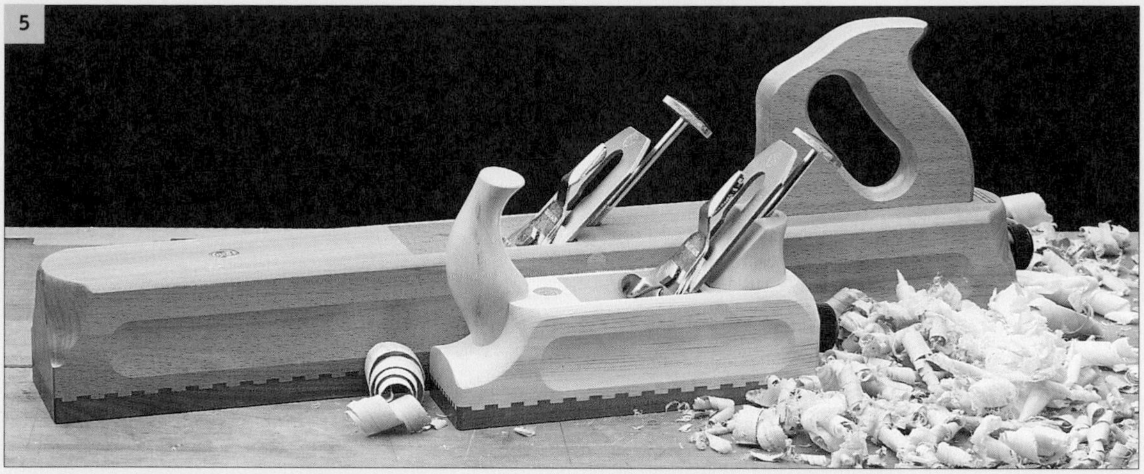

5

5 Primus trying plane and smoothing plane

These planes combine the wooden bodies of traditional wooden planes and the mechanisms of metal-body planes. The long-body trying plane (background), the largest plane available, is ideal for making accurate, tight, edge joints. It can also be used to level surfaces on particularly large boards. The smoothing plane (foreground) can be used with the grain or against it to remove high or rough spots.

6 Lie-Nielsen scraper plane

A handsome tool, this plane is made from super-tough cast ductile iron, solid bronze and brass, steel, and cherry wood. It excels in producing a spectacularly smooth final finish on flat surfaces, even ones that have very difficult wood grain.

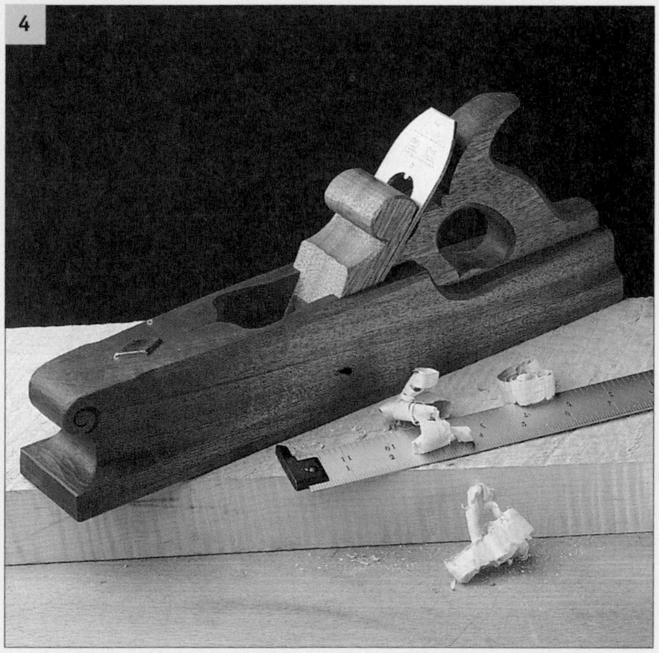

4

6

SCRAPERS AND BURNISHERS

The cabinet scraper has a frame with two handles to hold the scraper blade. Both the spokeshave and a scraper blade cut a shaving. The spokeshave shaving is just bigger and longer.

THE SCRAPER IS ONE OF WOODWORKING'S MOST UNDER-appreciated tools; however, it is one of the oldest tools used by man. A type of stone scraper was used in the Stone Age. Woodworkers not familiar with the scraper and the little miracles it can produce assume that using one is similar to sanding, which is arguably most woodworkers least favorite way to spend time in the shop. The scraper, which is only a thin piece of steel, excels at smoothing (even polishing) a surface that has been planed but still has grain tear-out (such as where the grain is wild).

Whether held by hand or in a frame, the scraper works by cutting, not abrading, the wood. The blade is given a small angle, or hook, along the edge—usually by the woodworker—and this hook cuts a tiny shaving as you pull or push the tool across the surface while holding it at a 15- to 30-degree angle. Usually, you should bow the scraper by pushing your thumbs against the back as you grip the sides with your fingers. This concentrates the cutting action.

Although long strokes with the blade are sometimes used, more often than not, short rapid strokes are used to concentrate on a specific area you are trying to get absolutely smooth. You can work in any direction at all. If you feel that a given direction is not working well enough, simply work at a different angle to the grain.

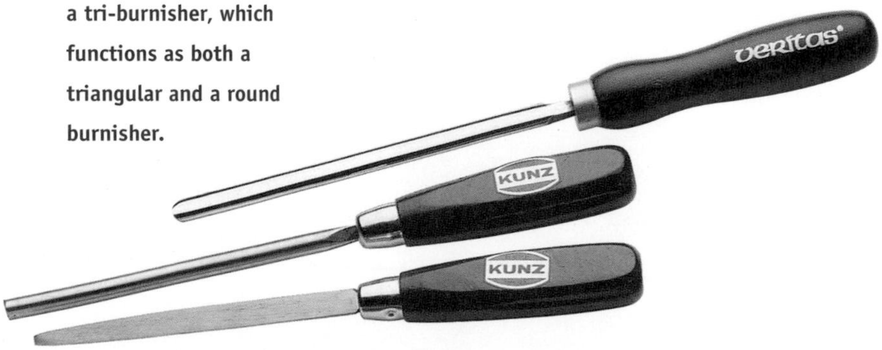

Burnishers come in a variety of profiles. From bottom to top: a triangular burnisher, a round burnisher, and a tri-burnisher, which functions as both a triangular and a round burnisher.

Scrapers are made using relatively mild steel. If the steel were as hard as that used for plane blades and chisels, the woodworker would not be able to form the cutting hook, this tool's key feature. Although most scrapers have flat edges and measure about 4 x 6 inches (100 x 150 mm), they can also be found with a curved gooseneck or convex shape. (There are even some miniature ones, sized specifically for musical instrument makers.) The curved ones are obviously invaluable in working hollowed areas such as chair seats.

Some specialist tool dealers even have scrapers in a variety of steel thicknesses, because very thin steel is often excellent for making very light cuts. However, because the steel used is relatively mild, it dulls more rapidly than other wood cutting tools do.

Preparing the hook with the burnisher

A lot has been written about the proper technique for preparing a scraper for use, but it is simply a matter of first getting both sides of the edge that will be doing the cutting clean and smooth (without burrs), using stones or smooth files, then giving them a few strokes with the scraper burnisher.

Burnishers come in a variety of forms, but all are about 6-inch- (150-mm-) long rods of very hard, highly polished steel. The rod is triangular in shape for rectangular scrapers, or round or pear shaped for curved scrapers. To use a burnisher, with the scraper held on a flat surface, stroke it along the face of the tool, at its edge, and repeat on the other side; then stroke the same surfaces with the burnisher held at an angle, using even pressure.

As you do this, you are turning the edge of the scraper and forming a very small hook. All this sounds more complicated than it really is, but once you get the hang of it, preparing the hook will become second nature.

Turning the edge of a scraper is not necessary, however, if it is held in a frame (called a cabinet scraper or scraper plane). In this case, grind a bevel on the edge. The heavy force put on the edge through the frame works the same as a hook.

Another scraping tool

A special form of scraper is known as a decorative beader. In this case, the scraper steel, which is held in a special frame, has a shaped edge. Repeated motion along the edge of a piece of wood will cut a decorative edge, such as a bead or a reed (a type of multiple bead).

Shown below are a variety of scraping tools. The first one to add to your tool collection is the rectangular scraper. You can add the others as you need them for special projects.

1

2

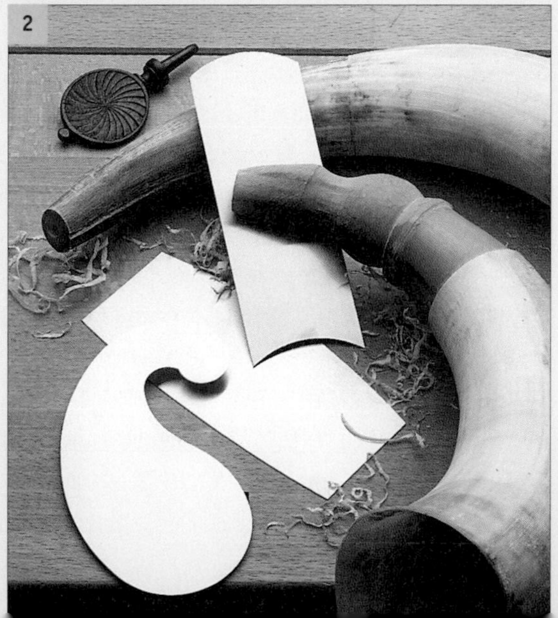

3

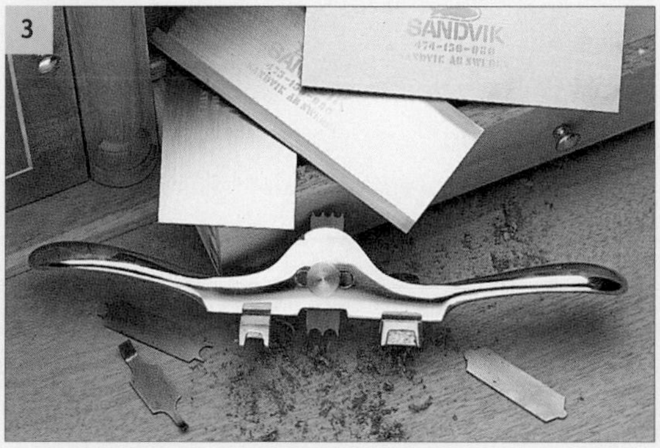

4

1 Beading tool/scraper blade holder

Using this beading tool (top), you can do beading, reeding, and fluting with confidence. You can use one of the standard cutters, or file a custom one to add fine details. Metal blades get hot from the friction of scraping. The wooden body of this scraper blade holder (bottom) provides a comfortable way to hold the blade.

2 Curved scraper blades

To complement your flat rectangular scraper, consider purchasing a set of curved scrapers. This set allows for a wide variety of hollow and convex shapes, and the blades are available in two thicknesses.

3 Scraper blade/bronze beading tool

These rectangular scraper blades (top), which set the standard by which others are measured, have polished edges and come with protective sleeves. A deluxe model has precision-prepared edges. The bronze hand-finished beading tool (bottom) holds a wide variety of scraping cutters for beading, reeding, fluting, and producing decorative molding.

4 Scraper blade conditioner

This effective and comfortable-to-use tool combines the four functions to prepare the edge of a scraper blade: stoning, filing, edge consolidation, and burnishing the hook.

This 1850 wood engraving shows a "circular planing machine" that was used during the building of the Crystal Palace in England.

A pair of push blocks are essential for keeping your hands away from sharp cutting edges.

PLANERS, JOINTERS, AND SHAPERS

THE FOUNDATION OF ACCURATE WOODWORKING IS GETTING THE material to be straight and square, which is called stock preparation. Each step in woodworking is dependent on the attention to detail of the previous step. Glue-up, which is the final construction stage, is dependent upon the accuracy of the joint-making process, which is completely dependent upon the accuracy of the stock. An initial lack of accuracy will be compounded as work progresses.

It is important to understand the properties of wood to appreciate why you should prepare the stock with a planer and jointer. Wood is a complex material, which swells and shrinks as humidity fluctuates. If wood were a static material, preparing accurate stock would be a simple matter. But wood is constantly changing. Water plays an important role in the life of the tree, and a large percentage of green wood is water. As woodworkers, we interrupt the natural process of decay by drying wood, then trying to keep it dry with protective finishes. However, nature always has its way. Wood never dries completely; instead, it attempts to remain in equilibrium with the atmospheric humidity.

After the wood is sawed from the log, the water in the board is exposed to air and the moisture evaporates. The board continues to lose moisture until it reaches equilibrium with the environment. As wood dries, it shrinks. The board shrinks in some dimensions more than others. The new growth and much of the moisture are near the outside of the tree, so that wood shrinks the most.

As wood dries, a number of changes take place in the shape of the board. A major factor is the difference between the higher moisture content in the sapwood, or outside of the tree, and the drier inside heartwood. Drying exerts force on wood, especially around the middle of the tree, which contains the least moisture. These opposing forces can actually crack the board. It is impossible to stop the board from deforming as it dries. "Warp" is a general term that describes a board that has not remained straight during the drying process. By sighting down a corner, you will quickly see what type and how much warp there is in the board.

The combination of warping and shrinking is wasteful. A board that is surfaced to a finished ¾ inch (19 mm) is usually cut at a 1-inch (25-mm) or 1⅛-inch (30-mm) thickness at the sawmill. The extra ¼ inch (6 mm) or more is allowed for shrinkage and warpage. That extra ¼ inch (6 mm) of material may seem like a lot of waste, but you must remember that the board may lose ⅛ inch (3 mm) of thickness in the drying process. A wide board may warp ⅛ inch (3 mm) or more during the drying process. If the tree had a lot of internal stresses, ¼ inch (6 mm) excess material may not even be enough to salvage a long board.

Choosing wood

Wood is usually available in three forms. The first is rough lumber, which has not been processed since it was cut at the sawmill. The lumber will have coarse surfaces and will undoubtedly be warped to some degree. The second, surfaced lumber, has been planed so that both faces of the board are parallel to each other and smooth. This is also known as "surfaced two sides." Often, material is planed at a mill to be 1/16 inch (1.5 mm) oversized. The bulk of the material has been removed with an industrial machine, but it still allows the woodworker to do the final planing.

This allows any slight warp that has developed since the initial planing to be removed.

A third option is to buy wood that has already been processed, which is called "surfaced four sides" (S4S). The problem with completely surfaced wood is that it is already at the standard thickness, and it still may warp. This means that removing the warp would require that the finished piece be thinner than the standard thickness.

The ideal situation is to avoid wood that has already been planed to its final thickness and do your own planing. Bring wood into the shop for about a month before it is to be machined, and allow it to equalize with the shop's humidity and temperature. Make all of, or at least part of, the furniture and put the finish on it. The finish will moderate the tendency of the board to warp and decrease the seasonal expansion and contraction.

Dos and don'ts

Do plan ahead. Use extension tables and have push sticks ready.

Do adjust the guard and use it, and adjust the fence correctly.

Do lubricate the machine and wax the tables often.

Do pay attention to the grain when feeding the wood to avoid tear-out.

Don't take a deep cut or force the wood.

Face jointing

The first step in machining rough stock is to establish one flat face with cuts made on the jointer. The jointer is a machine with two flat tables, with a cutter head spinning between them. The infeed table is lower than the cutter head and is adjustable for the depth of cut. A fence controls the edge of the board. It is also used for squaring the edge of the board.

The jointer provides the woodworker with edges on workpieces that are straight and square to the faces, a vital element for accurate joinery.

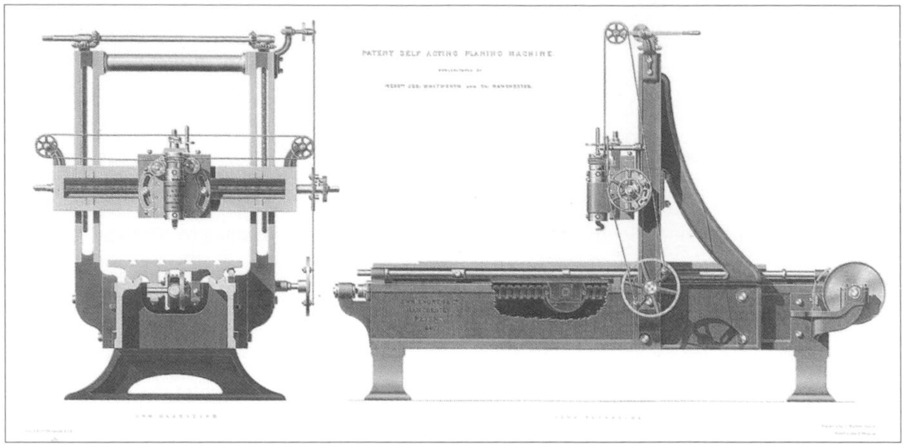

The English inventor Joseph Whitworth patented this planing machine in 1839.

Pay attention to the direction of the wood grain. Jointing against the grain causes a rough surface and tearout. The wood is positioned on the infeed table and fed into the cutter head. The difference between the infeed table and the top-dead-center of the cutter head is the amount of material that is removed from the board. Don't try to remove too much material from the board at one time.

You can minimize any tendency of a warped board to rock from side to side by putting the concave side down on the infeed table. To stop a twisted board from rocking back and forth, take light passes off the opposite corners until the board rests flat on the table. Each successive pass removes material until that surface is flat. The face becomes the reference point for making the opposite face parallel and the edges square and true.

Always use the jointer guard and keep your fingers away from the cutter head. A push stick not only protects your hands, but also gives you more control of the board.

Craftsman's tips

If possible, avoid planing wood that has been processed with an abrasive sander, because the knives will dull rapidly from the grit in the wood. Also avoid planing dirty wood; the dirt will quickly dull the knives. Clean the wood with a wire brush if there are any signs of dirt. If you glue boards together, they should be planed within 24 hours—otherwise, the hard glue line will nick the knives.

Thickness planing

The next step is to make the opposite side of the board parallel to the flat reference side. The machine for this task is the thickness planer. As the name implies, it planes the board to a specific thickness. Whereas the jointer is hand fed, the thickness planer is power fed.

Place the board on the adjustable table, and the feed rollers will pull the board into the cutter head. Adjust the depth of cut, and you are ready for the next pass. Occasionally, the board may bow because planing releases tension on one side of the board. If it has bowed or cupped, re-joint the concave side again, but be careful not to remove too much material. After you get a parallel and true second face, you can continue to plane the board to the appropriate dimension.

The next step after each side of the board has been planed to the desired thickness is to square an edge on the jointer. Again, if possible, use the concave side on the jointer table. Check to make sure that the jointer fence is square to the table. Keep pressure down onto the table and into the fence as you guide the work pass the cutter head.

Many experienced woodworkers allow the wood to settle by partially processing the wood, then allowing it to stabilize for a month in the shop environment before final machining. The wood is cut to size and planed to between 1/16 inch (2 mm) and 1/8 inch (3 mm) oversize and is then piled with sticks spaced between each board. This allows air to

> KEEPING BLADES SHARP
>
> *Retouch the knives often with a diamond hone or a small stone so that you are always using sharp knives. If there are nicks in the blades, you can loosen one blade and move it slightly so that the nicks don't line up with each other.*

pass around the boards so that they reach equilibrium with the environment. After the boards have reached equilibrium, they are surfaced again to remove any warp that appeared during the acclimatization process.

Choosing a machine

The design of jointers and planers has evolved over the years, and they vary according to the place of origin. North American machines are usually individual pieces made from cast iron. The machines made in Asian countries are similar in design to the American machines. Europeans have taken a different approach and have designed combination machines that are both jointers and planers, which share a cutting head. This design saves money and space. In fact, it is often possible to get a European combination machine for the price of an individual jointer. Another area where Europeans have made progress has been in cutter technology. There are now quick-change cutter designs that allow the blade to be changed in minutes. This saves time and a lot of frustration.

Reading the grain

Annual growth rings in trees create a design, which is often referred to as "grain." The grain is determined by the growth rings. A circular end-grain pattern can be seen at the end of a log, and the grain can indicate the position of the board in the log. When surfacing with a jointer or planer, cut with the grain instead of against it. Cutting from the right direction leaves a smooth surface, while cutting in the wrong direction lifts or tears the grain and leaves a rough surface.

For successful cabinetry, the face of the wood must be flat, a task the planer (foreground) is designed to accomplish. This model also converts to a jointer.

"[There] are no short cuts to good craftsmanship. The recognized stages have to be worked through as skills build up.... To try to skip leads only to disaster. And not only to disaster; it misses much of the pleasure."

CHARLES HAYWARD, *WOODWORKER* MAGAZINE, JULY 1962

The standard approach for reading the grain is to observe the direction of the grain along the edge of the board. This will give you a feeling for which way the grain is running. If it rises markedly in one direction or the other, you will need to plane the board "uphill" to prevent the blades digging in. Checking each board in this way may be time-consuming, but you only have to do it once. If you detect tear-out, reverse the direction of the board and try it again. There may be boards in which there is no tear-out no matter which direction is used. A lot depends on the type of wood.

Stationary shaper

With the popularity of the plunger router and router tables, the shaper has been out of fashion in recent years. However, a heavy-duty shaper can swing more substantial cutters then a router can, taking deeper cuts and working nonstop all day. It makes clean shapes that need little or no sanding.

The shaper combines elements of the router and the jointer. The work is fed along a cutter, which shapes wood in the same way as does a cutter on a router, while it is guided against a fence—as a board is guided on a jointer. This machine excels in cutting decorative edges and making finger joints in the edges of boards. A variety of cutters is available to cut different shapes.

This is not a tool to take lightly. Always ensure that the cutter is firmly locked in place, and use the guards and hold-downs. Use the push sticks to keep your hands out of harm's reach, and watch out for kickback. As with the jointer and planer, it is important that you use only sharp cutters.

Crisp, sharp decorative shapes are best achieved with a fast, rotating cutter. The stationary vertical shaper is the machine of choice in the well-equipped shop.

Planers, jointers, and shapers are each designed to do specialized tasks in the woodworker's shop. There are a variety of accessories available to help you get the best results from these powerful machines. The most essential acquisition is certainly the hone. The other accessories can be purchased on an as-needed basis.

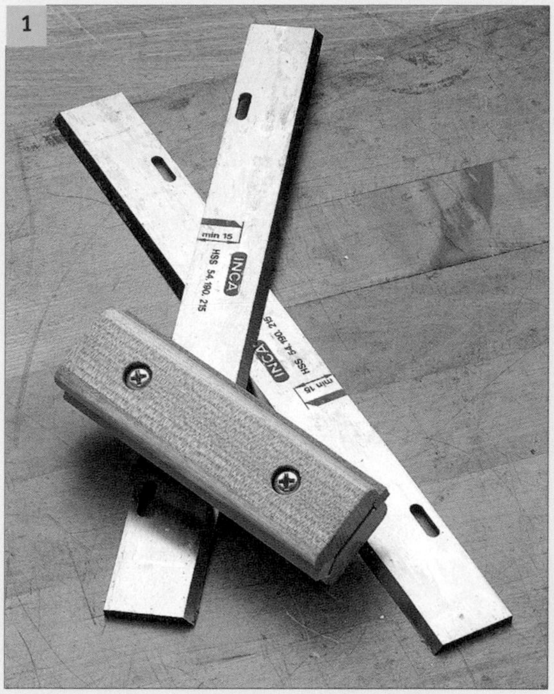

1 Jointer and planer hone

Although this special hone designed for a jointer and planer will not help you regrind a dull edge, it will re-hone a cutter that needs a little bit of "touch up" in order to get back into reasonable working condition. One side is 200-grit aluminum oxide and the other is 400 grit. Lubricate with a drop or two of oil.

2 Shaper sliding table

By installing a sliding table on your shaper, you will have a more versatile work surface. This system has a double track, which is bolted to the ends of the rails of the machine. Its table surface measures 13 x 20 inches (330 x 510 mm) and travels 54 inches (1370 mm).

3 Planer blade-setting jig

The body of this bronze jig is machined from aircraft-grade aluminum. It fits all two-blade cutter heads and three-blade heads with a gap in the head of ⅜ inch (10 mm) or less. A second version fits larger three-blade heads. Although primarily designed for setting thickness-planer blades, it can be used to set jointer blades.

TRIMMING AND OTHER PLANES

This 19th-century shoulder plane came supplied with a box for storage.

ALTHOUGH CALLED TRIMMING PLANES, TOOLS IN THIS CATEGORY are used to cut and fit woodworking joints. This job can be done after the basic parts of the piece are correctly sized and accurately trued to shape (mostly, straight and parallel sided with square corners and edges). Also included are other planes that can trim or shape the work.

Historically, there is a whole group of tools essential to the work of cutting joints. Each trade, of course, developed these tools to suit the demands of its specialized work—whether it be house building or coopering. It would not be unusual for a shop to contain dozens of planes.

Even today, joints can often be cut and fitted from scratch faster by using hand tools than by using machinery. But this advantage is more theoretical than practical, for many traditional trimming and joint-cutting planes have essentially disappeared from the workplace.

The style of joints have not changed, whether they are mortise-and-tenon joints, rabbets, or dadoes, but the tools used to form them today are most frequently power tools (for example, routers). This is especially true in the case of highly specialized hand tools such as the following planes:

- plough or dado planes, for cutting dadoes
- rabbet planes, for cutting rabbets
- dovetail planes, for cutting sliding dovetails
- matched planes, for cutting matched joints such as tongue-and-groove or rule joints.

Among this group of 19th-century planes are a pair of left- and right-hand coachmaker's plough planes (left and center), used to make grooves in curved parts, and a rabbet plane.

This rabbet plane (left) has a ⅜-inch- (10-mm-) wide blade, which is ideal for trimming narrow dadoes and rabbets.

The shoulder plane (above) has a manganese bronze body. The bullnose plane (above left) has machine-squared sides.

WHAT TO LOOK FOR

Because of the finish work these special planes are called upon to do, it is especially important that the ones you choose be well made. When selecting one, make sure it is solid and that the blade has little or no side-to-side movement. Most important, pick one that is the right size for the job at hand.

Unlike surface planes (see pages 84–99), most often these special joint-cutting tools were single iron planes, sometimes fitted with small scribing cutters to slice the top layers of the fibers ahead of the main blade if the work was to be done across the grain. The blade was also often set in the body in a skew position, because the resulting shearing action would aid the fineness of the cut.

For the modern-day woodworker, the most important, even vital, role that trimming planes can now play is in adjusting joints for a good fit. For it is the shoulders (these can be thought of as the interior "corners") of the joints and their mating faces (the larger interior flat surfaces) that do the real work of maintaining a good fit and ensuring a long life for the finished product. Good fitting is no less important today than it was 200 years ago, and trimming planes are unsurpassed for this work.

The best trimming planes are all prized by woodworkers for their function and usefulness. Older ones can often be acquired at a flea market or an antique auction. Stanley, in Sheffield, England, still makes a number of planes, which are sold by specialist mail-order catalogs. In addition, there are several firms in Britain and in North America that make a high-quality version of some styles. There are also a few German firms that still make trimming planes with a traditional wooden body. The blade of a trimming plane should be as sharp as possible—even more so than for a surface plane. (See page 96 for information on sharpening a blade.)

Shoulder, chisel, and rabbet planes

Today, the most common trimming planes are those known as shoulder planes. These are narrow-bodied all-steel planes, ranging in width from ⅜ inch

Block planes are invaluable tools for any woodworker. The blade on the block plane in the foreground is set at a low angle.

(10 mm) to 1¼ inch (32 mm). The blade is kept very sharp, and the tool is used one-handed with short strokes. The shoulder plane has a relatively long nose to aid stability. The nose section on some of those available, such as Stanley's no. 92 and no. 93 models, can also be removed, effectively turning the plane into a chisel plane.

The chisel plane is designed with a blade that extends in advance of the body, so the plane can be used to reach to the farthest edge of a "stopped" joint. (An example of this is a stopped dado—a flat groove across the grain of a wide board that does not continue all the way to the other side.)

Perhaps the most exotic of all is the side rabbet plane, whose sole purpose is to increase the width of a long rabbet or dado incrementally by shaving the sides of the joint. These unusual planes are

"Craftsmanship can be like a living thread running through a whole lifetime: in its early stages a challenge, in its later stages rewarding with the feeling of mastery it brings...."

CHARLES HAYWARD, *WOODWORKER MAGAZINE*, JANUARY 1966

This chisel plane can be used to reach all the way into the corner of a joint to get it absolutely clean and crisp.

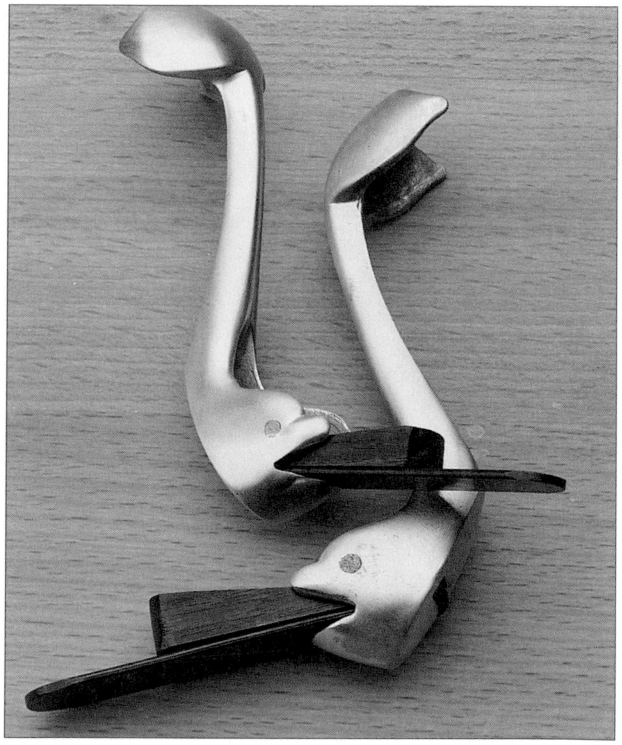

These small violin planes make tiny cuts in the wood. They can be used for decorative work, but were originally intended for making instruments.

Once a staple in any toolbox, the chisel plane (above) is superb for removing glue and trimming work.

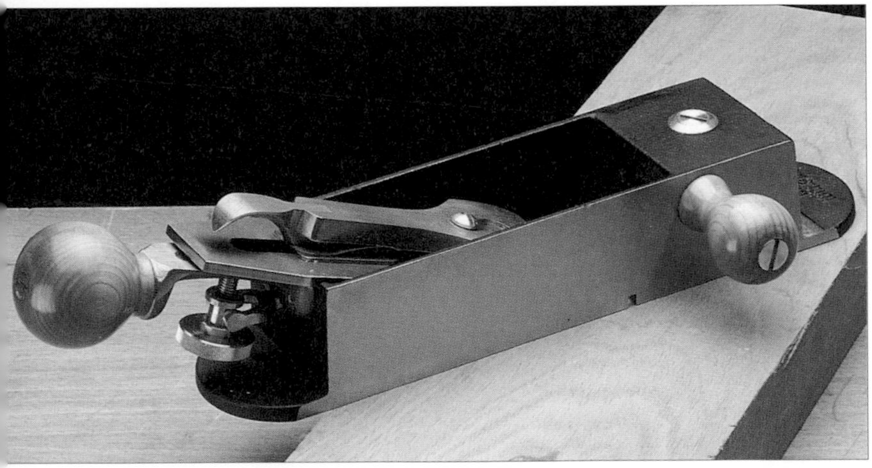

The boxy construction of the miter plane allows it to be used on its side. The side knob can be positioned on either side of the body.

The rabbet plane has a fence to guide it along the work. The blade can be repositioned to the front of the plane for bullnose work.

either fitted with two blades, pointed in opposite directions on the body so that the plane can cut both sides of the groove, or are purchased in a pair, one plane for each side.

The block plane

One can argue that a block plane is really a small surface plane, but the fact that it is a one-handed tool makes a strong case for it to be considered as a type of trimming plane. What distinguishes it from all the other trimming planes is its relatively wide blade. This tool first appeared as a staple after the development of an iron-casting technology for plane bodies late in the 19th century.

Block planes were once made in a variety of sizes but today the blade widths available are 1¼ inches (32 mm), 1⅜ inches (35 mm), and 1⅝ inches (40 mm). Body lengths range from 5 inches (125 mm) to 6 inches (150 mm) and the blade angle is set at 20 degrees (standard) or 12 degrees (low angle). Block planes excel at rapid cleanup work on wide boards, at larger joint trimming, and in work on end grain. In fact, they are the most common type of plane in any toolbox or woodworking shop.

What trimming plane should you use?

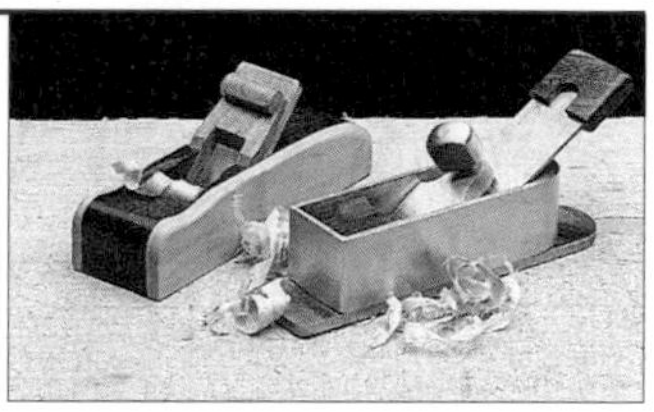

Good-quality trimming planes are best purchased from a reliable dealer.

ACTIVITY	TYPE OF PLANE
Cutting and trimming joints	There is a large number of choices for this type of work. Most of these trimming planes (for example, Stanley no. 92 or no. 93) are relatively short (up to 5 in/125 mm long) and narrow (with blades up to 1 in/25 mm wide, but frequently narrower), being typically used one-handed. A few (such as a large shoulder plane) are long enough for two-handed work. In all cases, it is very important that the blade be used very sharp. If the area is very small, you can use a violin plane, but these special tools have a curved sole, so be careful.
Cutting rabbets (grooves with the grain)	You can use a trimming plane of the proper size, a rabbet plane, or a combination plane (see pages 124–125) fitted with a straight blade. These last two alternatives have the advantage of a fence to guide you. The width can be enlarged when fitting the joint by using a side rabbet plane.

ACTIVITY	TYPE OF PLANE
Cutting dadoes (grooves across the grain)	Use a Stanley no. 71 or no. 271 plane. The width can be enlarged when fitting the joint by using a side rabbet plane. You can also use a combination plane (see pages 124–125); dadoes are often made in the middle of a board, so first remove the fence.
Cutting moldings on edges	Use a combination plane (see pages 124–125) or antique molding plane. (Today this kind of work is done almost exclusively with a router; see pages 126–133). Or use a beader, a type of scraping tool (see page 101) that can produce beautiful small-scale decorative edges on boards.
To cut in a recess for a hinge plate	The plane used for this work is a butt mortise plane, designed to make a recess to fit a hinge.
Cutting miters or shooting an edge	Use a block plane, a special miter plane, or any plane with a side warranted square to the sole.

Shown on these pages are only a few of the hundreds of trimming planes still available today, mostly from specialist woodworking shops and mail-order catalogs. They command a premium price but will last a lifetime. The planes included are all new models, but if you are able to find a second-hand plane in good working order at a flea market, there is no reason that you cannot use it in your workshop.

1 Lie-Nielsen side rabbet plane set
The planes in this set are perfect for cleaning up or widening a groove that's just a little too narrow—or for trimming the width of a rabbet. The shoe in the front can be removed to allow access in tight places.

2 Stanley no. 93 plane/Clifton three-in-one plane
The Stanley no. 93 trimming plane (top) has more heft than its classic no. 92 plane; the removable top allows it to be used as a chisel plane. The Clifton three-in-one plane (bottom) has detachable nose pieces, as well as shims to vary the mouth depth. Its sides and bottom are machined square.

3 Chisel plane, block plane, and scraper set
All three tools are about 2¾ inches (70 mm) long and made of solid brass with rosewood infill. The blade of the chisel plane (top left) sits at the front of the plane. The blade of the block plane (bottom) is at a 27-degree angle. The scraper (top right) has an adjustable blade. These are ideal for touch-up work.

4 Edge-trimming block plane
Cast in manganese bronze, this plane is a remake of the Stanley no. 95 plane. It has an integral 90-degree fence and is effective for squaring surfaces, either with or across the grain. The plane comes in right-hand and left-hand models.

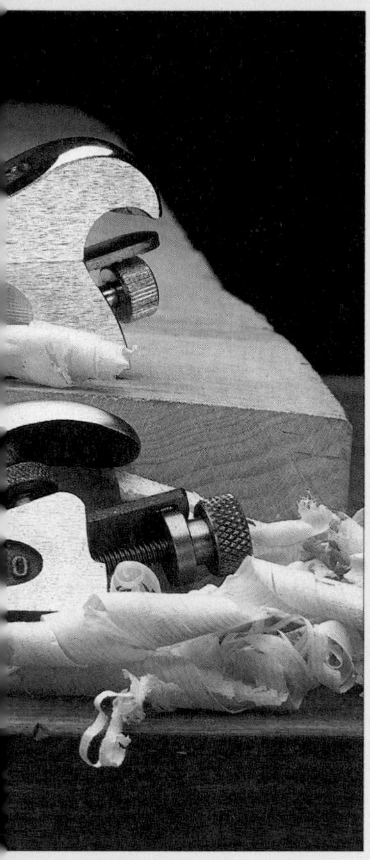

5

5 Skew blade rabbeting block plane

This plane is handmade at Lie-Nielsen. The blade is at a skewed low angle, which allows smoother, more accurate work than with a normal straight-fitted blade. The body is machined of manganese bronze, and the steel right-hand side is removable, allowing the plane to be used in a rabbeting mode with the adjustable bronze fence.

6 Wooden block plane

This traditional-type German block plane has a white beech body with a lignum vitae sole. A hole in the blade slips over a pin driven by a fine screw shaft. Adjustments can be made by rotating the large knob. The plane is extremely comfortable to hold in the palm of the hand, and the fingers fit naturally over the large knob.

4

6
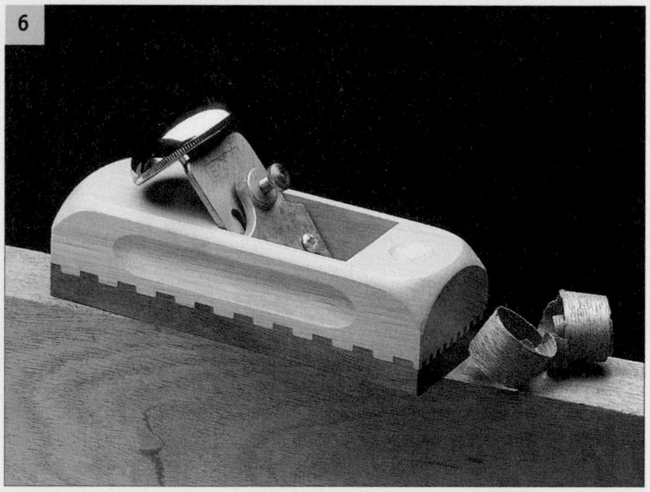

A Venetian carpenter is using a drawknife to shape a gondola oar in this Dutch painting by Jan van Grevenbroeck (1731–1807).

DRAWKNIVES AND SPOKESHAVES

LIKE PLANES, DRAWKNIVES AND SPOKESHAVES—ALONG WITH inshaves and scorps—have a sharpened edge on a blade to cut and shape wood. The drawknife, basically a naked blade with two handles, probably dates back to the 2nd century AD, when shipbuilders and other woodworkers used it in their trades. The spokeshave, which has a blade enclosed in a body, evolved from the drawknife. Closely related to these tools are the inshave for hollowing work—which is similar to the drawknife but with a U-shape blade—and the scorp, a small, one-handle hollowing tool.

Drawknives

There is evidence that the Vikings used the drawknife to build their ships and might have introduced it to Russia, but the drawknife does not seem to have found its way into the Western European workshop until the late 17th century. Traditionally, the drawknife was used by coopers, wheelwrights, gunsmiths, shipwrights, and makers of Windsor chairs. It provided them with the capability to rough-dimension their material and quickly shape finished parts. Today, among green woodworkers (those who work with unseasoned wood), the drawknife is an indispensable tool. It can be used after wood is riven, or split, to remove excess material at the corners in preparation for turning on the lathe, and it can be employed to cut decorative chamfers. It excels where a plane cannot get to the work, a chisel cannot provide enough control, and an adze produces too rough a result. Some woodworkers completely form and shape furniture with the drawknife.

Generally measuring between 8 and 10 inches (200 and 255 mm) long, the blade is shaped like a chisel in section and sharpened along its long edge. The tool is controlled by two handles set in the same plane, but at right angles to the blade. With this tool, a woodworker can quickly remove great large slivers of wood along the grain or produce a beautiful shimmering surface—not quite smooth, but gently faceted and attractive to the eye.

The drawknife has no fences to guide the blade or depth stops to control the amount of material removed. And since it has no body to support the blade, it is designed to cut effectively along a curve, create a hollow, or shape a flowing contour. Every aspect of the tool's performance is completely controlled by the expert hand of the woodworker—the depth of the cut, thickness of the shaving, and the angle.

Today, there are a few companies that still produce drawknives, and there is a supply of antique drawknives available. When purchasing a tool, pay special attention to the handles, making sure that they are long enough, that they feel comfortable, and that they are set at a good angle for drawing the blade over the work. To get a good slicing action to remove rough work, hold the tool

REPRODUCTION SPOKESHAVES

Many of the original spokeshaves were employed in specialized trades for specific tasks, such as cutting to a small radius, scooping out a hollow, or shaping to a specific contour, but as these trades died out, so did the use of their tools. Today's traditional woodworkers often search for these old tools to use for their work, which puts them into competition with antique tool collectors. This has created a demand for the revival of some tools.

Although based on an antique design, the reproductions often have a new feature, such as a more sensitive blade adjustment mechanism or longer wearing hi-tech blades. Sometimes a design might be "sized" for larger modern hands. The extra attention paid to these tools is reflected in their cost.

firmly, with the blade level to the work but at an angle. You will have better control of the tool if you use the end of the blade. To remove large amounts of wood, use a series of short strokes, sliding the knife back between each stroke.

Inshaves and scorps

The inshave is, essentially, a "crooked drawknife." Once part of a cooper's tool kit, used for shaping the insides of a barrel, this tool is the ideal choice for hollowing chair seats and bowls and for carving.

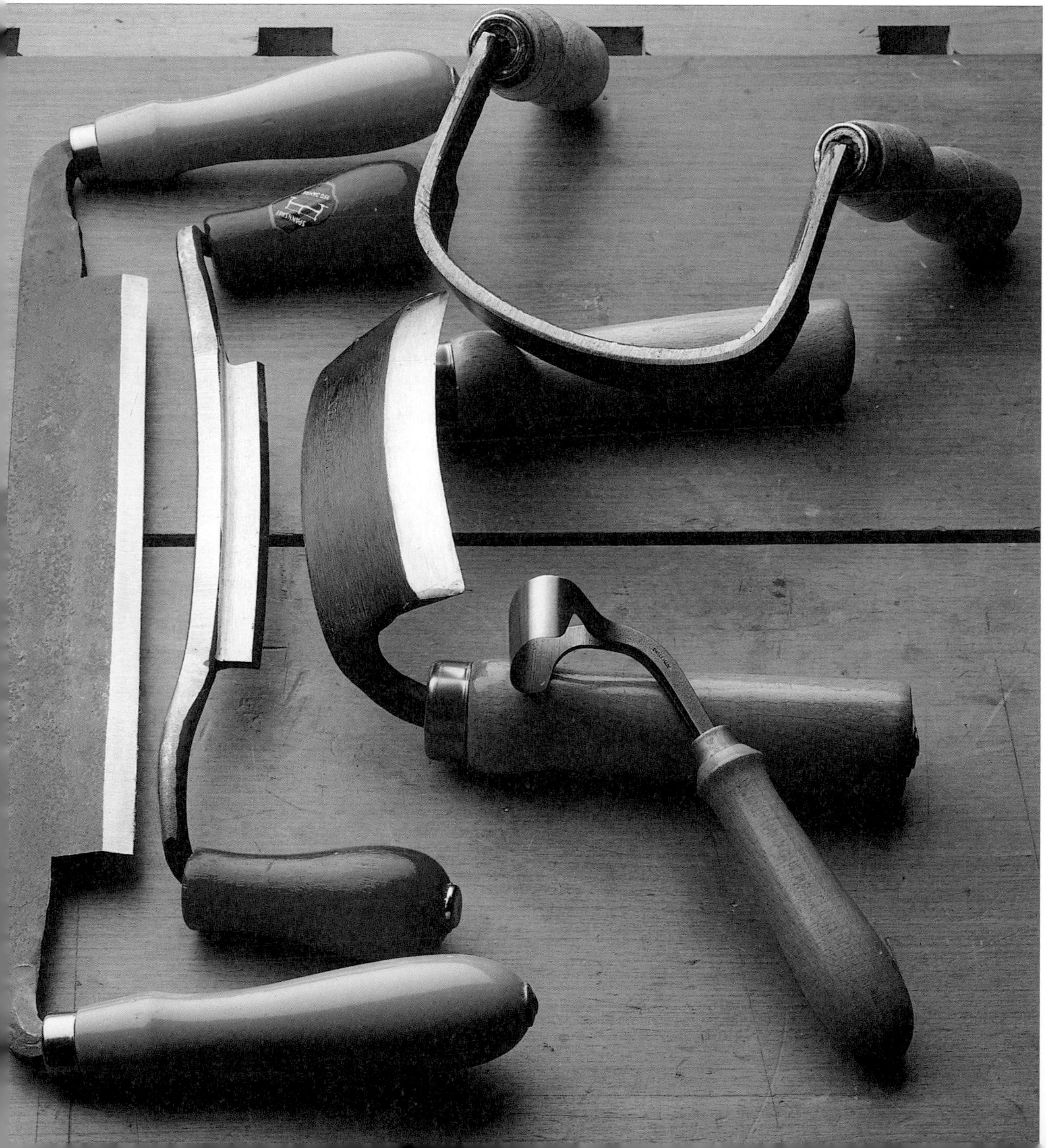

This collection of shaping tools includes two types of drawknives (far left) a pair of inshaves (top and center left), and a scorp (bottom right).

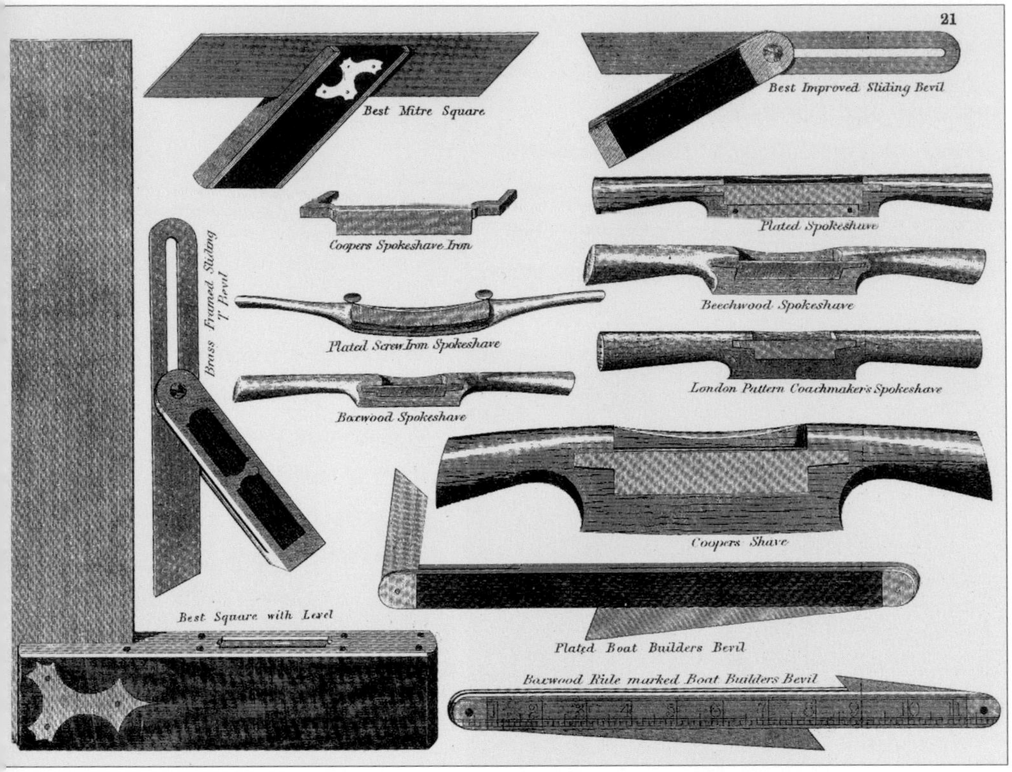

A small sample of the variety of spokeshaves (center and right) available in the 19th century can be seen in this 1889 *Sheffield List*.

It has a curved blade with tangs bent at an angle to bring the handles in line with the blade. It is used in the same way as the drawknife.

The scorp is a type of inshave on which the blade forms a complete circle, about 2½ to 4 inches (63 mm to 100 mm) in diameter, attached to a handle. It, too, was part of the cooper's tool kit and was used for scooping out wood.

Spokeshaves

This tool, like the drawknife, is used principally to shape curves and round edges. But unlike the drawknife, the spokeshave's blade is set into a body that controls the depth of cut (thickness of the shaving) and maintains a constant cutting angle—two factors that have an important effect on the finished surface. The spokeshave is, in many respects, like a plane, but with a short sole. It comes in an almost endless variety of shapes, materials, and sizes. Today, with the resurgence of hand-tool woodworking, it is enjoying enormous popularity. You would probably find at least one in the toolbox of every serious woodworker.

Traditionally, the body of the spokeshave was made of wood. The bulbous center section was hollowed out to allow a shaving to pass through and drilled to support the blade tangs. These tangs were at right angles to the blade and passed through holes drilled at an angle into the wooden body, keeping the blade in tension. The blade could be advanced or retracted by tapping the projecting tangs with a small hammer. Flanking the center section was a pair of handles. These usually arched up, away from the body, providing clearance for the knuckles while cutting near the surface of the work.

Athough the process sounds difficult, with a few minutes of practice, any woodworker can properly set up and use the tool. The early spokeshaves were thoughtfully designed. The handles are smooth and easy to grasp, making control of the tool almost effortless. And the blade is carefully sized to the body, giving the craftsman full effect for any extended effort. The tangs passing through the body provide stability and smooth, chatter-free performance, and leave a beautiful surface. The lower cutting angle of the blade cuts difficult grain more smoothly—an asset when much contour shaping involves cutting tough end grain.

However, these early spokeshaves were prone to the shortcomings of most wooden tools. Usually the sole wore out, making a smooth cut very difficult. Later, this was avoided by the installation of a brass wear plate just in front of the blade, which prolonged the life of the tool. Another problem was the U-shape blade. Because of the right-angle projection of the tangs, this blade was difficult to sharpen. And when the blade eventually wore out, replacement blades were difficult to obtain.

Metal-body spokeshaves

By the end of the 19th century, manufacturers in England and the United States were producing metal-body spokeshaves. Early examples had gun-metal bodies and wooden handles. Today, most commercially available spokeshaves are made of cast iron. A popular design, produced by Stanley and Record, has become the standard. A metal spokeshave is durable and will not wear out, warp, or twist out of shape (although it might break if dropped). Another unique characteristic is the flat blade, which is hung on two knurled nuts that travel on threaded posts, which simplifies the adjustment of the blade.

If you need a general-purpose spokeshave, suitable for a range of tasks, a Stanley no. 151 would probably serve well. But today there are many interesting—and beautiful—alternatives.

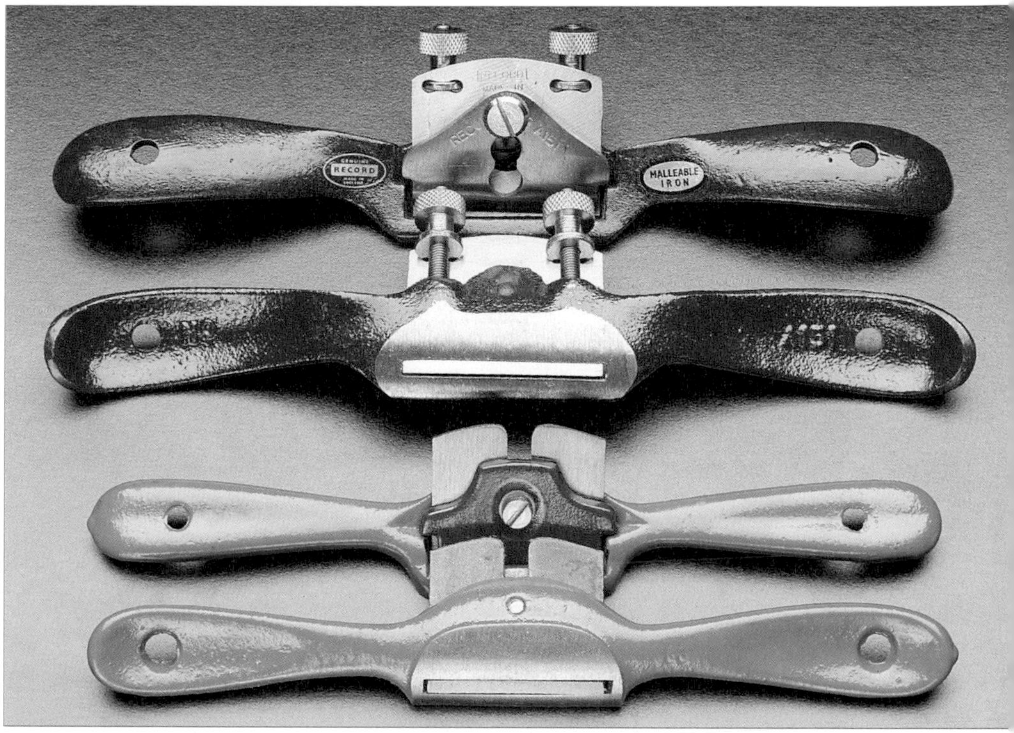

The spokeshaves (above, top) are adjusted by thumbscrews or use a screw (above, bottom).

The spokeshaves below includes a half-round spokeshave (top left), a convex—or radius—spokeshave (top right), a cooper's spokeshave (center), and the adjustable chamfering spokeshave (bottom).

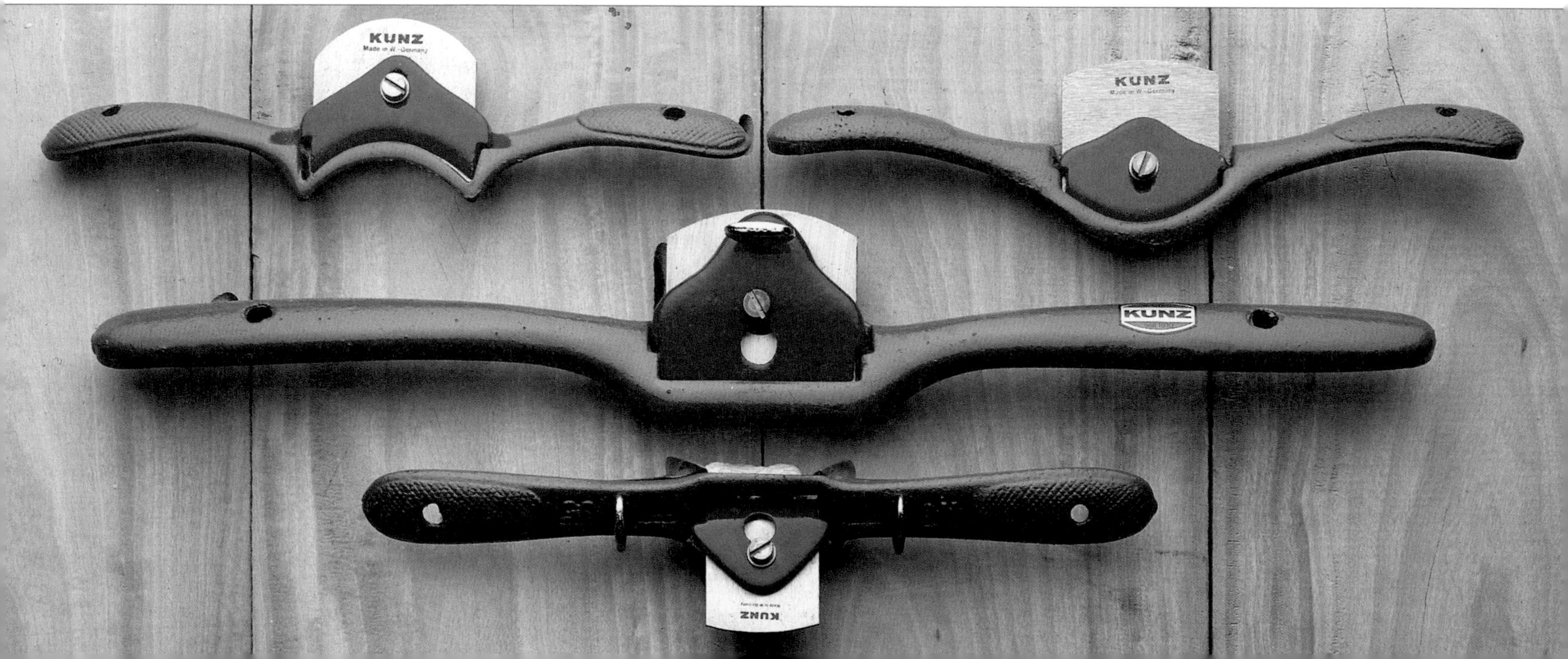

A drawknife can be a useful addition in most woodworking shops, even if only for creating chamfers or rounded edges on wood. If you plan to do any carving or shaping of wood, a standard spokeshave will also come in handy. However, if you spend a lot of time shaping wood, you may want to invest in a number of different spokeshaves and, perhaps, a scorp. The inshave is the best tool for shaping a chair seat and for other hollowing work.

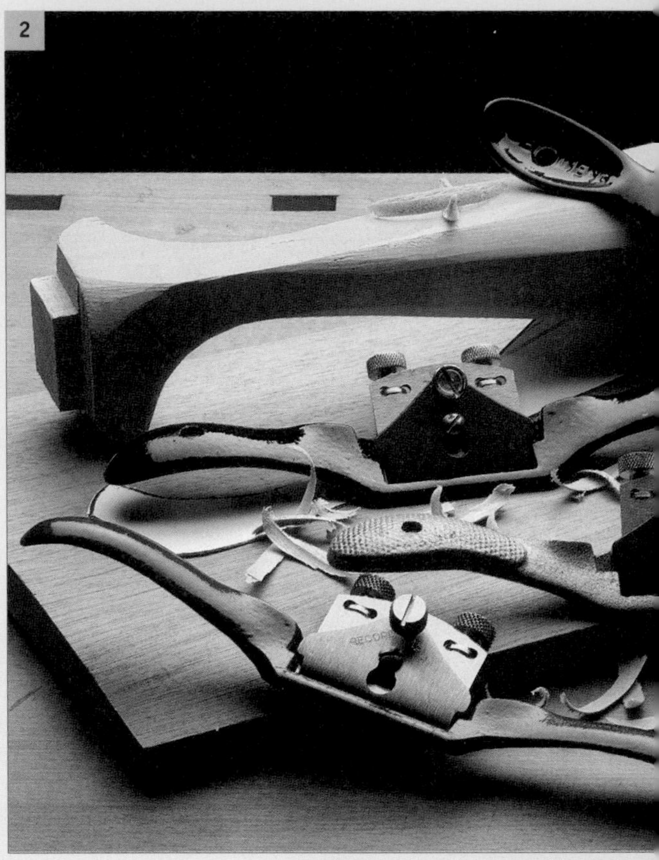

1 Inshave and Sheffield drawknives

The inshave (bottom right) has an 8-inch- (200-mm-) long blade and beech handles that are canted out slightly for more leverage, control, and clearance. The Sheffield drawknives include one with a straight blade (top), which has a slight upward bend to aid its control, and one with a curved blade (center); the ends curve downward slightly for a faster cut.

2 Adjustable spokeshaves

From top to bottom: the Stanley no. 151 (with a flat face) and no. 151R (with a round face) spokeshaves, which have adjustment knobs at both sides for precise blade control; the Stanley no. 151, made of malleable iron, a material that is essentially unbreakable (also available in the no. 151R version); and a Record adjustable spokeshave, which is available with either a flat or round face.

3 Scorps

These hand-forged scorps include (from left, counterclockwise) a flat carver's scorp, a $\frac{3}{8}$-inch (10-mm) micro carver's scorp, a curved carver's scorp, and a $\frac{3}{16}$-inch (5-mm) micro carver's scorp.

4 Forged drawknives

These French drawknives come with leather cases to protect the sharp blades. The set includes a drawknife with a flat blade, one with a concave blade, and one with a convex blade.

5 Clifton spokeshaves

Made of malleable iron, these concave and convex spokeshaves are virtually unbreakable. They have a fine adjustment mechanism.

6 Wooden and brass spokeshaves

The wooden spokeshaves (top) have a brass wear plate in front of the blade; the top model has a flat face and the bottom one a curved face. The small brass spokeshaves (bottom) come with flat, round, and spoon-shape soles.

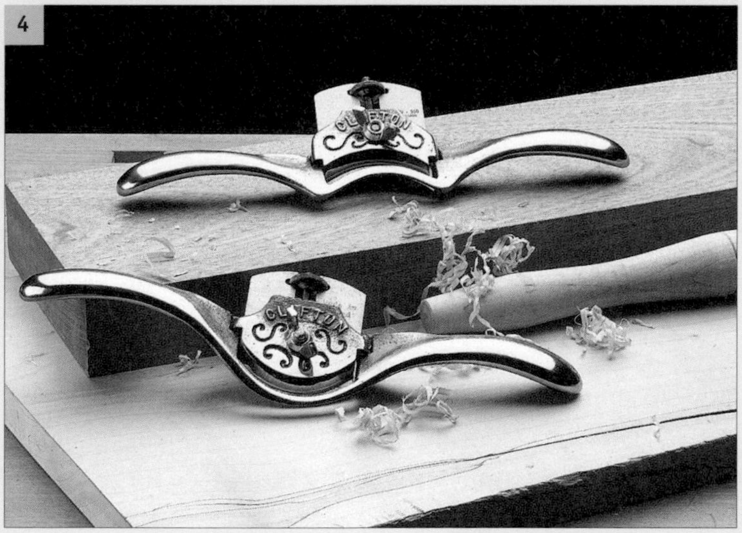

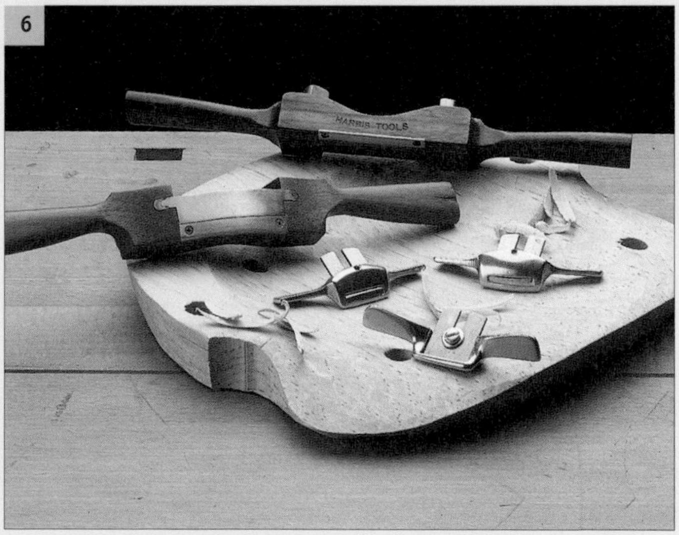

Multiple cutter tools

The precursor of the router, the combination plane comes with interchangeable blades.

Woodworkers have always needed to cut flat-bottom grooves in boards, with the grain and across it, for joinery and assembly—for example, to make dadoes and rabbets. Routing, or plough, planes have long been used for this purpose.

Early wooden varieties of routing planes had one cutter, but in the late 18th century, designs were perfected, allowing the same plane—both wooden and subsequently iron models—to carry many sizes of flat cutters. As designs and castings of the iron models improved in the late 19th century, these were made to carry shaped cutters to cut molding and decorative edges on furniture—until then only possible with dozens of molding planes. Ultimately, in the 20th century, the electric router replaced all of these in most shops.

MULTIPLE-BLADE PLANES

THE IDEA OF A PLANE CAPABLE OF CUTTING MORE THAN A single profile must have been shared by many 19th-century woodworkers. There are surviving prototypes proving that a number of artisans wrestled with the notion. Probably the first product of this idea was the combination match plane, also called a "push-and-pull." It was fitted with two cutters set in opposite directions. With this one plane, the woodworker could cut both the tongue and groove portions of a joint. It has little practical use in a modern workshop, but antique models are available and can be fun to use.

One type of multiple-blade plane is the plough plane, which has been used by woodworkers since the 16th century. The model above was made in London in the mid-18th century.

One of the first multiple-blade planes involved a metal skeletal body, which supported the blade and was fitted with a wooden handle. They had interchangeable blades and matching wooden soles—each blade profile had a supporting sole to provide thorough support for the cutter. Theoretically, if the cutter was supported both in front and from behind, the resulting work would yield more usable molding of good quality. Eventually, it was realized that the interchangeable soles were unnecessary, and, once the designer was freed from this notion, the development of the multiple-blade plane took off.

The Stanley no. 45 combination plane

The first successful incarnation of the multiple-blade molding plane was the Stanley no. 45 combination plane, first advertised as "Traut's Patent Adjustable Beading, Rabbet, and Slitting Plane." The plane was introduced in 1884 and sold worldwide until 1962. Instead of the interchangeable soles, Stanley simply "hung" the cutter between the main and auxiliary bodies. In practical terms, this meant that there was nothing to break the chip in front of the cutter and there was no sole profile to "track" along the edge. To obtain usable molding, the cutter had to be razor sharp and properly adjusted in the plane.

The no. 45 combination plane was an innovation, but it can also be seen as a complicated "Victorian contraption." Fitted with an assortment of blades, slitters, and matched cutters, it was advertised as capable of making an endless variety of moldings.

ROUTER PLANES

One type of plane in continued use since the 19th century is the so-called router plane. Descended from a much older tool known as an "old woman's tooth" (which has a wooden body and narrow blade held with a wooden wedge), this plane has an L-shape blade, which can be easily adjusted.

The router plane is used freehand to deepen a flat-bottom groove or surface, and because the blade is narrow (½ in/13 mm or less) it works equally well across or with the grain. The tool has interchangeable blades, including square, V-shape, and skewed blades. The standard model is 7½ inches (190 mm) wide, but a smaller 3-inch- (75-mm-) wide model can be used for creating grooves for inlays.

The Stanley Tool company claimed it was the only plane needed by a carpenter. It was Stanley's marketing that made this tool a success.

The no. 55 universal combination plane

The Stanley no. 45 combination plane was so successful that it fostered a few imitators. To keep ahead of its competition, Stanley developed the no. 55 universal combination plane. Introduced in 1895, this was the ultimate plane of its type. It offered a greater variety of cutters and allowed the execution of a vast range of moldings. Naturally, with this enhanced capability came some practical complications. This tool can be difficult to set up. With all its fences, guide rods, depth stops, and grips, it can take 30 minutes to set up and test for a single cut. And if even one of the settings comes loose during the work, the entire job can be ruined.

The expanded range and variety of cutters was made possible by the adjustable auxiliary side body. By adjusting the depth and position of this piece in relation to the cutter, you could provide support for the cutter. In addition to this development, supplemental "skates" could be placed on the rods between the bodies for additional support of the blade. The result was cleaner moldings, of greater variety, with less effort, and in less time.

In the modern shop

Both the no. 45 and no. 55 planes are challenging tools to master, and they have confounded many woodworkers. But mastering these tools can be satisfying, and they can prove to be the best tool for a particular job. For example, the no. 55 plane can be used to make or duplicate small quantities of a molding missing from an antique piece.

With the progression of the power router, both these woodworking dinosaurs have dropped from the woodworking scene, but they can be obtained in various secondhand markets and outlets.

Obtain new multiple-blade planes from a specialist woodworking tools dealer.

1 Combination planes and multiplane

The Stanley combination plane (far left, top) is supplied with 25 cutters. A fingertip cutter adjustment makes it easy to adjust. Although the inexpensive Record combination plane (far left, bottom) is sold with only one cutter, additional cutters are available. A worthy successor to the Stanley no. 45 and no. 55 planes, the Clifton multiplane (left) is equipped with as many as 40 cutters. The price of this tool reflects its complexity.

ROUTERS

NO TOOL HAS TRANSFORMED THE CRAFT OF WOODWORKING MORE than the router. The early models, which were developed in the 1930s, were huge and clumsy. The first usable models were small, using fixed speed ½ to 1 horsepower (hp) motors with collets that could only hold cutters (router bits) with a ¼ inch (6 mm) shaft. It took many years for a decent variety of cutters to be available, and it wasn't until the 1950s and 1960s before this new tool became popular.

The router's rapidly rotating bit can cut grooves in wood and work on edge decoration and shape. It has replaced the moulding plane and specialized planes for cutting flat-bottomed dadoes or rabbets, and it can be used to cut in curved areas, as well as on straight lines. The depth of cut is easily adjusted.

Router design

The basic idea is simple: A collet—a type of chuck—is fitted to the end of a high-speed motor shaft. A one-, two-, or three-wing cutter is inserted into the collet. The motor is attached to a base, and the cutter, or bit, protrudes through a hole in the base. The bit's projection is controlled by sliding the motor housing up and down inside a cast housing, which is attached to the base—usually a form of a rigid plastic 6 to 8 inches (150 to 200 mm) in diameter.

Gradually, larger bits with larger shanks came on the market, requiring more motor power and a larger collet. Motor power up to 5 hp is now available, with interchangeable collets that can handle the largest bits. The development of effective speed controls (with minimal loss of torque) means that the large routers can be fitted safely and effectively with the largest new cutters, which require lower speeds for proper use.

One of the biggest breakthroughs came when manufacturers developed the ability to braze tungsten-carbide tips (TCT) onto steel bodies. (This was an outgrowth of the development of TCT-tipped circular saw blades.) TCT bits last much longer than standard steel, even high-speed steel (HSS) and, because they are abrasion resistant, they are particularly important with the growth in use of artificial materials in construction.

The most significant development in design came with the development of the plunge router. This design has the motor housing attached in a spring-loaded fashion to two large rods fixed to the base. The motor housing can be easily adjusted by moving it up and down the rods, then locking it in position, or it can be "plunged" into the work (controlled by a position stop) from a non-cutting safe position—then withdrawn when the cut is completed.

Manufacturers have also improved router handle and switch design, so that these larger tools can be handled more safely and effectively. Inexpensive jigs and fixtures have also been developed to help guide the router and expand its capabilities.

All of these developments led to the creation of the router table, which uses the router fixed in an

The standard-base router (below) has a detachable fence fitted to it. The two handles, one on each side, help you maintain control of the tool as you guide it with the fence.

The plunge router can make cuts at a variety of depths without the need of making too many adjustments. This model has a depth-stop guide.

upside-down position underneath the table surface. The router table has a hole in it for the bit to protrude through, a fence to guide the stock, and often an inset miter track, so that a miter guide can be used. In many shops, the router table has replaced the shaper, and its relatively modest size and cost has brought shaperlike capability to shops that have never been able to afford or use a shaper.

Router bits

There is a wide range of quality and variety in router bits. Better bits are sharper, last longer, and work better. The shaft on a high-quality router bit is accurate, so it fits in the collet precisely. Router bits are divided into three categories: edge-forming bits, joinery bits, and pattern-routing bits. Edge-forming bits are used to create a decorative edge on the corner of a board. These bits include Roman ogees, chamfers, and roundover bits. The joinery bits include straight bits, spiral mortising bits, and dovetail, rabbet, and slot cutters. Pattern-routing bits are used to trim a workpiece to match the

Dos and don'ts

Do not store the router with the bit in the collet. After you finish using the router, release the bit and clean both the bit and the collet.

Do not leave the motor on when you are not using the router. This can prematurely wear out the bearings.

To maintain their sharpness, make sure you store router bits so that they do not touch each other.

Router bits come in an array of shapes and sizes such as the Roman ogee (top row, far right), straight plunge (bottom row, right), and dovetail (bottom row, left) bits.

These top-quality bits (above right) include, from left to right, straight plunge, tongue and groove, cove, bevel, finger joint, roundover, and plywood bits.

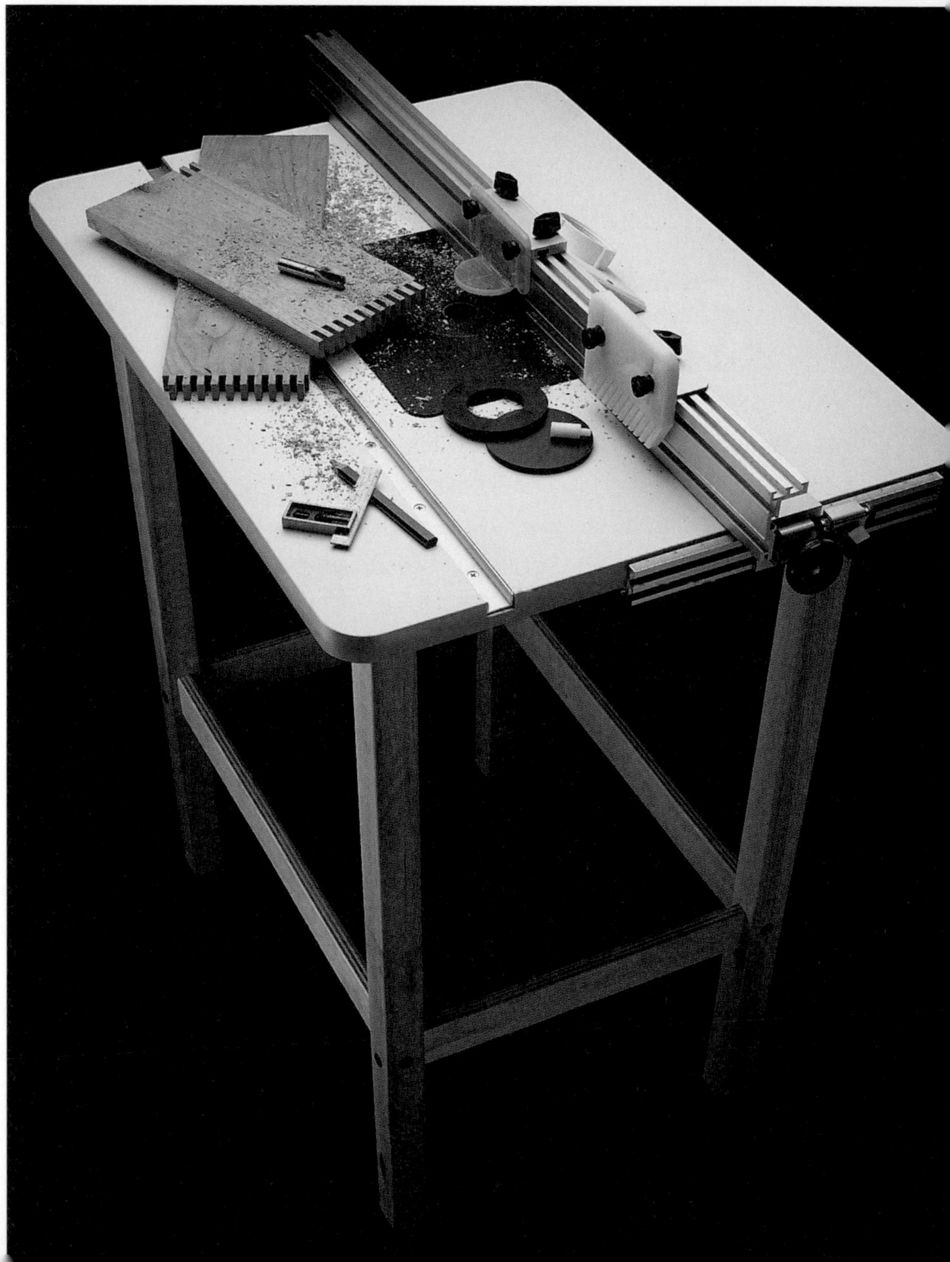

shape of a pattern. These are straight bits with a bearing, which contacts the pattern. The bearing is fitted between the shaft and the cutter or at the end of the bit, depending on if you want the pattern near the router or not.

With router bits, there is a choice in shaft sizes. The smaller shafts are ¼ inch (6 mm) in diameter; the large shafts are ½ inch (12 mm) Whenever possible, purchase the larger shaft size.

Router tables

The shaper (see page 106) was once used for most molding work. This heavy, stationary tool can absorb the kind of side thrust that you find in continuous production. In recent years, however, the distinction between the shaper and the router used with a router table has diminished. Larger, higher-power, variable-speed routers mounted on router tables can cut raised panels and rail-and-stile doors, once the exclusive domain of the professional shaper. Variable-speed routers permit large cutters to spin at a safe 10,000 to 12,000 RPM (revolutions per minute) range. You can now find a router, router table, and the necessary accessories for less than the price of a shaper.

The shaper and table-mounted router are called spindle machines, because the cutter is mounted on a spindle that sticks up through the middle of the table. There are advantages to having a cutter mounted in this way. It is easy to mount a fence to control the workpiece, and smaller pieces are easier to control. The most important advantage is safety. It is easier to see and feel what is happening to the workpiece and the cutter.

The best router tables feature a removable plate that fits into an opening in the table to allow for changing bits and making adjustments. You can make a wood fence, but extruded aluminum ones are the best, because they stay straight. If the aluminum fence has T-slots, it is easy to mount guards, zero-clearance fences, and hold-downs. When the fence is used, attach a guard to it.

A miter slot in the table helps to control cross-cutting operations. Some tables have adjustable miter extrusions for an accurate fit with the miter guide. The miter slot works well for straight cuts on the edge of the board, such as rabbets and grooves, or in the middle of a board such as a dado. You can use the slots for feather boards and other devices. Attach spacer block jigs to the miter guide to make dovetails.

Never feed the wood or a pattern into the cutter freehand. Wood can catch on the bit and kick back. Use a starting pin to avoid kickback. Rest the workpiece, pattern, or jig against the starter pin as you ease it slowly into the cutter.

The router can be used with a specially designed router table (left)—it is placed below the table, with the cutter above it.

Router maintenance

The collet, bearings, and bushings of a router wear with use, and they may need to be replaced several times over the life of the tool. Proper maintenance prolongs the life of the collet, but it will eventually need to be replaced. If all of your bits slip, the collet is probably due for replacement. If only one bit slips, it may be that the bit is undersized.

WHAT TO LOOK FOR

The mechanism that holds the bit is the collet. Collet design and quality should be the first consideration when buying a router. A model with a great motor and base, but an inferior collet is a bad investment. The inside of the collet is straight and holds the bit. The outside of the collet is tapered and fits into the cone at the end of the arbor shaft. As the nut tightens, the collet is pushed into the cone and the bit is squeezed tight. The compressive force on the outside of the collet is concentrated on the bit shaft.

The collet should be flexible enough that you can easily squeeze it with your fingers. Collet flexibility is directly related to how many slits there are in the collet—the more, the better. Also, the greater the surface area between the bit and the collet, the better. A long collet is better than a short one.

The best collet system is a self-releasing three-piece collet. The top of this collet usually has a ridge, groove, or keeping ring, which fits inside the nut. As the nut is loosened, it pulls the collet out of the cone. These collets are usually very long and made of high-quality polished spring steel, with a large number of slits. Because of their flexibility, they have a great deal of holding power—even on shafts that may be slightly undersized.

Fences guide the router along an edge—a circle jig can be attached to it.

Pitch and dirt can accelerate the rusting process. Pitch, sawdust, dirt, and rust decrease the ability of the collet to hold and release the bit. The collet should have as smooth a surface as possible on both the inside and the outside. The cone and cutter shaft should also be clean. Clean the outside of the collet with steel wool, a nylon pad, or a fine brass brush. The inside can be cleaned the same way, but the best tool for the job is a fine round brass brush.

Template guides are attached to the base of the router.

Router bearings last longest when they run under load. Turn the router off when you are not using it. When using a router table there is a tendency to turn the router on and leave it on. The best solution is to use a foot switch that is activated only when you stand on it. When you walk away the motor turns off automatically. Slower rpms and the soft-start feature found on some routers prolong bearing life.

Caring for router bits

The cutting edge of the bit is either steel or carbide. Sharpen steel bits on sharpening stones. Carbide-tip router bits require diamond abrasives. Small diamond hones are now available and are excellent for this task. Sharpen only the flat inside surface. Don't try to sharpen the shaped edge, because you can easily destroy the profile or wreck the balance of the cutter.

Before sharpening your bits, make sure they are clean. If the bit is in good shape, clean it with steel wool or a nylon pad. Scrape off any pitch or baked-on residue, especially from wood such as pine or cherry; then clean the bit with pitch and gum remover, oven cleaner, or ammonia. The shaft should be as smooth as a new bit. If the shaft is tarnished or rusty, clean it with steel wool or a nylon pad, then buff it with a metal polish. Or buff it with rouge on a buffing wheel.

Freehand routing

One of the primary uses of the router is to create a decorative edge on a board. The bit used for the cut is usually a decorative design with a bearing that rubs on the edge of board. The cutter follows any change in the edge to enhance the design. Instead of clamping and unclamping the board as the router goes around the edge, you should hold the work in place by positioning it on a rubber nonskid mat. The downward pressure of the router on the board also helps to keep the work on the mat.

You can use a fence attached to the bottom of the router's base to control the depth of cut and keeps the cutter parallel to the edge. Some factory-made fences are crude, but others are extremely well designed and user-friendly. The best fences have a micro-adjusting feature. You can use

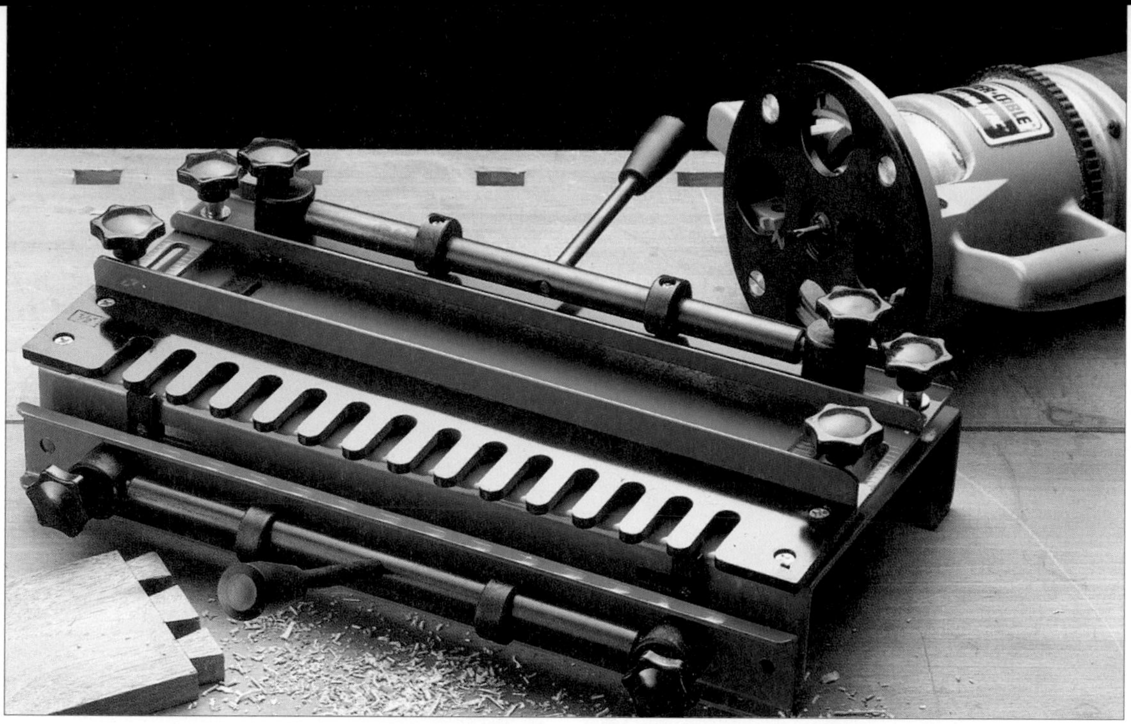

There are many types of jigs available for the router, including this dovetail jig, which acts as a template to cut flush, flush offset, and rabbeted dovetails. Look for one that is easy to adjust.

the fence on edge work, to space dadoes parallel to each other, and when fitting hinges.

Some of the deluxe fences have extension rods that accept a circle jig point. A large circle, such as a round table, is made in multiple passes with a straight bit in a router. For working on large panels, a substantial fence is needed. You can make one out of wood, but it will be cumbersome.

Several companies offer a light weight T square similar to a drafting square. The router is attached to a plate that slides on the T square. Stops limit the depth of travel for cuts parallel and adjacent to the edge. This allows the user to make square cuts for functional joinery or for decoration.

Router joinery

The router is often the tool of choice for joinery such as mortise and tenon or dovetails. In both cases a jig or fixture is used to control the router to cut the desired shape. The usual approach is to attach a collar to the bottom of the router. A collar is a tube that surrounds the cutter and fits into the jig. There are a variety of collars; some thread together and some are screwed to the base.

The most widely known jig for the router is for making dovetails. The wood is clamped into the jig in relationship to a plastic or aluminum comb. The router with the appropriate bit is guided by the collar. The collar slides in the indentations between the guide fingers to cut the dovetails. More sophisticated dovetail jigs have been developed to allow the size and spacing of the dovetail to be changed. The fingers are adjustable laterally to change the size of the cut.

Practice is required to use the router well. Remember that each jig or fixture has a learning curve. Don't expect to be cutting beautiful dovetails in five minutes. Use a lot of scrap and play with the tool to see what it wants to do. Then you can decide what you want to do.

"[We] are forgetting all the small hidden things which star the path of every good craftsman: the moments of intense pleasure when the work is going well and, even more, the moment when a difficult problem has been solved...."

CHARLES HAYWARD, *WOODWORKER MAGAZINE*, AUGUST 1962

There is such a huge array of bits, jigs, and other accessories for the router that it can be difficult to know where to start. The first items that you should invest in, after the router itself, are a set of standard bits and a fence. You can then gradually add to your router accessories when the need arises.

2

1

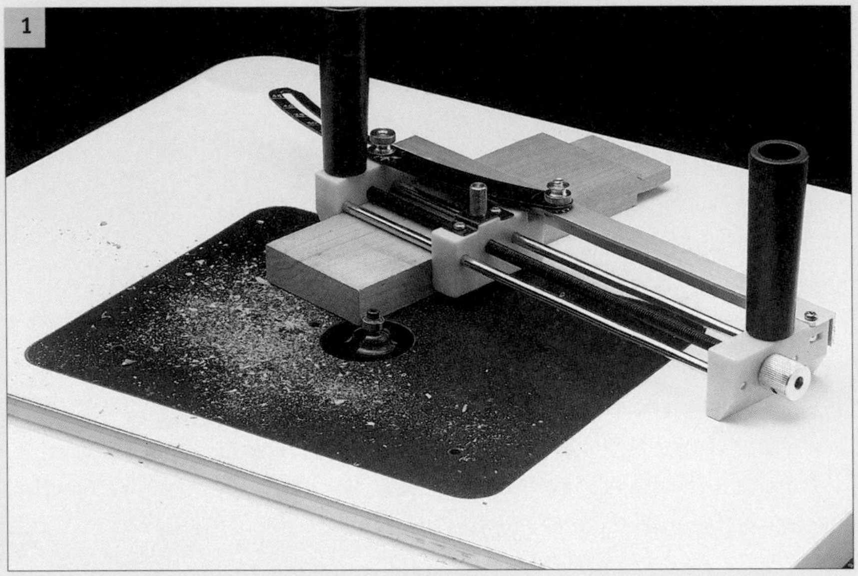

3

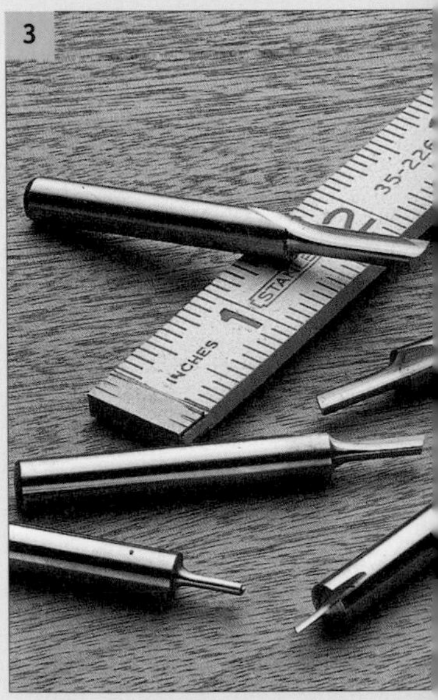

1 Safety control jig

Handling small pieces safely on a power tool can be tricky—and, at the least, make you a bit nervous. This control jig, for shaping small pieces up to 10 inches (255 mm) wide, clamps for a cut angle up to 45 degrees and keeps your hands away from the sharp edges. The jig has a quick-release clamp.

2 Professional dovetailing jig

By permitting varied spacing between pins, this jig lets you have the flexibility and character of hand-cut joints, but in a fraction of the time that hand work would take. The clamp bars hold the workpiece under paired guide fingers, which can be positioned anywhere to control spacing.

3 Small straight router bits

These small router bits are available in increments from 1/16 inch (1.5 mm) to 3/16 inch (4.5 mm). The obvious use is for inlay and decorative routing, but you will find many other applications, too. They can fit in places that larger cutters simply cannot.

4 Router bit bearing kit

With 4 top collars and no fewer than 13 individual bearings, this kit has it all. You'll never be caught short of what you need again when you want a bearing. You can even make your own top-bearing bits.

5 Trimmer router

A smaller version of the standard-base router, this tool is normally used for trimming plastic laminate, but it is also terrific for inlay and any work that requires small cutters. Its light weight gives better control, and a microset depth adjustment provides pinpoint bit accuracy.

6 Router depth gauge

To easily set the depth of a cut for your router, you can use this depth gauge. It has clearly marked 1/16 inch (1.5 mm) increments, from 1/8 inch (3 mm) to 1 inch (25 mm).

Chisels and carving tools

Flatback chisels can be found in all woodworking shops. These tools are invaluable for creating perfect joinery.

One of the most essential tools used to carve, or shape, wood is the chisel, which has a cutting edge along the end of its blade and is fitted with a turned handle. It can be struck with a mallet to sever tough wood fibers or pushed with controlled hand pressure to gently pare wood. Chisels can be separated into two categories. Flatback chisels are tools often necessary for the final stages of a project, when they are used to carefully remove small amounts of wood, thus ensuring the perfect fit of joinery and hardware. "Carving tools" is the term used for chisels—and their close relatives, gouges—that are employed specifically for woodcarving techniques.

Other types of carving tools include carving knives, which are popular for chip carving, rasps and files, and the rotary cutter/grinder. These tools are often found only in a woodcarver's workshop.

Robert Sorby
R. Sorby Sheffield England
Robert Sorby • Sheffield • England
SPANNSÄGE
150 JAHRE
MADE IN W.-GERMANY

Socket chisels made before the mid-18th century often had six-sided handles.

FLATBACK CHISELS

CHISELS HAVE BEEN USED BY WOODWORKERS IN NEOLITHIC TIMES. By the Bronze Age, the metal blades—both tang and socket ends—were being cast in stone molds. The Romans made firmer and mortise chisels. Paring chisels were first developed in Germany in the 16th century, usually with square or hexagonal handles—but without a ferrule. The firmer chisel, often with a splayed blade, appeared in the 17th century. It wasn't until the 18th century, however, that chisels acquired turned handles with a ferrule.

All chisels have a rectangular blade. One end of the blade has either a tang or a socket, which is fixed to the handle, and the other end has a cutting edge ground to a 25- to 35-degree bevel. The blade must be in perfect alignment with the handle, and the back of the chisel blade (opposite the beveled side) should be completely flat—ergo, the flatback chisel. This enables the woodworker to achieve absolute control over the tool.

The width of the blade is used to describe the size of the chisel. Today, chisels are commonly available in sets of four: ¼ inch (6 mm), ½ inch (13 mm), ¾ (19 mm), and 1 inch (25 mm). These sets can be expanded, beginning with a 1/16 inch (1.5 mm) chisel and extending up to a 2 inch (50 mm) chisel.

Tang or socket

There are two basic designs for attaching the blade to the handle. One is to drill a hole in the end of the handle to accommodate a pointed tang. Most modern manufacturers employ this method, which involves drilling a hole large enough to accept the tang, but small enough to hold it tight. Because of the possibility that inserting the tang into a too-small hole could split the handle, a cup-shape ferrule is placed around the entrance of the hole.

The other method involves fitting a tapered end on the handle into a reciprocal socket in the blade. This method is favored for chisels that are heavily struck with a mallet, because the socket style is the strongest possible way to attach the handle to the blade—but it is also the most costly.

You want a handle that is securely attached to the blade, so that it won't separate or become loose. Handles often break after years of use and need to be replaced. Sometimes a custom-made handle can be shaped to suit your hands or designed to better suit the nature of your work.

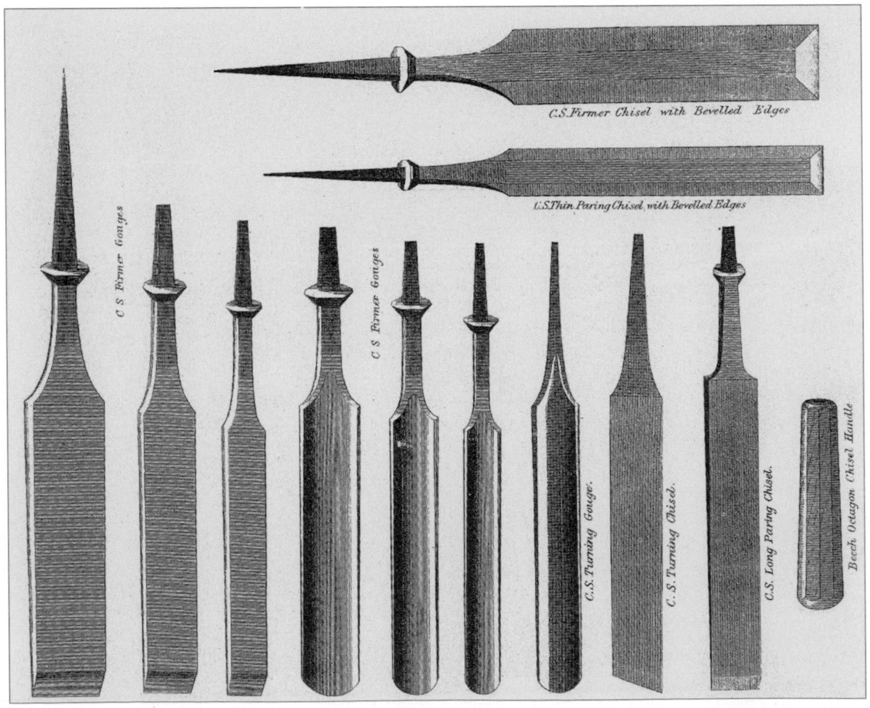

This illustration from the 1889 *Sheffield List* shows a variety of flatback chisels, along with turning gouges.

Types of chisels

Chisels are categorized according to shape, blade thickness, and use. The difference between firmer chisels and paring chisels is that firmer chisels have blades with straight sides and paring chisels have beveled edges along the sides of the blade. Paring chisels are used for fine work. They are rarely struck with a mallet, so their blade is slender and lighter. Many paring chisels have a long blade, which gives the user better control while working and the ability to work in tight spots without the handle getting in the way. (Butt chisels and bevel-edge chisels, which are used for more basic work, share many characteristics with paring chisels, but they have shorter blades.)

Mortise chisels have thick sections and heavy handles and are designed for heavy work. They can be driven into solid wood with a mallet. Firmer chisels straddle between paring and mortise chisels. They have a flat blade, but straight unbeveled sides. They can be hit with a mallet for heavy work or used for paring and fitting. There is also a variety of special-purpose chisels, including corner chisels, with a right-angle blade; dog-leg chisels, some with skewed blades; crank-neck chisels, with an offset handle; and drawer-lock chisels, with a slender blade.

The manufacture of chisels

The main difference between chisels is in the quality of the steel used and in the quality of the handles. Low-carbon steel is too soft to develop and retain a sharp cutting edge. High carbon steel is hard enough for a good edge, but too brittle for it to last. So, ideally, steel for a chisel blade must contain just enough carbon to develop a durable cutting edge, yet retain the toughness to survive repeated blows from a mallet. Some manufacturers add special alloys, such as vanadium or chromium, to the mix. A delicate balance is needed to produce a chisel with a long-lasting, razor-sharp edge.

The heavy-duty socket firmer chisels (right) and bevel-edge chisels (left) have extra-long blades.

The owner of this 18th-century tanged chisel would have made his own handle—only the blades were available for sale.

Some chisels come with plastic tips to protect the cutting edge. To combat rust, store your chisels, such as these butt chisels, in a thick canvas roll, which helps absorbs any moisture near the tools. You can apply camellia oil or another lubricant oil to the blades.

What to look for

The important factors to consider when shopping for chisels is the type of work you'll be doing with them and how the handle feels in your hand. Are you going to make fine furniture or built-in cabinetry? Maybe your interest is in making stringed instruments, boat building, or modelmaking. Each of these specialities might require a different tool.

Everyone enjoys a beautiful tool. Burnished steel darkened to a deep patina and a handle fashioned from an exotic chunk of wood can make a chisel beautiful to behold. But the tool should also feel right in your hands. It should lie easily in your palm, becoming an extension of your arm and hand. After using the chisel for prolonged periods, your hands should not become fatigued or cramped. You should be able to grip the chisel firmly and guide it easily.

The chisel should be reasonably well balanced, with a good relationship between the size and length of the handle and blade. The length of the blade can be important to effective use and performance. A long blade is easier to guide when

NEW VERSUS OLD CHISELS

Some excellent chisels can be found at secondhand tool dealers, yard sales, and flea markets. But, as in any secondhand market, the buyer should beware. Handles are sometimes an indication of quality (that's if the original hasn't been replaced). A fancy handle design with beads and scoring, fitted with a leather washer, is a good sign. Decals and other manufacturer's marks are indications of light use or good care.

A blunted or slightly bent tang is not a serious problem and can be straightend easily. However, excessive rust and pitting can be a problem, making a sharp and long-lasting edge impossible. Also look out for cracks in the blade, which might indicate improper use.

"A craftsman is one who understands his tools and his material and uses them with skill and honesty. It does not matter whether his tool is a chisel or a planing machine, it is the work that he does with it that counts."

THOMAS HIBBEN, *THE CARPENTER'S TOOL CHEST*, 1933

paring joints. And a long blade can be easier to sharpen, as the handle does not get in the way.

Many woodworkers find wooden handles more attractive and nicer to hold. Also, wood is the traditional material for handles, and this historical aspect of tool design is often appealing. However, wooden handles can chip, split, or become loose, requiring repair or replacement. Plastic handles avoid these problems. During manufacture, the tang of the blade is permanantly set into a durable plastic grip; they are virtually indestructible. However, plastic handles can grow shabby. Although the handles won't break easily, they are susceptible to scratches and discoloration that can transform a once-gleaming tool into an eyesore.

Conditioning a chisel

Wooden handles frequently become loose. The wood fibers can become compressed by the tang as the handle is twisted during use. Sometimes the handle will shrink as the wood dries. To fix this condition on a tang-style chisel, set several glue-coated slivers of veneer in the hole before resetting the blade. In a socket chisel, the problem can be that the tapered end of the wooden handle no longer conforms to the socket taper of the blade, causing the two to separate. Sometimes the tapered end of the handle can be reshaped with a rasp or file.

The back of a chisel blade should be absolutely flat. If it curves upward, the edge is raised off the surface and the chisel will not cut. If it curves downward, the edge is unsupported and the chisel will dig into the wood. Either of these conditions will prevent the chisel from cutting efficiently and can affect the woodworker's control over the tool.

The remedy is to flatten the back of the chisel. This can be accomplished by rubbing the back of the chisel against a flat abrasive surface such as a coarse honing stone or a slab of glass covered with wet/dry abrasive paper. Once the back of the chisel is covered with uniform scratches, progress

The long blade of a paring chisel (top) must have a flat back to be successfully pushed along the work surface. If you purchase chisels with a plastic handle (bottom), make sure they are of good quality.

Among the special-purpose chisels is the crank-neck chisel, which is ideal for paring work in recessed areas.

to finer honing stones. Eventually the back of the chisel will be both flat and polished. Although polishing the back won't necessarily improve the performance of the tool, it should extend the life of the cutting edge.

Sometimes the sharp corners of a blade can cut you. These sharp corners are easy enough to blunt by wrapping 220-grit wet/dry paper around a small block of wood and gently beveling the sharp corners running along the length of the blade. Two or three passes is usually all it takes.

Sharpening and honing a chisel

No matter how much you've spent on your chisels, if they are not sharp, they are useless. Sharpening chisels is a two-step process. First, grind the blade on a slow-speed bench grinder (see page 229) to restore a square edge with a 25-degree bevel across the entire cutting edge. The grinder should be fitted with a jig designed to maintain the proper angle of the bevel in relation to the abrasive wheel, while allowing enough lateral motion, so that the blade can be passed across the wheel. Typically, a chisel's edge will take a minute or so to regrind. You do not have to regrind the chisel every time you resharpen.

When the edge comes off the grinder, close examination will reveal a ragged cutting edge. All the grinder does is prepare and shape the chisel. Now the chisel must be honed on abrasive stones to achieve a razor-sharp edge. Most woodworkers can get by with just a few stones. Keep a coarse 400-grit stone for the removal of shallow nicks. When it's possible, repairing the edge on a stone is preferable to returning the chisel to the grinder.

The remaining two stones should be a medium 1000-grit stone and a fine 4000- to 6000-grit stone. As the edge is passed from the coarse to the

The blades of Japanese chisels (right) are made of durable laminated steel, with the cutting edge having a constant hardness along its entire length. As is the Japanese style, the flat side is partially concave to reduce friction and aid in keeping the back flat.

medium, then the fine stone, the edge becomes brighter, more reflective. This process usually takes about three minutes. The use of a honing guide is recommended. This is an accessory that supports the chisel at the desired angle and prevents it from rocking. Any movement away from the desired angle might result in a rounded-over edge.

Using a chisel

A chisel can be used with the bevel either up or down, depending on the operation performed. If the chisel is laid flat on its back, the chisel should travel straight forward, along the surface. You might employ the chisel in this manner to clear out a flat mortise for a hinge or to trim the cheek of a tenon. You can also use the chisel bevel-side-down. In this case, the bevel controls the depth of cut. The more upright the chisel is, the deeper the cut.

No matter how sharp the edge of the chisel is, the best results are obtained with a careful paring stroke, taking small cuts. When paring a piece of wood, use a lateral cutting motion to slice the material neatly, which presents minimal resistance and leaves a smooth surface.

Which chisel should you use?

Most work can be accomplished with a few of the basic chisels, such as the firmer, bevel edge, paring, and mortise chisels, but some unusual tasks may require a special chisel.

ACTIVITY	TYPE OF BLADE
Cutting dovetails and other fine work in cabinetry	Bevel-edge chisels can navigate the tiny spaces without inadvertently damaging your work. These chisels are easier to manipulate when trimming fine joinery.
Cutting and fitting joints in hard woods, such as oak, heavy work, or paring and fitting	The heavier blades found on firmer chisels can keep the chisels from flexing under heavy work loads or the blows from a mallet. These chisels can also be hand driven for more delicate work such as paring and fitting.
Hanging doors and fitting interior fixtures	A set of shorter butt chisels will work well. Generally made of softer steel, these are better suited for the rough-and-tumble nature of construction work and interior carpentry.
Heavy work such as cutting tough crossgrain wood fibers	Mortise chisels can be effectively driven into solid wood with a mallet. They are designed to withstand the constant heavy blows.

ACTIVITY	TYPE OF BLADE
Cleaning up and squaring mortises	Special-purpose corner chisels have a right-angle blade designed for trimming corners in mortises and other square holes and corners.
Cleaning up dadoes and other difficult-to-reach recesses	The small dog-leg chisels have a straight blade or skewed blade, either to the right or left, and they are used like a paring chisel for final cleanup.
Levering out waste material in mortises	Swan-neck chisels have an angled blade suitable for getting into the bottom of a mortise. The blade can be held flat against the surface of the work with the handle clear above it.
Cleaning up corners of lock mortises	Drawer-lock chisels have a slender right-angle blade for working in the tight, narrow corners typically found in lock mortises.

Your first acquisitions, depending on the type of work you plan to do, should be a set of mortise and and bevel-edge chisels or a set of firmer chisels. A basic set usually consists of four chisels, but you may want to expand it to suit your preferences. Choose ones that feel comfortable in your hands. You'll also need a wooden woodworker's mallet. You can add specialized chisels to your collection as you see fit.

1 Blue Chip and cabinetmaker's chisels

The squared-off high-impact plastic handles on the Blue Chip chisels (left) prevent them from rolling. The steel hoops at the end of the stained beech handles on these cabinetmaker's chisels (right) protects the handles so they can be struck with a mallet. The set comes with a storage box.

2 Crank-neck chisels and Japanese butt chisels

These crank-neck chisels (left) have a shorter blade than most, which makes them easier to use then the traditional long-blade variety. The Iyoroi butt chisels (right) have a hollow-ground flat back and sharpen quickly, without removing much steel.

3 Lignostone mallets and mortise chisels

Made of layers of beech laminated under high pressure, lignostone mallets (left and top) have great impact strength and tremendous resistance to cracking. The mortise chisels (right) have extra large handles, which are also shock resistant. The blades have a deep cross-section to allow easy levering.

4 Bevel-edge chisels

The octagonal boxwood-handle chisels (left) are carefully hardened and tempered and are a delight to use. The gilt-edge chisels with rosewood handles (right) have tapered solid brass bolsters, which fit tightly into the handle.

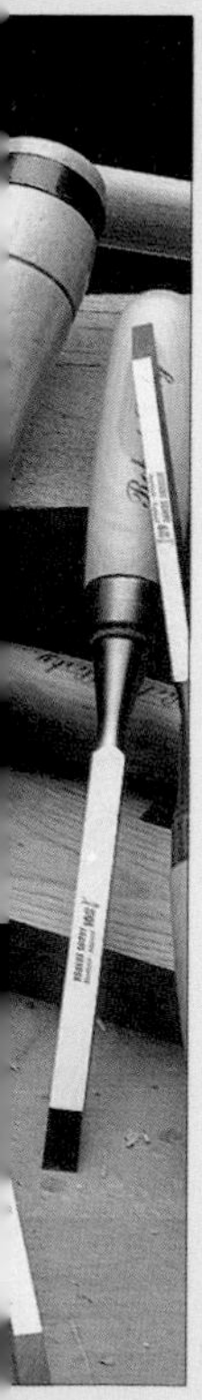

5 Paring chisels and registered mortise chisels

The paring chisels (top) have rosewood handles, which should be gripped with both hands for paring. Rectangular in cross-section, the blades of the registered mortise chisels (bottom) are tapered from the shoulder to the bevel. The ash handles are steel hooped and have leather shock washers.

6 Firmer chisels and woodworker's mallets

The firmer chisels (left) have handles large enough for two-handed use and double hoops to protect the handle when struck with a mallet. The traditional red beech wooden mallets (right) have an angled face and chamfered handle to ensure that the striking force will be applied with maximum efficiency.

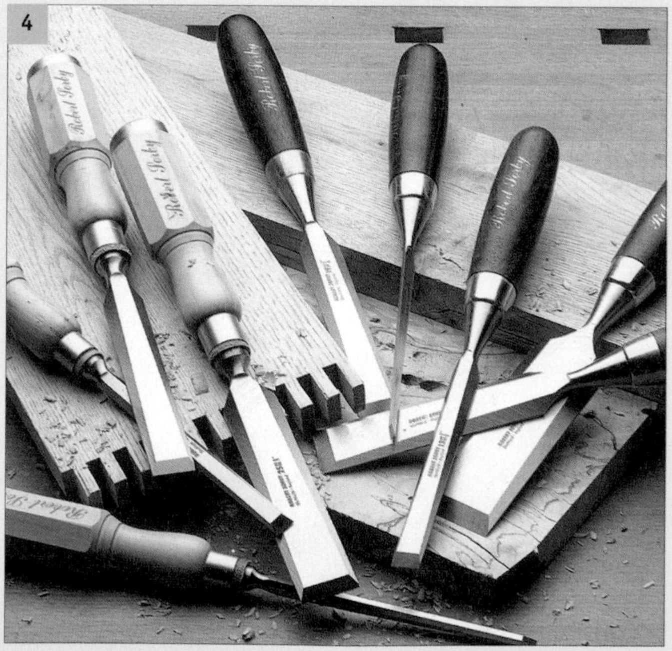

1

3

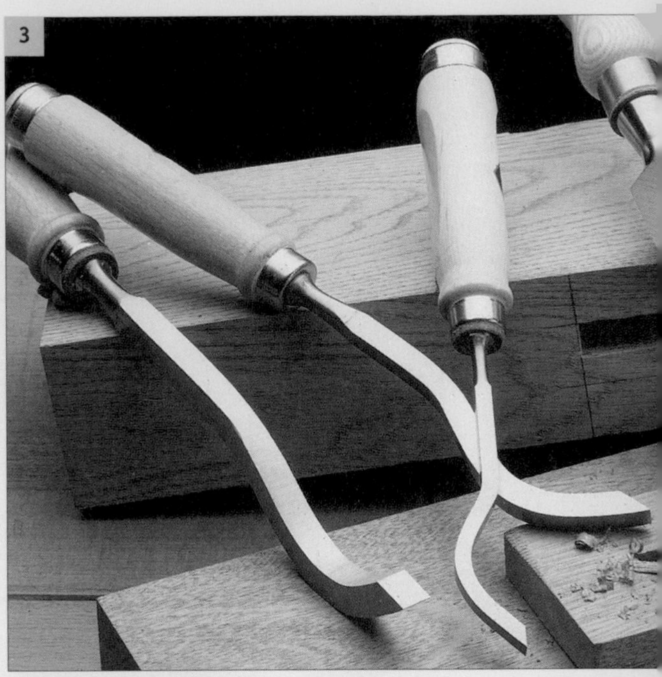

2

4

7 Japanese mortise hooks

You can use the Japanese mortise hook to clean out and pare interior areas of joints that would otherwise be difficult to work on. The body of the chisel is slightly curved backward to provide extra clearance in constricted areas.

8 Skew chisels

The paring action of the skewed blades allows the most precise kind of cutting action, and the point allows you to reach into places in which a regular straight-blade tool would have trouble.

5

9 Swan-neck chisels and corner chisels

The unusual but useful swan-neck mortise chisels (right) are carefully forged from square bar stock. The shape allows you to place the cutting edge against the bottom of the mortise and clean it smoothly. The corner chisels (left) have double-hooped ash handles to withstand the impact of a mallet blow. They are ideal for cleaning up corners.

10 Japanese mortise chisels

The laminated steel construction of these well-crafted chisels is harder than on any Western-designed tool, and the socket/tang design of the red oak handle provides extra strength, so that you can use these chisels with a mallet.

11 Dog-leg chisels and blind nailer

The skewed blades on the dog-leg chisels (top) are ideal for furniture makers to trim jointwork and for undercutting. The blind nailer (bottom) is a unique tool that allows you to set nails or brads invisibly by slicing a chip of wood from the surface, which is glued back in place after the nail or brad has been installed.

12 Clean-out chisels

These special chisels have short blades bent to the right and left to clean out corners, grooves, and dadoes.

6

CARVING TOOLS

THE CHISELS OF THE WOODCARVER WERE ORIGINALLY THOSE OF the carpenter and joiner, but over the centuries carvers have devised a range of shapes to enable them to carve things that would otherwise have been impossible, would have taken too long, or would have been crudely finished. There are now more than 600 separate carving chisels and gouges (chisels with a curved blade) available.

Carving uses three principal kinds of cut: stabbing, long flowing, and short scooping. In stabbing, the shape of the chisel is left in the wood such as in chip carving or in setting down a relief pattern. Long flowing cuts may be used in the process of removing waste wood and in creating a finish. Short scooping cuts are used for both shaping and texturing. Another cut involves sliding the chisel edge sideways like a knife.

Below is a collection of parting, or V, tools. From left to right are three straight-blade chisels, a long bent chisel, and two short-front bent chisels.

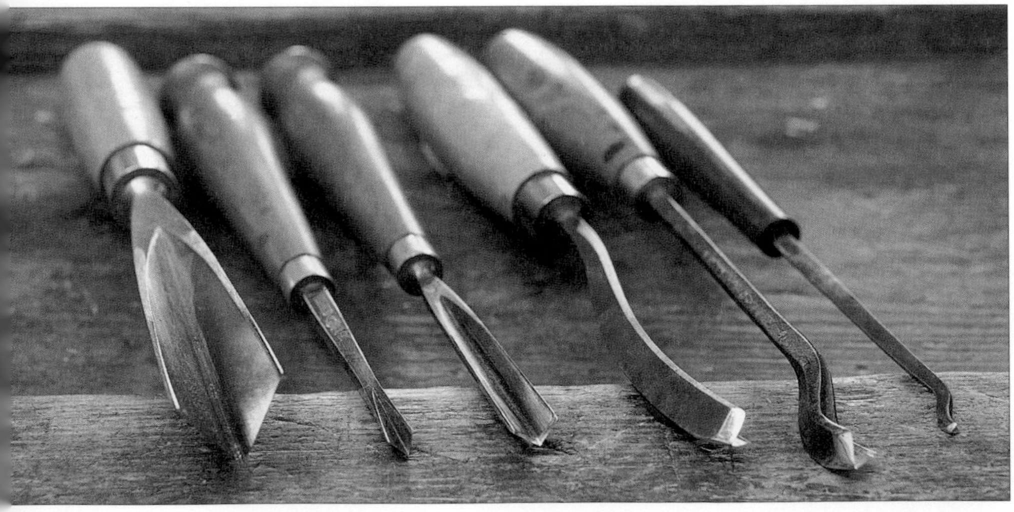

The numbering system

The basic shapes of the edges of the tools are numbered according to either the London or Sheffield system or in some similar system that different European manufacturers use. There are about 19 separate shapes, which are usually represented in catalogs by the marks they stab into the wood. The width of edge may range from 1/32 to 3 1/8 inches (0.75 to 80 mm).

Since 1900 reputable manufacturers have stamped a number on the shank of each chisel to indicate the shape. Not every maker's shapes are exactly the same as another's, but they all agree that the first 11 shapes run from completely flat to U-shape. After that, the numbering varies considerably. Some manufacturers make certain shapes only on request and others have shapes not included in the Sheffield system, which is the numbering given below. The uses described are typical, but most chisels can do many jobs.

- No. 1 is a straight-edge chisel. It is beveled on both sides, which gives it a low angle of entry to the wood for paring while keeping reasonable strength at the edge. It is also ideally suited for stabbing center lines in incised letters. It is not suitable for smoothing a flat surface wider than itself.
- No. 2 is a skew, or corner, chisel, straight-edged and beveled on both sides but cut on an angle so that its point can be used to cut into corners. The obtuse angle is used for chasing and paring; it works like a knife. At least one manufacturer includes this as a no. 1 chisel.
- No. 3 is the flattest of the gouges. It is ideal for smoothing a flat surface because its corners can be kept from digging in. It can also be used for stabbing a gently curved outline such as on an ornamental leaf or stem.
- No. 4 is slightly deeper and is used for the same purposes as a no. 3.
- No. 5 is a very popular shape because it can be

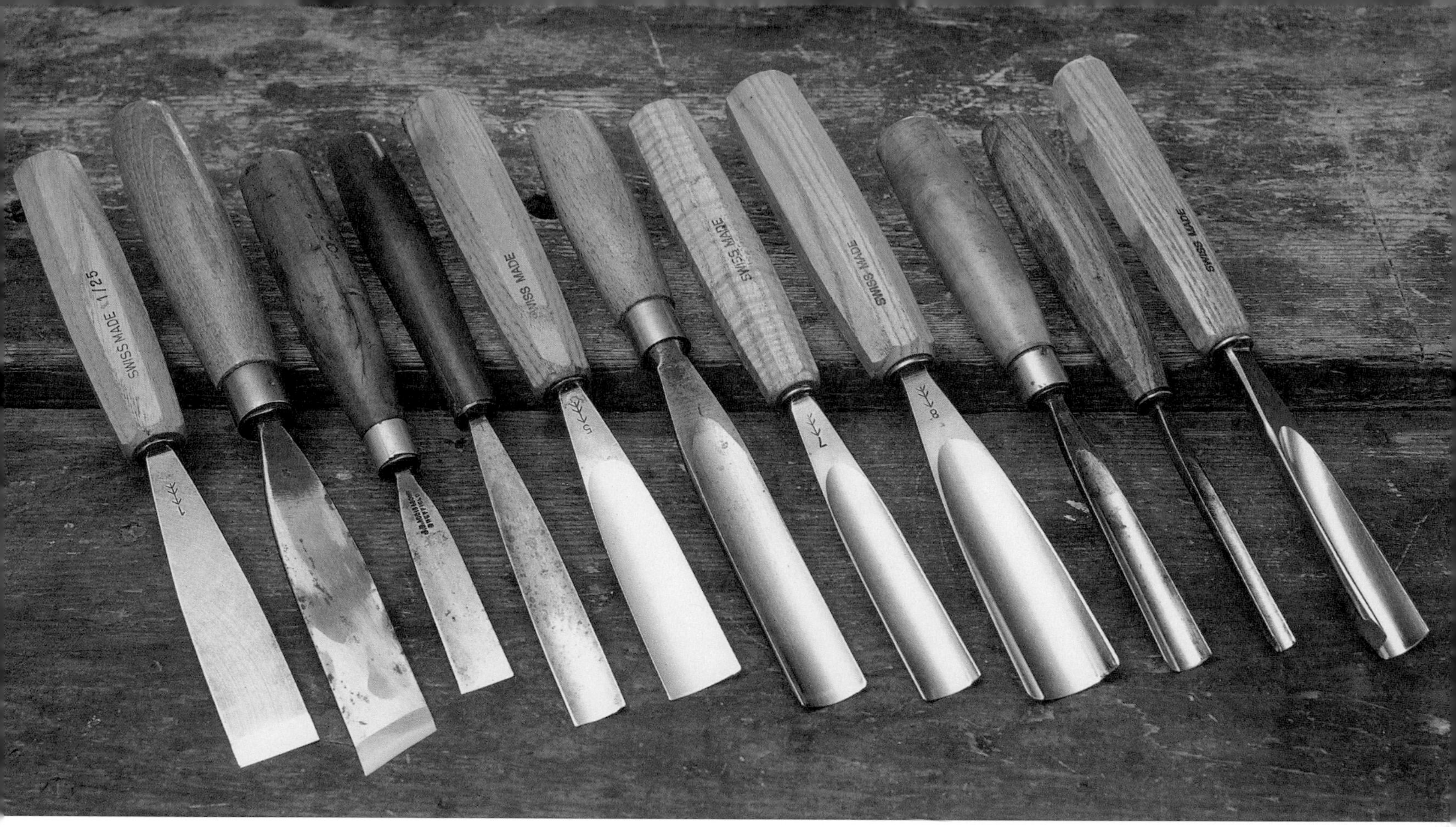

used both for removing waste wood and for stabbing outlines.

- Nos. 6 and 7 are used in the same way as the no. 5 chisel. No. 6 is particularly useful in shaping the eggs in an egg-and-dart molding.
- No. 8 is particularly useful for shaping beads, berries, and center bosses. It is less than a semicircle. The bigger sizes are useful for removing large amounts of waste.
- No. 9 is virtually a semicircular shape. Like the no. 8, it can be rotated in the wood to mark a circle or twisted as it is driven through the wood to give a smooth action in removing waste.
- No. 10 (a fluter) forms a shallow "U" and is used in cutting flutes and removing waste.
- No. 11 has a deep U-shape. The smaller ones, called veiners, are used for leaf veins. The larger ones can be used confidently to cut across the grain for shaping or waste removal, because the corners can be kept clear of the wood to avoid splitting.

Parting tools

The parting, or V, tools come in 45-degree, 60-degree (the most popular), and 90-degree angles. They are never very sharp on the heel of the V, because the inside shape is slightly rounded at the bottom. The outside of the angle must be rounded to match the inside. One manufacturer also makes them with a rounded middle for specialized use. Parting tools are used for cutting outlines, for cutting crisp angles between forms where stab marks might go too far, and for carving hair and various ornamental textures.

The wing parting tool is now rare but is useful for carving grooves into which the sides curve down such as in reeding, for veins on the top surfaces of leaves, and for wrinkles in skin. Macaroni and fluteroni tools are also rare. Macaronis, essentially two right-angle V tools in one, may be used to carve hair. They can also carve various square profiles where the inside corners need to be clean. Because

Carving tools are identified by numbers, which are correlated to the shape of the blade. The tools above are arranged from no. 1 to no. 11 (left to right). The two chisels below are both no. 11 tools, but they are different sizes.

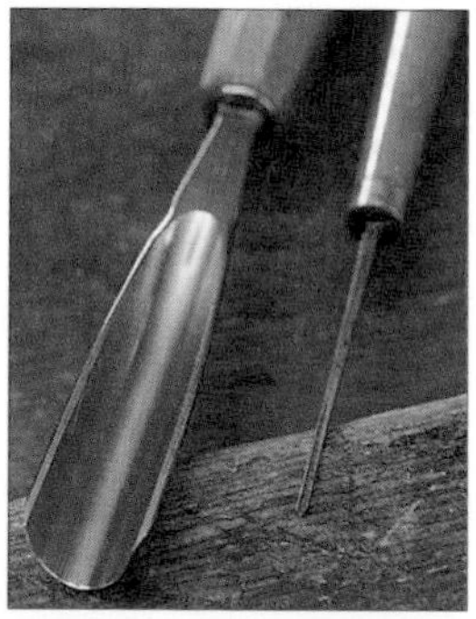

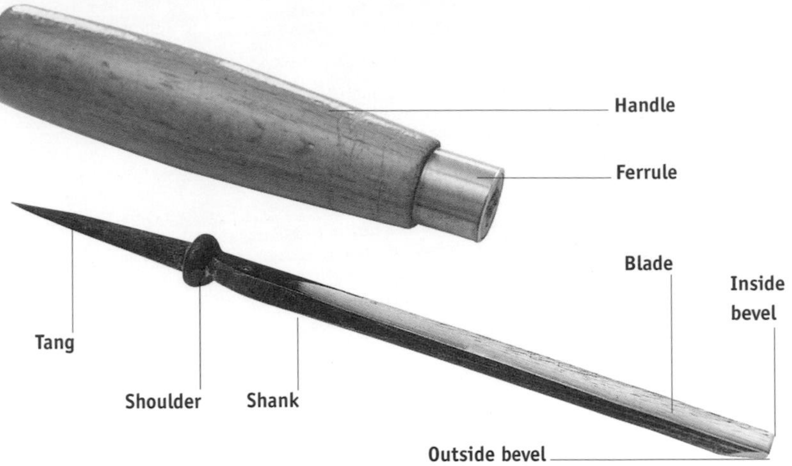

Shown above are the components of a chisel or gouge used for carving.

they are beveled on the outside, they can be used to produce flat surfaces that are wider than the chisel edge. The fluteroni has a rounded square section; it can be used in the same way. A variation of the fluteroni is the backeroni; it is hollowed beneath.

About the blades

Although most carving tools have straight blades, all the end shapes of the blades are also available in long and short-front bent blades. Long bent tools are used for long hollows such as bowls where a low angle of entry is possible. Short-front bent chisels in the flatter shapes are called grounders, because they are used for making flat backgrounds in relief carving. Deeper short bent gouges, known as spoons or spoon bits, are useful in making deep scooping cuts and hollows along inside curves. Nos. 1 and 3 to 11 and fluteronis are also available as backbents. These are particularly useful for convex shapes along inside curves such as on plant stems and animals' tails. The backbent fluteroni is valuable for carving the ribs on acanthus foliage.

The blades of all these tools, except the short bent ones, are available with parallel sides, and they come in the allongee pattern, with a long taper from the edge to the shoulder. Probably the most versatile is the fishtail, or spade, chisel, which has the edge splayed to a 60-degree angle at each corner. Although unsuited for heavy work, they enable crisp cutting into corners and facilitate delicate work. Halfway between these tapered tools is the long pod; it combines strength with versatility.

Newcomers are the skew gouges invented by Fred Cogelow, which work with a knifelike action; you need a left- and right-hand tool for every shape and size. There are various other peculiar shapes, which combine a chisel with a knife action.

Japanese chisels hold sharp edges, but they are suited for only short scooping cuts and stabbing, and they will not accept an effective inside bevel.

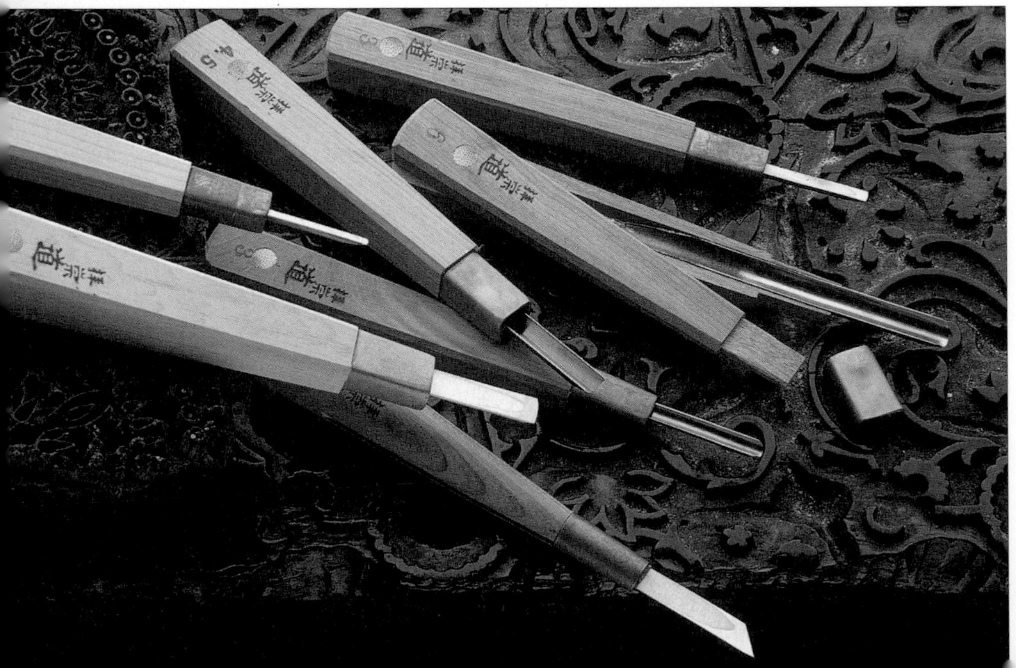

Choosing a chisel

A good chisel is made of well-tempered, good-quality metal. It is accurately shaped and of even thickness from side to side, fairly slender, and comfortable to hold. Some makers play for safety by making tools unnecessarily thick. This makes them unwieldy, difficult to use in confined spaces, and prolongs sharpening because more metal needs to be ground away. The blade should be directly in line with the handle. If bought without a handle, the tang should be in line with the blade and sharpened to a point with square sides, so that it can ream its own perfectly fitting hole in the handle.

Shallow scooping cuts are best made with the two gouges on the far left; deep scooping cuts are best made with one of the other gouges. The two on the near right are backbent gouges.

Cost may not be a reliable indicator of quality. An experienced carver can recommend makes that are consistently good such as the Swiss Pfeil chisels and the Henry Taylor Sheffield-made Acorn brand tools. Some makes are consistently soft, but frequent mechanical polishing will maintain sharp edges. In Britain less expensive secondhand chisels by Addis and by Herring Bros. are still available. Most of these are of the highest quality.

The shape of the handle may be a tapered cylinder, octagonal, or any shape devised by the carver for comfort and quickness of recognition on a crowded bench. Handles with waists often denote carpentry chisels and inferior metal. Beech, ash, and boxwood are the most commonly used woods.

Using a chisel and mallet

On small work, it is usual to push the chisel by hand, both hands being engaged with the tool or one holding it and the other striking it with a mallet or the base of the palm. This last method can damage the hand but many professionals use it.

Mallets may be used on delicate work but are essential for roughing out and large carvings. The weight of the mallet needs to be comfortable to the user as well as effective. Some mallets are sold by diameter instead of weight. The most durable wooden ones are turned from lignum vitae. They are heavier than beech, the next most common. Mallets of wood-polymer composites, rubber, nylon, soft iron, or bronze are also available. Metal ones will wear out chisel handles faster.

Chisels are potentially harmful, because they should be sharpened to a razor's edge and are often driven with force. The carver should never work directly toward any part of the body. A chisel should be put down carefully when not in use. Becuase the edge is sharp, it is also easily damaged. It is foolish to shorten the life of the tool through careless handling. Carving chisels are sharpened in the same way as flatback chisels (see pages 140–141). Gouges are rolled from side to side; use a slip stone to sharpen an inside bevel or to remove the burr if there is no inside bevel.

The fishtail blades of these chisels are used for fine work. The three chisels on the left are true fishtails, but the three on the right are not, as they don't have the śame curved flare. They are allongee and two long pod chisels.

There are hundreds of carving tools to choose from, so deciding what you need can be overwhelming. Although carving tools are often sold in sets, it can be more beneficial to buy them individually as you need them. Secondhand tools can be of superior quality, but may need new handles.

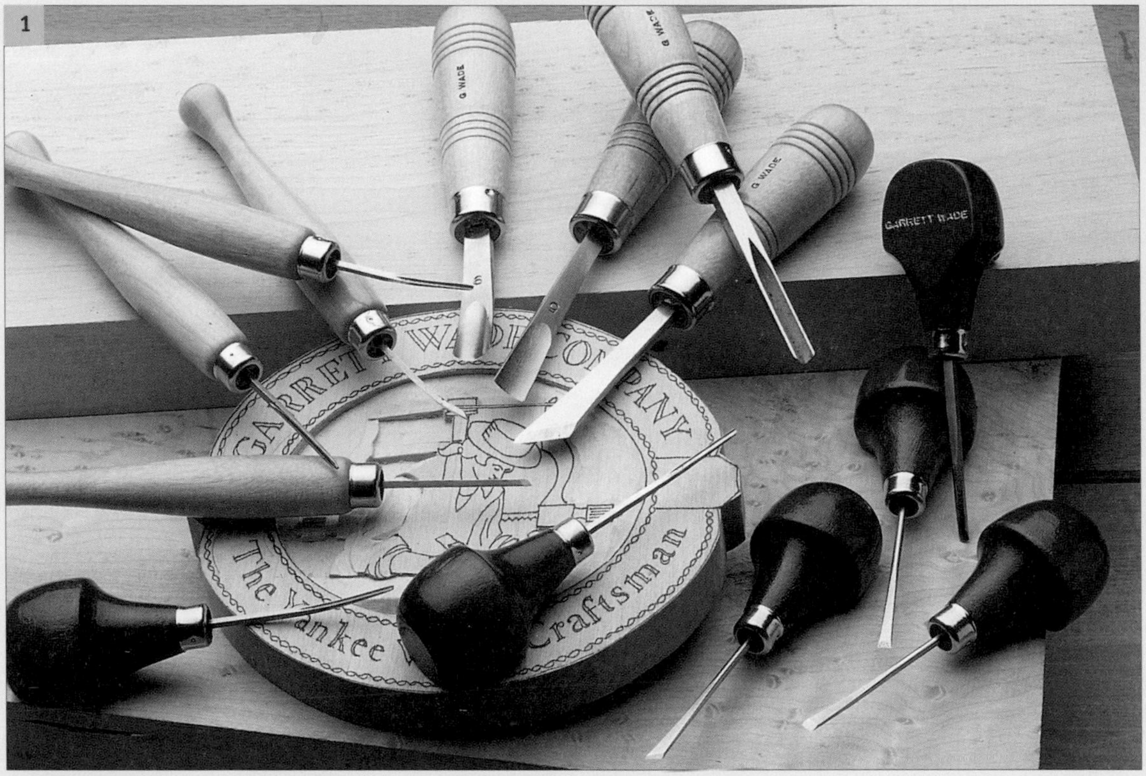

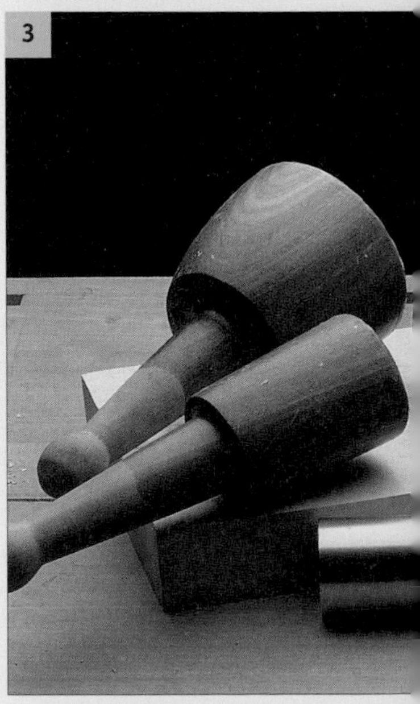

1 Miniature carving tools

The blades of these so-called micro tools are no narrower than on the smallest standard tools, but they are shorter, often with stubby handles that fit comfortably into the palm.

2 Henry Taylor carving set

These tools are available in sets or individually. They all have a black working finish except on the inside of the blade, which has been dull-polished. They have been hand forged and have octagonal, pau marfin-wood handles.

3 Carver's mallets

The alemendro mallets (left) are made of a special tropical wood that is more stable than most woods and less likely to crack. The mallets have a slightly bulged convex shape characteristic of all the best traditional British carving mallets. The heavy-duty mallets (top right) are made from beech laminations using high-strength thermosetting resins for extra strength. The solid brass-head mallets (bottom) have a phenomenal balance. They are held near the head to produce a less tiring strike.

4

4 Hooked skew chisel

This chisel is designed by Ray Gonzalez and made by Ashley Iles. It can be used wth a slicing motion or for chip carving.

5 Macaroni and wing parting tools

These tools are difficult to find, but if you see one in a flea market or elsewhere secondhand, it will be well worth the investment. These tools are useful for detailed carving work.

6 Flexcut chisel

This American-made tool bends as it is pushed into the wood, but has a springlike action, which allows it to come up readily at the end of a stroke.

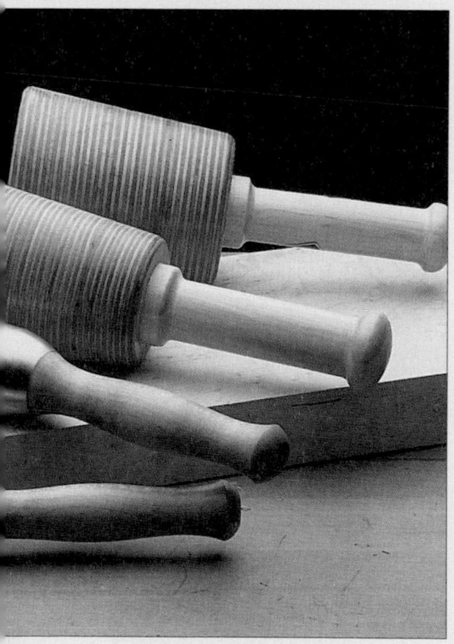

5

6

KNIVES FOR CARVING

IF THE STURDY OAK FURNITURE OF EARLIER CENTURIES HAD any decoration at all, it was usually the work of woodcarvers, specialized craftsmen with a respected role in most cabinet-making workshops. This work may have been done with the use of chisels and gouges (see pages 146–151) or—for example, as in the case of chip carving—with knives. As a trade, carving began to decline in the 19th century and, instead, became a hobby.

As often happens when enthusiastic amateurs create a market, there are now dozens of knives offered in contemporary woodworking catalogs. But curiously, expert carvers and whittlers are likely to claim that they rely on just a couple of their favorite knives, which, more often than not, have lasted them for a lifetime.

The basic knives

One of the most basic of carving knives is the bench knife, with a thin, straight, pointed blade between 1⅞ inches (48 mm) and 3 inches (75 mm) long. For some carvers, this will be the only tool used. It cuts the lines that create the borders into the wood, clears waste, and shaves and whittles. The longer-

These Canadian carving knives are shaped to be comfortable and provide a good feel for proper knife control.

blade versions are sometimes called Sloyd knives; the shorter ones offer finer control when needed.

A stab knife, held like a dagger or an ice pick, incises stop cuts. It is dug into the wood, then rocked to extend the line. Having started with these basic knives, the woodcarver may go on to experiment with more complicated blade shapes—knives with curved blades and angled skew tips, and hook knives, sometimes double-edged, for easing the waste wood out of spoons and small bowls.

Comfort in the hand is the all-important consideration. Beechwood, often treated with linseed oil, is a favorite material for handles. Choose forged steel and high carbon-steel blades for strength and their ability to hold a razor edge for long spells of work. Straight-blade bench knives may be of laminated steels, with softer metal sandwiching the cutting edge.

There is a type of knife with one handle and a variety of blades. One brand has an anodized aluminum handle and skew, concave, and convex curved blades that fit into a finger-tightened collet. The blades can be honed many times before they will require replacement.

When choosing carving knives, consider the comfort of the handles and the shape of the blades you plan to use.

1

2
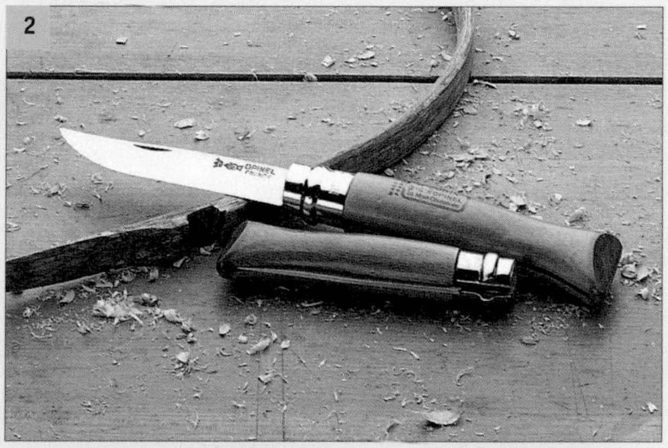

3

1 Multiple-blade knife
A variety of blades, including some gouges, fit into the knurled collet on the wooden handle, which is shaped for comfort.

2 Opinel knife
These French knives have an old-fashioned, positive locking ring to keep the blade open or closed, and comfortable wooden handles. They are suitable for whittling work.

3 Swiss chip-carving knives
The set of chip-carving knives in the canvas roll have superior and durable cutting edges. The stabbing chip knife at top has a special shape to enhance the stabbing action.

RASPS, FILES, AND RIFFLERS

The patternmaker's rasp is the most effective type of rasp used by woodworkers today. The patternmaker's rasps below, one with slightly coarser teeth than the other, are prized for their cutting action.

THE RASP IS ANOTHER OF THOSE TOOLS THAT ONCE CAME IN A great variety of forms to serve specialized needs—for coachbuilders, wheelwrights, and gunstock makers. There was even a baker's rasp, for scraping the burned crust from a loaf. In appearance, the baker's rasp was similar to the modern microplane—a patented design by Surform not yet 50 years old—whose versatility and popularity have contributed to the decline of woodworking rasps.

Rasps are valuable for smoothing curves, shaping edges, and cleaning up blemishes close to screws, nails, and hardware such as hinges. Rasps may be 8, 10, or 12 inches (200, 255, or 305 mm) long. They have two flat faces, or one flat and one half round, or they may be cylindrical, like a knife-sharpening steel. (This shape was once known as a rat's tail.) The surface of hardened steel is covered in teeth, which are hand cut on high-quality rasps.

The fewer the number of teeth, the more fiercely the rasp works. A so-called wood rasp is the roughest, with a tooth pattern called coarse, or bastard; a cabinet rasp is second-cut or smooth; a pattern-maker's rasp—the smoothest—has smaller teeth, which are cut randomly to reduce the tendency of the teeth to slide along ruts made on earlier strokes.

Files and rasps are similar in shape and are described by the same nomenclature. The difference is in the surface pattern. Instead of teeth, files have ridges—tiny blades—cut diagonally across the face, either single-cut or in the crisscross pattern

This set of woodworker's files and rasps (right) includes rat-tail rasps, which can be found in the canvas roll (near right) and a cross-cut file (far right). The file card can be used to clean both files and rasps, and the handle can fit onto any of these tools.

known as double-cut. A traditional, and patient, craftsman might use a file to smooth off the work of a rasp, because it gives more control. Files are more commonly used in the workshop to sharpen saws.

Both tools are sold without handles, but because the tang at the end of the tool comes to a sharp, hazardous point, you should always fit a handle over it, or make one out of dowel. Rasps and files are designed to be pushed, not pulled.

These tools need regular cleaning. You can use a file card, a double-sided brush with wire bristles of different densities: on one side, the bristles loosen debris; on the second side, they clean. Some Japanese-made rasps avoid this need. They consist of narrow saw blades, with fine teeth on one edge, coarser on the other. Waste falls through the gaps.

Rifflers and other variations

Rifflers are delightful tools used by woodcarvers (but also stonemasons and metalworkers) for detail carving and cleaning up intricate work in awkward spaces. Usually 8 inches (200 mm) long, they have pointed, tapering, curved ends with rasp or file surfaces. The central shank is sometimes swollen, to make them easier to hold. A set of eight will have these profiles: oblong, flat, oval, triangular, square, round, knife, and half-round.

Recently, a new tool has been developed called a microplane. It has the same facility for cutting as a rasp. The rasping surface is a replaceable, perforated plate, which has an appetite for wood, fillers, man-made boards, soft metals, laminated edges, and plastics. The basic frame design copies a plane, for two-handed use, but shaver, block plane, and rasp styles are available, and there are blades of different sizes and half-round blades.

The patternmaker's rasp is the most useful tool for the woodworker's shop, but these other types can earn a place at the workbench, too.

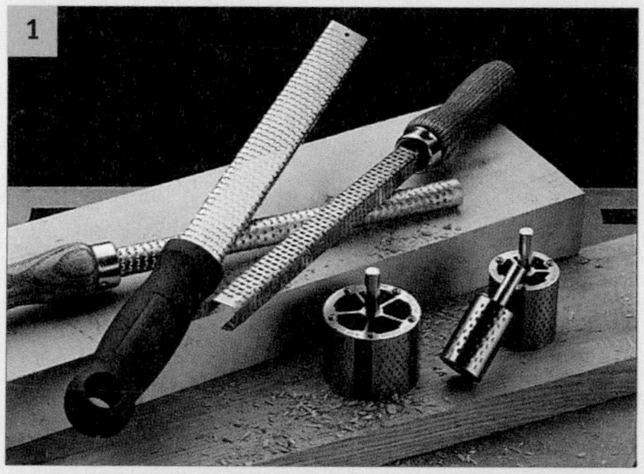

1 Microplanes
Wood chips can easily pass through the "throat" of the miniature plane blades, ensuring free cutting at all times. These tools are as rigid as traditional rasps. One type comes with a handgrip secured to an aluminum holder, which accepts three different blades.

2 Rifflers
The rifflers in this inexpensive set are capable of doing detail work, although they won't have the smoothness of cut available with high-quality and more expensive tools. However, they won't require a great investment, and they can be handy to have around the shop.

3 Curved rasps and file frame
The German-made curved rasps (top) are called stair rasps, because they were designed to shape a baluster. The special float file frame can be used on wood with a straight or skew cutting motion to produce an exceptionally smooth surface; it cuts rapidly.

ROTARY CUTTER/GRINDER

MACHINES THAT MOVE SMALL BITS AND ABRASIVE WHEELS IN A rotary manner have, for the last 50 years, played a significant role in woodworking—particularly carving. The earliest, and most powerful, of these drive the bit, cutter, or grinding wheel (frequently at high speed, up to 30,000 rpm) via a flexible shaft. At one end of the shaft is a motor, which sits on a bench or hangs from a hook. At the other end is the handle into which the bit is inserted.

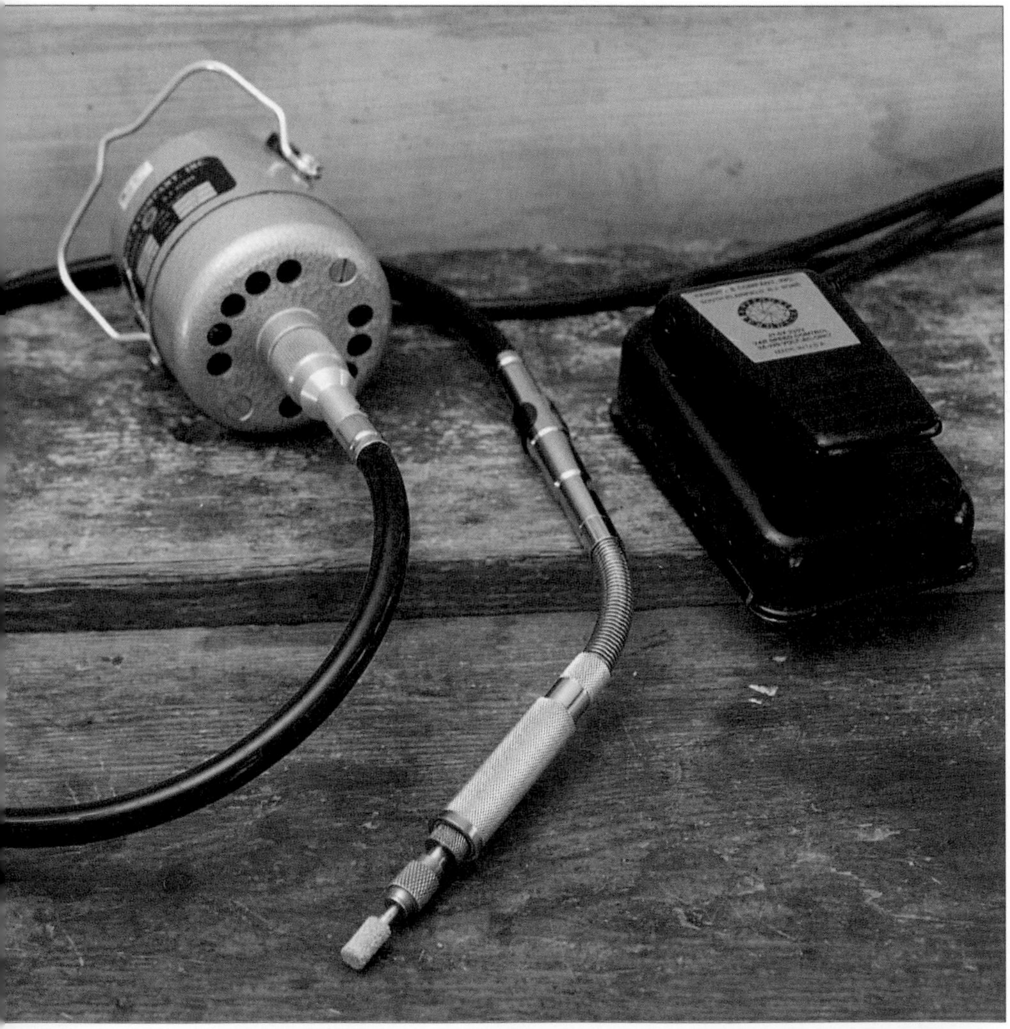

The professional rotary cutter/grinder will have a handle to hang the motor on a stand and a foot pedal to control the speed of the rotary bit.

Typically, the motor speed can be easily varied by means of a manual control or a foot switch/control.

Today, many of these larger machines are still made and sold, but other companies also make small hand-held units for which the there is no flexible shaft. These necessarily have much less power but are also much easier to use and are much less expensive. Dremel is probably the most familiar brand available in today's market.

There are hundreds of accessories available for grinding, drilling, cleaning, polishing, sanding, cutting, carving, engraving, and routing. The secret for exploiting the potential of each and all of them is practice—finding the right speed for different tasks and materials, learning when two-handed control is necessary, as in persuading the tiny cutters to cross the wood grain, and recognizing the relationship between speed and pressure. Firm but delicate control can be achieved, because the cutting and grinding edges are used sideways, stroking the work instead of boring into it.

Woodworking applications include making miniature mortises and tenons required by modelmakers. Some wood carvers specialize in using these tools to make intricate carvings, particularly of birds.

Tungsten-carbide cutting bits are for shaping and smoothing hardwoods. Holes as small as 1/48 inch (0.5 mm) can be drilled. Sanding bands in a range of grits fit onto approximately 1/4 inch (6 mm) or 3/8 inch (10 mm) drums; they are ideal for enlarging holes and removing debris around intricate shapes. There are cutters for engraving shapes and lettering in hardwood and a range of routing bits that can be used with a router attachment. Emery cutoff wheels, about an inch (25 mm) in diameter, will slice through thin sheets of plywood, but only along straight lines as they tend to break up on curves.

There are also accessories for working on materials other than wood such as metals, plastics, ceramics, stone, glass, and leather. When using these accessories, bear in mind that small is necessarily fragile, and you should handle your work and the equipment with care. These tools have been designed to operate at a high speed to replace the need for using heavy pressure. When using the tool, always use protective eyewear and a dust mask.

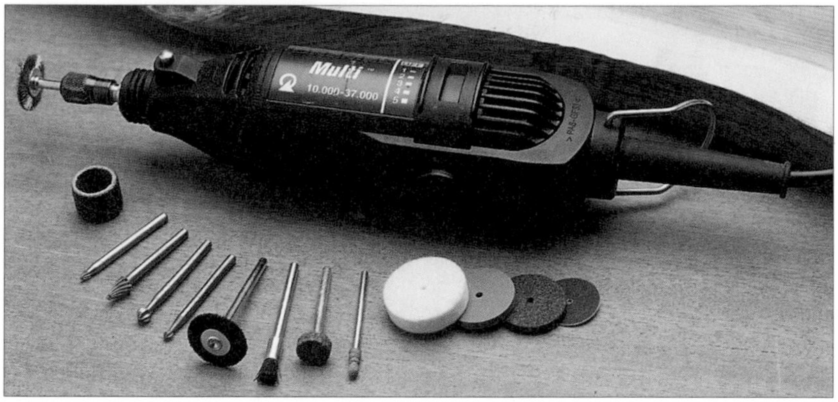

The original rotary cutter/grinder was made by Dremel. It comes with a huge variety of bits to perform a diverse range of activities.

A model operated by a foot pedal provides the best control. You'll need a basic set of accessories. Purchase specialized ones as you need them.

1 Rotary rasps

Designed to fit a ¼ inch (6 mm) collet or properly sized chuck, these rasps are used primarily in carving to roughly shape stock.

2 Miniature grinding wheels

You will probably find dozens of ways to use these grinding wheels: from reshaping a gouge to fitting hardware to fixing machinery. They will grind almost anything, including hardened steel and ceramic tile.

Turning tools

The scrapers, skew chisels, and gouges used in turning, known as turning tools, have blades in a variety of shapes.

Woodturning is a manual operation, and turning tools, apart from the motors on lathes, are essentially hand tools. Becoming an expert turner takes practice and perseverance, but is well worth the trouble. Once you know how to turn, you can make legs, pedestals, chair parts, knobs, tabletops, balusters, tool handles, mallets, pens, lamp bases, bowls, breadboards—the list is endless.

Turning projects are classified as spindle turning or face turning. Spindle turning is used primarily to make furniture parts; face work, to make bowls. Many of today's bowl makers are turning sculptural works of art prized by collectors and museums. For the most part, turners use different tools for the two types of turning. Beginners start with spindle turning to learn the basics of tool control and movement around the lathe, then move on to face work. This chapter provides an introduction to the tools used in both types of turning.

LATHES

This *c.*1760 French engraving (far right) from Diderot's *Encyclopédie* shows an assistant turning a huge wheel, which rotates a lathe for a woodturner.

THE EGYPTIANS ARE KNOWN TO HAVE USED THE LATHE—A TURNING machine, which is used to shape wood, metal, ivory, and other materials into a round form. In Great Britain there is evidence of wood-turning dating as early as the fourth century; and in Germany a guild for woodturners had been established by 1180.

The lathe has two spindles to hold the workpiece. On the left, as you face the lathe, the headstock houses a motor-powered spindle. On the right, the tailstock houses an unpowered spindle. The position of the tailstock can be moved to increase or decrease the space between the two spindles. Between the headstock and tailstock is the tool rest base, which holds the tool rest, where the woodturner places the cutting, or turning, tools (see pages 164–167). All these parts are supported on the lathe bed.

The work created on a lathe falls into two categories: spindle turning and face turning. In spindle turning, the workpiece is held between the two spindles by centers. The headstock center, which does the "driving," has prongs to securely hold the work. In face turning, the workpiece is secured only to the headstock, using either a faceplate or a chuck system.

Early lathes were powered by human or mechanical energy. Today, they are powered by electric induction motors, typically in the ¾ to 1½ horsepower (hp) range. Power is transferred from the motor to the headstock spindle by a belt rotating over pulleys. On older versions, the woodworker adjusted the turning speed by shifting the belt among different-size pulleys, a system in which speed could be adjusted only in fixed increments. Modern lathes often allow for infinite speed adjustments by using a variable-size pulley with a V-belt, by adjusting the speed of the motor, or by a combination of these two methods. Motors that run in both directions are useful for sanding and other purposes.

Faceplates are useful for mounting a large workpiece; however, they also leave holes in the workpiece.

The tailstock slides along the lathe bed and is secured with a quick-release assembly. The tailstock's spindle usually rides on a screw mechanism so it can be tightened to the workpiece with a handwheel. This allows for the quick mounting and dismounting of the turning blank. The tool rest base also has a quick-release cam that facilitates locking and unlocking. The tool rest fits into the tool rest base and is secured with a threaded handle.

In the past, the best lathes were made of cast iron. This is still the ideal material for lathes, because its heavy weight dampens the vibrations caused by turning. Recently, structural steel has become popular as a material for lathes; and some of the best lathes made today have welded structural steel parts. Steel lathes are cheaper to construct because the parts don't need to be cast in a foundry. Lathe beds can also be made of steel tubing, wood, or even aluminum.

Size

Most lathes can carry only workpieces that fit between the spindles and the lathe bed. If the spindle centers are 6 inches (150 mm) above the bed, the lathe has a 12 inch (305 mm) swing. The maximum diameter for the workpiece is a little less than the swing, because the tool rest base is in the way. To work wider pieces, such as tabletops and large bowls, some lathes allow "outboard turning," or face turning outside the lathe bed. Either the headstock rotates relative to the lathe bed or the headstock spindle has a screw attachment on the left-hand side, away from the lathe bed.

The distance between the headstock and the tailstock (or the distance between centers) will determine how long a workpiece the lathe can handle. Full-size lathes typically have 36 to 39 inches (915 to 990 mm) between centers; mini-lathes and bowl lathes, 12 to 24 inches (305 to 610 mm).

This homemade English lathe, made in 1804, has a treadle and flywheel mechanism that has been designed to be moved from side to side to align the drive with the headstock.

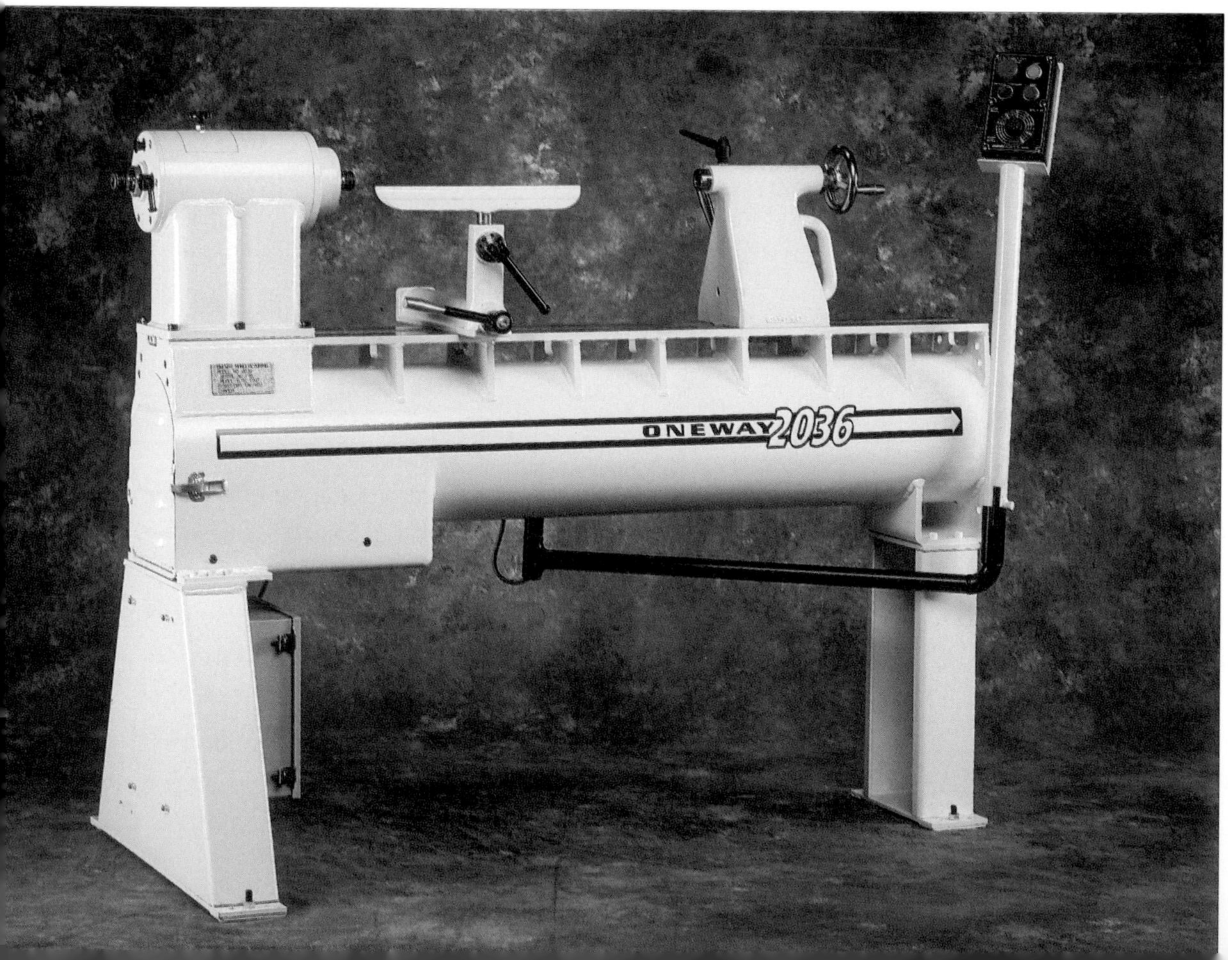

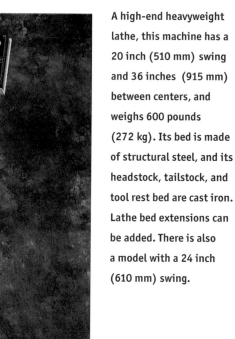

A high-end heavyweight lathe, this machine has a 20 inch (510 mm) swing and 36 inches (915 mm) between centers, and weighs 600 pounds (272 kg). Its bed is made of structural steel, and its headstock, tailstock, and tool rest bed are cast iron. Lathe bed extensions can be added. There is also a model with a 24 inch (610 mm) swing.

This inexpensive Delta lathe, with a 12 inch (305 mm) swing and 36 inches (915 mm) between centers, has a bed, tailstock, and tool rest base made of cast iron. The headstock assembly is covered by a plastic cover, but underneath it is mostly cast iron. It weighs 125 pounds (57 kg) and is a good beginner's lathe.

The larger the diameter of the spindles, the larger and heavier a workpiece the lathe can safely carry. Standard lathes have 1 inch (25 mm) spindles, which are adequate for all except the largest work.

Accessories

Both spindles are hollow and have a taper front-to-back called a Morse taper, which holds accessories. The great majority of lathes use a medium-size, or no. 2, taper, and nearly all accessories are made to fit the no. 2 taper.

You can also attach work to the headstock using a mechanism such as a chuck, which screws onto it. Spindles are threaded on the outside, usually with 8, 10, or 12 threads per inch (25 mm), to accommodate chucks and faceplates. The typical 1-inch- (25-mm-) diameter spindle with 8 threads per inch (25 mm) on the outside would be designated as a "1 by 8." Some headstocks have indexed wheels inside, with holes where a pin can be inserted to lock the spindle in place. This system is useful for carving flutes or reeds.

What you should look for

It is more important to have first-rate tools and accessories than to have the best-quality lathe. You should choose a lathe that is sized for the work you

Dos and don'ts

Do not use a dead center on the tailstock. A dead center, which does not turn, creates friction and may burn the work. If the lathe comes with a dead center, upgrade it to a live, or revolving, center.

Do set up your lathe in an area with plenty of lighting (adjustable task lights are best). Set up the grinder where you can reach it without moving away from the lathe.

expect to do and that can mount the accessories you will need to use. If you are a beginner, don't start out with a large lathe, even if you hope to do large work. You can get more from a smaller lathe than you would expect, and you can always upgrade to a larger lathe later.

The weight of the lathe is an important indicator of its quality. The heavier the lathe, the more it dampens vibration, and the easier it is to use. Other features that will give you more control over the work are variable-speed motors and bidirectional motors.

Unless you have a good reason to do otherwise, buy a lathe that accepts the widest range of accessories. The lathe should have 1 inch (25 mm) spindles with no. 2 Morse tapers and 8 threads per inch (25 mm) on the outside of the headstock.

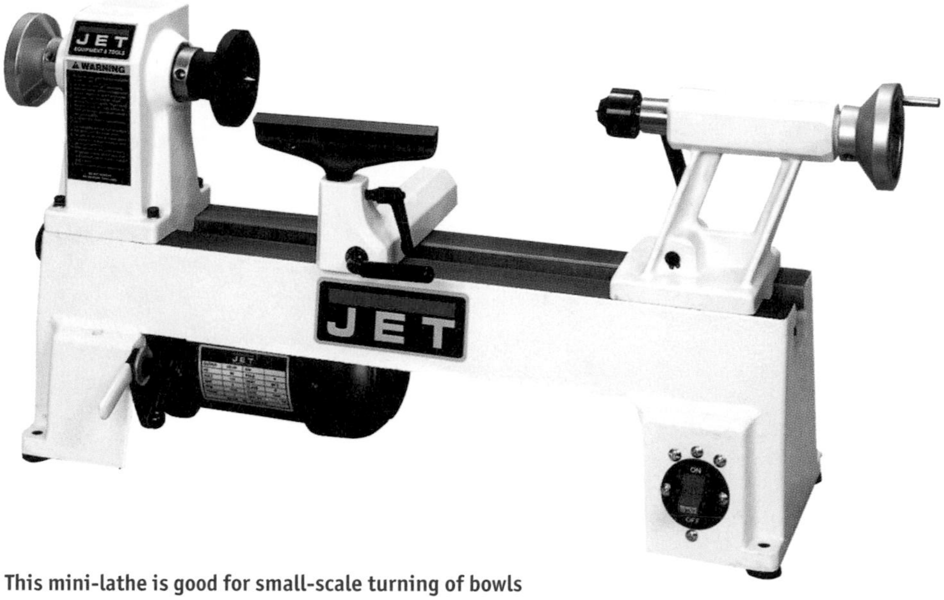

This mini-lathe is good for small-scale turning of bowls and pens. It has a 10 inch (255 mm) swing, and 14 inches (355 mm) between centers.

Once you purchase a lathe, you'll need certain standard accessories to get started, including drive centers, chuck systems, and faceplates.

1 Chuck systems

The One-Way Chuck/Stronghold systems are easy to use and good at handling larger bowl work. The One-Way system features a four-jaw self-centering scroll mechanism, and the much larger Stronghold system uses a geared chuck.

2 Two- and four-prong drive centers

The prongs on these centers, which fit onto the headstock, ensure a positive bite, and the short pin length aids in repositioning the work without reducing holding capacity. The centers are made of high-quality steel.

3 Revolving cone center

Designed to fit onto the tailstock, this cone center is a 60-degree live center that rotates with the work, so it doesn't require lubrication. It is fitted with dustproof top-grade bearings.

TURNING TOOLS

LEARNING TO USE TURNING TOOLS AT A LATHE IS LIKE LEARNING A dance—body position and movement are the keys to success. As the lathe (see pages 160–163) turns the workpiece toward the woodturner, the turning tool is levered by the tool rest and the wood comes into contact with the cutting edge. It is important for the novice to spend time watching experienced turners, either in person or on one of the many videotapes available, to pick up the techniques necessary to achieve the desired attractive results.

The basic tools

Modern turning, or cutting, tools are made of high-speed steel, known as HSS, which can tolerate the heat generated by turning without losing its temper, and so stay sharp longer. Turning tools can be divided into four basic categories: gouges, scrapers, skew chisels, and parting tools.

This British engraving of a boy asking a woodturner for a job was published in London in 1875.

Gouges are used with the bevel rubbing against the work, cutting down into the grain of the wood. They typically cut long curls of material. Spindle and roughing-out gouges are used for spindle turning, and bowl gouges are reserved for bowls and other face work.

Scrapers are used mostly for bowl and face work. (They tear out the grain if they are used for spindle work.) When scrapers are presented perpendicular to the work, they cut long shavings, just as gouges do. The American woodturner Del Stubbs developed a technique called sheer scraping, in which the tool is presented at an angle to the work. With sheer scraping, the burr on the scraper creates small thin curls and gives an exceptional finish in endgrain.

The most difficult cutting tool to master, but the most rewarding when you do so, is the skew chisel. Used mostly for spindle work, it is rectangular in cross section, with a bevel ground on both sides. This tool is difficult to use because it has a tendency to catch and make deep gouges in the work. Skew chisels with oval cross sections have been introduced in an attempt to make the chisel easier to control. Although an oval tool may be easier for the beginner, the rectangular design allows the expert to use the tool to its full potential.

Once mastered, the skew chisel gives the best finish of any cutting tool. It can also get into tight corners to make very clean details, but don't think it is just a detail tool. Experts use this tool to roll beads, push long curves, and even turn a square blank to round. Richard Raffan, an Australian woodturner, has introduced a method of grinding the tool so the cutting edge is gently curved. This makes the tool more versatile and makes curves easier to execute.

The blade on this 18th-century turning tool, which is showing signs of corrosion, is held to the handle with a ferrule.

Parting tools are used to cut spindles to length and, in conjunction with calipers, to size diameters when you are working from a pattern or duplicating by hand. Square and diamond profiles are available; the diamond profile is more versatile. An extra-wide parting tool, called a bedan, is useful in sizing tenons. Ultra-thin parting tools are helpful when you do not have much waste to spare.

Open bowl forms are hollowed out with bowl gouges and scrapers. Hollowing tools allow you to turn closed forms as well. Some have curved ends that can get around the lip and under the shoulder of the bowl. Others are straight, with an embedded carbide tooth for hogging out waste. Many have detachable arm braces, which help control the tool in delicate operations. The development of hollowing tools and the techniques to use them have advanced the art of the wooden bowl. Modern bowl makers are turning closed forms with ultra-thin walls of astonishing delicacy.

Start with a basic set. For spindle turning you will need ¼-inch (6-mm) and ½-inch (13-mm)

Among the turning tools below are (from top to bottom) a round-nose scraper, a skew chisel, a spindle gouge, a roughing-out gouge, a pair of parting tools, a scraper, and a fluted parting tool. The calipers (right) are for duplicating spindles.

The three most common styles of calipers used by bowl turners are (left to right) hourglass, inside/outside, and bow tie.

spindle gouges and a 1-inch (25-mm) roughing-out gouge, a skew chisel, and a parting tool. For bowl work, start with ¼-inch (6-mm) and ½-inch (13-mm) bowl gouges, then add a mini-gouge for small beads and other details, and a scraper.

Dos and don'ts

Do hold a cutting tool by grasping the top of the handle with your dominant hand. Tuck the handle under your forearm, and pull your arm tight against your body.

Do hold a tool in only one hand. This is more comfortable and helps you cut more accurately. It also frees up your nondominant hand for other purposes—stabilizing the end of the tool at the tool rest, cradling the spinning work to dampen vibration, or stabilizing the outside of a bowl wall and sensing the thickness of the wall as you hollow.

Don't move the tool with your arm. Instead, move it by shifting your weight back and forth and arching and straightening your back. The leg and back muscles have a larger range of motion than the arm and hand muscles do, and their motion is more flowing. Using your legs and back to move the tool allows long, flowing, and uninterrupted cuts.

Turning accessories

In addition to rulers, sizing tools are used to lay out the details of the work. This is especially important when you are duplicating pieces—for example, making a matched set of table legs or salad bowls. Dividers are used to lay out circles on face work and the locations of the elements on a spindle. Calipers are used to determine diameters and thicknesses of walls. A number of styles are available to perform different tasks. For example, bow tie calipers are critical for measuring deep narrow forms, the hourglass style is for reading the wall thickness of a bowl, and the inside/outside caliper is helpful for chucking work and sizing lids.

Other than tool technique, nothing improves the finish of the work as much as power sanding. Power sanding discs fit into the end of a power drill (see pages 174–183). The combination of the drill's rotation with the rotation of the lathe, together with the turner's motion, results in a motion similar to that produced by a random-orbit sander (see pages 212–213). Discs can be changed quickly, from coarse- to fine-grit paper. Power sanding doesn't eliminate the need for hand sanding (see pages 210–211), but it is much faster on long, gentle curves and on straight surfaces. You should use hand sanding for fine details that power sanding tools would otherwise round over.

Turning tools should be sharpened regularly as you work. It is quickest to use a bench grinder (see pages 228–229), which produces an edge that can be used without further polishing in only 10 to 15 seconds. A useful grinder accessory is an adjustable tool rest, which allows you to position the tool accurately so you will get a single-facet grind on the tool face. There are also sharpening systems on the market, which include special jigs to hold the tools, but these can be expensive.

Buy the best-quality turning tools, starting with six or so tools and adding more as you need them for specialized applications. A few good tools are worth more than a rack full of inferior tools.

1

2
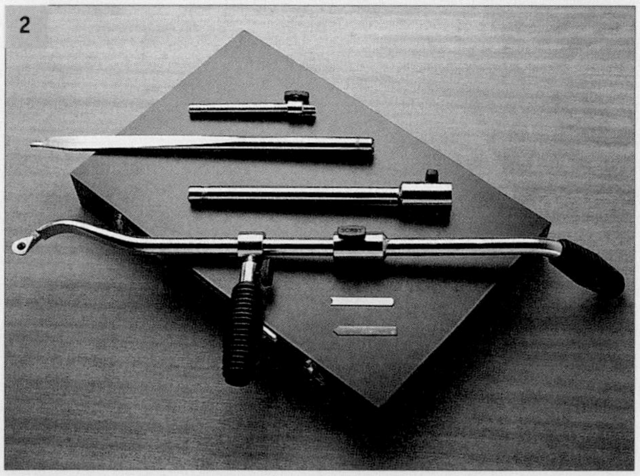

3

4

1 Heavy-duty scrapers

The thick blades of these Robert Sorby chisels reduce vibration. The group includes two skew chisels, a half-round side cutter, and a round-nose scraper.

2 Deep hollow turning system

Robert Sorby produces this specialized system, which was designed by woodturner Dennis Stewart. It includes a slicer, reversible hook, swivel tips, chattertool cutters, scraper blade, main handle, side handle, and shank.

3 High-speed steel turning tools

This representative group of Henry Taylor high-speed steel turning tools includes a round-nose scraper, roughing gouge, standard skew chisel, and bowl gouge. The tools can be purchased individually or in sets.

4 Henry Taylor carbon steel tools

Although not as durable as high-speed steel blades, carbon steel has been the traditional material used to make turning tools for centuries. These tools are sold individually.

Hole-boring tools

Both manually and electrically powered drills require bits, but not the same types. The auger bit (right, top) is for a hand brace, the Forstner bit (right, bottom) is for a power drill.

The first woodworking task to be taken over by power tools was the boring of holes. With the arrival of the variable-speed drill, even purists had to admit that here was a modern helpmate whose result was indistinguishable from the woodworker's traditional brace and bit. (Some say that tool owes its development to surgeons, who used it for trepanning—boring holes through skulls—in the 16th century.)

The brace and hand drill—and the awl and gimlet—still belong in the tool rack. They are unfussy, are easy to manipulate, and can often find the spots power tools cannot reach. There is no risk of high-speed friction causing bits to lose their temper or burn fine woods. There is also a sense of calm control that power tools noisily overwhelm.

BRACES, DRILLS, AND BITS

St. Joseph, portrayed as a medieval carpenter, is using a brace in this painting by Robert Campin (*c.*1375–1444).

THE SIMPLEST, MOST BASIC HOLE-MAKING TOOLS ARE THE AWL, bradawl, and gimlet. The awl has a sharp, pointed spike used for leaving a mark in wood (see pages 26–35). The bradawl has a chisel tip, which is stabbed into the wood, across the grain, then twisted to sever fibers and start a hole for a screw or a larger tool. A gimlet is threaded and can make deeper holes (see page 172). An auger is simply a gimlet that is larger—3 feet (92 cm) long or more. It is used in house contruction and by boat-builders.

Braces

Unlike the gimlet and auger, the brace has a hand-cranked frame, which can be continuously turned to bore a hole. In fact, it is this hand-cranked leverage that makes the brace the most powerful of the boring tools, and its low-speed torque is often more useful than the output of a power drill. Even at the bottom end of the variable-speed range, bits on a power drill can dull and fine wood can burn.

Braces first made an appearance in a wooden form in the 15th century, and metal versions have been found that date to the 16th century. However, wooden braces (they were once known as bitstocks) remained prevalent until the mid-19th century. The original wooden brace had an inherent weakness in its design: the "arms" of the crank were made in the cross grain of the wood, which would break under pressure. Metal plates, often made of brass, were added to these areas to strengthen the crank. In 1848, John Cartwright took out a patent for a brass-frame brace, in which wooden infill was used between a divided brass frame. Other improvements came about when a rotating handle was added to the crank and improvements were made to the pad, or chuck, design.

Braces were once available in a variety of formats and sizes, but now they almost invariably have the same styling and the same 10 inch (255 mm) sweep—that is the diameter of the frame's turning circle. Pressure is applied through a second, dome-shape handle at the end of the tool. Old-time artisans using a brace for heavy work would wear a breastplate to comfortably apply full body weight.

Today's braces vary in price, which is an indication of the tool's quality and the intricacy of its working parts; these include ball races in the handle, a ratchet mechanism, which allows the chuck to "freewheel" in places too restricted for a full circular sweep, and a cam ring that reverses or locks the action. Bits designed for use in braces have square shanks that seat in the notches of two jaws—the traditional pattern. Look for a model with a four-jaw chuck, which will give a more secure hold on round-shank bits. Don't overlook the capability of a brace and screwdriver bit when a large screw seems unshiftable, one way or the other.

Hand drills

The first type of hand drill, which was used in Egypt as early as 2500 BC, is the bow drill. It had a bow string, which was wound around a bobbinlike stock. When the worker moved the bow from side to side, the bit held in the stock rotated. A later version, the pump drill, worked along the same principle, but it used a push-and-pull motion to drive the bit. The pump drill is the predecessor to the Archimedean drill, which uses a pumping action up and down along a spiral shank to drive the bit. This hand drill is recognizable in its descendants, the ratchet screwdriver (see pages 194–195) and the push drill, which is still manufactured by the Stanley Tools. It

This English-made brace has a chuck designed to take a variety of bits, including the auger bit (top center) and half-reamer chair bit (bottom).

ANTIQUE BRACES

For collectors of antique tools, braces offer particularly rich pickings. The reason is that the adjustable chuck, which allowed bits to be changed speedily, did not come into general use until the second half of the 19th century. Before that, the woodworker needed maybe half a dozen braces, each fitted with a different-size bit. Many of them have survived, and because they were generally made to suit the needs of the craftsman who was to use them, the styles and forms are varied and personal. The materials used were sometimes extravagant and splendidly decorated—sterling-silver frames with ivory inserts, brass and ebony, maple and whalebone, antler horn and burr walnut.

A more sparely designed model from the early 20th century can be useful because of its small size. The undertaker's brace, carried discreetly in the pocket, was used to screw down the coffin lid quickly and quietly after the family viewing of the body.

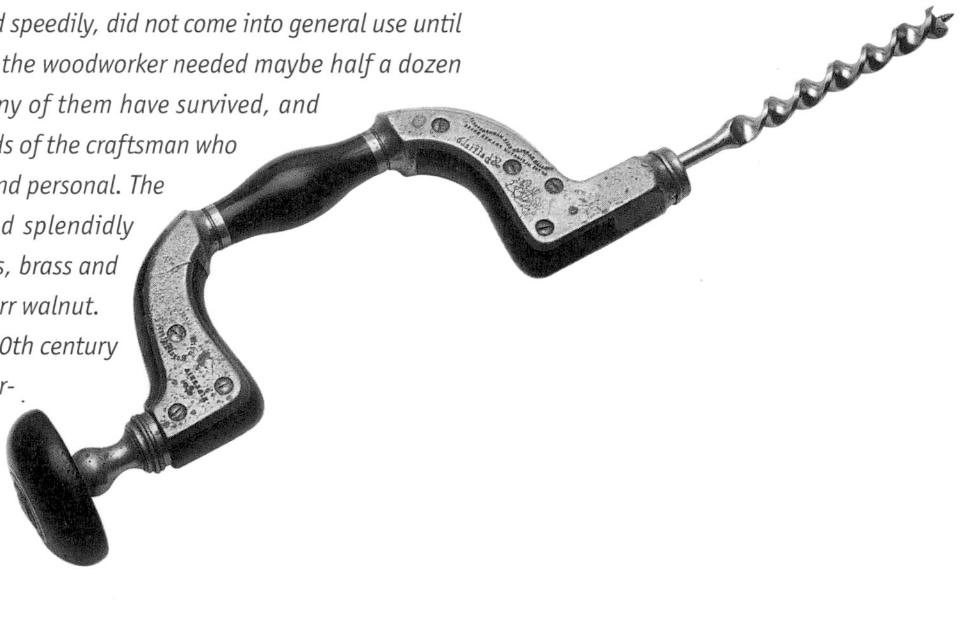

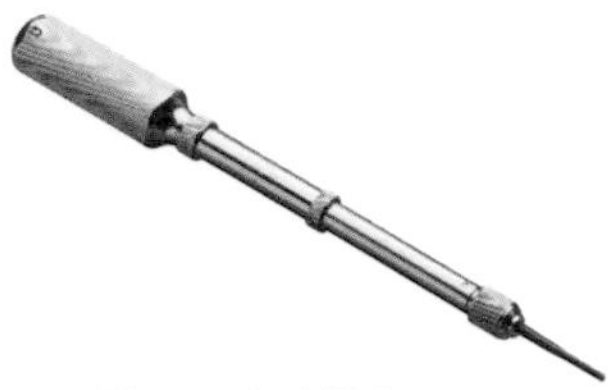

The push drill has a spring-loaded frame, which is pushed in and out to quickly cut a hole for screws. Extra bits are stored inside the handle.

requires only one hand to operate and is best limited to making small holes.

The "eggbeater" style of hand drill, which is the type most often associated with the term "hand drill," originated in France in the late 18th century. It takes bits up to ⅜ inch (10 mm) in diameter and rotates the chuck through a geared drive wheel and bevelled pinions (for durability and smooth operation, two pinions are better than one). Small pistol-grip models are designed for starting pilot holes in confined spaces. Avoid plastic parts; cast aluminum wears better, but cast-iron parts are best.

Bits

What engineers call "drills," woodworkers call "bits." The exception is the twist drill. At the pointed tip of a twist drill there are two cutting edges, which lead into spiral flutes that clear away the waste. Bit sizes range from 1⁄16 inch (1.5 mm) to ½ inch (13 mm). The tip angle of drills intended for metalworking is slightly different from that of woodworking drills; if buying just one set of twist drills, choose the more flexible machinist's type.

Dowel bits have a point at the tip for accurate location, but the fluting ends in two spurs, so that the outside of the hole is cleanly cut. Like twist drills, these bits are intended for use in a hand drill. Bits that make larger holes—up to 3 inches (75 mm) is possible—require a brace or powered drill press.

A center bit is for boring shallow holes up to 2 inches (50 mm) across. There is a lead screw for central location, one spur to score the edge of the hole, and another to cut into the work. Expansion bits are adjustable. A flat bit works like a revolving chisel centered on a pointed tip. An auger bit is the most accurate for drilling deep holes, having a helical twist, which keeps it in line and resists the tendency of a point-dependent tool to follow the grain of the wood. A Jennings-pattern auger has a double helix for better clearance of waste.

Countersinks may be separate hand tools or bits for drills. They make seatings for screw heads and chamfer and deburr the edges of holes.

Higher-priced bits are worth the extra money. They will be ground from solid bars of high-speed steel; the point angles will have been checked for accuracy and the fluting for concentricity.

Use small hand files to resharpen them. Remove as little metal as possible, and only from inside edges, to avoid changing the diameter. If unsure which edges need to be sharpened, use the bit slowly in a piece of softwood and watch its action.

GIMLETS

The best tool for starting a screw hole is the gimlet. Although a huge variety of gimlets has been developed—usually for different trades, such as the brewer's gimlet, farmer's gimlet, ship gimlet, and wheeler's gimlet—the design is much the same. The gimlet has a T-bar handle, is tipped with a screw point and thread, and has fluting along the shank to clear away the waste. The screw point pulls the tool into the wood, which pushes the fibers apart. After the tool enters the work, it then cuts shavings to enlarge the hole.

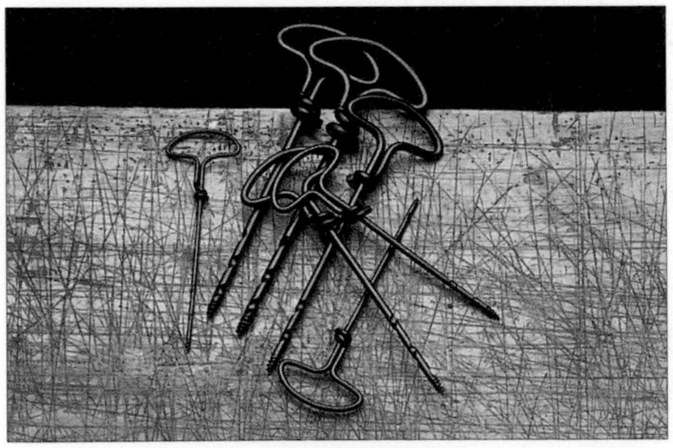

If you plan to work with fine woods, you should invest in a good-quality brace, whether a new model or one that is secondhand but still in good condition. The hand drill can be useful for drilling small holes where you can't fit a power drill.

1 Short swing brace, joist brace, and breast drill

The top-of-the-line short swing brace (left) uses an all-steel ratchet to control the chuck and has a sweep of only 6 inches (150 mm), which makes it the choice for tight-space driving and drill jobs. The joist brace (center) is also designed to work easily in confined spaces. The ratchet allows you to turn the chuck head with only a small arc of movement, and the long handle provides added leverage. The breast drill (right) operates at two speeds and has an adjustable breast pad.

2 Auger set

The bits in this auger set are forged from a single piece of special bit steel. They have double-cutting spurs and a long screw to ensure steady pulling power and clean cutting.

3 Hand drill

The cast-iron frame, double pinion gear, and wooden handles are all signs of the high standards achieved in this eggbeater-style hand drill. It will provide many years of service.

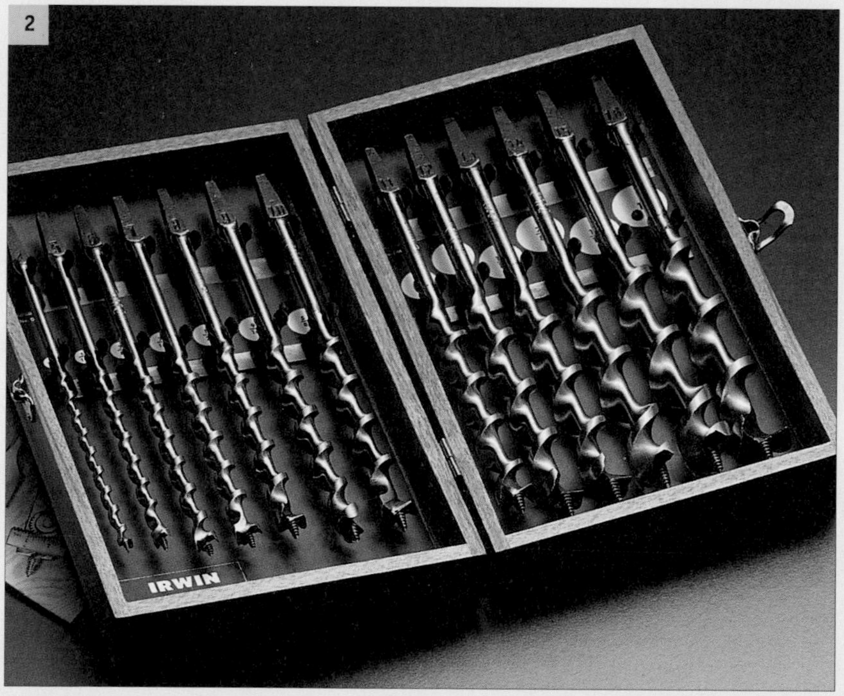

POWER DRILLS

A drill gauge will help you determine the size of your drill bit.

THE ELECTRICALLY POWERED HAND DRILL WAS FIRST DEVELOPED in Germany in about 1895, but it wasn't until the 1940s before small, reliable, inexpensive electric motors became available. It was only after World War II when the power drill became the first hand-held power tool to become commonplace in the average home.

Today, the power drill is usually the first portable tool purchased and the most frequently used hand power tool found in the woodworking shop. It is used for drilling holes, screwing, doweling, sanding, mixing, and sharpening. The options are almost endless. Determining the drill that is best for you depends upon what type of work you do and what features on the drill are best for this work.

Power drills may be divided into three basic categories, depending on their use. The first of these is the light-duty drill. This drill is used for everyday purposes such as drilling holes in walls for hanging pictures and shelves and for light sanding. The next category, the medium-duty drill, can be used for installing sheets of wallboard, building bookcases, or removing paint or corrosion with a wire brush attachment. The final category is the heavy-duty drill, which is able to perform construction tasks such as house framing, deck building, and home remodeling. Once you have determined which drill category best fits your needs, deciding whether you want a corded or cordless drill is your next step.

Older power drills had to be bulky to encase the motor and gears that drive the bit. These parts have become smaller with modern developments in technology, allowing newer models (opposite page) to have a streamlined design.

Cordless drills

Recent technological advances in rechargeable batteries have spurred the sales of cordless drills. Batteries for cordless drills hold a charge longer and have shorter charging times than in the past. The cordless drill also offers many advantages over corded drills. The simple fact that there is no cord to get tangled in while you are standing on a ladder is a strong selling point. Another advantage is that once the batteries are charged, a local power supply is not necessary. This is great for new construction where electrical outlets may not yet be available.

Unfortunately, the latter advantage is also the drill's biggest disadvantage. The fact that you are using a rechargeable battery means that at some time it will need charging. If you do not have an extra battery available, you will have to wait while the battery charges. You will find charging times ranging anywhere from 15 minutes to 12 hours. Even if you have purchased more than one battery, running back and forth to switch the batteries may not be very appealing, especially if it means climbing up and down stairs or a ladder. Another disadvantage is that as the battery is drained, the drill loses power. If you are doing a repetitive job, such as hanging sheets of wallboard or driving large quantities of screws into your new deck, this could become a very large inconvenience.

One of the most useful features on a cordless drill—but one that is not available on all models—is the clutch. It usually takes the form of a rotating collar located just behind the chuck. The collar is marked with a number scale, which varies, depending on the manufacturer. The collar is rotated to align a mark on the drill with a number on the scale. When the drill attains the set torque, the drive is disengaged and the chuck stops turning. The main use of the clutch is to vary the depth of a screw head.

A speed setting is available on some corded drills, but for the most part this is a feature that is reserved for the cordless drill. A high and a low

The batteries of new cordless drills can run longer and need less time for recharging than those of the original models.

Dos and don'ts

Do make sure that a corded drill is unplugged before you change any accessories or attachments.

Do regularly inspect the cable and plug on a corded drill for signs of wear and damage.

Do use protective eyewear if there is any danger of a twisting bit or other accessory throwing debris toward your eyes.

It's easy to lose a chuck key, but among these four-way chuck keys, you should be able to find a replacement key that will fit your chuck.

speed switch is usually found on the top of the drill. Corded drills often have their speed settings located on the trigger itself. The low setting—which is the preferred setting for driving screws—supplies more torque than the high setting. For more speed, use the high setting, which is the setting to use when drilling holes and sanding.

The motor and other features

The best indicator of the power of any type of drill is its amperage rating. If it's power you want, go with the drill with the highest rated amperage. This rating will be found on the side of the drill. Another way to rate your drill is by the maximum torque rating. Torque rating is usually found in the owner's manual that accompanies the drill.

The chuck is located at the very front of the drill and is designed to hold the drill bit. Three jaws inside the chuck are opened or closed to release or grab the bit. The method in which the chuck is opened or closed is the only difference in chuck design from one model to another.

The stop collar is fitted onto a drill bit to prevent a hole from being drilled any farther than desired. The set shown below uses radial clamping pressure to hold the bits in place.

Chucks may be split into two categories: keyed or keyless. A keyed chuck uses a small gear on a handle called a chuck key. The key is inserted into the chuck and turned. This rotates a matching gear on the chuck, opening or closing the jaws. The keyless chuck is simpler to use. To adjust one, you simply hold onto the chuck body and pull the trigger on the drill, which opens or closes the jaws. The keyless chuck is usually coated in plastic or rubber for better grip and will hold the bit much tighter than a keyed chuck. The time saved in searching for a lost key makes the keyless chuck more appealing.

A drill may also be categorized by its chuck size, or capacity. The capacity is measured by the maximum-size diameter bit the drill will accept. A drill with a ⅜ inch (10 mm) capacity will handle all bits up to and including ⅜ inch (10 mm). You may find bits with reduced shanks to fit in smaller chucks. These may work well in standard applications, but if you are dealing with a lot of torque, a larger shank size is suggested.

Forward/reverse switches are usually a lever or push-button type. A switch operated with the same hand as the trigger will be the most useful. Forward/reverse switches located on the back or top of the drill requires two hands and are cumbersome to use in tight places or when on top of a ladder.

The power lock is available only on corded drills. This lock will be useful if you use your drill for sanding or mixing purposes. For safety reasons, make sure the lock is not located where it may be accidentally engaged. Letting go of a locked drill may cause serious damage to the user and anything in the vicinity.

Manufacturers are adapting tools to satisfy consumer demands. Some of these tools include a standard body that takes interchangable parts such as a hand drill that can be turned into a saber saw

WHAT YOU SHOULD LOOK FOR

There are more choices when it comes to power drills than for any other power hand tool on the market. Do a little research and find out what options are available. The heavy-duty drill is very powerful and may include features not found on other drills.

If torque is your major concern, a corded drill is what you need. Mixing drywall mud or driving large screws into hardwood will drain your cordless battery in no time. The corded drill provides both constant and endless power. Some corded drills may come with a lock, which allows the trigger to be kept in the "on" position. This feature is wonderful when sanding or mixing. Another advantage of the corded drill is that the lack of a battery decreases the weight of the drill. If the drill is going to be used for any length of time or in an overhead position, the lighter weight will be welcomed.

The cordless and the corded drill each has advantages. There is certainly a rationale for having more than one drill. Owning both a cordless and a corded drill is ideal.

GOOD

A good cordless drill will have a battery that can be quickly recharged and that will keep going a relatively long time.

BEST

A corded power drill with a comfortable hand grip can be used for hours without interruption. The hammer action allows you to drill into hard materials such as masonry.

There is a huge variety of bits available for the power drill, including these brad point bits. They are tungsten carbide tipped for a longer cutting life, and the wide flutes expel wood chips to prevent clogging.

or sander. However, a word of caution: these tools may be satisfactory for light-duty work, but they are not a substitute for a good power drill.

Fit and comfort

Taking into consideration all the features and benefits, one factor still remains. Is the drill comfortable to hold? Drills can be split into two main body types: the pistol-grip style and the T-handle style. Cordless drills may fall into either of these categories, but most corded or impact drills are of the pistol-grip type. On a T-handle drill, you will find the handle placed closer to the center of the drill body. This offers better balance and control over the drill.

Switch placement is another consideration. A poorly located speed or forward/reverse switch can be an inconvenience or even a safety hazard. A keyless chuck with an uncomfortable grip may cause slipping or blisters.

You should not overlook the weight of a drill. Some drills weigh in excess of 5 pounds (2.3 kg). A heavy drill can be more fatiguing, and if your job requires long hours with the tool, this could be a factor when it comes to comfort.

Accessories

There are dozens of accessories designed for the drill. One of the better ones is a drill guide, which holds the drill accurately at 90 degrees or at an

"The true craftsman will accept every kind of working experience as a natural part of the job and so get the best out of his tools, his time and himself."

Charles Hayward, *Woodworker* magazine, August 1960

This drill guide gives you drill press control with any handheld drill. It can be set to drill at an angle and has V guides to hold round stock.

The benchtop model Multico mortiser has an accessory that turns the machine into a horizontal drill press.

angle. Drill stands can be used to hold a drill in a stationary horizontal or vertical position. You may want to use a horizontal drill stand with a flexible shaft extension, which allows you to do detailed work with rotary bits that are normally used with the rotary cutter/grinder (see pages 156–157). Other accessories are available in the form of depth stops, sanders, wire wheels, and a buffing pad.

Nothing is as frustrating as a dull drill bit, especially when drilling hard material such as metal. There are a number of sharpeners on the market that can quickly restore the tip of the drill to its original shape.

The drill press

Although it is not an absolute necessity, the drill press is a handy tool to have in the workshop. It was originally designed for hole-drilling operations in the metalworking trades, but most woodworkers use it to drill, sand, and make mortises. It is a very simple machine with a motor attached to a rotating shaft through a step-pulley system. A lever moves the chuck and the drill bit up and down.

The drill press consists of a base, column, table, and head. The base supports the column on which the head is mounted. The table slides up and down

A drill press is useful in any woodworking shop. This benchtop model is suitable for a small workshop. Larger capacity floor-standing models are also available.

the column, allowing adjustment of the space between the table and the drill bit. The motor mounts on the back of the head, and a series of pulleys changes the rotating speed of the chuck. A guard covers the front of the pulleys. Two styles of drill presses predominate in woodworking shops: a bench model, which mounts to a stand or bench, and a floor model, with a longer column so that the base rests on the floor. A bench drill press has less space under the chuck than the floor model.

Chuck size is an important consideration. Most machines are equipped with ½ inch (13 mm) chucks, which allow you to use any tool with a ½ inch (13 mm) or smaller shaft. Correct speed is important when drilling, and most machines offer four or five speeds. The general rule of thumb is that the larger the bit diameter and the harder the material, the slower the spindle speed.

The head is the cast-iron piece that houses the movable quill, which contains the revolving shaft. The chuck, which holds the drill bit or accessory, is connected to the end of the shaft. The feed lever lowers the quill and, therefore, the bit into the workpiece. A quill clamp locks the quill when sanding or routing. The tool holder for the drill press is a three-jaw chuck. A handy new type of chuck is the keyless chuck, which can be tightened by hand. Most drill press accessories have straight mounting shafts that fit directly into the chuck. A fence stabilizes the work and aligns an edge of the workpiece with the drill bit, which is important when making holes parallel to the edge.

You can also adapt a drill press to make mortises. Many hollow-chisel mortising attachments consist of a square hollow fixture with sharp corners and a bit that rotates inside the fixture. A bracket holds the fixture onto the quill. To work efficiently, the attachment must be sharp and correctly adjusted.

Craftsman's tips

When choosing a bit, consider the size of the hole to be drilled; the size of the shank (it should be as large as possible); whether you need a flat bottom hole; what your rate of entry will be (production work requires wide flutes to get a clean hole); how clean you want the hole to be; the direction of the hole (with or across the grain); and the type of wood you are drilling.

Which drill bit should you use?

It is always a good idea to have many different types of bits, so you can experiment to see which one is best for a given task. (See *Craftman's tips,* opposite page, for specific advice.)

ACTIVITY	TYPE OF BLADE
Making fairly neat holes in most materials; making holes in soft metals	When you think of a drill bit, one usually envisions the ubiquitous twist bit. It's a multipurpose bit that's not particularly good at drilling in anything but mild steel. On the other hand, a twist bit makes holes fairly well in almost any material, they're inexpensive, and you can buy them everywhere.
Clean cuts in wood, especially for doweling	Brad point bits are simply twist bits that have been modified to cut wood well. The lip, or the cutting edge, of the twist bit has been cut back so that the tip of the bit is now a true point and the very edge of each lip is edged to serve as a perimeter knife. The design cuts wood more efficiently and cleanly. It is ideal for doweling.
Making large holes in soft wood	Spade bits are one-piece bits with a flat body and a single long central point. These are usually used in the contruction trades, because they are efficient at making large holes in soft wood.
Larger, clean cuts in wood	Multispur bits are used for drilling clean holes larger than is possible with a standard brad point bit. The outside surface is shaped with cutting teeth. A central point stablizes the bit, an opening exhausts the chips. These bits are very efficient and make a very clean hole. An added feature is the ability to sharpen the outside cutting teeth by using a file.
Making clean flat bottom holes and cutting holes that overlap	The Forstner bit is similar to the multispur bit, but it doesn't have the teeth on the rim, so it cuts more slowly. The rim is sharp and doesn't wander during the cut, so it can be used for overlapping holes. The Forstner bit produces a high-quality flat bottom hole.
Drilling screw holes for hinges	The Vix bit is a small drill housed inside a spring-loaded tube, which is attached to the drill. The tube is pointed so that it fits inside the screw hole of of a hinge. This design allows the screw hole to be perfectly centered.

Drill bits

The design of drill bits has evolved to allow for greater specialization. All you have to do is decide what you want and there is a drill bit that can do it. Most types of metal- and wood-cutting drill bits work well in a power drill or the drill press. You may want to experiment with the type of wood, speed, and depth of cut until you are satisfied with the result. If drilling a deep hole, retract the drill bit occasionally to allow for waste removal.

The only drill bits that should not be used in the drill press are bits with a screw point. These are designed for slow drilling, in which the screw pulls the bit into the wood. If a screw point is used on the drill press, it pulls the bit into the wood very quickly, so the drilling process is too aggressive and can possibly tear the work. A potentially dangerous side effect is that the screw point can pull the work off the drill press table and cause the workpiece to rotate if it is not clamped down.

There are dozens of bits and accessories available for the power drill. Start with the basics, such as the standard brad point and twist bits, along with a few Forstner or multi-spur bits. Other accessories, such as a drill guide, collar stops, and sanding discs, can also be of great help in the woodworking shop. Specialized items, such as the Vix bit and doweling jig, can be added if you plan to use them a lot.

1 Countersink and multi-spur bits

The countersink bits (left) create an exact, smooth conical hole for flathead screws. The multi-spur bits (right) are guided by the rim instead of the center to bore holes cleanly, even when overlapping holes.

2 Vix bits and countersink/counterbore combination set

When drilling screw holes for hardware, Vix bits (left) ensure that you drill perfectly centered holes. The combination set (right) includes taper bits to drill holes shaped like screws. Each bit includes an adjustable stop collar and countersink/counterbore so that you can prepare a screw hole in one operation.

3 Drum sanding kit

This custom kit has deluxe quick-lock drums, which can be expanded to grip the sleeve simply by turning the rubber cylinder by hand. The drums come in a variety of sizes and each one comes with three sleeves—one each of 50-, 80-, and 120-grit paper. Replacement sleeves are available.

4 Expansion bit

These bits have an adjustable cutter to drill holes in a variety of sizes.

5 Circle cutter

This specialized bit, which is indispensable to toy makers, bores holes or wheels up to 5 inches (125 mm) in diameter. It is best used in a drill press.

6 Self-centering jig and plug cutters

The jig (left) centers a bit to drill holes for dowels. The plug cutters (right) cut an oversized taper on the top of the plug, which are used to fill dowel holes.

7 All-in-one drill and driver sets

Each drill bit has a thread-on countersink. The depth is set by tightening the collar. A drill/countersink fitting snaps on the combination bit. Drill and countersink your hole, then snap off the fitting to drive the screw.

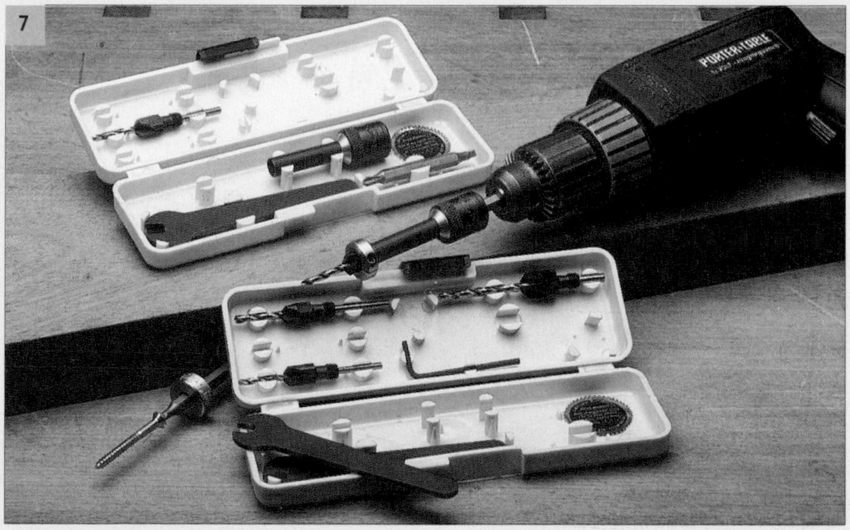

MORTISING MACHINE

THE MORTISE AND TENON JOINT IS ONE OF THE MOST ANCIENT and one of the strongest structural joints in woodworking. However, although the tenon side of the joint is relatively easy to form, the mortise (either square-ended or round-ended) can be time consuming and difficult to make by hand.

Mortising machines were developed late in the 19th century and early in the 20th century to cut square-end mortises, but these were typically large floor-standing machines that were suitable only for a large shop or furniture factory. Such large machines continue to be made today.

Modern machinery

In the early 1980s, however, an English firm, Multico Ltd., developed a small-scale, bench-top mounted mortise machine that is suitable for use by the serious amateur or small professional shop—thus revolutionizing the use of this style of joint in modern woodworking. Multico's design has since been extensively copied by many machine makers in the Far East, and the result has been a proliferation of machines of this type. Although they vary in quality and in design, the choice now available on the market is an advantage for the woodworker who wants to make furniture using square-end mortise-and-tenon joints.

Some machines come with a conversion kit that allows you to convert the mortiser into a small drill press, and with the additional of end drill brackets, it can be used as a horizontal borer.

As an alternative to the traditional square end mortise, a round-end joint can be cut with a straight router bit (using a suitable jig) or with a special "mortise bit" (essentially a long milling cutter) mounted on the side of a table saw or power planer.

The mortise machine can make mortises in stock up to 4 inches (100 mm) thick, up to 4 inches (100 mm) from the edge of the work.

These hollow square-mortise chisel bits have a tapered ground, so they will not jam in the cut. The mating drill bits have a single- or double-spiral twist to lift the shavings as they rise in the barrel.

BISCUIT JOINERS

IN MANY WAYS BISCUITS ARE THE IDEAL JOINT. THEY ARE VERY strong, and biscuit joinery is easy to do and requires very little accuracy. The system is also very versatile and relatively inexpensive.

During the 1950s a Swiss cabinetmaker set out to discover a new joint for his production work. He wanted the joint to have holding qualities that no other joints of that time possessed. As with any joint, strength was a concern. Ease of setup and speed were also needed for a mass-production environment. Overshadowing all of these was the need for a joint that would work with man-made products. The biscuit joint met all of these requirements. It has since become one of the most widely used ways of joining two pieces of stock. Today, the biscuit may be found in a variety of joints, including face miter, face frame, corner, edge miter, edge-to edge, and T-joints. The biscuit joint has become a staple for the hobbyist, as well as for the production line.

The biscuit joiner is a small portable machine that is designed to be hand-held against the board. A small circular blade is advanced into the board, leaving a small round cut into which the biscuit fits. The cut is made on both mating pieces. The body of the machine—which contains the cutter—is attached to a spring-loaded fence, and the blade is not exposed when the machine is not cutting.

Pre-made wooden biscuits are available to fit into the slots made by the biscuit joiner.

The biscuit joint

The joint could not be simpler. A compressed wooden biscuit is glued into two oversized half-oval cuts in the wood. The slots are cut larger than the biscuit, so the two workpieces may be slid side-to-side, allowing the edges of the stock to be aligned before clamping. This means that the final positioning of the joint is done after the gluing, not before. The other benefit of the biscuit comes into play in the glue set-up period. During this time, the moisture of the drying glue is absorbed into the compressed wooden biscuit, which causes it to expand and create an even stronger joint. A biscuit soaked in water and placed in the workpieces without glue will also expand to hold the joint together by itself.

The biscuit joint may not replace the dovetail for beauty or the mortise and tenon for strength, but its combination of adjustability and holding power, along with its compatibility with MDF (medium-density fiberboard), plywood, and particleboard have changed the shape of woodworking forever.

Assembly and finishing tools 3

Hammers and nail sets
Screwdrivers
Glue applicators
Clamps
Pliers and wrenches
Abrasive papers and wools
Power sanders
Brushes and other applicators
Finishes

Assembly tools

Hammers may be seen as the center of attention in construction work; however, they are also indispensable in the woodworker's shop.

One of the wonders of fine old furniture is the rarity of assembly hardware such as screws and nails, nuts and bolts. Instead, the individual pieces of the furniture were shaped and connected in an order that brought them into stable tension—each piece supporting the other, with dovetails and tenons wedged into position and the whole assembly held together with only the merest whiff of glue.

That approach is still an option for the woodworker, but today's armory of hammers and punches and nails, screws and screwdrivers, clamps, and adhesives brings ambitious projects that were once unachievable for the weekend enthusiast within reasonable reach. These tools are not new inventions, but their adaptations, applications, and capabilities have found their way into today's woodworking shop.

VAUGHAN
VAUGHAN

The claw hammers above have handles made of hickory and hand-forged polished steel heads.

These nail sets have knurled shanks, which are comfortable to hold.

HAMMERS AND NAIL SETS

NO TOOL HAS A LONGER HISTORY OR HAS TAKEN MORE VARIED forms than the hammer. The straight-face, fist-size rock of prehistoric times became a forged metal implement that helped to build Rome, and by the heyday of hammers, a century ago, every trade had its own stylized versions. There were hammers for glaziers, thatchers, slaters, saddlers, plumbers, cobblers, even toffee makers and grocers, whose model had a claw for prying open boxes of tea or butter or cheese. And tool catalogs of the day always showed a ladies' hammer, a light and elegant thing intended, presumably, for securing the upholstery tacks the housemaid's dusting had loosened.

In today's workshop, two hammers will serve most purposes: a heavy claw hammer and a "Warrington," named after the English town where it was first noticed. This is lighter, with one end of the head shaped into a rounded wedge (a flat peen, which may also be spelled pein or pane) for starting tacks and nails without finger damage.

The claw once had more significant usefulness than it does now. Well into the 18th century, nails were handmade—and valuable. Unwanted buildings would be burned down, rather than demolished, to allow the iron nails to be recovered more readily. The claw on the hammer allowed the carpenter who bent a nail to immediately recover it so that he could beat it back into shape without changing tools.

Basic hammer design

Hammers come in various weights for different jobs. A good weight for a general-purpose, curved-claw hammer is 12 to 16 ounces (350 to 450 g). In a quality product, the head will be drop forged, with the tempering less hard around the rim of the hitting area. This prevents "spalling"—chipping of the edge from misjudged blows. Its balance should be such that the hammer will sit on its claw with the handle at an angle of 45 degrees. The strength and shock-absorbing qualities of the handle are crucial. Fiberglass and rubber-encased steel are available, but the comfortable flexibility, and good looks of hickory or ashwood are best.

Peen hammers weigh half as much. A cross peen is usual; a straight peen, parallel to the handle, may be preferred. The hammering end usually has a flat surface, but there are models with crowned, curved faces, allowing small nails to be gently buried without leaving a rim mark. Other models have faces with square, hexagonal, or octagonal sections. Smaller and lighter still, are so-called tack and glazier's hammers; they are good for tacking brads to hold backings in picture frames or fitting sprigs around glassed areas. A ball-peen hammer has a hemispherical face for shaping light metals.

Inevitably, the Japanese have a slightly different take on hammer design and manufacture. One face is flat, for driving nails and striking chisels; the other is slightly crowned, to make the final flush blow to a nail. The steel tempering reverses Western practice—the softer metal is at the center to absorb shock. Japanese hammer handles are longer and slimmer, usually of white oak.

Other designs

Steel-head hammers are for striking hard materials such as nails. Mallets are for working wood without damage, including the wooden handles of chisels. Indeed, that is the main function of the carpenter's mallet; the woodworker can pay attention to the cutting edge of the chisel or

Traditional woodworker's hammers, the Warrington hammers (shown with a small sledge hammer, top) have a flat cross peen suitable for striking small nails.

gouge, confident that the broad, rectangular face of the mallet is unlikely to miss its target.

A beech or boxwood mallet is a valuable tool for gently driving mortises and tenons together and the fine alignment of dovetail joints—as well as for disassembly, when misjudged work has to be taken apart before the adhesive dries. Rubber-, leather-, and plastic-head hammers also serve these uses. One variation, the dead-blow hammer, is partially filled with heavy granules, whose movement add to the force of the strike and prevent recoil.

In wood-frame building construction, carpenters use oversize versions of these tools, called "persuaders." The ultimate one is the sledge hammer, which takes its name from an old word for "slay," showing its lineage from a weapon of war.

"Man is a tool-using animal. . . . Without tools he is nothing, with tools he is all."

THOMAS CARLYLE (1795–1881), SCOTTISH HISTORIAN AND POLITICAL PHILOSOPHER

Nail sets

Sometimes there is the need for intervention between hammer and nail, in tight spaces and when nails are to be sunk below the work surface. This is the job for a nail set, a type of punch, often made of chrome vanadium steel. The tip may be a point, a flat, or a tiny cup, which permits firm location on the nailhead. Sliding nail sets have the striking punch in a sleeve, which also holds the nail or tack. Besides offering accuracy of location, they ensure that tacks will not buckle.

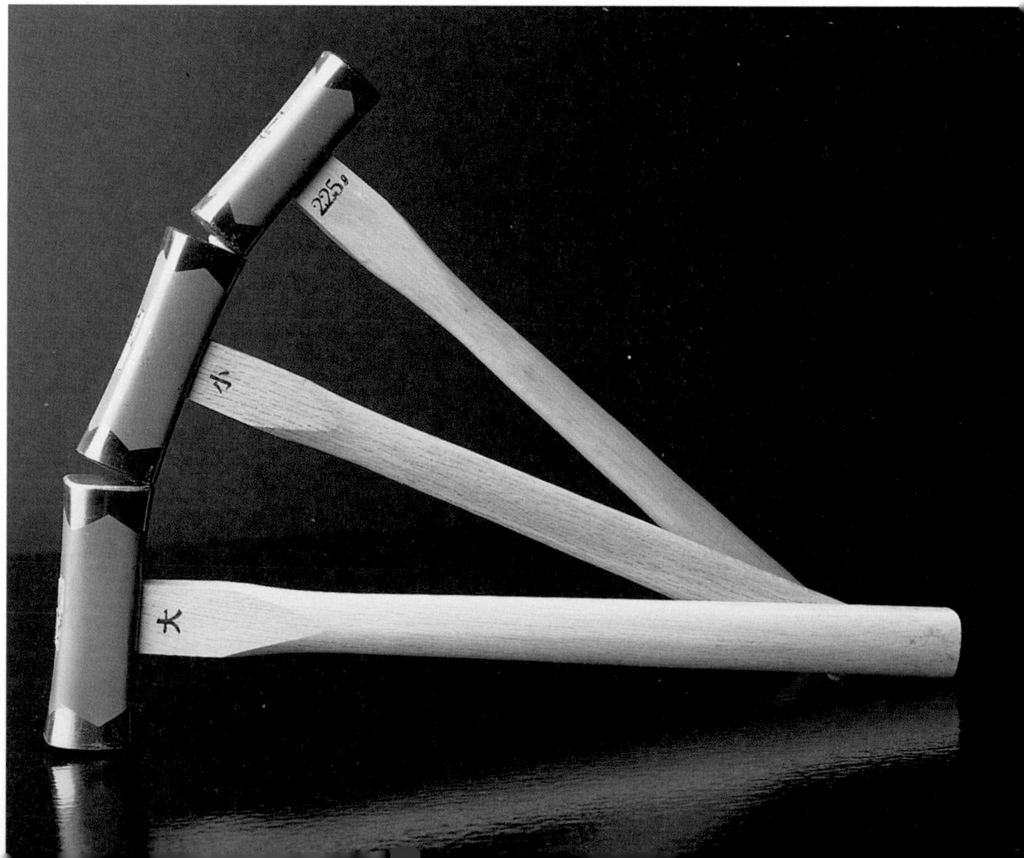

These Japanese square-head hammers are especially well balanced. They have chrome-plated heads (unusual for Japanese hammers) and white oak handles.

Most woodworkers will find it essential to have a curved-claw hammer and a few Warrington hammers in the shop, as well as some nail sets. Other types of hammers can be acquired for more heavy-duty work, including renovation work around the home. Some hammers have special features or are designed with decorative elements that should be considered before coming to a decision as to which hammer would be best for you.

1 Hi-tech hammer

Shown with complementary crowbars (one is a high-quality standard type and the other has a swivel head), this unique hammer has a head that can be tilted up or down by up to 15 degrees. This allows you to hit a nail dead-on in the most confined areas, where a straight blow would otherwise be impossible. This facility also maximizes the leverage that can be applied to remove nails.

2 Framer hammers

A type of ripping hammer, these hammers are designed for energetic people who use their hammers often. They have a centerline balance and long handle grip to take the strain off the user's arm. The faces have been specially treated to make them particularly hard. The hammers are also available with a smooth face or with serrations, which are crush ground to ensure that every tooth is the same hardness.

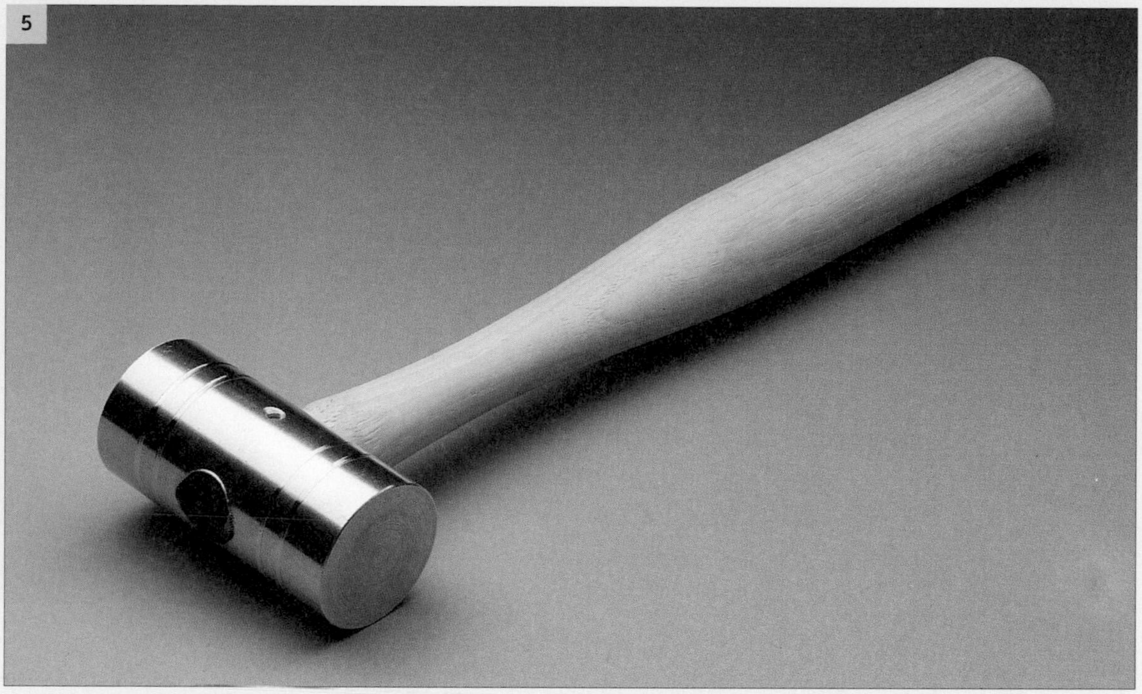

3 No-bounce thumper

When you really want to "whack" something with your hand, such as when assembling mortise-and-tenon joints, reach for this simple tool instead of picking up a hammer. Filled with steel shot pellets, it has the same no-bounce effect of a dead-blow hammer. This tool comes in two sizes: the smaller one has a medium-soft face on both ends; the larger model has a hard steel face like a hammer.

4 Solid steel hammer

An extremely strong tool, this hammer is forged out of a single piece of steel, which makes it essentially unbreakable. It has a fully polished head, and the wrapped leather handle is suprisingly comfortable.

5 Brass-head hammer

Solid brass is very heavy, and this gives these hammers great balance. They are particularly suitable for metalwork because the brass heads are "kind" to metal surfaces.

6 Cushioned-grip nail sets

Designed by an industrial tool maker, these ingenious nail sets have cushioned grips, which fit over the shank of the tool to protect your hands, allowing you to concentrate on the job without worrying about your knuckles. Available in five sizes, from 1/32 inch (0.75 mm) to 5/32 inch (3.75 mm), the tips are cupped and chamfered.

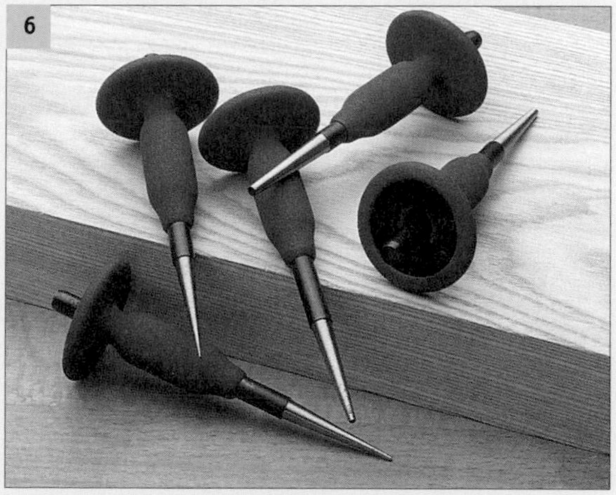

Yankee screwdrivers are available in different lengths, but they all take the same bits, including these single-slot and Phillips bits.

SCREWDRIVERS

EVEN THE MOST MALADROIT HOUSEHOLDER FINDS A USE FOR A screwdriver—as a can opener, paint stirrer, chisel, punch, candlewax scraper—which accounts for the abuse so many screwdrivers suffer. Because the condition of the tip is crucial, that damage makes them ineffective for their purpose.

Screws (threaded but without points) and screwdrivers were first used by gunsmiths, early in the 17th century. It was a century or so before screws with pointed ends could be machine-made and woodworkers recognized their potential as fasteners. The first screwdrivers (then called turnscrews) were discarded rasps and files, even swords, with one end fitted into a handle, the other ground to size. Round blades came from the spindles of worn-out knitting machines. The modern, stubby, crutch screwdriver, indispensable for applying high pressure in restricted spaces, looks almost exactly like the one a gunsmith would have supplied with a new shotgun 300 years ago.

The neat and effective turning of a single-slot screw requires that the screwdriver tip fits exactly to the width of the screw slot. The workshop, therefore, will require three screwdrivers: one for 12–16 gauge screws with a 10-inch (255-mm) blade; one for 6–8 gauge screws, a few inches (5 cm) shorter; and one for 3–4 gauge screws, for which a long, thin electrician's screwdriver, itself copied from a piano maker's screwdriver, will do.

There is a bewildering range of versions of these basic carpenters' screwdrivers, with blade sections round, square, or flat, and with waisted blades (a "London" screwdriver) or flared tips. Most of the variations come in the construction of the handles, mostly plastic moldings, occasionally rubber-sleeved, claiming some ergonomic justification or another. As a handsome display on the workbench, and with a long reputation for blister-free comfort, the traditional round or oval handle in polished beech, ash, or boxwood is hard to beat. The preferred blade material is chrome molybdenum, zinc-coated to prevent corrosion.

Ratchet screwdrivers are easier to use one-handed; the handle can be rotated to its starting position while the blade stays still. The Yankee spring-loaded spiral-drive screwdriver employs a pump action and comes into its own when there is

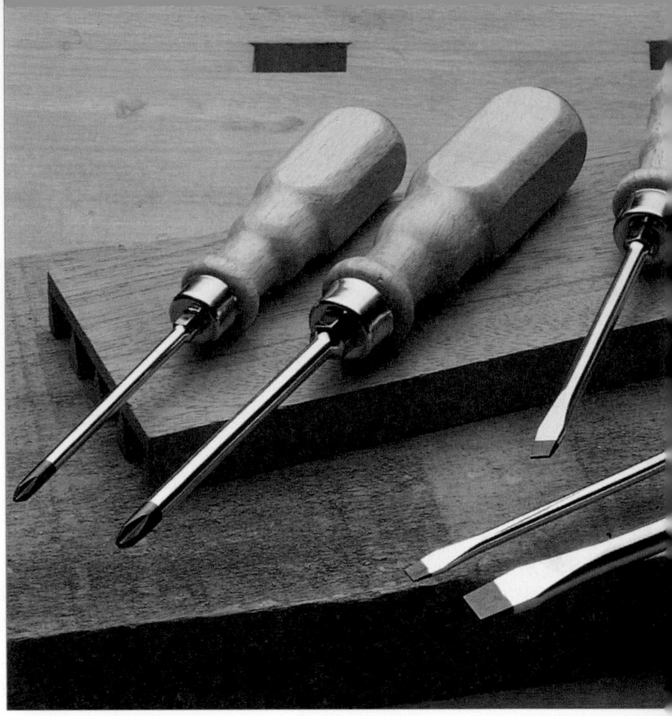

Dos and don'ts

Do not use a screwdriver with a tip that does not fit the screw. You could strip the screw—wear away the slot in the head—which makes the screw difficult to remove.

Do not hold the screwdriver at an angle to the work surface if you want the screw to go in straight.

a lot of screw driving to do. Both these mechanical drivers have a thumbslide to set a clockwise or counterclockwise—unscrewing—movement.

Single-slot screws are traditionally preferred when the screw head will show in the workpiece. But cruciform, crosshead screws—Phillips and Pozidriv are the best-known patent names—are often easier to work with. Fixed-blade screwdrivers in all sizes are available for them; ratchet and spiral screwdrivers usually have interchangeable bits, and the offset screwdriver—a short double-angle metal bar for working in very tight spaces—has a crosshead drive on one end.

These German-made screwdrivers (left) have a steel blade that runs all the way through the beech handle for durability. They are fitted with hexagonal flanges below the handle for extra torque when needed (use pliers or a wrench).

The first screwdrivers to choose are those that turn single-slot screws—the most common screws found in the woodworker's shop. Choose screwdrivers that feel comfortable to hold. If you plan to turn a lot of screws, consider one with a ratchet mechanism.

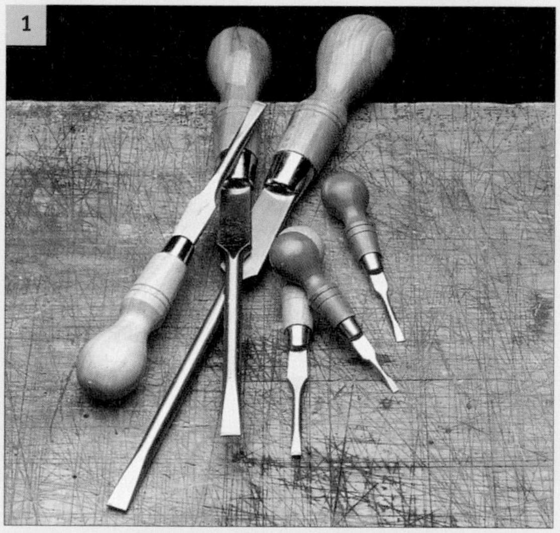

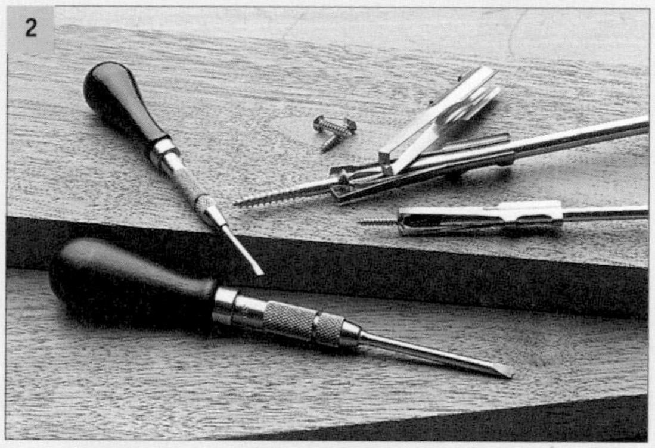

1 Cabinetmaker's screwdrivers
The blades of these screwdrivers are specifically designed for the slots in wood screws. Part of the shank is flat to accommodate a wrench if extra torque is needed.

2 Small screwdrivers/screw holders
The screwdrivers on the left have gunsmith-style barrels and small straight blades, which fit small screws. The holders on the right clip to the end of your screwdriver and the screw clips to the holder.

3 Ratchet-action clutch drivers
The multispeed driver (top) can be used in two speeds, and the handle has two positions—straight grip or pistol grip for extra leverage. The "Skew" driver (bottom) provides action at the tip at a 105-degree angle to let you get into hard-to-reach places.

Polygun TC
3M

GLUE APPLICATORS

ASSEMBLING IS A JOB WELL LEFT TO THE END OF THE WORKING day. Modern adhesives dry fast, but it's a good idea to walk away from the temptation to unclamp before a few hours have passed.

There's still work for traditional hide glue to do, particularly in repairing old furniture. New glue should be compatible with the original glue left in the wood fibers. That requires a glue pot, either a double boiler and a heat source or an electric glue pot. The appropriate brush has stiff bristles in a round ferrule, with an adjustable wire bridle to prevent spreading. Disposable paintbrushes will do, but bind them near the tip with string or brass wire.

Adhesives often have applicators in their container cap. Also available are squeeze containers that offer a variety of nozzles for dowels and biscuit joints, plus a roller for delivering an even spread over larger areas. Disposable plastic syringes come in useful, particularly to fill small gaps.

An old-timer's tool, a toothing blade, roughens a surface to increase gluing efficiency; and for those hide-glue jobs where a number of bonds have to be made simultaneously and a little extra open time is valuable, applying a decommissioned hair drier to the work surfaces can delay the setting.

Hot-melt glue guns are of limited use to the woodworker. The adhesive does not penetrate wood fibers but sits as a layer on the surfaces; it does not sand down well or absorb coloration. Hot-melt glues were developed for bonding disparate materials and for strengthening unseen joints. That's their contribution to the home workshop.

Glue brushes are ideal in the workshop, and containers can be helpful, depending on the glue you use. A glue gun is useful if working with materials other than wood.

If you do a lot of gluing, you should consider purchasing special applicators to make your job easier. A glue pot is essential for heating traditional hide glue.

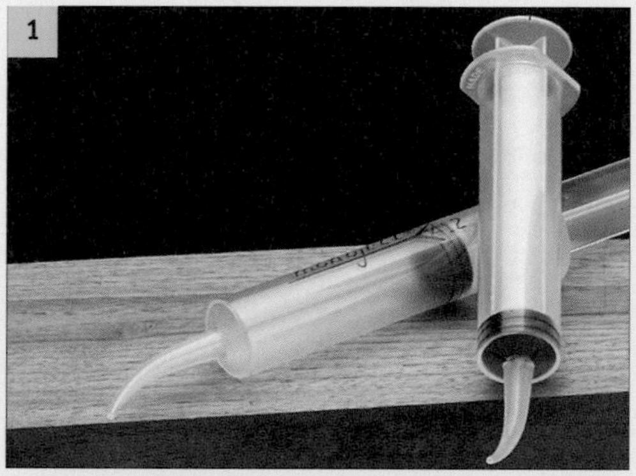

1 Glue syringes
These unbreakable plastic syringes have a curved tip to assist when applying small amounts of glue into tight areas. You can use any type of glue in the syringes.

2 Electric glue pot
Real traditional hide glue must be kept at a reasonably constant temperature. This thermostatically controlled pot keeps glue in the ideal temperature range, without the use of a water jacket.

3 Deluxe glue applicator
This kit includes a container with a roller attachment and a variety of nozzles, which can apply PVA (white) glue in a number of applications, including dovetails, biscuits, and dowels.

On the C clamp, pressure is applied by turning the T-bar handle.

CLAMPS

This German illustration, printed in 1840, shows two cabinetmakers (right) assembling a piece of furniture, with the help of wooden-frame clamps.

IN THE DAYS OF FISH GLUES—WHEN THE WORKSHOP WAS OFTEN damp and chilly—the work had to be left overnight for the glue to set, so the ability of a clamp to apply great and continuing pressure was paramount. That's no longer the case. More important is that the clamp's hold is firm and true, and that it can be applied quickly, before our modern, fast-setting adhesives set. There is a profusion of ways to approach this goal, and most of them are well worth trying.

It is not surprising that novice woodworkers often remark on the sheer numbers, and variety, of clamps available for service in an expert 's shop. There, clamps are considered to be extra pairs of hands, with a role in testing assemblies and in glue-up; as the helper stabilizing the other end of a board as you work on it; and acting as a filing clip on parts for tomorrow 's assignment. The usual wisdom expressed by most woodworkers is that they can never have too many clamps.

When a new-model clamp appeals to you, it is a good idea to buy two or more. Pressure evenly spread is more satisfactory than a single powerful squeeze. When assembly work is about to start, make sure that plenty of clamps are near at hand, with enough clamp pads if the work surfaces need protection (wood on wood is okay, but metal on wood can mar the wood's surface). Before applying adhesive, check that pieces mate well—clamps are to hold, not to force.

This North American clamp, dated 1790–1830, applies pressure between the screws—not at the end of the jaws, as hand screws do.

Types of clamps

C clamps, called G clamps in Great Britain, are the most widely used of all clamps. Small ones, for modelmakers, may have just a 1-inch (25-mm) capacity. It is worth having a selection of sizes, in pairs, up to 12-inches (305-mm) capacity, with varying throat depths. When choosing a clamp, look for a good-quality screw thread. The frame may be forged or cast—forged is better. A useful bolt-on accessory is an edging clamp, for holding lipping or other trim onto a face edge. Sometimes that feature is incorporated in the C clamp; this is known as an edge clamp.

For large work, bar, or sash, clamps are required. In the United States, the bar is a pipe, threaded at one end so that the clamp head can be screwed onto it, and with a cam-action lock on the tail slide. In Great Britain, an adjustable screw head is fixed at one end of a piece of steel, usually a yard or a meter long; the other jaw, the tail slide, is appropriately positioned by a pin through one of the holes spaced along the bar. On speed clamps, both the jaw and the tail slide move along a bar and friction-lock when the jaw screw is tightened. Trigger-action

A trigger-style handle allows you to quickly position these speed clamps (right) to the work. Twist the handle on the movable jaw to adjust the pressure.

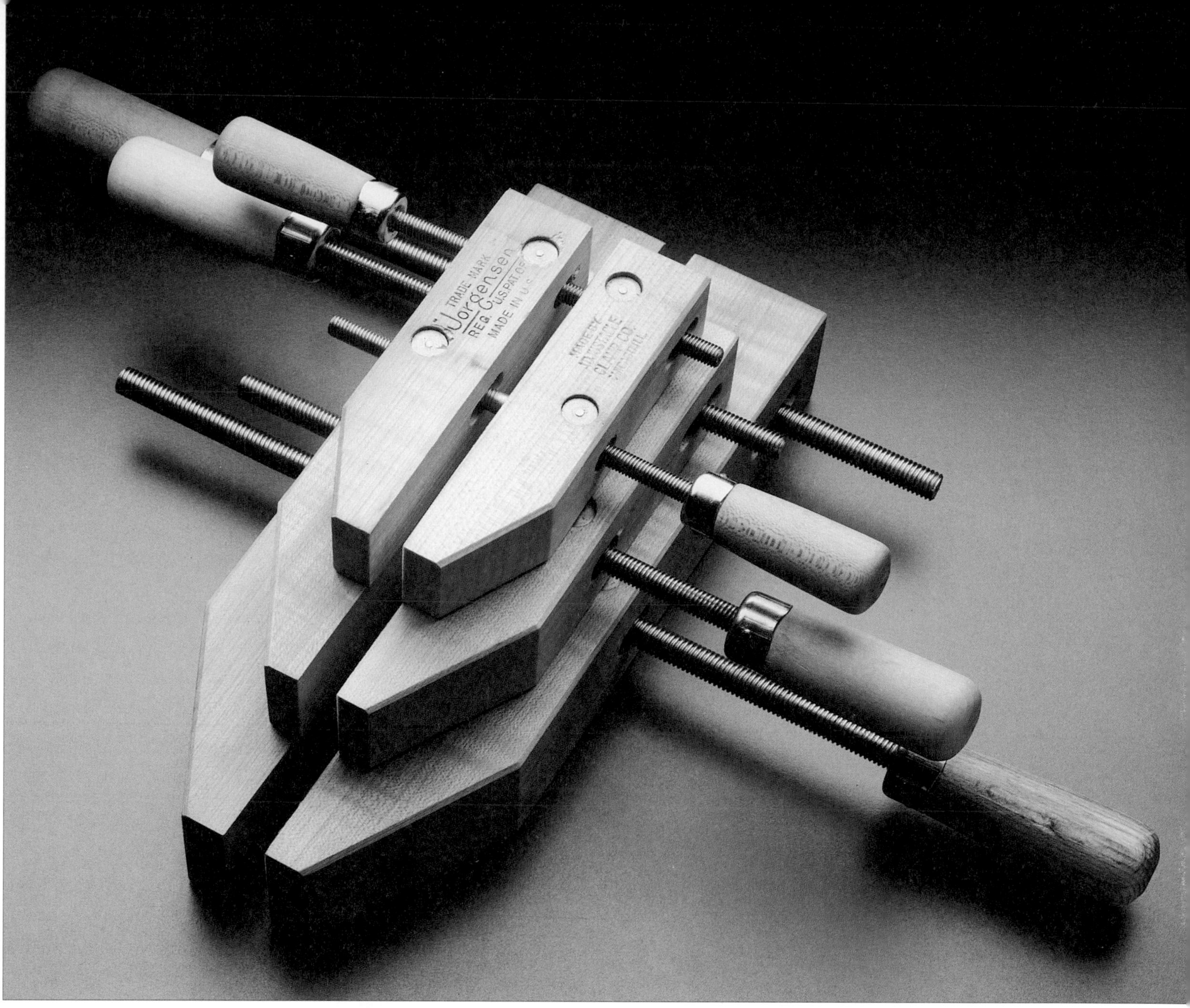

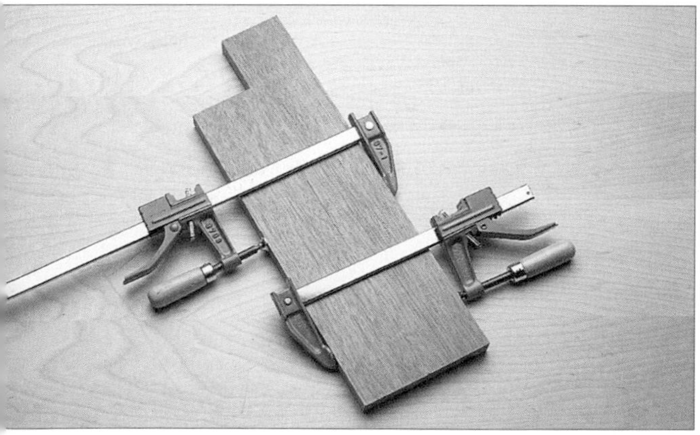

Craftsman's tips

In most situations requiring clamps, more is better. For good-looking, sturdy joints, place clamps to apply pressure at regular intervals along the surfaces being joined. Locate the clamp jaws on thin softwood strips, above and below the workpiece, to protect the work and spread the pressure.

By holding the handles and rotating them one over the other, you can adjust the jaws on these hand screws (above) independently. They can be set parallel to each other or at an angle.

Once the pipe clamp is positioned on the work, the handle is turned to apply gentle pressure.

clamps have the merit of allowing one-handed setting. Clamp head sets are for use on a home-made lumber cut to any suitable length and drilled to take the head and tail pins. The clamp will be as strong and true as the lumber selected.

"CLAMP" OR "CRAMP"

In Great Britain, the word is, or was, "cramp"; in the United States it is "clamp." It is said that Dutch settlers popularized the tool in America, and their word clampe *was adopted and anglicized. The British word probably derives from the notion "to cram."*

Modern British tool catalogs are often ambivalent about the word, heading the relevant pages "Clamps/cramps," then calling all but the industrial-size tools "clamps."

Tools provide a "link with our past, the human past, the hand."

JIM DINE, AMERICAN ARTIST (1935–)

When the need is for a lot of clamps applying modest pressure, the fret clamp is economical and effective. This is a simple U-bend of flattened steel with a screw adjustment to a swivel pad.

When two boards are to be joined to make a wide panel, a four-way clamping system applies pressure to the faces to prevent bowing. In this situation, the simplest of all clamps, pinch dogs, can do very well. Simply heavy-duty staples with wedge-shape legs that straddle the joint, they draw the work closer together the deeper they are driven in.

The most handsome member of the clamp family, the beech or maple hand screw, is not as favored as it once was, perhaps because it requires more careful treatment than its metal successors (it all too readily glues itself onto the work). Long wooden jaws with a deep reach are adjusted by two threaded steel rods held in pivoting inserts. It is a particularly useful tool when the outsides of the parts being brought together are not parallel.

Spring clamps work on the clothespin principle and can truly serve as a third hand in many situations. A miter clamp will deal with one right-angle corner at a time or hold a T-joint in position. Cord, webbing, or steel band frame clamps will hold four-, six-, or eight-angle corner blocks in place until the adhesive sets. Simple versions apply a tourniquet to the cord around the corner blocks; more sophisticated models ratchet up the tension to a chosen setting on a dial.

Which clamp should you use?

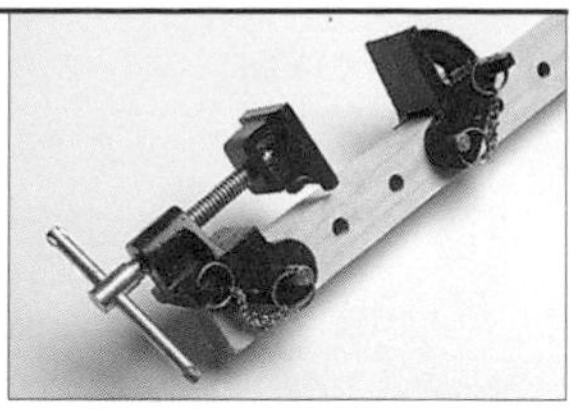

Some clamps can be used for a variety of jobs; others are specialized for one type of activity.

ACTIVITY	TYPE OF CLAMP
Hold large frames and carcasses together and true while adhesive sets	Pipe and bar clamps are ideal for boards being joined to make wider panels. The length of the pipe or bar needed will depend on the size of the project. In most home workshops, clamp head sets bolted onto a slim length of hardwood will do, made more rigid, if necessary, by being screwed onto a wider base plate of softwood. The virtue of speed clamps lies in the rapid sliding action to a close fit, which then requires only a minimal twist of the jaw screw, or leverage on a cam to achieve working pressure. Trigger-action clamps can be operated with one hand. Some allow the fixed jaw to be unclipped and reversed so that the tool spreads, instead of squeezes. Others have accessories for holding mitered and other corners.
When laminating or veneering	Use C clamps at 6-to-8-inch (150-to-200-mm) intervals on top of protective softwood strips to ensure gap-free edges. Smaller ones grip the workpiece 1 inch (25 mm) or so in from the edge; deep throat versions of the larger clamps have a reach equal to the jaw opening—up to 6 inches (150 mm). On the premise that you can never have too many, collect C clamps at garage sales and flea markets, where they can be bought for pennies. Be sure the frames are not distorted and that the jaws align.
Securing lipping or trim to a face edge	Use an edging clamp, basically a C clamp with a screw-adjusted shoe in the center of the frame.

ACTIVITY	TYPE OF CLAMP
Bonding strips into curved forms and temporarily holding pieces together for pre-assembly checks	Fret clamps, which work along the same principles as C clamps, are lighter and much less expensive—however, they are also much less strong. When applying fret clamps, use them side by side by side, and close together.
Small work where light pressure is needed	Spring clamps, the "paperclips" of the workshop, are handy for organizing small pieces of an assembly at the make-ready stage, for applying pressure to glued mortise and tenon joints, and for holding springy elements out of the way during intricate assembly. The jaws of spring miter clamps have sharp points, which can hold the mitered corners of picture frames while adhesive sets.
Assembly and preparing complex work without parallel sides	Hand screws are traditional tools that connect two wooden blocks using two tensioning screws to apply even pressure across a wide face. They are useful when the outside edges of the work are not parallel.
Frames and other objects with corners	Miter clamps hold corners in place while the adhesive sets. They will also hold L- and T-joints. Four corners—for example, on a large picture frame—will all need to be clamped at the same time. With frame clamps, a strap applies tension around the whole assembly, with plastic corner blocks taking the strain. Apart from 90-degree blocks, 120-degree and 135-degree blocks can be obtained to secure six- and eight-sided frames. Strap and web clamps can also be used. These are ideal for clamping repairs to chair rungs.

Woodworkers often have dozens of clamps in the workshop. When starting your own collection, begin with eight or more bar clamps and an even number of C clamps. For some projects you'll need clamp jaws with deep throats—the distance between the end of the jaw (the shoe) and the back of the jaw—to apply pressure toward the center of the work; other projects will require shallow throats to avoid putting too much strain on the work.

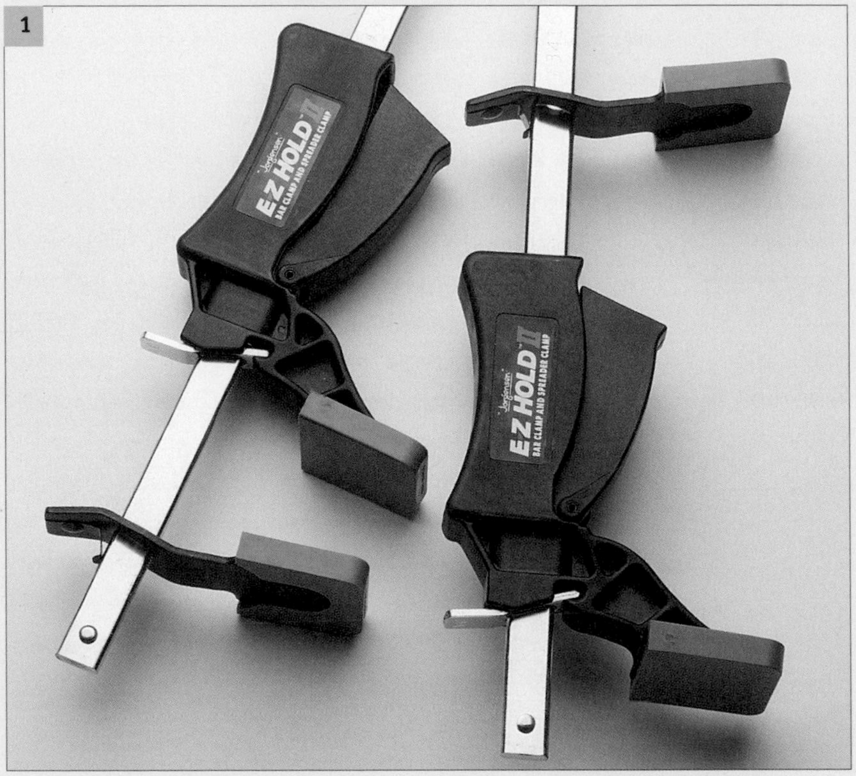

1 Squeeze clamps

These light-duty clamps can be applied with one hand, using an automatic advancing squeeze handle. One jaw can be reversed and positioned on the other end of the bar, so that the clamp can be used to spread pressure.

2 Pipe-clamp heads

The heads for the pipe clamps include (from bottom to top) a standard head, which can be fitted onto any length of pipe; a reversible head, which can apply or spread pressure; and a double pipe head, which is ideal for edge-gluing situations such as when gluing a table top.

3 Cam-action clamps

Suitable for light gluing and veneering tasks, these clamps have a cam, which acts as a lever to apply light or heavy pressure to delicate work. The wood jaws have cork faces to protect the work.

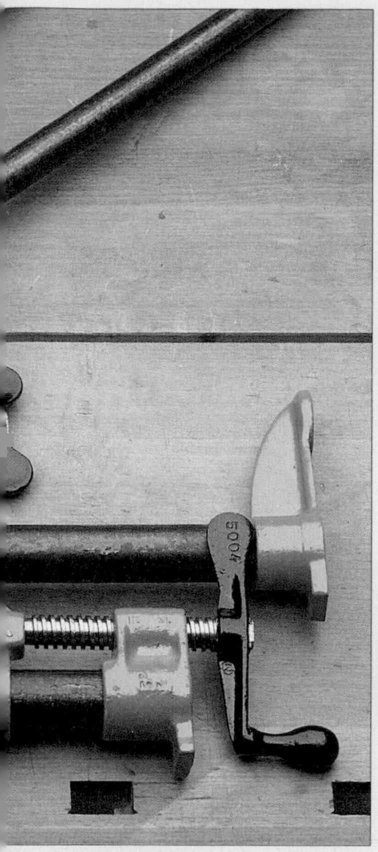

4 Hatakane clamps

Superb lightweight clamps made of brass (far left) and steel, these Japanese clamps have a sliding tail that is easily positioned. They have a clamping depth of ⅞ to 1¼ inches (22 to 32 mm), which is ideal for small-scale projects.

5 Clamp jaw extenders

The 8-inch- (200-mm-) deep jaws, used in conjunction with pipe clamps, slip over your standard black pipe or bar clamp.

6 Universal clamps

Designed for cabinet framework, the universal clamp can be secured to the edge of the work to hold two pieces together. It is available in different styles. The clamp at top is ideal for holding drawer supports to the furniture case and for supporting shelves; the clamp at bottom is suitable for holding butt joints.

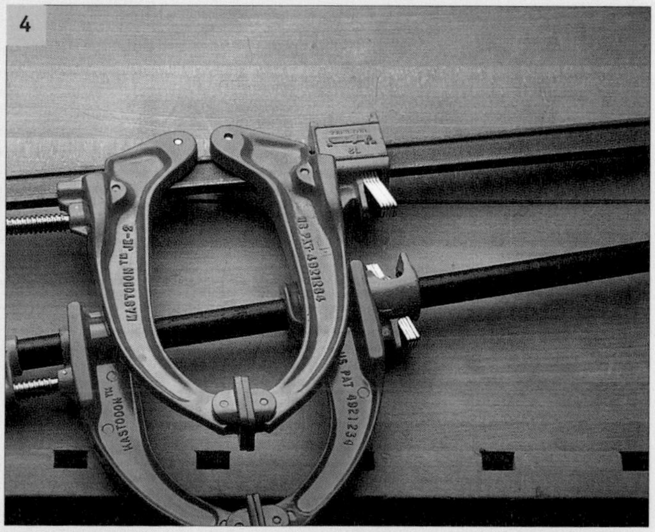

7

8

9

7 Multi-angle clamp

This versatile assembly clamp is ideal for miters and work with multiple angles, even for round or oval objects. It comes with a nylon webbing clamp and pressure corners. Pull the web through the clamp to set it up, lock the webbing clamp, and apply final pressure with the screw handle. You can use the clamp with or without the corners.

8 Spring clamp

It's very useful to have small spring clamps to temporarily hold a form or template to a workpiece—or for a number of other reasons. The tips and handles are coated with plastic to protect the work and your hands.

9 Frame clamp

In this astonishingly simple clamping system, long threaded rods screw into four corner blocks, and the whole assembly is quickly closed up to the frame by sliding speed nuts along the rods. A quick, locking twist applies the final pressure. Each corner piece has an inside channel to allow for squeezed-out adhesive.

10 Brass parallel clamp

When you need to hold two smaller pieces in postion, this small clamp can do the job without getting in the way.

10

11

11 Pinch dogs

The perfect tool for edge gluing, pinch dogs are used by simply hammering them into the butt ends of pairs of boards. You can then clamp up the middle of the boards without worrying about slippage or position.

12 Spring clamp set

The package includes six different sizes of pointed spring clamps, which are fitted in place by a spring-action tool that spreads them apart. The clamps are ideal for holding together mitered corners.

12

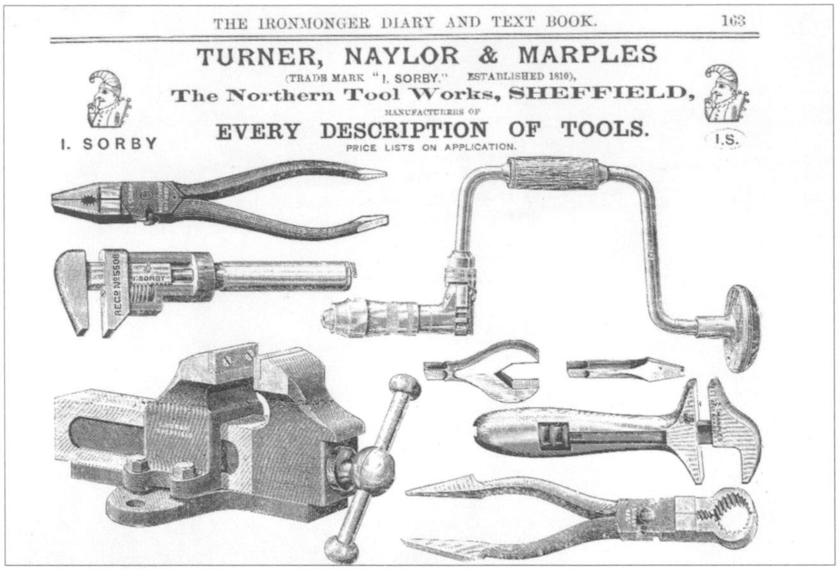

PLIERS AND WRENCHES

PLIERS AND WRENCHES RARELY RATE AN ENTRY IN WOODWORKERS' manuals, yet it is hard to imagine a workshop without them. They are found in most basic tool kits and are used substantially by mechanics, plumbers, machinists, and home builders. Many woodworkers are unconscious of how often they reach for pliers or a wrench to resolve a tricky problem. Besides being a necessity for maintaining large shop equipment, such as a table saw, pliers and wrenches can be used as a third hand to hold an object or to twist a difficult-to-turn object.

The mechanical principle—long-handled leverage through a pivot to control a jawed grip—had its first artisan application in the blacksmith's tongs, which have extra-long handles to allow a powerful and comfortably distant hold on white-hot metal. Miniaturization and refinement of the tool has made possible clock making and the elaborate working of precious metals.

In this family of tools, only pincers are specifically made for woodworkers—for disassembly rather than assembly. They are designed for the remedial work of removing unwanted brads and small nails in situations where the claw hammer's style would be too crude. However, with the crossover of materials that may be included in a woodworking project—for example, sheets of metal bolted to a wooden frame—some pliers and wrenches are finding their way into the workshop as an artisan's tool.

There is a range of smaller pliers, of which the most useful type for the woodworker is probably the long-nose pliers. They have extended, tapering jaws that can manipulate small items of hardware and reach into awkward spaces. They are excellent for handling miniature parts. Some of these pliers are

Along with the vise and brace, this 1884 advertisement (above) shows a variety of pliers and wrenches available to the ironmonger (hardware store owner).

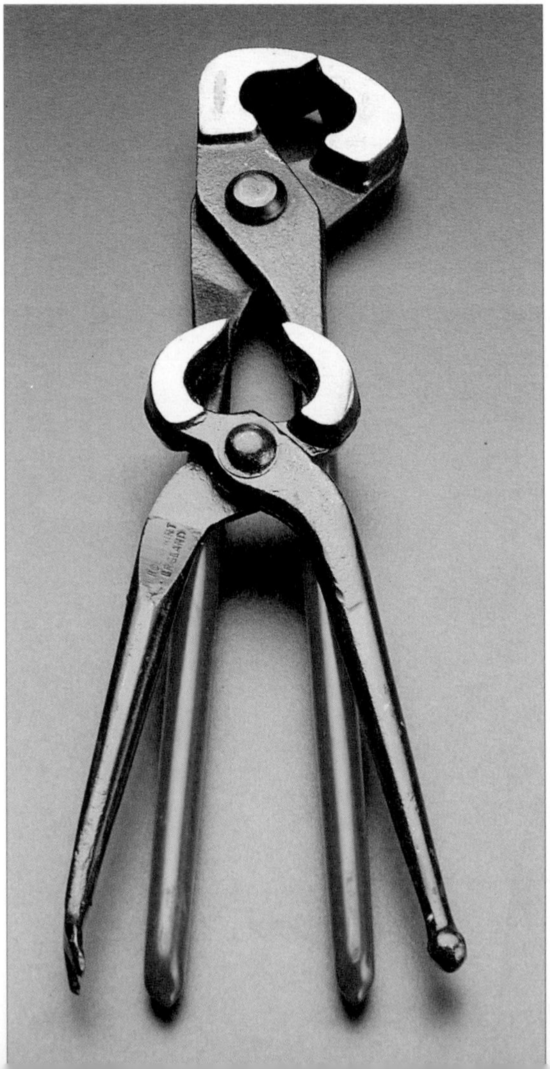

These pincers, basically large nail pullers and cutters, have a smooth rounded head and extra-long handles. The large pincers have an offset head to pull nails like a claw hammer.

adapted for use by electricians. They have cutting ends, which are useful for cutting thin wires.

General-purpose or combination pliers grip, twist, and cut. They should be made of chrome vanadium or carbon steel. The larger the pliers, the greater the leverage and effectiveness of the cutting action on wire and nails. On standard models, the handles are PVC (polyvinyl chloride), or vinyl, coated. More thickly cushioned, heavy-duty grips can reduce fatigue from frequent use, and insulated handles protect the user from potential shock when working around electricity or on electrical appliances.

Wrenches can be defined as fixed or adjustable. The former may have an open or closed "box" end, which fits around nuts to tighten or loosen them. Available in a variety of sizes, these must be matched, so that the box is the right size for the nut. The latter type has one fixed and one movable jaw, which may be lockable. This tool can serve as an emergency clamp, or, as with many other types of wrenches, be used for turning objects. If using a wrench on wood, you can prevent it from damaging the surface by applying masking tape to the jaws. You should avoid using excess pressure.

This adjustable wrench has a jaw that is moved with a worm gear. The faces of the jaws are parallel for turning nuts and bolts.

You won't need to acquire pliers and wrenches for your shop for most general woodworking projects. However, some of these tools are useful to have on hand in an emergency, including standard and long-nose pliers and an adjustable wrench. There are many other types of wrenches also available.

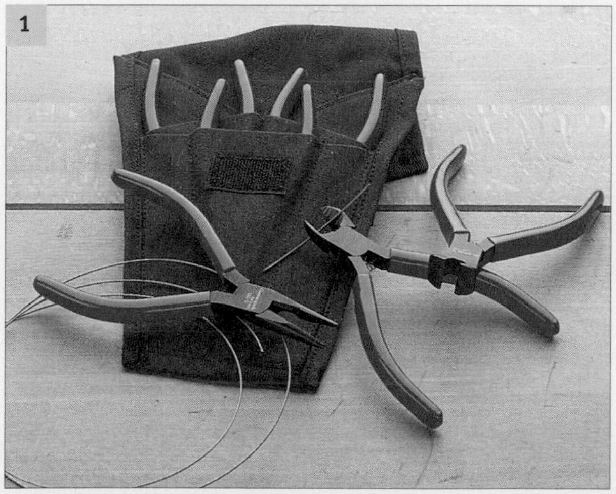

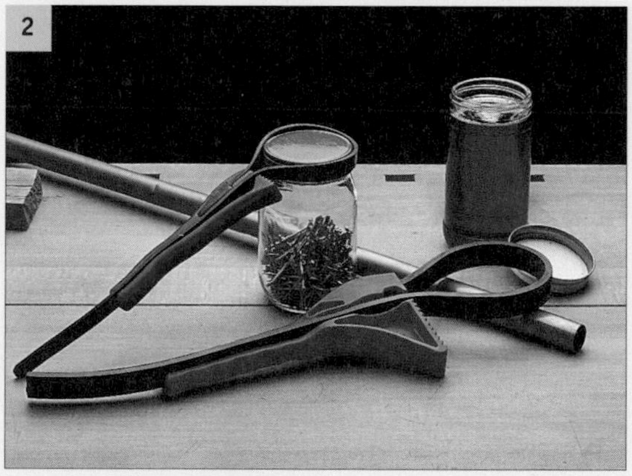

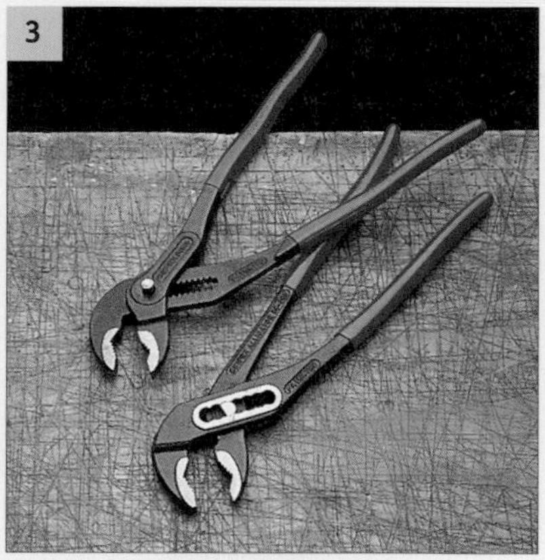

1 Bench cutters

This set of French cutting pliers includes a diagonal nipper, an end-cutting nipper, and needle-nose pliers (a variation of long-nose pliers) with side cutters.

2 Rubber strap wrenches

The rubber straps on these wrenches (based on similar tools used by plumbers) fit through the plastic handle. The strap will grip almost any shape and any material without leaving a scratch or mark.

3 Slip-joint adjustable wrenches

The width of the jaw on these wrenches can be adjusted to hold items of different sizes. The long handles provide additional leverage for extra turning power.

Finishes

Some finishes are best applied with a brush, which should usually be of top quality for the best results. Other finishes are best applied with clean, lint-free rags.

It's probably fair to say that almost no aspect of woodworking is more overlaid with mystique than that of finishing. Before a woodworker begins a project, he or she is likely to have made the most careful plans for the physical construction of the piece. However, the same person may well have only the most superficial idea of how the piece is going to be finished. This oversight in planning is made all the more remarkable by the fact that the finishing part of a project is every bit as important to the beauty of a piece and its durability, as is its construction.

For the best results when considering the finishing process, the woodworker should consider not only the products that will protect the work and the number of coats to use, but also the surface that the finish will cover and the tools used to apply the finish.

ABRASIVE PAPERS AND WOOLS

A CRUCIAL STEP IN WOOD FINISHING IS SURFACE PREPARATION. Scratches, dents, and roughness in the surface will show up clearly and even be magnified once a finish has been laid down—especially if any stain is applied. The only time when you will probably not care about the smoothness of your finish is when producing a "faux-antique" finish. In this case, the darker dents, for example, will look artful, because this is the way a naturally "distressed" piece of furniture looks after decades of use.

Surface smoothing is most commonly done by sanding—using flexible paper with various grades of small-particle abrasives glued to it. There are many different types of sandpaper manufactured: aluminum oxide-, silicon carbide-, and garnet-coated papers—and even ceramic- and diamond-coated papers. Although these various types of abrasives applied to paper make the traditional term "sandpaper" a misnomer, it is still in popular use. The most common abrasive used in woodworking is aluminum oxide. It can be easily obtained in good quality at a reasonable price.

Always start with the coarsest grit you need to remove the deepest scratches or dents, and move as quickly as possible to finer grades. If in doubt about how coarse a grit you need to start with, lean in the direction of a finer grade and switch if it is not doing the job. Stop sanding when you get a decently smooth surface (usually 150-grit paper will do the trick). If you use sandpaper that is "super-fine," you can, depending on the type of wood, clog the pores with fine particles and prevent the subsequent stain or top coats of finish from soaking in or adhering to the surface properly.

When sanding flat surfaces, it's good practice to wrap the piece of sandpaper around a flat sanding block (you can buy these, but any scrap piece of wood can work just as well). This keeps the pressure even. But never use such a stiff block when sanding curved or rounded parts, because you will quickly ruin the detail—instead, simply hold the sandpaper in your fingers or your palm.

Abrasive papers have the following features:

- Paper backing is available from "D" to "A" weight. "D," the stiffest, is rarely used in a woodworking shop. "A" is the most flexible and most common.
- Aluminum oxide has man-made particles available from 50- to 320-grit paper.
- Garnet is made with natural particles and comes

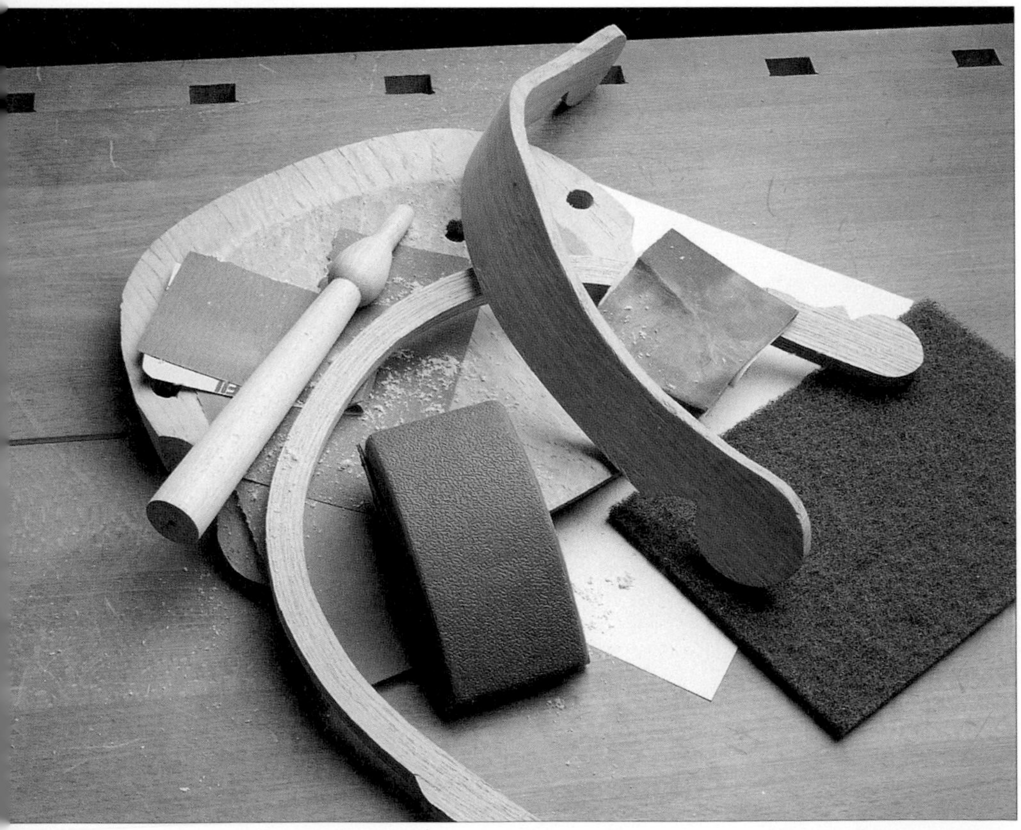

The curved sanding block is suitable for guiding sandpaper on curved work such as a chair seat. The abrasive-free nylon pad is ideal for fine work often done with steel wool.

in 120- to 320-grit paper. Some woodworkers prefer garnet papers to aluminum oxide paper.

- Silicon carbide is typically used with waterproof papers in grits from 220 to 600. It can also be used to polish metals, using oil or water as a lubricant.
- Diamond- and ceramic-coated papers are industrial alternatives used on metals.

Metal wools

These are very fine strands of metal that are formed into pads or rolls. Very coarse steel wool can be used to smooth raw wood surfaces prior to finishing, but a far more common use of steel wool (000- or 0000-grade) is in "rubbing down" a finish between coats. This removes the specks of dust that will have clung to the surface before the finish has dried completely, and it also prepares the surface for the next coat of finish. Wools are available as follows:

- 00-grade steel
- 000-grade steel
- 0000-grade steel
- Bronze, which is softer than steel and roughly equivalent to 0000-grade steel wool.

All woodworkers shops should be well stocked with aluminum-oxide sandpaper in various grits from coarse to fine, as well as the 000- and 0000-grade steel wools. Other types of abrasive papers may come into play for specialized tasks, and these can be acquired as needed.

1

2

1 Flexible sanding pads
Extremely useful for turners, these pads are great for anyone who has to sand curved surfaces. They are available in a variety of grits and can be used either wet or dry.

2 Norton coated abrasives
The manufacturer of these top-quality papers has taken care to provide uniform-size grits that are free from impurities and uses a strong resin to bond the abrasive granules to the paper.

POWER SANDERS

SANDING IS THE LAST STOCK PREPARATION TASK BEFORE THE final job of applying a finish. Sanding prepares the surface for the finish and also removes any rough areas or nicks. The better you are at sharpening the blades and teeth of your hand tools and using them, the less sanding you will have to do before finishing. When moving the wood, in gluing, and during assembly, you should always pay special attention to what you are doing so that you avoid damaging the surface, causing yourself additional work. The corners are especially susceptible to damage.

Giving the entire piece a final hand sanding with a fine-grit paper (see pages 210–211) to create a uniform surface will always be the final stage of surface preparation. But before you reach this stage, you can use power sanders to do the bulk of the surface preparation. They will substantially speed up the sanding process. For years there were just two styles of power sanders available: for rough and for finish sanding.

This orbital sander is equipped with a dust bag to catch the sawdust, and it has a handle at the front of the tool to assist you in controlling it.

Sanders for rough work

The tool of choice for aggressive sanding is the belt sander. It has a rotating cloth belt with grit on one side, which is used to remove material in a hurry. However, this sander is difficult to control. It should be used carefully—you can easily remove more wood than you want, especially when using a coarse grit. An improvement to the tool is a frame that surrounds the belt, making it easier to control on a flat surface. However, even with a fine grit, a belt-sanded surface needs more work.

Sanders for fine work

The orbital sander has traditionally been the tool of choice for finish sanding operations, using a fine-grit paper. The machine rotates the paper in a small circle. However, if the paper is too coarse, it will leave a small circular pattern in the wood. The real problem is that you may not be able to detect the swirl pattern until the finish has been applied. A clever adaptation of this design is a small hand-held profile sander, which has a triangular pad that is great for corners and tight spaces.

In recent years the random-orbit sander has been developed. It mimics the aggressiveness of the belt sander but has the finishing ability of the orbital sander. It has a round base that rotates and an internal cam mechanism that also rotates in a small orbit similar to the orbital sanders. The two rotating motions cancel out any scratch or swirl patterns. With fine-grit paper, it leaves a better finish than the orbital model. The random-orbital sander removes wood quickly and, correspondingly, produce the smoothest, most scratch-free finish. If you are going to have only one power sander, it should be the random-orbit sander.

Which sander should you use?

The random-orbital sander is the most useful type of power sander to have in a woodworker's shop, but the belt and orbital sanders have their place, too.

ACTIVITY	TYPE OF SANDER
Rough sanding	You can use either a belt sander or random-orbital sander with a coarse-grit paper.
Finish sanding	Choose an orbital or random-orbital sander with a fine-grit paper.
Sanding in a corner	The orbital sander will work for this task. You can also use a profile sander with a triangular pad.
Sanding with or across the grain	Any sander will do for sanding with the grain. Use an orbital or random-orbital sander for working across the grain.
Sanding a finish, stain, or filler	You can use either an orbital or random-orbital sander with a very fine-grit paper.

It's the woodworker's personal preference when it comes to choosing sanders, but the random-orbital sander is probably the most useful sander for the woodworking shop.

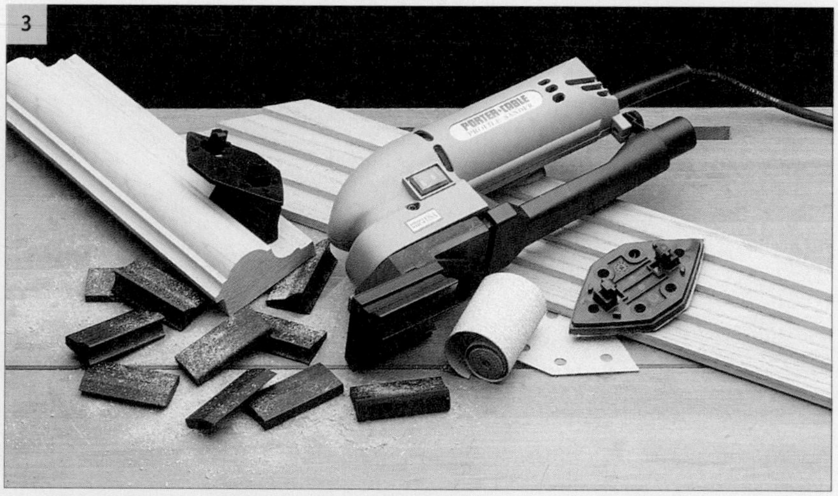

1 Palm sander

This small sander is made for one-handed use, with the base held flush to the work.

2 Random-orbital sanders

The variable speed feature on the random-orbital sander (top) lets you adjust the speed to suit the work. The random-orbit palm sander (right) includes a dust-collection system; the dust-collection kit (foreground) can be fitted to random-orbit sanders.

3 Profile sander

Detachable pads can be attached to this special sander to allow it to sand a variety of shapes and profiles.

BRUSHES AND OTHER APPLICATORS

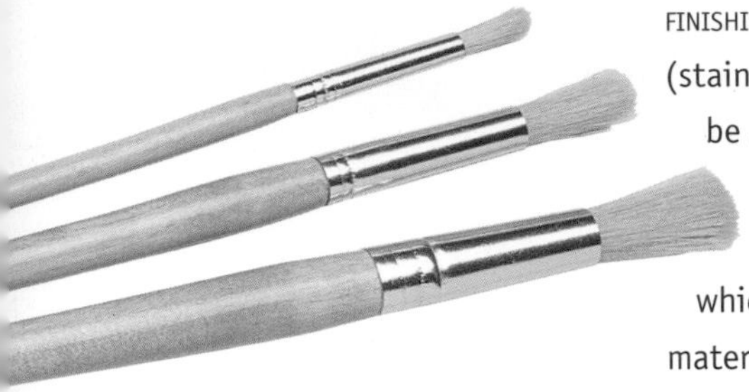

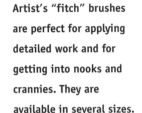

Artist's "fitch" brushes are perfect for applying detailed work and for getting into nooks and crannies. They are available in several sizes.

FINISHING MATERIALS, WHETHER THEY ARE COLORING AGENTS (stains and dyes), sealers, or final top coats, can be applied in only one of three ways: spraying, wiping, or brushing. All these techniques are used by all types of furniture makers—but which one is preferred depends on both the material being applied and the setting. A high-volume factory making a series of pieces often relies on spraying, because it is fast and minimizes hand labor. The end result, however, usually does not have much "character." A smaller shop will typically wipe or brush on the finishing materials because spraying takes capital equipment, can be messy in a small space, and can require the use of safety spray booths. Recently, a new spraying technology has become available. HVLP (high-volume, low-pressure) equipment has made spraying an option even for hobbiest shops.

Finishes that are volatile—those that dry very fast—are usually sprayed. One example is nitrocellulose lacquer. If a lacquer is brushed, because of the speed in which it dries, it will not flow out smoothly. Spraying is accomplished using a high-pressure air compressor and a spray gun or a HVLP sprayer. The end result is essentially the same, although HVLP equipment is easier to use, especially in the smaller shop.

Other finishes, notably oils, such as Danish oil and tung oil, are best applied using a wipe-on technique with clean lint-free rags, because the

Natural bristles, such as red sable (bottom) and striped badger (center), are the best brushes for certain types of finishes.

excess has to be wiped off anyway. However, brushing-on remains the staple method of applying a finish in most small woodworking shops.

Brushes for finishes

A traditional brush comes to mind when considering brushing on a finish, but foam applicators can also be used. They are cheap and disposable (just throw them away after one use). Surprisingly, they can often do a fine job, especially with a self-leveling material, such as paint, which flows evenly onto the work.

Other materials, such as varnish, require a very good brush in order for the job to look good. In general, a better-quality brush, such as a natural-bristle brush set in a hardwood handle, will always produce a better result than a cheap one.

Fiber brushes generally have artificial bristles such as polymer. Best-quality brushes will have all-natural bristles and will give much better results with demanding materials such as varnish. In addition to having natural bristles, better brushes have little or no "fill" in the center of the brush—that is, they will be bristle all of the way through. This greater concentration of bristles holds more finish material, allowing you to work faster. Better brushes will also often have "chisel-cut" tips, which apply material more smoothly. You should look for a stainless steel ferrule, which won't rust. In general, choose a natural-bristle brush for oil, varnish, and polyurethane and synthetic-bristle brushes for water-base finishes.

As soon as you've finished using a brush, clean it in the appropriate solvent and reshape it. Once the brush has dried, fold clean paper around the bristles to help retain their shape.

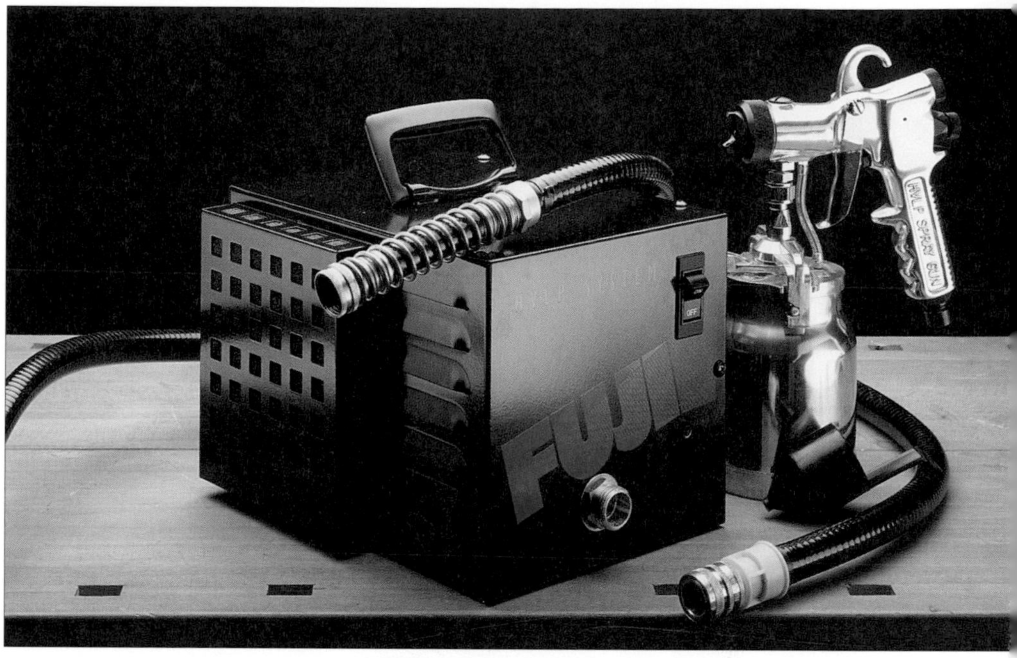

This high-volume, low-pressure spraying system produces a flow of clean, dry air that eliminates brushing, saves material, and makes for a faster drying time. It is suitable for everyday use.

Tools for special finishes

A variety of other tools, including special brushes, are used to create special effects with paints or other coloring agents such as glazes. Such finishes are often called "faux" (or fake), because they create an illusion on the surface of the wood. A graining tool leaves an impression of wood grain in a painted surface. Other effects can create an aged appearance or even imitate marble. A stencil brush has bristles held in a cylindrical shape and a flat tip to pounce paint through a stencil. These tools are used with paints and glazes suitable for furniture.

Craftsman's tips

Almost all bristle brushes, even the best, lose some bristles when new, but the better ones will not continue to do so. Before using a new brush, you can work the bristles back and forth across the palm of your hand to dislodge any loose bristles.

You should choose your brushes based on the type of finish that you want to apply. If you plan to work extensively with oil-base finishes, invest in a set of high-quality brushes—and take care of them. Choose specialized brushes only when you need them for a particular project. Disposable foam pads are always handy to have on hand, as is a reasonable supply of clean, lint-free rags, which can also be used for wiping up glue spills and squeeze-outs.

1 Traditional finishing brushes

These French brushes have natural bristles that extend from tip to handle, with none of the filler used by some other manufacturers. The bristles are securely bonded so that only a few come loose. The ends are uniquely hand cut in a double curve.

2 Disposable natural-bristle brushes

Made in China, these brushes are so inexpensive that you can really throw them away after use with a clear conscience. They can, of course, be cleaned and used again, but if you forget to, it won't be a great loss.

3 Detail brushes

The red sable brushes (near right) are suitable for small detail work for all types of finishes, paints, and stains. They are ideal for blending and matching stain and grain patterns. The ox-hair flat brushes (far right) are excellent for sign painting, and woodworkers will also find them handy for staining, painting, and varnishing molding and other hard-to-reach areas. They are flat in section and taper to the point.

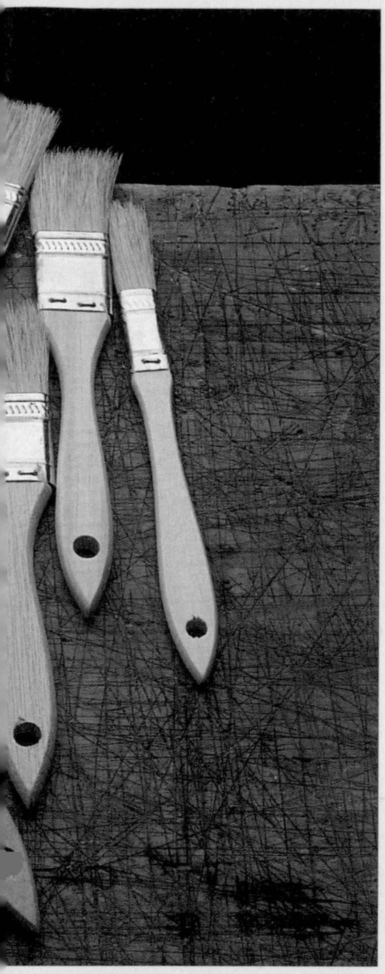

4

4 Disposable foam brushes

Available in three sizes, these foam brushes are just the thing for applying stain and sealer coats—allowing you to save your good brushes for the top coats.

5 Double-thick flowing brushes

The longer and thicker stock bristles make these superb natural-bristle brushes ideal for flowing types of finishes such as varnish, shellac, lacquer, and enamel. Remove any loose bristles by tapping gently against the palm of your hand. Never use them sideways, and do not poke or jab the brush.

5

FINISHES

THERE IS AN ARRAY OF FINISHING PRODUCTS AVAILABLE, AND choosing among the various types of staining or coloring mediums (if the wood is to be colored) and selecting the correct top coat is as important as, for example, the careful cutting and fitting of exposed joints. The craftsman should think through his objectives for wear resistance, toughness, flexibility, moisture resistance, and for beauty and clarity of appearance.

There is no automatic "right answer" to the question of which type of finish to choose. Yet, even with so many decisions to make, it is often at the last minute that the woodworker will purchase "some stain" and a "bottle of shellac" or a "can of varnish," paying little attention to the purity of the ingredients, the compatibility of the various solvents, or any real idea of what he wants the finish to accomplish.

As any good cook knows, the quality of the ingredients is every bit as important in producing a superior meal as the preparation itself. This is no less true in woodworking when "laying down," or applying, a superior finish. And it will produce no comfort to know that every manufacturer's formulations are different, the quality of the ingredients notwithstanding. Questions to consider include, What is the purity of the ingredients in the finish? What about the thinners (reducers) or drying retarders? Are the top coat solvents really compatible with what has gone on the piece before? (If the stain and top coat can be dissolved by the same material, they are compatible.) Here is a short course in finish materials and techniques essential in choosing and applying a finish.

Dos and don'ts

Do make sure you follow the manufacturer's recommendations for drying times—without exception.

Do make sure you follow all safety procedures, including providing adequate ventilation and wearing the appropriate respirator and other safety equipment, whenever you work with finishing products.

Don't apply finishing products to your workpiece until you have made sure that the work area is as clean as possible. Dust and other small debris will ruin even the most carefully applied finish.

Understanding finishing basics

The main purpose of a finish is to create a protective barrier between the wood and the environment. A good finish will keep out dirt and grime, slow the natural shrinking and swelling of the wood, and prevent decay. The type of protection a piece of furniture needs depends on the wear and tear it will be subjected to. For example, an occasional table in an out-of-the-way corner could be protected with a shellac finish, which might be preferred for the appearance of the finish. However, this type of finish would not do on a coffee table on which you would often place glasses and cups, because heat and liquids can damage a shellac finish.

The other principal reason for finishing wood is to enhance its beauty, to bring out the depth and richness of the grain and color and to highlight details. In the end, the character of the finish chosen will have just as much effect on the final appearance as the wood itself.

Gloss and texture

The gloss that you achieve—how much the finish shines—is not really a question of what is used, but how it is used. Almost any finish that is

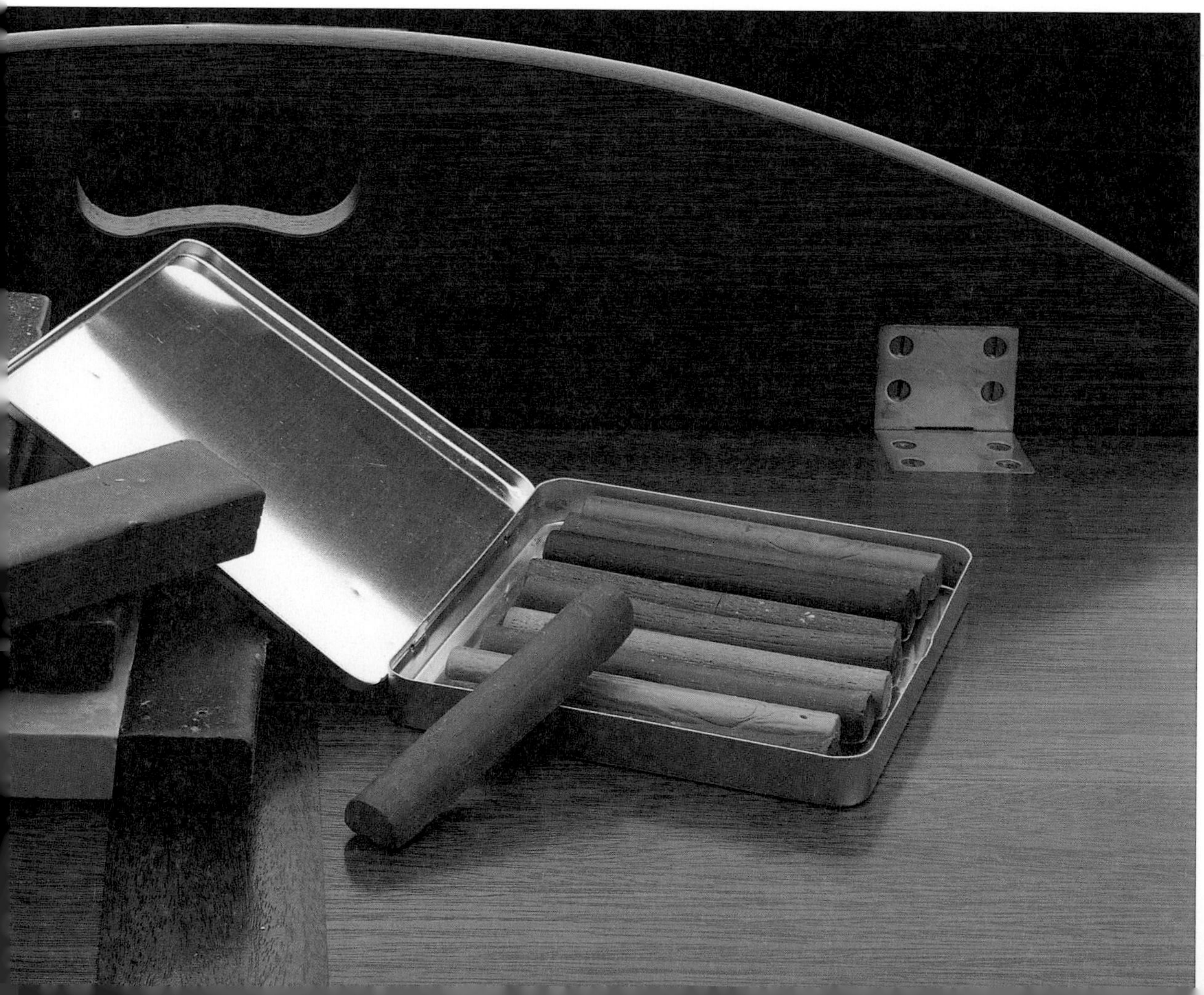

A small sample of the variety of stain colors can be seen in these "touch-up" sticks and crayons, which are used to make repairs to a damaged finish. The butler's table that they sit on is coated in a gloss finish.

properly applied in a sufficient number of coats and then polished can produce a mirror gloss. It can then be dulled to a satin or even a flat coating by rubbing it down with abrasives or steel wool.

The texture of the wood surface is as much a part of how your furniture looks as is its color or sheen. A varnish will tend to level itself, filling the tiny pores and irregularities in the wood, to create a smooth, flat surface with just a few coats.

Thinner finishes, such as shellacs and oils, tend to transmit wood texture to the eye and touch more faithfully, and oils will create a "warm" look. But texture is determined not only by the final film. Fillers, too, can be used to fill the pores, allowing a much flatter, smoother surface. This generally gives a more formal look to furniture and a higher gloss.

The finishing process

Work with the best materials that you can afford, good brushes (see pages 214–217), clean rags, and a well thought-out plan. Coverage for all finishes ranges from about 125 to 200 square feet per quart (11.5 to 18.5 sq m per liter). It depends mostly on how thickly each coat is being applied and the surface to which the coat is applied. Raw wood will soak up a lot of the first coat of finish, but each succeeding coat will go farther.

Here are some rules of thumb that will help:

1. Prepare the wood carefully. Do a final hand sanding, with the grain, using a fine abrasive paper. Dust afterward with a tack cloth.
2. Use good brushes and equipment, and keep them scrupulously clean. A cheap brush that

For the best results, some finishing products require the use of sandpaper or steel wool between coats to help create more of a "mechanical grab" for the following coat. Buffing with a clean, lint-free material is sometimes the final step.

continually sheds bristles, or a spray gun that spits and sputters, will waste time and materials and add needless frustration to the job.

3. It is usually wise to make the first coat of any finish a highly thinned "sealer coat," which will penetrate well, provide a good base for other coats, and allow the craftsman to sand off the "fuzz" (or raised grain) easily.

For lacquers, use a sanding sealer. Otherwise, use a thinned mixture of the final top coat. (Very thin shellac can be used under any top coat except lacquer, polyurethane, and water-base finishes or on exterior surfaces.) The use of a "sealer" coat is a very important step. It not only seals the wood pores to prevent the finish from seeping in, but it also seals in a stain so it won't bleed through as you finish your project.

4. Multiple thin coats are always better than a few heavy ones, especially with varnishes. Drying will be faster and more uniform, coverage more complete, and the appearance better.

A thick layer of finish will skin over and dry from the outside in. Trapped solvents are released at a progressively slower rate, because they have to travel through the thickening outer layer of finish.

5. Remember that wood is a natural product, and its grain and pores are not uniform. An area may look dry—even though it has just been coated. That dry spot has finish on it, but the spot is absorbing the finish faster than the rest of the piece. Let the finish dry completely, then re-coat it. After a few coats, the problem will disappear.

Drying—a critical part of finishing

Allowing a finish to dry undisturbed is the most important way in ensuring its success. As a general rule, thinner coats of finish and more of them produce a better drying finish, one that is more flexible, that is harder, and which has better adhesion between layers—and it will look better.

The process of drying must be understood thoroughly. Its importance cannot be overstated. "Pushing" dry times by putting another coat on too quickly causes the most finishing problems. It may look dry, it may feel dry, but it may not be dry. Using a piece of furniture before it is really dry may damage the finish. Drying is a curing process. Dry-to-the-touch has nothing to do with a finish actually being cured.

Applying another coat before the previous coat dries may cause the finish never to dry properly. Many finishes actually dry from the outside in. For a finish to dry, first the solvents must evaporate. The time this takes depends upon three things: the thickness of the finish (thinner finishes will allow solvents to evaporate more quickly); the type of solvents used (lacquer thinner and alcohol evaporate very fast, water more slowly, mineral spirits slower still); and the humidity.

Another process that takes place in some finishes (oils, for example) is a chemical reaction—oxidation, in which oxygen combines with the chemicals in the finish. The rate of oxidation is related to thickness of the finish, the type of finish,

> "This seasoning and mellowing of a man's work by the passage of time is one of life's choice gifts. Time, which deals ruthlessly with the mean and shoddy, adds a beauty that is all its own to good sound work."
>
> Charles Hayward, *Woodworker* magazine, October 1957

and to the humidity. (Note: Most varnishes will contain some oils.)

As you perform each finishing step on your project, also perform them on a small scrap piece of the same wood. You can then test the scrap piece to see if it is dry without risking damage to your work. An easy test is to lightly sand an area of the scrap piece. Most hard finishes, when dry, give off a white powder when sanded. If the finish is gummy, if it rolls up or slides under the sandpaper, it isn't dry.

Follow the golden rule—experiment

It is a very sound idea and good practice (good professionals do it) to always experiment on a piece of scrap wood before applying the product to the work, preferably finishing the scrap piece completely. Use the same type of wood as the work to see how the products will act on it.

Select several wood tones of one type of stain plus a few brighter colors, and test them on the scrap wood. A color that looks atrocious on a light colored wood can look spectacular on a darker wood. Write down what was done, so a record is available for the next time. Test-finish top coats in the same way, on both raw and stained wood.

REMOVING OLD FINISHES

Reclaimed wood can sometimes be used to create a piece of furniture. If it was previously protected with paint or a finishing product, the first step is to strip it. Use one of the purpose-made products on the market for a finish. If the wood was painted, you can use a heat gun. Wire-bristle brushes (right) can be used to help remove the finish or paint.

Safety matters

Virtually all products used in finishing have some degree of inherent danger associated with them. These dangers include, but are not limited to, solvent inhalation in high concentration, flammability, caustic products or acids, which can cause burns, and poisons.

All finishing materials dry by means of either a chemical reaction (oxidation in oils or varnish) or solvent release (as in shellacs and lacquers), or a combination of the two; and these create fumes. Adequate ventilation is certainly one of the most important requirements when finishing. Specially designed respirators (see pages 238–241) can also be of considerable help, perhaps, most importantly, when spraying.

Observe all safety precautions when finishing. Those solvents that are more flammable obviously require greater care in handling than those that are merely combustible. In addition to having adequate ventilation to keep vapor concentrations at a low level, you should not allow smoking, arcing fan motors, hobnail boots, or any other source of a potential spark in the work area.

Furthermore, rags used in applying finishes that dry by oxidation (all oils, for example) are subject to spontaneous combustion. The process of oxidation generally produces heat, and in a confined space this can be sufficient to set the rags on fire as they are drying. Be sure to wash them after use or "hang them out" so that the oxidation process does not result in heat buildup.

In addition, some solvents can cause skin irritations; or, if ingested accidentally, severe nausea or worse; or, if splashed in the eyes, blindness. You should always wear proper gloves, a suitable apron, and eye protection when working with such products.

Chart of finishes

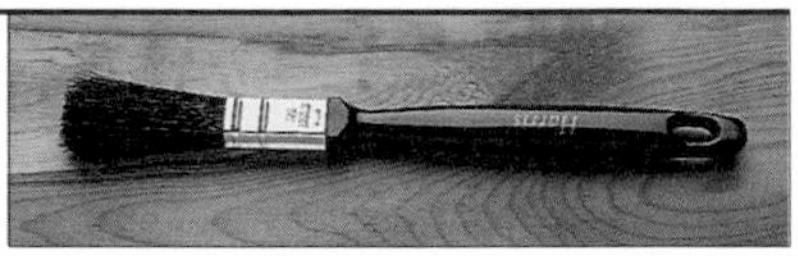

ACTIVITY	TYPE OF FINISHING PRODUCT
Surface preparation	Use chemical finish removers ("paint remover") or a heat gun to remove prior, unwanted finish. (A special remover is needed to take off an old organic-base finish.) You can also use a mechanical brush. To lighten the wood surface, apply beach—which can also be helpful in removing old stains such as ink. Use sandpaper, scrapers, and steel wool to abrade and smooth the surface. A tack cloth will remove fine dust particles from the surface after sanding.
Choosing coloring agents	Most coloring agents are made of finely ground color particles, or pigments, suspended in a carrier (such as oil), with small amounts of a binder to hold the pigments to the surface after the carrier evaporates. Wood can be dyed (like fabrics), using coal tar-base or metallic-base derivatives. Often used professionally, these usually come in powder form to be dissolved in alcohol or warm water, and they are easy and safe to use if the directions are followed. Dyes impart a clarity and transparency to the wood surface because there are no particles of color (pigment) to obscure the surface. Some dyes are specially formulated so that any grain raising is minimized. Certain chemicals (such as bichromate of potash) are used by professional restorers because of the extraordinary depth and quality of color they produce. The use of chemical dyes, which react with the wood itself to produce these beautiful results, is less common than it was decades ago, but they are still available for the adventurous hobbyist. Be sure to experiment first and take all safety precautions.
Filling wood pores	Wood fillers are not used to fill holes or imperfections in the surface, but are finely ground, transparent silex particles used to pack the pores of open-pored woods, such as oak, when the finisher wants a smooth surface. Depending on the desired result, filling is done prior to or after coloring.
Selecting sealer and top-coat materials	These are what is commonly thought of as "the finish." The variety is extensive, and categories are often "intermixed" in modern finishes as the manufacturers strive for the simplest and most mistake-proof means to achieving the desired result. All sealers and top coats comprise two basic elements: a carrier (such as mineral spirits, other chemical solvents, water, ether, oils) to carry the film or resin as it is rubbed, brushed, or sprayed on the surface, and a resin or other filmlike substance, which tries to stay on the wood. Some manufacturers produce finishes with an increased water-base (nonsolvent) content in an effort to reduce solvent harm to the environment and meet new mandated government regulations. Types of sealers and top coats include: oils (including tung and linseed oil), lacquers (these can be brushed or sprayed), varnishes, urethane and polyurethane, shellac, epoxy, waxes, and paint.
Polishing and touch-up and repair	For polishing, you can use wax, liquid polishes, steel or bronze wool, felt pads, powdered abrasives (such as pumice and rottenstone), and padding lacquer. Touch-up and repair work can be achieved with wax- and shellac-base sticks or crayons. Be careful to choose one that matches the color of the work.

The workshop

4

THE IDEAL WORKSPACE

A SATISFYING WORKSHOP IS LIGHT AND WELL-VENTILATED, clean and neat, has a view of the outside world, and does not get too hot or too cold. (As well as being uncomfortable, temperature extremes may damage your inventory of adhesives, paints, and varnishes.) As long as you have a minimum space of 8 x 10 feet (245 x 305 cm), you can set up a small, basic workspace.

The truly ideal workshop is beyond the reach of many, with space, time, and finance putting a limit to most woodworkers' ambitions. Furthermore, as a workspace is used, fresh ideas for adapting it to suit the woodworker's personal style will continually emerge. But in planning, and dreaming, you should consider certain criteria.

Planning the workspace

If you have the space and the money to build, or have built for you, a workshop, the first consideration should be the siting. It should be far enough away from family and neighbors to avoid creating a disturbance from noise and dust pollution, but close enough to the home to connect with its heating and electricity systems. The preferred construction materials are brick and lumber—concrete and metal sheeting create condensation, which corrodes tools and chills the air. A wooden floor with a nonslip surface treatment is comfortable, sound-deadening, and provides some protection against breakage if tools or workpieces are dropped.

A high ceiling helps the easy movement of long workpieces—bear this in mind when siting the entrance door. For many woodworkers, part of the garage is commandeered as the workshop, in which case, there's no access problem. But if the workshop is situated in some other space, be sure that large sheets of material—a 4-x-8-foot- (120-x-240-cm-) sheet of plywood, for example—can be delivered.

Natural lighting is restful and is the best lighting for woodworking. You can supplement it with fluorescent lighting placed high, using non-stroboscopic tubes—the pulsing type can mislead the eye into the belief that moving machine parts are stationary. Large, fixed power tools should have their own, individual spot lighting. Fit lamps with adjustable or flexible arms over work surfaces. A light shone low and diagonally on a board being planed or painted will highlight any ripples and blemishes in the wood.

There should be plenty of power outlets to avoid trailing cables. Consider suspending

There is plenty of room to maneuver around the workbenches and other work stations in this busy cabinetmaker's workshop, an 18th-century illustration from Diderot's *Encylopédie*.

cords from the ceiling over key work areas. Make sure all outlets are properly grounded. Avoid using extension cords, but if you must use one, make sure it has a higher capacity than that of the tool's cord.

Organizing the workspace

Positioning the main workbench is the first priority when organizing your shop. If there is just one source of natural light, place your workbench where it will benefit from this lighting. Make sure there is enough room to move around the bench. If there can be space on both sides to take the overhang of long workpieces, perhaps with the support of roller stands (see page 246), so much the better.

Large stationary machines also need space—can that 4-x-8-foot (120-x-240-cm) board be safely and comfortably fed through the table saw? Where there is not ample room, consider mounting such machines on wheeled bases, with flip-lock wheels, so that they can be moved into an open space when needed and moved against a wall when no longer required.

Ample storage is another feature of a satisfying work area. If the ceiling is high enough, fit a row, or rows, of large U-shape brackets to hold long pieces

In this woodcarver's workshop, there is lots of storage space, and the room gets ample natural light. A cabinet on wheels in the background provides a flexible work surface, allowing the tools to be readily at hand.

A homemade tool rack provides individualistic storage space for the tools used most often in this woodworking shop.

A magnetic tool rack can hold a variety of steel or iron tools—and these can be changed as the woodworker changes the tools he uses.

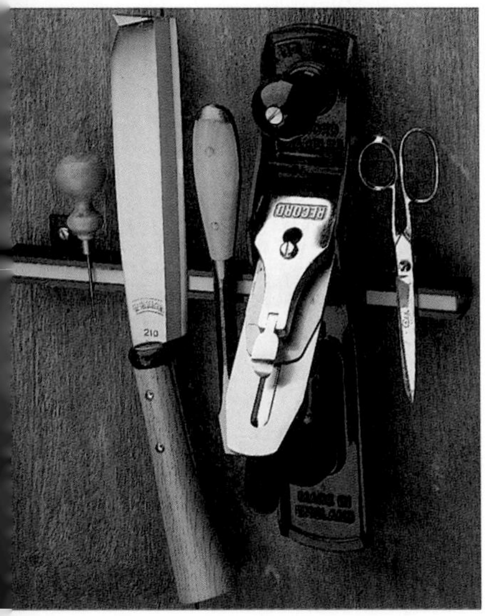

of lumber; otherwise, they should lie on closely spaced brackets against a wall (not on shelves, which prevent air circulation). Stand any large sheet materials upright—for example, in a gap between a wall and a line of floor cabinets.

The most flexible shelving systems are those constructed of vertical standards, slotted to take shelf-support brackets of various lengths. Paints, thinners, adhesives, solvents are all shelf items—so long as they are placed on high shelves, out of the reach of children. (If this is not possible, lock them away in a cabinet.) Glass or plastic jars recycled from the kitchen, clearly labeled to identify their new contents, are ideal containers for shelf displays of screws and nails, nuts, bolts, and washers.

Store hand-held power tools in cabinets, which helps keep dust out of motors. The hand tools most often used belong within easy reach of the workbench, in drawers underneath or on the wall behind it. A favorite method of storing hand tools is to fit sheets of pegboard on studs screwed to the wall, and hang the tools on the variety of available brackets and clips. A piece of plywood fitted with glued-in dowels can also be used, but it is less flexible as tools come and go out use. Some workers draw outlines of the tools on the board so that they can return the tools to their rightful places.

The bench grinder—a shop essential

A good bench grinder is necessary in any woodworking shop. All such shops are home to an array of cutting tools, such as planes and chisels, with blades that must be periodically sharpened. The bench grinder is the best tool for the first stage of the sharpening process, which is to create a bevel on the edge of the blade. Early models were powered by foot, but today's bench grinder, which can be mounted on a bench or a pedestal stand, has a housing that protects a motor, which turns a grinding wheel made of an abrasive stone. On some models the wheel is held in a vertical position (these often have two wheels, so that different wheel grits can be used at the same time), but other models use the wheel in a horizontal position.

The tool is held on a tool rest at an angle to create the bevel. The angle used depends on the type of tool—you should follow the manufacturer's instructions. The friction of the tool rubbing on the stone creates heat, so the work needs to be cooled down with water. Using light pressure when holding the tool reduces the amount of heat created.

The grinding wheels can become damaged. Before installing a wheel on a grinder, lightly tap it with a screwdriver and listen for a ring. If it produces a buzzing noise instead, the wheel is cracked or chipped and should be replaced. Always stand to the side of the grinder when turning it on—the wheel can sometimes shatter and cause an injury. Bench grinders can also be fitted with wire wheels for scraping off paint or rust on metal, and with a buffing wheel for polishing metals.

Health and safety

Always consider health and safety issues. Wear the appropriate safety equipment, and have a first-aid kit, fire extinguisher, and smoke alarm—even a panic button if you work alone with high-risk power tools (see pages 238–241).

Special aluminum oxide grinding wheels (left, background) minimize the burning of cutting tools. You should use wheel dressers (left, foreground) to clean and true a grinding wheel.

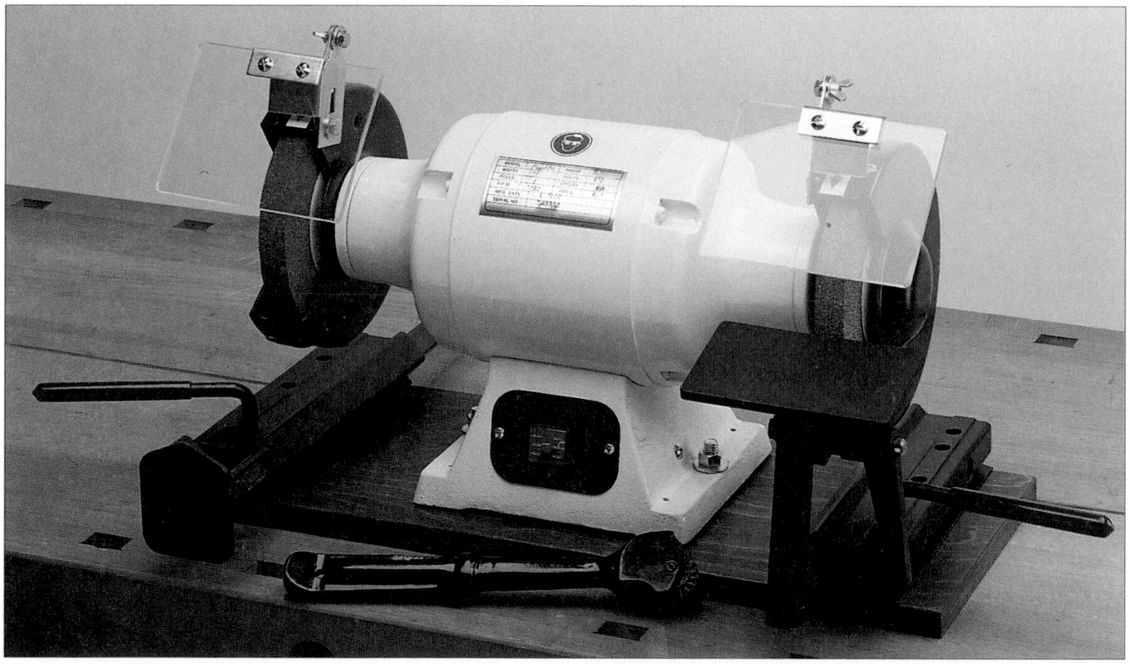

Every woodworking shop should have a bench grinder to keep edge-cutting tools sharp. A slow-speed model will keep the grinding wheels relatively cool. Even if your bench grinder is equipped with guards, as shown here, you should still wear eye protection.

WORKBENCHES

A WORKBENCH SHOULD BE THOUGHT OF AS SIMPLY ANOTHER TOOL, and it is arguably the single most important tool in any woodworking shop. It can also be the most expensive purchase that you are likely to make for a piece of non-machinery woodworking equipment. As a result, many craftsmen postpone this investment in favor of a greater variety of other tools. There's nothing fundamentally wrong with this strategy, but it does delay the important benefits that can be gained by using a good bench.

An early form of workbench, which had four splayed legs supporting a thick plank, was used by the Romans. L-shape holdfasts or pins driven into the top of the workbench were used to hold the work in place. This simple workbench remained in use through medieval times.

By the 17th century, an L-shape cleat made of a block of wood was fastened to the bench and used to support the work, along with a wedge and a peg secured in one of a row of holes in a bench leg. Eventually, a screw replaced the wedge. This system was replaced by a type of vise with wooden screws and horizontal jaws.

The traditional form of the vise was developed in the 18th century, where a vise with a vertical jaw was used in Britain. In Continental Europe, workbenches were also built with an L-shape vise, and it was the Germans who brought the workbench to its current sophisticated level of development. (For more information on workbench vises, see pages 234–237.)

One unique feature on this workbench is the slots along the edge of the bench to store the tools that you most often use such as chisels and a hand saw.

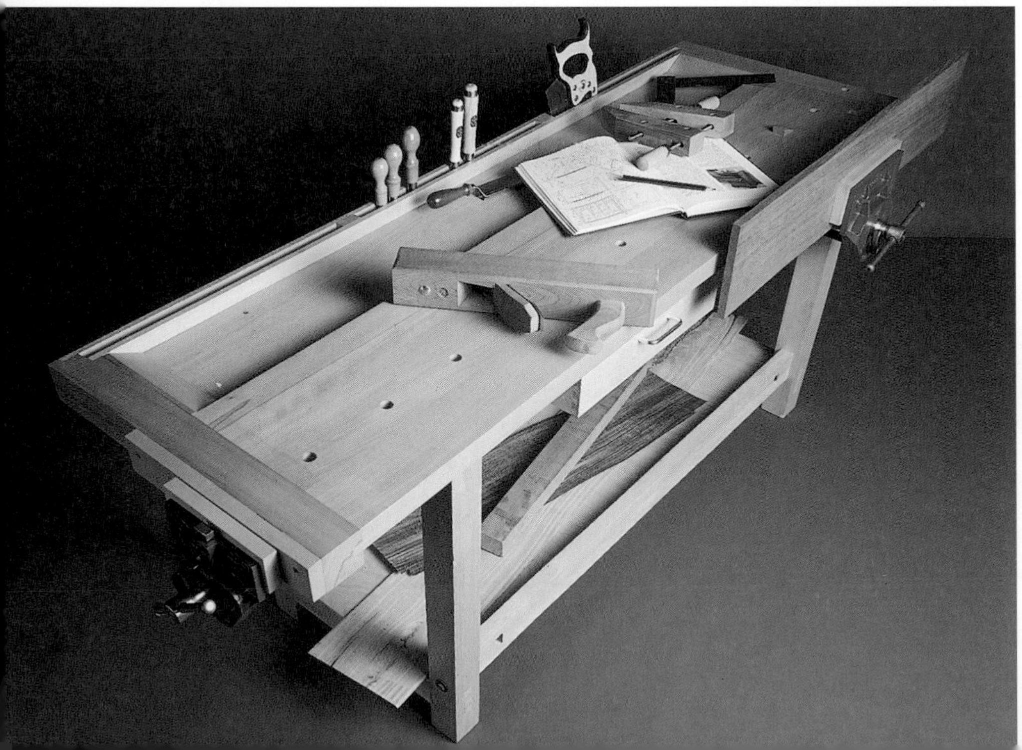

Manufactured workbenches

Today, a manufactured, fully equipped workbench is known worldwide as a European-style bench. Wooden workbenches are made in a number of countries. There are a few sources in Britain, but in the main, the best benches come out of Germany, France, and Sweden, although Zimbabwe—with its English craftsmanship tradition—produces some excellent European-style benches made of superior, unique African hardwoods. The German and French benches typically use European red beech, an excellent wood for constructing benches because of its stability and weight. The Swedish production uses mostly pine and birch, because that is what is available economically in Sweden. The bench top is normally at least 2 inches (50 mm) thick, so as to hold up to hammering and other hard knocks.

Some workbenches have L-shape vises on the front side, and others have full-width vises on the end. Some benches are fitted with English-style, cast-iron, quick-release vises, and others use single- or double-threaded rods running into castings to provide a clamping function. Some benches have drawers, but most do not (for reasons

WHAT YOU SHOULD LOOK FOR

A first principle in deciding what type of a bench to add to your shop is that its top should be made of wood timbers and that it should be as big and as heavy as can fit in your shop and as your budget can afford. (This is a lifetime investment, so extra funds paid out at this time will continue to have a value for many decades.) A good bench should have good, strong vises already fitted to it, or other arrangements for surface clamping; but other things being equal, this is one of those cases in which bigger is simply better. A heavy bench is better than a lighter one, and a larger one is better than a smaller one. Beyond size and a reasonably flat top, other considerations are whether or not the frame of the bench contains some type of storage, in the shape of cabinets and drawers or shelves.

BEST

The best workbench will have a flat worktop and steady frame supporting it, and it will be very long and heavy.

GOOD

A good workbench will be heavy enough and can provide storage space underneath to keep hand tools readily available.

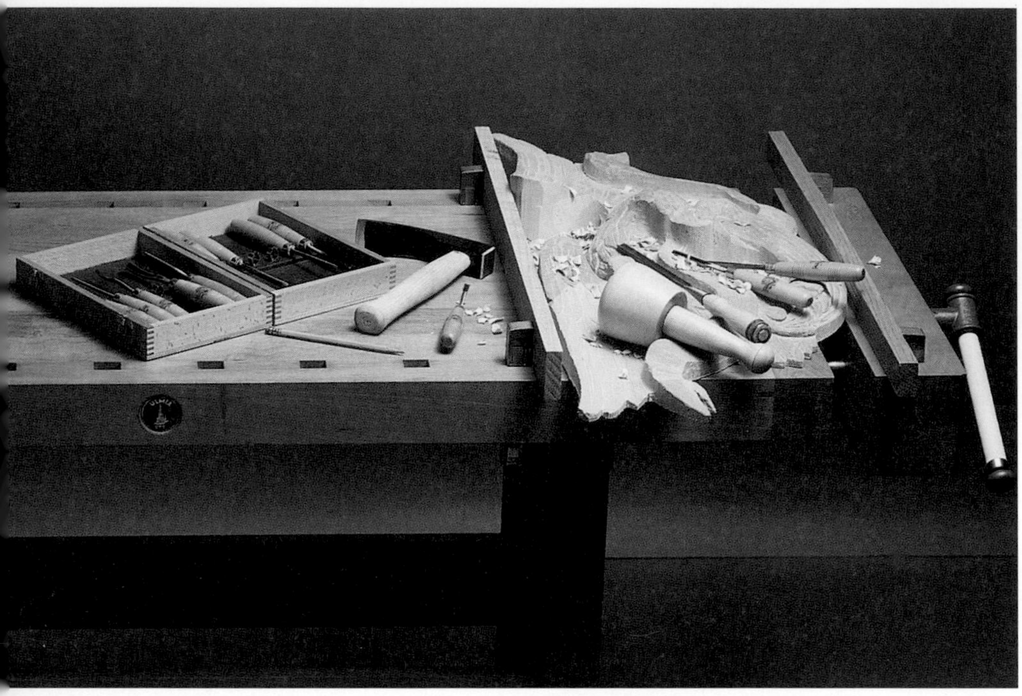

The woodworker's vise can be seen on this workbench, which is being used by a woodcarver. A pair of wooden strips supported by bench dogs are being used to secure the workpiece in place.

of cost). There is no "right" or "wrong" to any of these features—just personal preference and local tradition. You are best guided by your own personal tastes and requirements.

Homemade workbenches

Many craftsmen prefer to build their own workbenches, of course; and there are many sources of published designs, including woodworking books and mail-order firms. One bonus of building your own workbench is that you can customize it to fit the space available in your workshop and to suit your individual needs. If you do decide to go this route, you should try to use thick hardwoods for the top. Hard maple, red beech, and oak are all good choices. The legs and bridging stretchers can be of any material, but the fittings should be bolted or wedged together and, therefore, able to be retightened from time to time.

You should add vises to the edges of the bench and holes in the top for bench dogs and holdfasts. You can also install a tool tray along the side of the bench, or a shelf or drawers within the framework to suit your style of work.

You should bear in mind, however, that building a good workbench is a substantial project, and once you pay for all the wood and hardware—not to mention the time necessary for building it—you may not save anything over purchasing a workbench made by a manufacturer. The most reliable supplier for good-quality ready-made models is typically a specialist mail order firm.

SHOOTING BOARDS AND BENCH HOOKS

There are simple homemade jigs that can aid the woodworker when working at the workbench, including shooting boards and bench hooks. The shooting board is used to hold work while it is being hand planed to trim an edge. It consists of a wide board with a shorter board attached on top to create a rabbet of about 3 inches (75 mm). The lower edge of the rabbet side of this board is undercut to create a groove to allow the accumulation of sawdust. A length of wood called a stop is attached to the top of the short board at one end. To use a shooting board, the work is placed on top of the short board, pushed against the stop, and aligned with the rabbet end. The plane is laid on its side to make passes along the edge of the work. Other versions of the shooting board are designed to trim splayed or mitered pieces.

The bench hook is basically a homemade workbench accessory made of a board of hardwood, with a rectangular block of wood attached on each end, but on the opposite side of the board. By hooking one of the blocks on the edge of the workbench or in a vise, you can use the other block to hold the work in place. The bench hook may be shorter than the work to avoid damaging the surface of the workbench.

You will need to purchase only one workbench—and it should last you a lifetime. Before choosing a model, make sure you have enough space for it to fit into your workshop and for you to move comfortably around it.

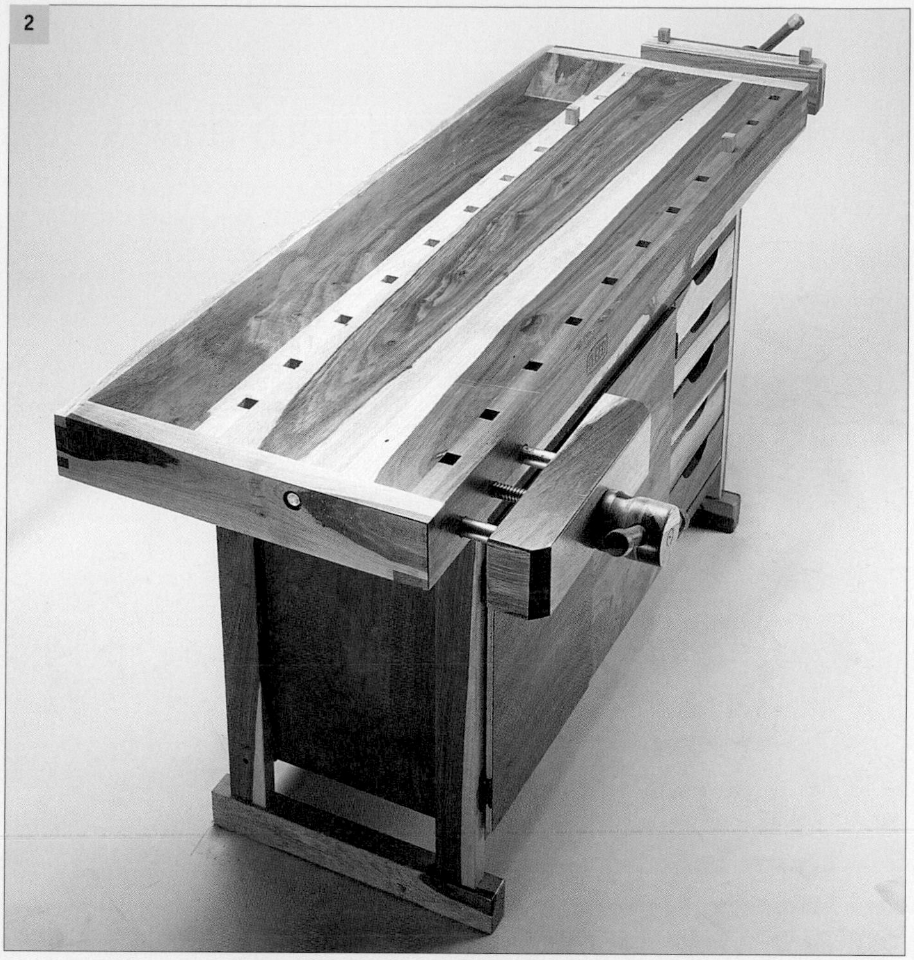
2

1

3

1 Small shop workbench

Made of teak and with one tail vise, this small workbench is suitable for the occasional woodworker. The double row of dog holes allows for maximum clamping flexibility.

2 Large cabinet workbench

This medium-size workbench has drawers and a cabinet for ample storage of tools. The top is large enough for real cabinet work, and the vises are well constructed. Because it is made of teak, it is much heavier than other comparable benches.

3 Traditional European-style workbench

This workbench is made of brown muninga, an African hardwood, which is as strong as beech and is also stable and resistant to splitting. The bench top is set on a traditional European bench leg and stretcher set.

VISES, BENCH DOGS, AND HOLD-DOWNS

THE KEY FEATURE OF MOST WORKBENCHES IS THE PROVISION for built-in vises, whose jaws are flush with the worktop. Many vises are made of hardwood, matching that of the bench. The one on the front of the bench has as its main purpose the holding of long boards against the apron, to be steadied at the other end of the bench by a hand clamp so that there is stability for planing and finishing edges.

The tail-end vise is, for right-handed workers, on the right side of the bench, at the front. The moving jaw has a horizontal L-shape, forming two clamping surfaces, one at the end of the bench, the other partway along the front apron. Its most effective use is in conjunction with bench dogs to hold boards flat for surface treatment.

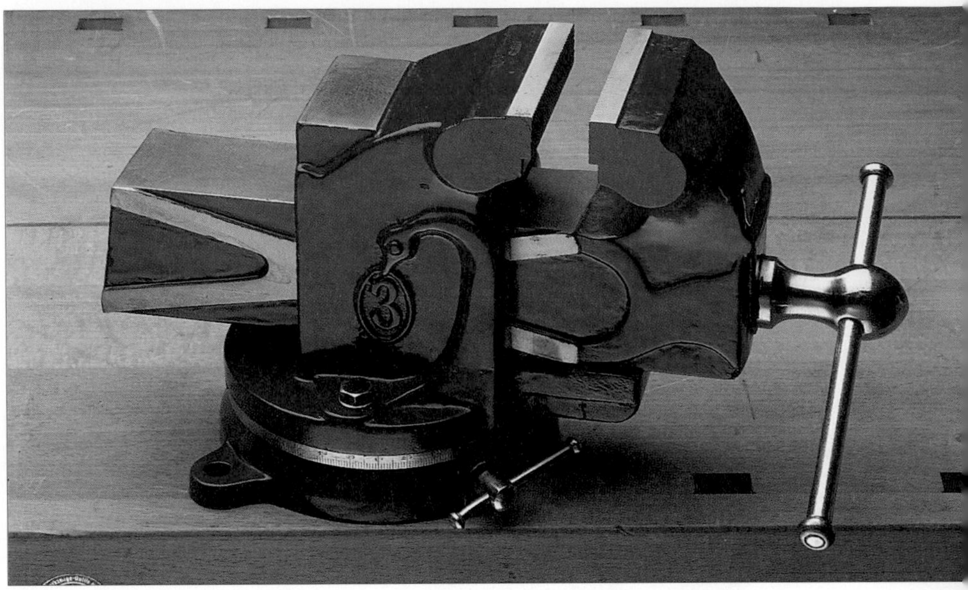

Both types of vises can be bought separately to install on a homemade workbench. They are bolted to the underside of the bench, using spacers if necessary to keep the jaws flush with the worktop. The rear, fixed jaws can be recessed into the worktop. You should position them over—or as near as possible to—the legs of the workbench, so that there is maximum stability when a vise is holding work that will be receiving blows from a mallet.

Sensible dimensions are 7–10 inches (178–255 mm) for the jaw width, 2–4 inches (50–100 mm) for the jaw depth, and 8–15 inches (200–380 mm) for the open capacity. Bear in mind that these add-on vises will probably be made of cast iron instead of hardwood, so the open capacity should allow for protective wooden inserts that will also take holes for bench dogs. Look for vises with holes drilled and countersunk in both jaws so that wooden plates may be permanently fitted.

Such vises have a central tightening screw, which is operated by a T-bar, sometimes with a quick-release mechanism, and steel guide bars on either side. The wider the jaw width beyond the guide bars, the more useful the tool is for holding work vertically, down to the floor, where the work can be steadied at ground level by a hold-down set into the bench leg.

Smaller vises, deriving from mechanics' and machinists' tools, are designed to be screwed, bolted, or clamped to a worktop. One design popular with woodcarvers can rotate on its base and has deep, swiveling jaw faces to hold oddly shaped workpieces. These smaller vises may be

Even in a woodworker's shop a machinist's vise is useful for holding metal pieces and to provide an anvil surface for striking metal.

This jeweler's pedestal vise (far left), which was probably made in the 19th century, functions much in the same way as a woodworker's vise. This model has a swivel base and was used for light-duty clamping.

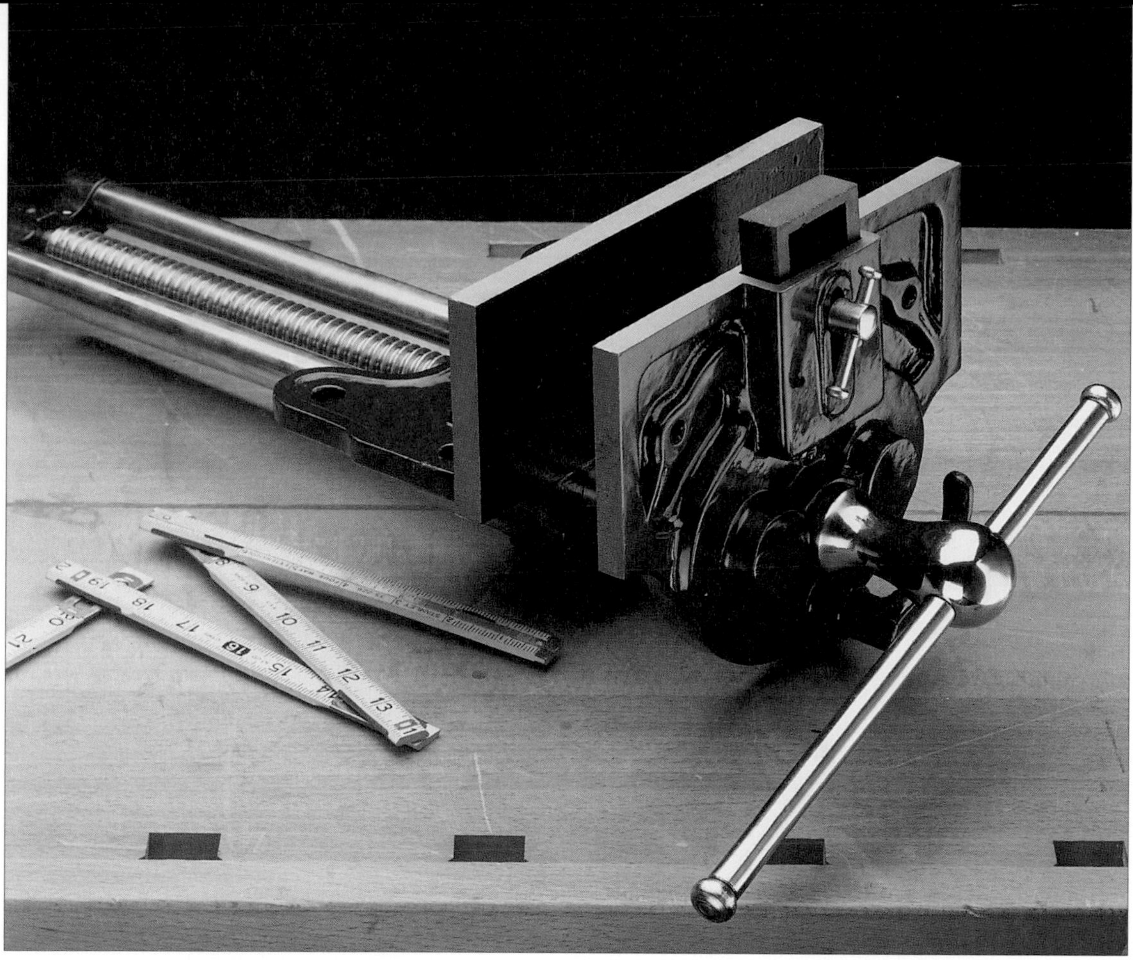

A cast-iron woodworker's bench vise with a quick-release mechanism is the best investment for a workbench, especially for a homemade model.

mounted on their own suitably sized, wooden T-plates, which can be quickly clamped into the bench's main vise when needed.

Bench dogs and hold-downs

Other workbench devices for holding work include bench dogs, which are simply posts of metal or wood—sometimes square, usually round—placed in holes evenly spaced along the edge of the bench. With the workpiece placed firmly against the appropriate dog, the tail-end vise, with its own dogs in position, can be tightened to hold the work.

Proprietary dogs may have spring clips set in the shanks or leaf springs to secure them in the bench holes. They are usually 4½ inches (115 mm) long—shorter ones are called puppies. Homemade pegs serve perfectly well; plane a flat surface on one side so that they can be wedged into position. Make them of hardwood for strength; to protect fine work, glue on faceplates of cork.

The hold-down (see page 236) is essentially a clamping jig to hold work onto the workbench. One version has a shaft that fits into a bench-dog hole with an arched arm to hold down the work. Another model hooks onto a mounting bolt and uses a T-bar to adjust the pressure put on the work. Mounting bolts can be installed anywhere on the bench.

Bench dogs are often used and sold in pairs. Among the variety here are two pairs of brass bench dogs and two pairs made of laminated wood.

A workbench should have a minimum of one woodworker's vise, but a second vise is preferrable. You should invest in a good one for it to last a lifetime. Other types of vises can be an added bonus for holding smaller workpieces, especially if you do delicate work. Bench dogs and hold-downs are always useful to have on hand. Several pairs of bench dogs are advisable, both square types and round ones. One or two hold-downs should be sufficient in most workshops.

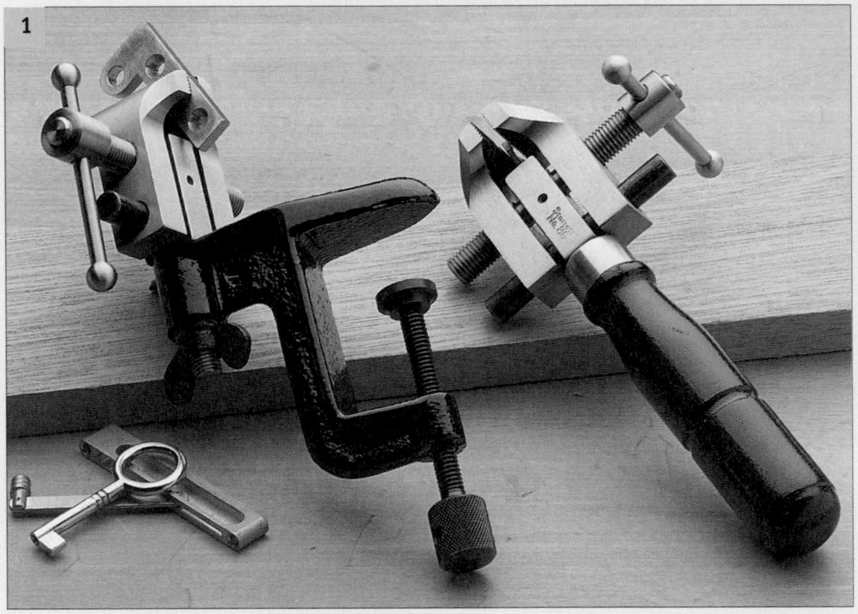

1 Combination hand vise
Indispensable for holding all types of small parts securely while you work on them, this hand vise can be fitted on a handle to be hand held or on a clamplike mechanism to secure it to a work surface. The clamp spindle is threaded into both jaws, allowing them to be opened and closed quickly.

2 Clamp-on vise and machinist's vises
The clamp-on vise (left) is ideal for the occasional woodworker. It clamps to a worktable, but also has predrilled holes for permanent mounting. The miniature machinist's vises are ideal for small-scale work; the V grooves will hold round stock.

3 Hold-downs and bench dogs
The hold-downs (top) wedge firmly into holes drilled into the benchtop. To give yourself the ability to use them in a variety of places, drill several holes. The bench dogs (bottom) are used together with a bench vise. Drill a hole on top of the vise and several others in line with the first to use these dogs.

4 Surface-mounted bench stop
A simple large thumbscrew allows you to open this bench stop into a raised position to hold work against it, then close it back flush with the surface when finished. You'll need to make a mortise in the bench to accept the stop.

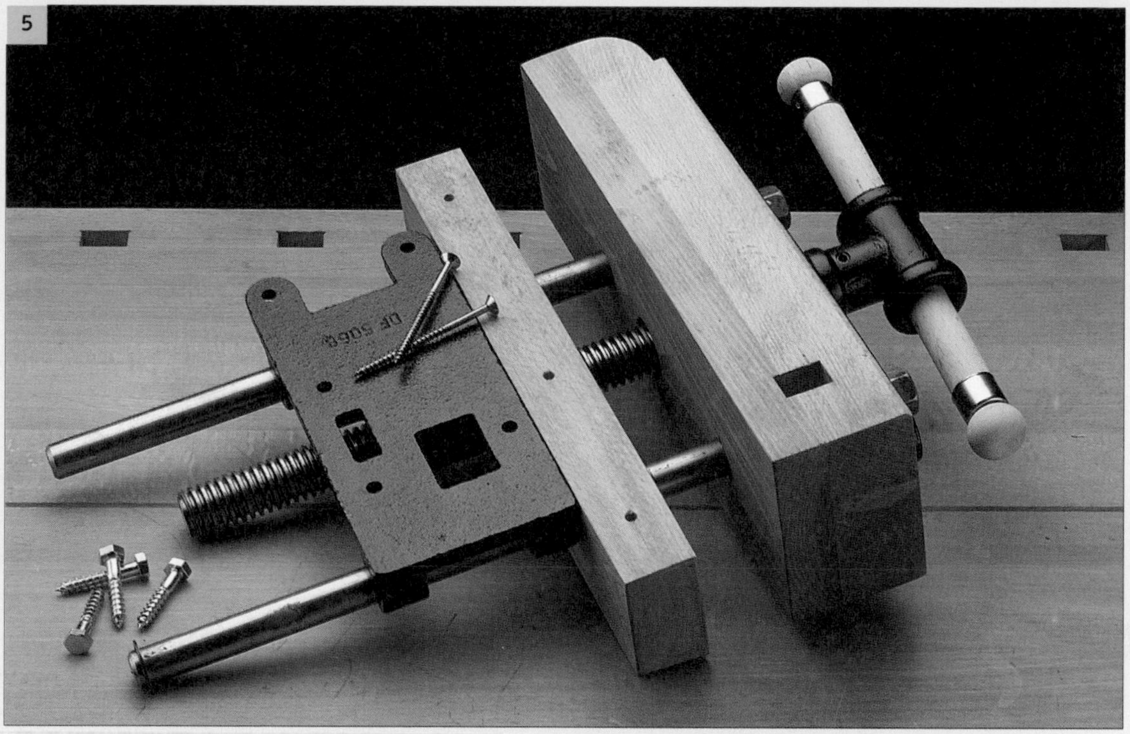

5 Preassembled European bench vise

Most European workbench vises are supplied as only the hardware, with the woodworker supplying the wooden parts; however, this model has been completely supplied and assembled by the manufacturer. It comes with a wood face and beech handle, and it can be easily attached to the front of the workbench.

6 Square and round bench dogs

The steel square bench dogs (left) are best for holding squared work, while the round aluminum bench dogs are ideal for holding unusually shaped stock. Both types of bench dogs are fitted with steel springs.

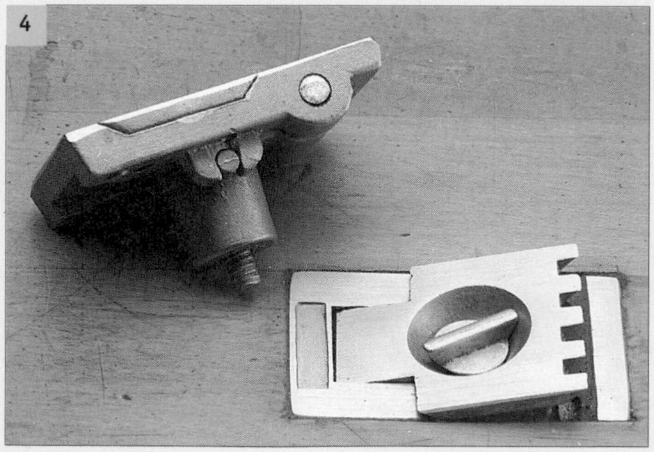

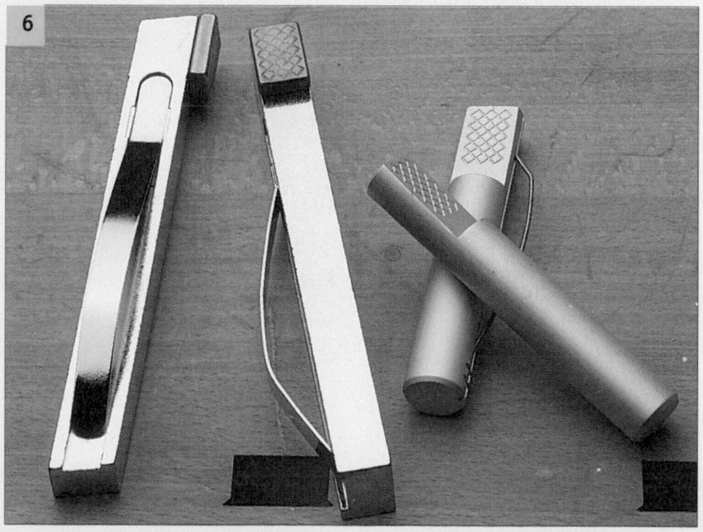

WORKSHOP SAFETY

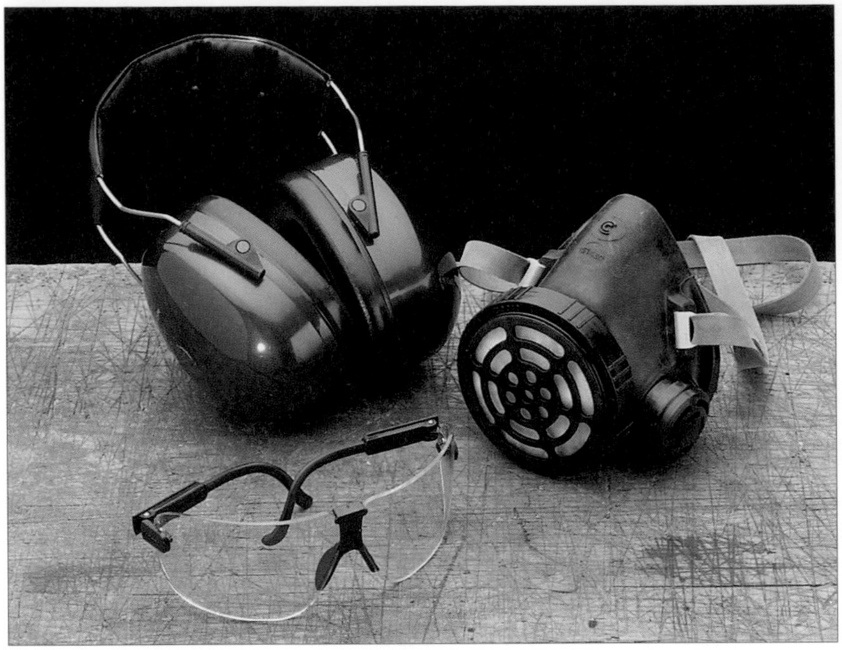

There are many activities in a woodworking shop that call for some form of hearing, eye, and lung protectors. These should always be readily available—and used whenever necessary.

WORKSHOP SAFETY DEPENDS ON YOUR OWN COMMON SENSE AND judgment. A workshop is filled with sharp, loud, powerful, and flammable objects. A saw blade rotating at 3,500 rpm, for example, can send 1,000 teeth through your finger before you can react. However, woodworking doesn't have to be dangerous, as long as you follow practical working habits and operating procedures, take the time to maintain your tools, and practice fire prevention and personal safety. Whenever you are in the workshop, always follow these rules:

Working habits

- Think about safety with each move you make. Always know where your hands are at all times, and keep them away from all blades and cutters.
- To anticipate any problems and take precautions, rehearse the project completely before starting it. Assemble and prepare all the tools and materials.
- Provide adequate support for large projects such as cutting long stock. Ask an assistant to support the stock, or use a roller stand.
- Use clamps whenever possible so that your hands are free for controlling your tools.
- Provide plenty of lighting for your work. Poor lighting and shadows can increase fatigue.
- Before cutting your stock, look for loose knots; check old wood for nails or screws. Make sure that the stock is straight. Don't saw wet wood.
- Keep ample working room around you at all times. Cramped conditions can lead to accidents.
- Work on a level floor at a comfortable height, and keep your balance all the way through a cut.
- Don't overreach. You can lose your balance and lose some control over the tool. Don't draw any sharp-edge tool toward your body unless absolutely necessary. Never reach over the cutter on a tool.
- Avoid awkward procedures. Don't get your hands into positions where they can slip and be injured.
- Avoid potentially dangerous operations that you don't feel at ease performing.
- No matter how long you've used power tools, always use them with caution. Overconfidence can lead to accidents.
- Never operate power tools when taking medication or if you have had any alcohol.
- Don't rush a job. Work at a comfortable pace; take your time. Never work if you are upset or agitated.
- Don't become distracted or hold conversations while working. Keep children, visitors, and pets out of the work area—distractions lead to accidents.
- Keep your concentration on the work at hand. Don't daydream—watch out for this when doing repetitive, boring tasks. You should always take a break if you start to feel tired or fatigued.

- Avoid working where you can't be heard if you need to call for help.
- Never stand on a wet surface when using a power tool—a short circuit can lead to an electric shock.
- Don't smoke in the shop.

Operating procedures

- Always read and follow the manual or instructions that come with a tool.
- Use the right tool for the job; never force a tool to work beyond its capacity or your ability.
- Never leave a power tool running—turn it off. Keep tools unplugged when not in use. Unplug a tool before making adjustments or changing blades, cutters, or bits.
- Don't remove guards or other safety devices that come with a tool, but consider installing other safety devices that improve on the ones supplied.
- Use push sticks and featherboards to guide the work past blades and other moving parts. This is especially true when working with small pieces.
- Don't feed stock into any type of cutter before it reaches full speed.
- Don't take too deep a cut or force work into the cutter head or blade. If the cut is not smooth and doesn't "feel" right, something is wrong.
- You should not let go of the stock until it is past the cutter or blade.
- At the first sign of an unusual noise or vibration—a sign of a problem—quickly turn off the machine.
- Do not leave items not necessary for the operation of a tool on its table.
- When you finish making a cut, turn off the tool and let the cutter come to a full stop naturally if the machine has no brake; never slow down or stop a cutter with a piece of wood.
- Never touch a moving cutter. If a cutter stalls, turn off and unplug the tool before freeing the cutter.
- When using a power tool, always complete the operation you are working on and switch off the tool before responding to any interruption.
- Before plugging in a tool, make sure the power switch is off, tighten all of its clamps, knobs, nuts, and levers, and make sure its cutters are secure.
- Make sure cords and outlets are grounded and outlets have ground-fault circuit interrupters (GFCIs). If there is a power leakage, a GFCI stops the power immediately—fast enough to prevent a fatal shock.
- If you use an extension cord, make sure it is a heavy-duty one that is rated to handle more current than required by the tool.
- Keep cords away from cutting edges.
- Never use the power cord on a tool to carry it or to pull out its plug.
- Never use power tools in damp conditions.

Maintenance and repair

- Sharpen or replace any dull or damaged cutters as soon as possible. Never use cutters or blades that are cracked. Throw them away immediately. If there is more than one cutter on a tool, such as a jointer, change all the cutters at the same time.
- Disconnect the power before changing blades or cutters, making mechanical adjustments, or doing any maintenance—make sure the switch is off.
- Replace frayed or cracked cords and plugs. Never try to fix a cord with electrical tape.
- Before starting a tool, make sure all cutters or blades are properly tightened and all fittings and adjustments are locked in place. Keep all mating surfaces (such as collets and blade collars) clean and free of chips, sawdust, and resin.

- Remove adjusting keys and wrenches from a tool before turning on the power.
- Test the tool before using it.

Fire prevention

Good housekeeping is an important part of safety. Sawdust and wood shavings can accumulate quickly, causing a potential fire hazard—especially when combined with hot filings from a bench grinder. Fine sawdust drifting in the air can create an explosive atmosphere—and the dust can damage your lungs.

Clean up wood shavings and sawdust often. The essential shop equipment for this task is a wet-dry vacuum. It comes with a variety of hoses and can be attached to power tools to clear away shavings and sawdust as they are created. A mobile dust extractor, which can also be attached to some power tools, filters dust from the air and collects it into a sack.

Another potential cause of fire is the chemicals found in a workshop. Keep flammable substances in a cool, dry, fire-resistant area, out of reach of children. You should never store leftovers in your home; buy only the smallest amount necessary for the job. Extinguish gas pilot lights before using flammable substances indoors; do not smoke. The fumes—and the liquid—can ignite.

When disposing of rags and residue, allow natural oil-base finishing products to dry in an open can outdoors, away from people, animals, and flames—oil-base products can ignite if exposed to air and then confined. Once they are dry, take them to a hazardous-waste disposal area.

In case a fire does occur, install a smoke detector, and keep a fire extinguisher and fire blanket within easy reach, near an exit. A multipurpose fire extinguisher rated A-B-C is effective against most common fires in homes. Check the pressure gauge monthly; if it is low, recharge or replace the extinguisher.

Learn how to use an extinguisher before you need to use it. Aim the nozzle at the base of the fire (not the top) and pull the pin or release mechanism. Squeeze the handle and spray the contents from side to side until the flames are out. Don't allow the fire to come between you and an exit—if the fire gets out of control, you may need to leave quickly.

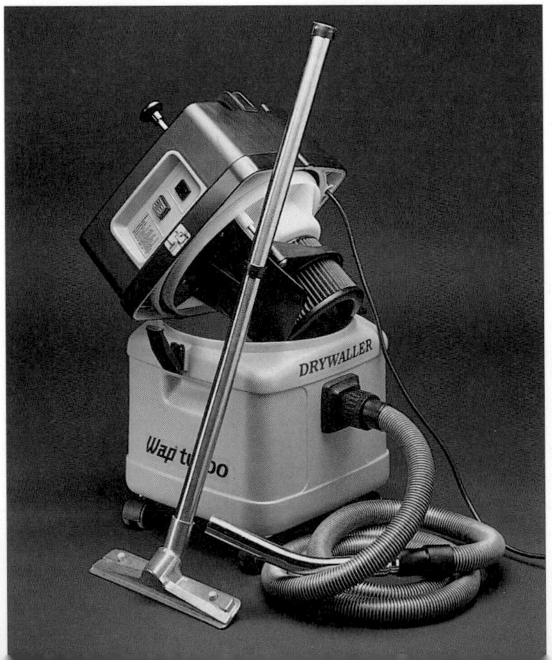

A shop vacuum is a must for most workshops. Look for one built for both wet and dry use. This model includes a hose, metal wands, and a floor-cleaning nozzle, and it has an accessory outlet.

Personal safety

Always be sensible in wearing safety equipment. It can save you from injury. Store items within easy reach to encourage you to use them. Sawing, chiseling, filing, grinding, and any other work that involves dust, projectiles, or splashes require eye protection. Safety glasses give general protection, but goggles are enclosed on the sides for better protection and can be worn over prescription glasses. For full protection, use a face shield.

Your hearing can be damaged by long-term exposure to loud noise. Hearing protectors that reduce but don't eliminate noise should be worn whenever you operate noisy machinery. Earmuffs are easier to take off and put on than earplugs and harder to misplace. Look for a noise-reduction rating (NRR) of at least 25.

A simple face mask labeled "NIOSH-approved" (approved by the National Institute for Occupational Safety and Health), will keep dust, non-toxic fumes, and paint spray from entering your lungs. A professional dual-cartridge respirator offers full protection against more toxic solvents, paints, adhesives, and dusts. Choose one that takes changeable color-coded cartridges to filter out specific toxic dusts and fumes.

Make sure your shop is well ventilated. When working with chemicals, open doors and windows and use a fan to move fumes away from you. Children, pregnant women, the elderly, and pets are susceptible to toxic hazards. You should always keep them away from your work.

Never wear loose clothing (including ties) or jewelry when using power tools; roll up long sleeves and keep long hair tied back. These can catch and draw you toward a rotating cutter. Wear sturdy shoes or boots with nonslip soles. Gloves are okay for handling lumber but not when using power tools. You lose the "feel" of what you are doing. When working with solvent-base products, wear chemical-resistant rubber gloves made of butyl or neoprene.

Store a standard, well-equipped first aid kit in your shop where it is easy to see and reach. Keep a bottle of eyewash solution (normally used for contact lenses) on hand to rinse out any chemical that gets into your eyes. If a chemical irritates your skin, wash it off with water. Seek prompt medical attention for a serious injury. Post an up-to-date list of emergency telephone numbers by the telephone.

You should always look for safety equipment that is rated suitable for the type of work you intend to do. For example, a simple disposable mask will not provide adequate protection for your lungs against fumes from toxic solvents. High-quality safety equipment should be available at a reliable home center.

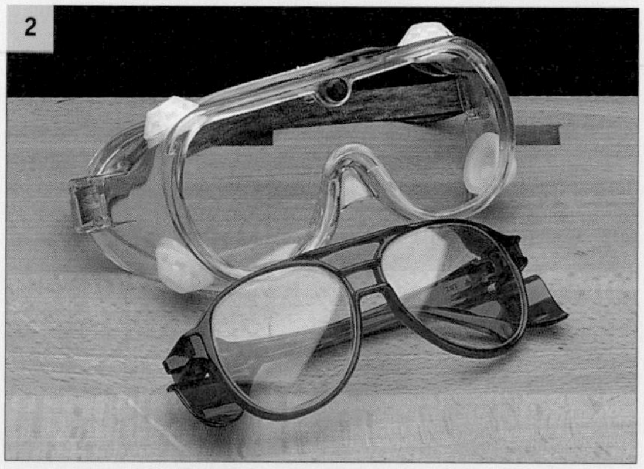

1 Peltor hearing protectors
The Peltor protectors use a dual shell design to provide great high- and low-frequency noise reduction, and they are also comfortable to wear. The headband design fits over your head; the back-band model fits behind your neck and could be worn with a hard hat.

2 Protective goggles and glasses
The protective goggles (top) have indirect ventilating louvers to reduce fogging and improve eye protection against chemical splashes and dust. The non-distorting safety glasses (bottom) have side guards fitted onto the ear pieces for extra protection.

3 Industrial respirator
This respirator comes with exchangeable cartridges and protects against dusts, mists, and vapors from sprays, paints, lacquers, and varnishes. The wide inner seal of the silicone face piece provides a comfortable fit.

MICROPEDIA

There are thousands of tools, and many of these are designed for other trades such as metalworking. Some of these tools, along with specialized woodworking tools, are described here.

Adze A sculptor's tool for shaping large pieces of wood, the adze has a gouge-shape blade held at a right angle to the handle. It has a long handle and looks similar to the ax.

Allen wrench The trade name for hex key (see Hex key).

Anvil Primarily a tool to help shape metal, the anvil is available in a variety of weights and shapes. The most common style is flat on top with a horn end protruding from one side. A small bench anvil can be useful in a woodworking shop for a number of odd jobs such as straightening nails or as a weight on top of a board for a small glue job.

Arkansas stone A natural sharpening stone for maintaining a blade's sharp edge, this stone generally comes in four grades—black hard, hard, soft, and Washita.

Articulated ladder Designed to suit a number of situations, this multipurpose ladder has self-locking hinges, which allow four sections to be positioned as a step or straight ladder, scaffolding, or in other arrangements for use in a stairwell.

Auger This hole-boring tool, which is used to make large holes, consists of a shank with an eye or tang on one end and a bit with a cutting edge on the other. The handle is usually fitted to the eye or tang to form a "T." There are dozens of types of augers available, from twist bits to reamer bits, for working in a variety of materials.

Aviation snips With their compound lever mechanism—which provides more control with less effort—aviation snips can easily cut sheet metal. All models can cut straight lines, but some can also cut left- or right-hand curves, or both.

Ax One of the oldest tools used by man, an ax, or axe, has two components—a handle and a blade fitted in line with it. The sharp edge of the blade cuts the wood, and the wedge shape of the blade forces the wood to split. The thickness of the wedge depends on the type of work the ax is intended for, usually for chopping wood or felling trees. In the United States, an ax used with one hand is known as a hatchet; the term "ax" is used for tools used with two hands. In Britain, a hatchet is a specific type of ax that has a little taper behind the cutting edge.

Bench stone Sharpening stone mounted on a workbench for honing the blades of woodworking tools (see Sharpening stones).

Blind nailer This tiny chisel cuts a sliver of wood to hide a nailhead. The nail is hammered in place before the sliver is glued down, back in its original position.

Box wrench A type of fixed wrench, it can fit only one size of nut or bolt because it has a completely enclosed head with a polygonal-shape opening. Standard and metric sizes are available. This type of wrench is stronger than an open-end wrench. Always use one of the correct size to avoid damaging the work.

Branding iron Once it has been heated, the head of a branding iron—which has writing, numbers, or a pattern in relief—is pressed against a wooden object to burn an image or mark into the wood. Originally, the head was attached to a long iron handle and heated over a fire; modern branding irons are heated with electricity.

Carpenter's tool belt A carpenter's tool belt is not technically a tool, but it is a handy garment to wear when working in the workshop. The belt is fitted with loops and pockets for holding tools and other items, keeping them within easy reach.

Carpet knife This knife has a special blade designed to trim carpets. It is especially useful for trimming carpets in tight areas such as around doorjambs. Use the back edge of the blade to push the carpet under baseboard or shoe molding.

Caulking gun A tool for holding tubes of caulk, adhesive, or similar material, this has a trigger handle that, when squeezed, forces a plunger to press against the tube, pushing out the material inside it. The tubes are interchangeable.

Cat's paw A tool for the home renovator, the cat's paw is a pry bar, with one standard head. The second head, however, has a wafer-thin tip that's pefect for precisely and delicately easing apart adjacent surfaces without damaging them.

Chainsaw As its name implies, this portable power saw has a blade in the shape of a chain with cutting teeth. The chain rotates around a steel guide bar as it makes a cut. The saw may run on gas or electricity. This is a powerful tool and can be dangerous in the wrong hands. It should be used only by those confident of their skills and always with care.

Chalk line This tool is basically a case filled with chalk and a reel of line between 50 feet (15 m) and 100 feet (30 m) long. As the line is pulled away from the case, it is covered with chalk. The line is held taut and then snapped against a surface, which leaves behind a chalked line. It is most often used on large surfaces for home renovation and building work. The chalk line often doubles as a plumb bob.

Chasing and repoussé tools These metalworking tools are essentially blunt chisels and punches, which are used to etch decorative designs into sheet metal. A special chasing hammer is designed to drive chasing tools.

Cold chisel Primarily a stone-cutting tool, a cold chisel has an integral handle and blade made of steel. The handle is struck by a hammer to cut a material (the user should always wear eye protection to prevent sparks flying into his or her eyes). You can use it to cut sheet metal, or to remove rivets, bolts, and nails, or to cut away at ceramic tiles adhered to a surface.

Countersink This hand-powered tool is basically a handle attached to a bit, which—like the countersink bit used on a power drill—shapes a screw hole to fit the head of the screw so it will sit flush with the surface of the work.

Dies and diestock These metalworking tools consist of a special wrench, the diestock, which turns a die to cut external threads on screws, bolts, and rods. The die is a small metal disc with a cutting edge in its center; some are adjustable.

Dowel former and pointer For the woodworker this accessory is a handy tool. The pointer can chamfer the ends of a dowel, which can then be forced through the steel die to perfectly size the dowel and add flutes for gluing purposes.

Edge tools A general term that refers to woodworking tools that have a sharpened edge or blade (without teeth) for cutting or shaping. Among this category are chisels and gouges, planes, spokeshaves, drawknives, and adzes.

Electrician's pliers This multipurpose tool is designed to perform several functions necessary for an electrician. The models vary, but they typically measure wire diameter, strip and cut wire, and crimp wire connectors. Some models can also cut machine screws.

Electrician's screwdriver The long shank of this screwdriver can reach into deep recesses in electrical appliances and equipment. The shank is protected with a plastic coating to prevent electrical shock.

Extension ladder Basically two or three straight ladders linked together, the extension ladder can be extended as much as 40 feet (12 m) for outdoor use. Some models have a pulley mechanism to help extend one ladder section above the other. Latches lock into place and support the raised sections.

Flaring tool This metalworking tool comes in two parts to create a flare in the end of a piece of flexible tubing (a type of pipe used in plumbing). A double-bar clamp has indentations to hold tubing of several sizes. A T-bar handle on the second part, when turned, forces a ram into the clamped tubing to flare it.

Float A building tool, the float has a rectangular steel or plastic flexible blade to evenly spread fluid materials such as concrete. A wooden float can be used for most applications, but a magnesium float is best for air-entrained concrete—that is, concrete with tiny bubbles.

Flooring chisel An all-steel chisel with a wide spade-shape blade, this tool is designed to cut along the grain of floorboards, then to pry them up. The blade is thin enough to reach and cut the tongue of tongue-and-groove boards.

Froe A splitting tool with a wedge-shape blade about 6–12 inches (150–305 mm), the froe has a round socket at the end of the blade, which fits around the handle. It is used to split wood lengthwise into shingles, a procedure that is often referred to as riving, cleaving, or rending. After the blade is struck into the wood, the handle is worked back and forth to make the split.

Glass cutter A wheel on this simple tool has a cutting edge to score a line in a piece of glass. The glass is then snapped by pressing down on either side of the scored line. If the section of glass being cut is narrow, a notch in the glass cutter can be used to snap off the thin strip.

Glazier's putty knife The flat chisel blade on this type of knife is intended for removing old window putty; the slotted V-blade is for applying and smoothing down new putty.

Hacking knife The thick blade of this knife can withstand hammering to "hack out" broken glass in a window frame by removing the old putty that holds the glass in place.

Hatchet A type of lightweight ax, the hatchet is used for chopping wood. There are many models available, with different-style blades, and some of these have a hammer head on the opposite side of the blade.

Heat gun By directing a blast of hot air, a heat gun can soften paint so that it can be scraped off or can soften tile adhesive to remove vinyl floor tiles. Start with a low heat setting and increase it as you work.

Hex key A type of wrench, the hex key consists of an L-shape rod with polygonal sides that fits into a recessed setscrew of the same shape. By inserting the short end into the setscrew and turning the key, you'll provide the most torque (turning power). You can use the long end to work in a restricted space. Hex keys are available in several sizes and in sets.

Hole saw This power drill accessory has a cylindrical, cup-shape saw blade with teeth, which is attached to a drill with an arbor. A bit in the arbor centers the saw before the teeth begin to make the cut.

Honing guide A jig that holds the blade of a plane or chisel at a constant angle during the honing process. You can choose one of several angles, depending on the type of blade being honed.

Hose clamp Traditionally used by plumbers around pipes, this clamp consists of a metal strap, which is tightened by adjusting a setscrew. It can also be used by woodworkers to mend a break in a spindle or chair leg.

Jack knife Basically a large pocket knife, the jack knife has a blade that folds into its handle. It is often useful in a woodworker's shop for a variety of small jobs such as marking wood.

Laminate roller Laminates need pressure applied to them to remove air bubbles and ensure good contact between the materials and the adhesives. The laminate roller—basically a smooth rubber or steel roller on a handle—is the suitable tool for this job.

Locking pliers To keep the jaws of these pliers locked in place, a locking mechanism is triggered by squeezing the handles closed. Releasing a lever allows you to open the jaws of the pliers.

Mandrel A cone-shape metal form, this metalworking tool is used to shape metal by bending it around the form. One common model is a ring mandrel, with graduated markings to make rings to specific sizes.

Micrometer Metalworkers work to precise dimensions, and they use a high-precision micrometer to measure outside dimensions on items up to 1 inch (25 mm) wide. The micrometer can measure in thousandths of an inch (hundredths of a millimeter). This tool is sometimes also used by woodworkers.

Miter trimmer The lever action of a long handle operates the blade of this tool, which is designed to cut baseboard and other molding at a mitered angle.

Monkey wrench Nuts and bolts can be turned with the smooth parallel jaws of this tool. It has an adjustable jaw, which is controlled by a worm gear.

Nail puller An embedded nail is difficult to remove with a normal claw hammer. The nail puller has a V-notch, which slips under the nail head and a long handle to provide extra leverage to pull up the nail.

Notched trowel The blade of this rectangular trowel, which is used to apply ceramic tile adhesive, has square notches. They leave ridges in the adhesive to give a better gripping surface for the tiles.

Oilstone A sharpening stone that uses oil as a lubricant (see Sharpening stones).

Open-end wrench The three-sided head of this type of wrench fits around nuts and bolts to turn them. It is not as strong as a box-end wrench, but it is easier to fit around the nut or bolt. These wrenches are sometimes available in sets, with a head on each end of the tool. There may be an overlapping of the sizes to allow you to use one wrench to hold the bolt as you use a second wrench to turn the nut.

Pipe cutter Shaped like a C clamp, the pipe cutter has rotating wheels on its jaws to cut copper or steel pipes. An adjustable jaw is moved by turning a threaded T-bar handle.

Planishing hammer Metalworkers use this two-headed hammer to flatten, shape, and add texture to sheet metal. The heads may have flat faces or a flat and a round face.

Plumb bob Basically a string with a weight at the end, the plumb bob is used to check that an item is straight vertically. (A weighted line will always be vertical.) A chalk line is often also used as a plumb bob.

Pneumatic tools Some tools use pneumatic, or air, pressure to operate, including the pneumatic drill and nailer. These are often used in the construction industry, which generally requires heavy-duty use of a tool.

Pop rivet Metal fasteners known as rivets—consisting of a pair of metal rings, one of which fits into the other—can be inserted into predrilled holes with this tool. The rivets can hold together metal to metal, metal to plastic, metal to heavy-weave fabric, or two or more layers of heavy-weave fabric.

Pruning saw A type of handsaw, the pruning saw is smaller than a panel saw but larger than a keyhole saw. Its teeth are specially shaped for cutting tree branches. On some models the blade can fold into the handle for safe storage.

Pry bar Often used by renovators, the pry bar has a curved blade to fit behind molding or between two sections of an object that are to be separated, while the long handle provides leverage to pry the sections apart.

Putty knife The flexible wide blade on a putty knife is used to apply and smooth wood putty and filler, spackling compound, and other materials. (Similar in appearance, a knife with a rigid blade can be used to scrap away paint, glue, wallpaper, and other materials.)

Ratchet wrench Usually with a boxed, or enclosed end, this wrench has a special mechanism that allows the user to move the handle back and forth without having to completely rotate the tool. It is a faster tool to use, saves on manual labor, and is ideal in tight spaces.

Raising hammer Metalworkers use this hammer to shape bowls, vases, and other objects that have a deep recess. The outer surface of the metal is struck with the tool.

Reamer A tool used for enlarging or smoothing a previously bored hole in any of a number of materials, the reamer has a cone-shape body. A pipe reamer, used by plumbers, has a T-bar handle. Reamer bits are available to use in a power drill.

Reciprocating saw The blade on this power saw moves in a rapid pistonlike motion to make rough cuts in wood, plaster, plastic, metal, and other materials. Several types of blades are available to use with the saw; the best one to use will depend on the work. The saw may operate at a single speed, with two speeds, or with variable speed.

Rod-threading kit There are three parts in this kit, which threads a wooden rod and creates a threaded hole to accept it. It consists of a tap to cut female, or internal, threads to match the male, external, threads made by the threadbox. A bottoming tap finishes off the female section.

Roller stand When working with large machinery, such as the table saw, the roller stand is essential for handling large boards or panels. It consists of a large stand (a pole supported by a base) with a roller above it in a horizontal position. The roller supports the work as it is moved toward the machinery.

Sawhorse Used to support a large workpiece, the sawhorse consists of a horizontal beam supported by a pair of splayed legs on each end. The sawhorse may be made of wood, have wooden components supported by metal brackets, or be made completely of metal. Some metal versions have fold-away legs. By placing a large sheet of plywood across a pair of sawhorses, you can create a temporary work surface.

Sharpening stones These blocks of natural or artificial stones have been dressed, or smoothed. They are used with an oil or water lubricant to sharpen the blades of woodworking tools such as chisels and planes. The majority are rectangular in shape, but other shapes, such as the slip stone (see Slip stone), are available. The stones come in many grades, from coarse to fine. There may be one grit on one side and a different grit on the other side.

Shave hook Removing old paint or varnish from molding or awkwardly shaped objects is made easier with a shave hook. This tool has three components—the handle, the shank, and the blade, which may be one of several shapes, including triangular, teardrop, and combination (for concave and convex surfaces). On some models, the blades are fixed to the handle, and you'll need to buy a set to have all the blades; on other models, the blades are interchangeable.

Slip stone A sharpening stone with an irregular profile, such as wedge or cone shape, this stone is used for honing curved blades such as those on gouges. Unlike other sharpening stones, this stone is moved against the tool, which is held stationary (see Sharpening stones).

Socket wrench Like the box wrench, the socket wrench has a polygonal opening in its head to fit over nuts and bolts to turn them; however, the head is much deeper, hence it is referred to as a "socket." The sockets are available in different sizes, and sometimes interchangeable heads can be used on the same handle. Some of these wrenches are ratchet driven—they have a mechanism that allows them to be turned back and forth instead of in one continuous direction.

Soldering gun Solder is melted onto metal pieces to bond them together. Solder is also used for joining stained glass. One method of melting the solder is to use a soldering gun, an electrically powered, pistol-shape tool that sends heat to a small tip when a trigger is pressed. Releasing the trigger deactivates the gun.

Soldering iron Like the soldering gun (see above), the soldering iron is used to melt solder; however, it does not have a trigger to control the heating of the tip. Both corded and battery-powered models are available. A smaller version, the soldering pencil, can be used for soldering electronic circuits and other delicate projects.

Sonic measurer An ultrasonic pulse is aimed at a flat surface up to 250 feet (76 m) away and, on its return, provides a measurement of distance.

Spatula A thin metal tool consisting of a shaft with a small blade, which can be one of several shapes. The blade is used for wax modeling, but spatulas are tremendously useful for woodworkers when it comes to delicate gluing and filling problems.

Strap wrench A claw at the end of the handle of this traditional plumbing tool holds a canvas webbing, or strap, which can be wrapped around cylindrical shapes, such as pipes, to turn them without damaging the work surface. To use this wrench, loop the strap around the work and back into the claw; with the claw pointing down, turn the wrench in the direction of the loose end of the strap.

Strop Some woodworkers pass a blade over a strop as a final finishing process to honing. The strop is a traditionally a block with strips of leather adhered to it; some versions also include a piece of slate. Strop paste—a fine abrasive paste—is used with the strop.

Tap Threaded holes can be made or restored in metal to accept threaded fasteners by using a thread-cutting tap, a type of bit that fits into a tap wrench, which has a T-bar shape handle to turn the bit.

Tile cutter Designed to cut ceramic tiles, this tool has a platform with a fence, against which the tile is rested. A handle with a cutting wheel is slid across the tile to score a cutting line; to make a clean break, the handle is then pressed down onto the tile to apply even pressure along both sides of the cutting line.

Tile nippers Looking very much like a pair of pincers or pliers, tile nippers have a cutting end to chip and trim contours and other irregular shapes in ceramic tiles.

Tin snips The scissorlike tin snips are designed for cutting lightweight sheet metal. The shape of the head determines the type of cut. A standard head makes straight cuts, a duckbill head makes curves, and a bullnose head makes notches in heavy stock.

Toggle clamp A mounting base allows this clamp to be attached to a bench or board to act as a quick-release hold-down. It comes in a vertical, horizontal, and straight-line design and is used in conjunction with other toggle clamps for repetitive template poistioning, production gluing operations, and holding stock on jigs.

Trowel The blade on this masonry tool comes in a variety of shapes for specialized tasks. In general, the tool is used for spreading mortar or similar material.

Tweezers Basically a pair of blades joined at one end, tweezers come in a variety of shapes and are ideal in the woodworker's shop for holding small parts and removing wood splinters.

Utility knife Often referred to as a mat knife or Stanley knife, this knife uses disposable blades for general-purpose jobs. Replacement blades are often stored inside the handle.

Vacuum clamp bed This device is designed to hold a workpiece securely to the workbench without using clamps or other objects that can interfere with the work, especially when using a router or when hand planing or sanding. A regular household vacuum cleaner or shop vac is attached to a pad, and the air suction it provides holds the pad and work in place.

Veneer roller A smaller version of the laminate roller, the smooth rubber or steel roller head presses the veneer in place, squeezing out any air bubbles and improving the bond between the veneer and the surface it is being attached to.

Waterstone A type of sharpening stone that uses water as a lubricant during the honing process (see Sharpening stones).

Winding sticks A pair of wooden boards, or sticks, that have been chamfered at the top edge, are used to determine if a board is flat or "winding," with an uneven surface. The top edge of the rear stick can be painted a light color to make it easier to see. The sticks are placed parallel to each other but at opposite ends of the boards. By looking along the top edge of the front stick, or gaffer, you should be able to see the top edge of the rear stick. If the board is flat, then the two edges will be parallel.

Wire brush A wire brush shaped similarly to a dustpan brush is ideal for scraping away caked-on oil and other debris on machinery parts, cleaning bolt and screw threads, and removing paint and rust from metal surfaces. The best ones have at least three rows of bristles and an offset handle.

Wire stripper Electricians use wire strippers, which—like a pair of pliers—have two handles and a pair of jaws to remove insulation from the end of a wire. More advanced models can also be used to cut wire and have sized holes to strip wires of specific dimensions.

Woodburning iron This is used to create designs in wood. An electrical element heats the tip of this tool, which darkens the color of the wood. The tool has interchangeable tips; some models have a rheostat to adjust the temperature of the tool.

GLOSSARY

Bevel The angle created where two surfaces meet, but not at a right angle.

Burr The remaining extremely thin strip of curved metal left on the edge of a blade after it has been sharpened. The burr is then polished off.

Calibrations Markings made at set graduations to be used for measuring.

Chamfer The angle created when two surfaces on a board meet at a 45-degree angle.

Chattering The noise created by vibration when using a tool on a workpiece. This is a sign that the tool, especially a large power tool such as a table saw, is being used incorrectly.

Collet Made of two or more sections, the tapered sleeve on a tool for holding the shank of a bit or other cutter.

Countersink To make a screw hole wider at the top to accept a screw head, so the screw sits flush or below the work surface.

Dado A rectangular groove, into which other work is inserted to form a joint.

Dovetail A flared end, designed to fit into a similar-shape recess, often used in a set to form a dovetail joint.

Feed The careful movement of the workpiece toward a cutter or blade.

Fence An adjustable guide used in conjunction with a tool to control the movement of the workpiece.

Ferrule A metal collar found on the end of a wooden handle into which a metal tang enters. The ferrule helps prevent the end of the wood from splitting.

Hardwood Wood that comes from broad-leaf, usually deciduous, trees such as ash, beech, and oak. This type of wood is typically hard to work; however, balsa, classified as a hardwood, is a soft, lightweight material.

Honing The process of sharpening the blade of a chisel, plane, or other cutter by using an abrasive stone.

Jig Either a homemade or manufactured device to hold a tool in the same position for repetitive operations or to cut numerous workpieces to the same size.

Kerf The cut made by a saw. Because saw teeth are set at an angle, the kerf will be wider than the blade.

Kickback The violent motion that occurs when the blade or cutter on a power tool throws the work backward, toward the woodworker, or when a jammed blade or cutter causes the tool to jump backward.

Knurled Describing the surface of a handle or knob that has been impressed with a series of linear indentations to improve the user's grip as the item is turned.

Miter The joint created when the ends of the two workpieces are cut at the same beveled angle, often—but not always—at 45 degrees.

Mortise A rectangular hole cut into a workpiece to accept a matching tenon.

Rabbet A step-shape recess along the edge of the workpiece.

Setscrew A completely cylindrical screw without a flare head; it sits below the surface of the work.

Softwood Wood from coniferous trees, including pine and cedar. Although most types are naturally soft and easy to work, there are some hard types such as yew.

Tenon A projecting rectangular tongue, which often fits into a matching mortise to form a joint.

Throat The distance between the jaw, head, or blade of a tool and its frame.

Torque A turning or twisting force.

Worm gear A threaded cylinder that moves along a rack of teeth when turned with the fingers. It is used to move a part of the tool.

DIRECTORY OF SOURCES

Listed here are companies that supply high-quality woodworking tools and related materials.

Garrett Wade Company
161 6th Avenue
New York, NY 10013
USA
1 (800) 221–2942
1 (800) 566–9525 (fax)
www.garrettwade.com

Advanced Machinery
PO Box 312
New Castle, DE 19720
USA
1 (800) 220–4264

Albert Constantine & Son
2050 Eastchester Road
Bronx, NY 10461
USA
1 (800) 223–8087
1 (800) 253–9663 (fax)
www.constantines.com

Axminster Power Tool Center
Chard Street
Axminster
Devon EX13 5DZ
England
44 (800) 371822
44 (1297) 35242 (fax)
www.axminster.co.uk

Bordet
23 rue Traversière
93100 Montreuil-sous-Bois
France
33 (0148) 58 28 39
33 (0148) 58–48–58 (fax)

Carba-Tec Pty. Ltd
40 Harries Road
Cooparoo, Queensland 4151
Australia
61 (07) 3397–2577
61 (07) 3397–2785
www.carbatec.com.au

Kim Carleton Graves
Wood turner
Carleton Woodworking
195 Adams Street #8G
Brooklyn, NY 11201
USA
1 (718) 399–1114
www.CWWing.com

Craft Supplies Ltd.
The Mill
Millers Dale (Buxton)
Derbyshire SK17 8SN
England
44 (1208) 871636
44 (1208) 872263 (fax)
www.craft-supplies.co.uk

Craft Supplies (USA)
1287 East 1120 South
Provo, UT 84606
USA
1 (800) 551–8876
1 (801) 377–7742 (fax)

Craft Woods
PO Box 439
Hanover, MD 21076
USA
1 (800) 468–7070
1 (410) 850–0519 (fax)

Dick GmbH
Donaustr. 51
94526 Metten
Germany
49 (0991) 910930
49 (0991) 910950 (fax)
www.dick-gmbh.de

Packard Woodworks
PO Box 718
Tryon, NC 28782
USA
1 (800) 683–8876
1 (828) 859–5551 (fax)

Rockler Woodworking & Hardware
4365 Willow Drive
Medina, MN 55340
USA
1 (800) 279–4441
www.rockler.com

The Japan Woodworker
1731 Clement Avenue
Alameda, CA 94501
USA
1 (800) 537–7820
1 (510) 521–1864
www.japanwoodworker.com

The Tool Shop
78 High Street
Needham Market
Suffolk IP6 8AW
England
44 (1449) 722450
44 (1449) 733683 (fax)

Tool Crib
PO Box 14930
Grand Forks, ND 58208
USA
1 (800) 635–5140
1 (800) 343–4205 (fax)
www.toolcrib.amazon.com

Wood Carvers Supply
PO Box 7500
Englewood, FL 34295
USA
1 (800) 284–6229
1 (813) 698–0329

Woodworker's Supply
1108 N. Glenn Road
Casper, WY 82601
USA
1 (800) 645–9292

BIBLIOGRAPHY

Abram, Norm *Measure Twice, Cut Once*
Little, Brown, New York, 1996

Blackburn, Graham *Traditional Woodworking Handtools*
B.T. Batsford Ltd., London, 1999

Blandford, Percy W. *Country Craft Tools*
Swan Hill Press, Shrewsbury, 1997

Burton, Mike *Veneering: A Foundation Course*
Sterling Publishing, New York, 2000

Chinn, Garry and John Sainsbury *The Garrett Wade Book of Woodworking Tools*
Gallery Books, New York, 1979

Duginske, Mark *Band Saws: A Workshop Reference*
Sterling Publishing, New York, 1999
— *Mastering Woodworking Machines*
The Taunton Press Inc., Newtown, CT, 1992

Dunbar, Michael *Restoring, Tuning & Using Classic Woodworking Tools*
Sterling, New York, 1989

Flexner, Bob *Understanding Wood Finishing*
Reader's Digest, Pleasantville, NY 1999

Frid, Tage *Tage Frid Teaches Woodworking Volumes 1 & 2*
The Taunton Press Inc., Newtown, CT, 1993

Gaynor, James M. and Nancy L. Hagedorn *Tools: Working Wood in Eighteenth-Century America*
The Colonial Williamsburg Foundation, Williamsburg, 1993

Hack, Garrett *Classic Hand Tools*
The Taunton Press, Inc., Newton, CT, 1999
— *The Handplane Book*
The Taunton Press, Inc., Newton, CT, 1997

Hasluck, Paul N. (ed) *Manual of Traditional Woodcarving*
Dover, New York, 1977

Hoadley, Bruce *Identifying Wood: Accurate Results with Simple Tools*
The Taunton Press, Newtown, CT, 1990

Jackson, Albert and David Day *Complete Woodworker's Manual*
HarperCollins Publishers, London, 1996

Jewitt, Jeff *Hand Applied Finishes*
The Taunton Press Inc., Newtown, CT, 1997

Joyce, Ernest *Encyclopedia of Furniture Making*
Sterling Publishing, New York, 2001

Korn, Peter *The Woodworker's Guide to Hand Tools*
The Taunton Press Inc., Newton, CT, 1998

Landis, Scott *The Workbench Book*
The Taunton Press Inc., Newtown, CT, 1998
— *The Workshop Book*
The Taunton Press Inc., Newtown, CT, 1995

Lee, Leonard *Complete Guide to Sharpening*
The Taunton Press Inc., Newtown, CT, 1995

Metcalfe, Peter (ed.) *The Woodworker's Handbook*
Marshall Editions Ltd., London, 1984

Nagyszalanczy, Sandor *The Art of Fine Tools*
The Taunton Press Inc., Newton, CT, 1998
– *The Wood Sanding Book*
The Taunton Press Inc., Newtown, CT, 1997

Odate, Toshio *Japanese Woodworking Tools*
Linden Publishing Inc., Fresno, CA, 1998

Onians, Dick *Essential Woodcarving Techniques*
Guild of Master Craftsman Publications Ltd., Lewes, East Sussex, 1997

Peters, Rick *Controlling Dust in the Shop*
Sterling Publishing, New York, 2000

Pye, Chris *Woodcarving Tools, Materials and Equipment*
Guild of Master Craftsman Publications Ltd., Lewes, East Sussex, 1994

Raffan, Richard *Turning Wood with Richard Raffan*
The Taunton Press Inc., Newtown, CT, 2001
(also companion "Turning Wood" video)
– *Turning Projects*
The Taunton Press Inc., Newtown, CT, 1991
(also companion "Turning Projects" video)
– *Turned Bowl Design*
The Taunton Press Inc., Newtown, CT, 1987

Rees, Jane and Mark *Tools: A Guide for Collectors*
Roy Arnold, Needham Market, Suffolk, 1999

Rogowski, Gary *Router Joinery*
The Taunton Press Inc., Newtown, CT, 1997

Rowley, Keith *Woodturning: A Foundation Course*
Guild of Master Craftsman Publications, Ltd., Lewes, East Sussex, 1999

Salaman, R. A. *Dictionary of Woodworking Tools*
The Astragal Press Inc., Mendham, NJ, 1997

Sinitsky, Diane (ed.) *The Basics of Craftsmanship*
The Taunton Press Inc., Newton, CT, 1999

Stankus, Bill *Setting Up Your Own Woodworking Shop*
Sterling Publishing, New York, 1993

Tolpin, Jim *The Toolbox Book*
The Taunton Press Inc., Newtown, CT, 1998
– *Working Wood*
Sterling Publishing, New York, 1996
– *Working at Woodworking*
The Taunton Press Inc., Newtown, CT, 1990

Walker, Philip *Woodworking Tools*
Shire Publications Ltd., Haverfordwest, Dyfed, 1996

Watson, Aldren A. *Hand Tools: Their Ways and Workings*
The Lyons Press, New York, 1982

Wheeler, William and Charles Hayward *Practical Woodcarving and Gilding*
Bell and Hyman, London, 1983

Whelen, John *The Wooden Plane*
Astragal Press, Mendham, NJ 1993

INDEX

Note: The page numbers in italic refer to items in the Glossary or Micropedia.

ACKNOWLEDGMENTS

t = top; b = bottom; l = left, c = center; r = right

All photographs in this book were taken by Dick Frank except:

6*l* Smithsonian Institution/Eric Long; 9*l* The Bridgeman Library, 9*r* Brown Auction Services; 18*t* The Art Archive/Archaelogical Museum Venice/Dagli Orti, 18*c* Clive Corless/Marshall Editions; 27 Fickett Road, Pownal, Maine USA; 28*b* The Colonial Williamsburg Foundation; 30*t* Mary Evans Picture Library; 40 Mary Evans Picture Library; 42 Science Museum/Science & Society Picture Library; 52 The Fotomas Index, 53 Delta Manufacturing; 58*t* Mary Evans Picture Library; 66 The Bridgeman Art Library; 68 Jeremy Hopley; 70*b* Jeremy Hopley; 72*t* Mary Evans Picture Library, 72*b* Advanced Machinery; 77 Eagle Tools; 81*t* Advanced Machinery; 81*bl* Advanced Machinery; 84*r* The Bridgeman Art Library/Ecole des Beaux Arts, Paris; 85*l* Mary Evans Picture Library, 85*r* Mary Evans Picture Library; 102*t* Ann Ronan Picture Library; 104 Science Museum/Science & Society Picture Library; 106 Delta Manufacturing; 108*b* Shelburne Museum, Shelburne, Vermont; 116 The Bridgeman Art Library/Museo Correr, Venice; 118 Mary Evans Picture Library; 124*t* The Colonial Williamsburg Foundation; 136*t* The Colonial Williamsburg Foundation; 136*b* Mary Evans Picture Library; 137*b* The Colonial Williamsburg Foundation; 146 Chris Linton, 147*t* Chris Linton, 147*b* Chris Linton; 148*t* Chris Linton, 149*t* Chris Linton, 149*b* Chris Linton; 151*t* Chris Linton, 151*bl* Chris Linton, 151*br* Chris Linton; 156 Chris Linton, 157*t* Chris Linton; 160*t* Mary Evans Picture Library; 161*t* The Colonial Williamsburg Foundation, 161*b* One Way Manufacturing; 162 Delta Manufacturing, 163*t* JET Equipment & Tools, 163*bc* Chris Linton, 163*br* Chris Linton; 164 Ann Ronan Picture Library, 165*t* The Colonial Williamsburg Foundation; 167*b* Chris Linton; 170 The Bridgeman Art Library; 175 Chris Linton; 177*t* Chris Linton, 177*b* Chris Linton; 180 Delta Manufacturing; 188 Chris Linton; 198*tr* AKG London, 198*b* Courtesy, Winterthur Museum; 206*t* Mary Evans Picture Library, 207*t* Chris Linton; 208 Chris Linton; 214*t* Chris Linton; 223 Chris Linton; 226 The Colonial Williamsburg Foundation; 227 Chris Linton; 228*t* Chris Linton; 234*b* Brown Auction Services, 27 Fickett Road, Pownal, Maine, USA

Marshall Editions would like to thank Robert Sorby and The Old Tool Chest for the loan of their tools.